South-East Asian Social Science Monographs

Bangsawan

Bangsawan

A Social and Stylistic History of Popular Malay Opera

Tan Sooi Beng

SINGAPORE
OXFORD UNIVERSITY PRESS
OXFORD NEW YORK
1993

Oxford University Press, Walton Street, Oxford OX2 6DP

Oxford New York Toronto
Delhi Bombay Calcutta Madras Karachi
Kuala Lumpur Singapore Hong Kong Tokyo
Nairobi Dar es Salaam Cape Town
Melbourne Auckland Madrid

and associated companies in
Berlin Ibadan

Oxford is a trade mark of Oxford University Press

Published in the United States
by Oxford University Press, New York

British Library Cataloguing in Publication Data
Data available

Library of Congress Cataloging-in-Publication Data
Tan, Sooi Beng.
Bangsawan: a social and stylistic history of popular Malay opera/Tan Sooi Beng.
p. cm.—(South-East Asian social science monographs)
Includes bibliographical references.
ISBN 0-19-588599-6
1. Bangsawan—Malaysia—Malaya—History and criticism.
2. Malaysia—Social life and customs. 3. Malaya—Social life and
customs. I. Title. II. Series.
ML1751.M4T34 1993
7.82.1'09595'1—dc20
92-25275
CIP

Typeset by Indah Photosetting Centre Sdn. Bhd., Malaysia
Printed in Singapore by Kim Hup Lee Printing Co. Pte. Ltd.
Published by Oxford University Press Pte. Ltd.,
Unit 221, Ubi Avenue 4, Singapore 1440

For Ci Yan

Preface

THE term *teater tradisional* (traditional theatre) has been used in
Malaysia to denote theatre which has existed for many generations and
which contains elements characteristic of the South-East Asian region.
These characteristics include plots which are episodic and didactic,
incorporating comical, farcical, melodramatic, and serious elements; the
absence of scripts; the mixture of a number of media (such as dance,
music, and drama); strongly typed characters; non-realistic settings; and
performance for community events (Brandon, 1967: 115–24). Based on
this definition, writers such as Rahmah Bujang (1975: 41–3) and
Mustapha Kamil Yassin (1974: 151–2) have described *bangsawan* as
traditional Malay theatre. The latter states: 'In spite of being played on a
proscenium stage in a closed theatre building, the *Bangsawan* retained
nearly all the characteristics of traditional theatre of this region.
Certainly *Bangsawan* cannot be taken as a new form....' (Mustapha
Kamil Yassin, 1974: 151–2.) This too is the Malaysian government's
view of *bangsawan*.

I intend to argue that *bangsawan* was in fact a *new* form developed in
the late nineteenth and early twentieth centuries. Although it showed a
continuity with the past, *bangsawan* acquired characteristics that were
different from traditional Malay theatre. In particular, *bangsawan* was
commercial in nature and was constantly innovating to suit the changing
tastes of the audience. It was 'modern' (*Saudara*, 11 April 1936), 'up-to-
date' (*Straits Echo*, 11 June 1926), and incorporated Malay, Western,
and other foreign elements. It was mainly because of its heterogeneous
character that *bangsawan* became the common local theatre for different
ethnic groups living in Malaya in the early twentieth century. The performers who were promoted as stars were multi-ethnic too.
Performances were advertised in the newspapers and radio. Indeed as
Camoens (1981) and Wan Abdul Kadir (1988) have suggested, *bangsawan* was popular urban theatre. This popular theatre witnessed the
development of the first popular music in Malaysia which incorporated
Malay, Western, and other non-Malay musical elements—music that
was innovative and that was disseminated through the mass media. In
form, *bangsawan* exemplified the multi-ethnic character of the society.

Since the 1970s, however, the Malaysian government has *created* a traditional past for *bangsawan*. Under state sponsorship, a popular type of theatre has been reshaped, 'Malayized', and institutionalized for new, national purposes. Accordingly, the changes in *bangsawan* from the early twentieth century to the 1980s are the focus of my investigation. This study aims to show that socio-cultural and political transformations and the exercise of cultural control by governments have affected musical form and cultural content. In particular, I wish to explain why in the early twentieth century, *bangsawan* was popular theatre which included Malay, Western, and other non-Malay elements, while today it has undergone a process whereby it has become labelled as traditional theatre.

In order to understand the changing characteristics of *bangsawan*, it has been necessary to draw together and reconstruct its social and stylistic history. As Blum (1975: 221) emphasizes, 'Comparative studies of the social and historical circumstances in which human beings ... devise meaningful symbolic structures remain the most useful type of work musicologists might perform.' The approach taken in this study is therefore not based solely on transcription and analysis except in as much as they help to isolate aspects of musical and theatrical change.

In the writing of history, I have been influenced by recent original historical works on popular culture published in British social history journals like *History Workshop* and *Past and Present* and books tracing the history of leisure and recreation in England (such as Bailey, 1978; Yeo and Yeo, 1981). These works challenge both the form and content of conventional academic writing of history which emphasize 'abstract empiricism', the belief that 'facts' speak for themselves, and 'history without people' (Samuel, 1981: xl, xvi). They also emphasize that recreational activities form an important part of social experience and that the study of the history of such activities will contribute to 'the broader exercise of reconstructing the kind of life lived by the ordinary people of the past'. They relate popular culture to the 'structure of society as a whole and the wider patterns of social change' (Bailey, 1978: 1) and are concerned with culture as a 'process involving both mediation and struggle' (Burke, 1981b: 224).

These developments in socio-cultural history are beginning to have an impact on ethnomusicology and anthropology which, in the past decade or so, have increasingly emphasized 'diachronic, processual' analyses rather than 'static, synchronic' ones (Ortner, 1984: 158). I do not wish to embark here on a long discussion of why ethnomusicology has generally avoided history and historiography to date. It suffices to say that some of the reasons are that (1) ethnomusicologists have felt they needed to focus on present-day situations for fear of cultures 'dying out'; (2) there is a lack of historical–musical data, as the oldest recordings available today date back only to the late nineteenth century; (3) the discipline had more urgent theoretical concerns such as field collection procedures, transcription and analysis, and the study of living music in its cultural context (Hood, 1971; Merriam, 1964); and (4) ethnomusi-

cology was reacting to the emphasis on the historical approach in musicology which had rejected the Euro-centric modernization approach in
the social sciences which had linked music history with the 'idea of
temporal–linear progress as embodied in Western civilization' (Chase,
1976: 234).

With the move to diachronic analyses, cultural and artistic forms are
now seen as processes rather than as products (Coplan, 1982; Nettl,
1980, 1985, 1986; Turner, 1986b). These forms are continually being
'constituted', 'constructed', and 'represented' (Cohn, 1980: 217–18).
Changes in 'small-scale societies' are related to changes in 'large-scale
historical developments' such as 'colonialism and capitalist expansion'
(Ortner, 1984: 158). As a result of these developments, there seems
increasingly to be a convergence between socio-cultural history on the
one hand, and what I would call 'socio-historical ethnomusicology/
anthropology' on the other.

This book has been written in full awareness of this emerging convergence. It relates the development of *bangsawan* to the wider patterns of
social and political change, and establishes in chronological order the ties
that link them. It shows how new art forms emerge when changes take
place in society and the new conventions and musical styles which
articulate these changes. Williams (1977: 132–3) writes that the
dramatic conventions of any given period are fundamentally related to
the 'structure of feeling' in that period, which he defines as 'social
experience which is still in process'. As a new theatre form and a
product of the times, *bangsawan* articulated the changes which took
place in Malayan society in the early twentieth century. In turn, as form
and product, *bangsawan* may be understood as a 'signifying practice'
through which a changing 'social order' was 'communicated, reproduced, experienced and explored' (Williams, 1981: 13).

Thus there were close correspondences between the dramatic form
and musical style of *bangsawan* and the political, social, and cultural processes. Influenced by Barthes's study (1972) of signs and signals, and
their meanings in film, theatre, art, photography, fashion, and other
types of mass culture, I shall illustrate the relations between the theatrical conventions of *bangsawan* such as the plot structure, scene types,
music, character types, costumes, and language on the one hand, and
the wider social and historical reality on the other. Attention is given to
themes of continuity as well as change.

Besides showing homologies between a particular theatrical form and
the changes in society, this work illustrates why 'syncretism' or the
'blending' of 'elements of two or more cultures' involves both 'changes
of value and of form' (Herskovits, 1958; Merriam, 1964: 314). As
Blacking (1986) and Coplan (1982) emphasize, the processes of musical
and cultural interaction are not mechanical. The argument that musical
cultures which have 'similar' (Waterman, 1952), 'compatible', and
'central traits' (Nettl, 1978, 1985) mix more readily than cultures which
do not have such 'central traits' is also questioned. As Kartomi (1981,

1987) asserts, it is difficult to agree on which 'traits' are 'central', 'similar', or 'compatible'. Further, one cannot objectively measure the degree of musical similarity or difference. Taking after Kartomi (1981), then, this work shows that it is *extra-musical* factors, such as the influence of Western theatrical troupes, commercialism, the mass media, and the relative openness of the society towards cultural interaction and change, that determine musical and cultural interaction.

In particular, intervention by governments and government institutions is an important factor affecting syncretism. This is especially salient in newly independent countries like Malaysia where many cultural forms and events are sponsored and organized by the State or State-controlled media and other institutions (Kimberlin, 1988; Shiloah and Cohen, 1983; Wallis and Malm, 1984). Cultural experts in government institutions may construct traditions which imply a continuity with the past. To be sure, these artificial traditions are created not only for political purposes (Hobsbawm and Ranger, 1983) but in response to a universalizing modernity (Kahn, 1992). However, the greater the extent of State intervention in constructing traditions, the less satisfactory will be the cultural synthesis.

Thus, I propose not only that there are links between musical–theatrical forms and socio-political processes but also that government intervention affects artistic syncretism. However, musical–theatrical forms are not mere reflections of socio-political circumstances. Cultural change in general and musical change in particular ultimately result from decisions made by the performers themselves. As proponents of the 'practice' approach (Bourdieu, 1978; Giddens, 1979; Thompson, 1978; Turner, 1986a; Williams, 1977) emphasize, human beings 'make' and 'create' culture and have the 'capacity to transform society and create new human environments' (Austin-Broos, 1987: xix). 'History is not simply something that happens to people, but something they make—within, of course, the very powerful constraints of the system within which they are operating.' (Ortner, 1984: 159.) Blacking further stresses that 'musical change' is the result of 'decisions made by individuals about music-making and music or about social and cultural practice, on the basis of their experiences of music and social life and their attitudes to them in different social contexts' (Blacking, 1986: 3, 7). Likewise, Treitler (1984: 369) notes that 'it is a weak notion of evolution in the arts that does not regard individual creation as the central factor of historical continuity and change.... Change is a result of individual creation.'

To understand human agency, it is therefore important to look at the musical resources available to performers and the 'conditions and perceptions that guided them in selection, recombination and creative elaboration' (Coplan, 1982: 116). The behaviour of performers, their own and others' perceptions of them as performers and of their products, their training, and their co-operation or competition are therefore important (Merriam, 1964: 33). Moreover, it is also pertinent to study the motives of performers, which are of course an important factor in all decision-making. In this study, performers are seen not only as 'striving for gains' but as 'experiencing the complexities of their situation and attempting to solve problems posed by those situations' (Ortner, 1984: 151). The types of restrictions a system places on performers and how they respond to these restrictions are investigated.

To a considerable extent, I have allowed the performers to speak for themselves and have drawn on their vocabularies. To capture these 'voices from below', I recorded the performers' perceptions of the changes in *bangsawan* from the early twentieth century till the 1980s. Quotations in the text are direct translations of the performers' responses. Drawings of costumes and sets were also based on the memories of the performers. In addition, a number of life stories were collected. In these interviews, I focused on political events which were significant in the history of Malaya, asking the performers what they were doing and what *bangsawan* was like at the time. The political events provided the framework for a chronology of the development of and the changes in *bangsawan*.

Recognizing that old people have a tendency to idealize the time when they were young, I have felt it necessary to include documents such as newspaper reports and advertisements, travel books, and old photographs as complements and checks of their oral accounts. In particular, the Malay and English press in the early twentieth century provided valuable sources. Newspapers carried advertisements of *bangsawan* troupes; and, as *bangsawan* was very popular, reviewers wrote about the plays, the performers, the audiences, the halls, and the settings of performances. A great variety of newspaper sources made it possible for me to compare and draw conclusions about the nature of *bangsawan* over a period of time.

To support the oral history, 78 r.p.m. recordings of *bangsawan* songs available were also employed. Although I recorded songs that the performers could still remember, these songs could not of course be assumed to be identical to those of the past. To establish the nature of the musical style of the early twentieth century, I relied heavily on transcriptions and analyses of selected 78 r.p.m. recordings of songs which, according to veteran performers, were representative of the musical style of *bangsawan* at that time. Aural studies of other 78 r.p.m. recordings were carried out while old handwritten music scores were used to further verify the musical style. It should be noted that musical examples were taken from gramophone records of the late 1920s and 1930s when gramophone technology first became widely available in Malaya. The records used were donated to Universiti Malaya by a *bangsawan* enthusiast, Naina Merican.

Direct participation through the study of musical instruments and performances with a *bangsawan* troupe, observations and recordings of performances of other troupes, and transcriptions and analyses of *bangsawan* songs performed by these troupes during the time of fieldwork further helped me to trace the changes in *bangsawan* in the 1980s.

Finally, it should be clarified that not every aspect of the music has been transcribed. Only particular traits—formal structure, instrumentation, harmony, vocal style, rhythmic articulation, and heterophonic ornamentation—are identified and shown in the transcriptions in order that the musical style of *bangsawan* in the early twentieth century and in the 1980s can be compared.

Universiti Sains Malaysia   TAN SOOI BENG
Penang
1992

Acknowledgements

THIS book would not have materialized without the help of many. I owe the greatest debt of gratitude to a number of veteran *bangsawan* performers, who not only afforded me their generous hospitality but also provided me with invaluable historical data on *bangsawan* and allowed me to tape the stories of their lives. I am especially indebted to Pak Mat who taught me the *rebana* (Malay frame drum) and the gong, passed his knowledge of *bangsawan* music on to me, and allowed me to travel with his ensemble. Pak Mat and his wife, Mak Halinah, made me their *anak angkat* (adopted child); a student cannot ask for more. I am also grateful to Pak Rahman B., who made it possible for me to meet other veteran performers in Kuala Lumpur. He introduced me to the *warung* (coffee-shop) frequented by veteran performers, where I spent many hours sipping coffee and talking about *bangsawan* with them. To Mak Minah and Pak Alias I express my thanks for permitting me to attend rehearsals and to perform with the Bangsawan Sri USM. I also wish to thank Tok Wan, Tok Bakar M., Tok Shariff Medan, Pak Rahim B., Pak Suki, Mak Menah Yem, Mak Ainon, Mak Saniah, Pak Abdullah Abdul Rahman, Pak Ahmad B., Pak Yahya Sulong, Pak Mahmud Jun, Pak Ahmad C. B., Pak Mat Arab, Pak Aziz, Pak Alfonso Soliano, Pak Ahmad Shariff, Pak Wan Pekak, Mak Marshita, Mak Kamariah Noor, Baba Gwee Thian Hock, and William Tan, who gave me many hours of their time. Since I conducted my research in 1985–6, Pak Alfonso Soliano and Pak Alias have passed away. To their memory, I dedicate this book.

Special thanks are extended to the following friends and colleagues. Ghulam Sarwar shared many of his field recordings with me and introduced me to *bangsawan*. Mohd. Bahroodin Ahmad assisted me in reading Jawi newspapers and contributed the fine drawings in this book. Yeap Jin Soo edited the manuscript. Khoo Khay Jin and Tan Liok Ee were important sources of advice. I am indebted to Margaret Kartomi, who supervised my Ph.D. thesis, an earlier version of this book. I would like to thank Joel Kahn, Ben Anderson, and Philip Yampolsky for their detailed comments. Thanks are also due to Barbara Hatley, Ashok Roy, Adrian McNeil, Patricia Matusky, Bronia Kornhauser, and Michael Kinnear.

I would like to express my gratitude to a number of institutions. This study was made possible by a graduate scholarship from Monash University and study leave from Universiti Sains Malaysia. I am also indebted to the following departments of Monash University: (1) the Centre of Southeast Asian Studies for providing me with a travel grant to carry out research in Malaysia and for providing an environment and facilities to complete this study; (2) the Music Department for lending me recording equipment; and (3) the Geography Department for preparing the map and plates. I owe a special debt to the library of Universiti Sains Malaysia for assisting me to track down old newspapers, and to the libraries of Universiti Malaya and Radio Televisyen Malaysia for allowing me to use their 78 r.p.m. records. The Research Unit of the Ministry of Culture, Youth and Sports also contributed some photographs of *bangsawan*.

I would like to acknowledge the *Review of Indonesian and Malaysian Affairs*, Vol. 23 (1989) and *Ethnomusicology*, Vol. 33, No. 2 (1989) in which small sections of this book have been produced.

Throughout the preparation of this book, I have greatly appreciated the encouragement I received from family members. They include my parents, my sister, my mother-in-law, and my sisters- and brothers-in-law.

Finally, Francis has been extremely supportive, seeing me through the agonies of thesis and later book writing and challenging me with his criticisms.

Contents

Preface   *vii*

Acknowledgements   *xiii*

Appendices   *xvii*

Tables   *xvii*

Figures   *xviii*

Map   *xix*

Plates   *xx*

Musical Examples   *xxii*

Musical Transcriptions   *xxiv*

1 *Bangsawan* in the 1980s   *1*

2 The Development of Urban Entertainment and Commercial Theatre, *c.*1880–*c.*1930   8

Changes in Malaya   8

The Growth of Urban Entertainment   9

The Development of *Bangsawan*   16

Bangsawan as Urban Commercial Theatre   18

Popularity of *Bangsawan*   25

3 Variety, Adaptability, Novelty, and the Spectacular, *c.*1880–*c.*1930   35

Variety   35

Novelty and Spectacle   40

Adaptability   44

4 The Promotion of Stars, *c.*1880–*c.*1930   60

Stars   60

Recruits of Various Ethnic Backgrounds   61

Learning to be Stars   64

Maintaining Star Status   67

Changing Troupes   68

Community Integration   69

Women in *Bangsawan*   71

5 **Development of the *Orkestra Melayu*, c.1880–c.1930**   *73*
   Development of the *Orkestra* or Band: The Incorporation
      of New Instruments   *73*
   Classification of *Bangsawan* Instruments in the 1930s   *78*
   Instrumental Combinations in the 1930s   *79*

6 **An Arena for Musical Interaction in the 1920s and
   1930s**   *83*
   Examples of Musical Interaction   *84*
   Summary of Musical Style   *98*
   Reasons for Musical Interaction   *99*

7 **Scene Types, Plot Structure, and Stock Characters
   in the 1920s and 1930s**   *103*
   Scene Types (*Babak*) and Plot Structure   *104*
   Dramatis Personae (*Watak*)   *110*
   Adaptation of *Hamlet*   *125*

8 **Categories of *Lagu* and Their Dramatic Uses in the
   1920s and 1930s**   *131*
   Rentak, *Irama*, and Dramatic Situation   *132*
   Irama Orang Putih   *132*
   Irama Melayu   *143*
   Irama Padang Pasir   *150*
   Irama Jawa   *155*
   Irama Hindustan   *159*

9 **Decline of *Bangsawan* since World War II and Its
   Revival in the 1970s and 1980s**   *165*
   The Japanese Occupation   *165*
   The Immediate Post-war Period, the Emergency, and
      Independence   *166*
   The 1960s   *174*
   The Implementation of the National Culture Policy and
      the Revival of *Bangsawan* by the State, 1970s and 1980s *175*
   The Malayization of *Bangsawan*   *178*

10 **Conclusion**   *189*

   Appendices   *195*
   Glossary   *232*
   Bibliography   *237*
   Index   *253*

Appendices

1 Musical Transcriptions   *195*
2 Synopses of Six *Bangsawan* Plays   *209*
3 Categories of *Lagu* and Their Dramatic Uses in *Puteri*
   Gunong Ledang   *229*

Tables

5.1 Classification of Instruments in the 1930s   *78*
8.1 The Relationship between Dramatic Situation and
     Rhythmic Pattern   *162*

Figures

2.1   Advertisement for the First Malay Film Made in Malaya   *11*
2.2   Advertisement for Pagoda Records   *12*
2.3   Advertisement for Chap Kuching Records   *13*
2.4   Amusement Park and Radio Advertisements   *15*
2.5   Advertisement for the Empress Victoria Jawi Peranakkan
      Theatrical Company, Indra Bangsawan   *17*
2.6   Proscenium Stage of the Drop and Wing Variety,
      *c.*1920–*c.*1930   *22*
2.7   Three Types of Side-wings for Different Scenes,
      *c.*1920–*c.*1930   *23*
2.8   Opera Tent Showing First-, Second-, and Third-class
      Seats, *c.*1920–*c.*1930   *24*
2.9   *Bangsawan* Theatre in the Amusement Park,
      *c.*1930–*c.*1940   *24*
2.10 Advertisement for Nyo Nya Bangsawan   *27*
3.1   Advertisement for a Chinese Play   *36*
3.2   Advertisement for Guest Artists Frank J. Sidney and
      Company, the Great Jumper and Whirlwind Tumbler,
      and the Philips Sisters Performing with the International
      Dramatic Company   *42*
3.3   Advertisement for Vaudeville Night   *46*
3.4   Advertisement for the Malay Play *Laksemana Hang
      Tuah*   *48*
3.5   Advertisement for the Malay Play *Hang Tuah and Tun
      Tijah* and the Hindustani Play *Noor-E-Islam*   *49*
3.6   Advertisement for *The Silver Mask*, a *Bangsawan*
      Adaptation of the Film *The Mark of Zorro*   *50*
3.7   Advertisement for Dja's Dardanella's *Fatimma*   *54*
3.8   Advertisement for the 'Exotic' Plays of Dja's Dardanella   *55*
3.9   Advertisement for the Indonesian Troupe,
      Miss Riboet's Opera   *56*
3.10 Advertisement for a Malayan Opera's Performance of
      an 'Exotic' Play from Hawaii   *57*
7.1   Backdrops of Malay/Javanese *Taman*, Arabic/Hindustani
      Taman, *Hutan Tebuk*, and *Hutan*, *c.*1920–*c.*1930   *105*

7.2   Backdrops of *Gua Batu, Istana, Istana Tebuk*, and
      *Rumah Kampung, c.*1920–*c.*1930   *106*
7.3   Backdrops of *Padang Pasir, Kayangan, Kampung*, and
      *Strit, c.*1920–*c.*1930   *107*
7.4   Movements of the Sultan, *c.*1920–*c.*1930   *113*
7.5   Hand Movements of the *Puteri* and the *Orang Muda*,
      *c.*1920–*c.*1930   *114*
7.6   Characters and Costumes in the Chinese Play *Sam Pek
      Eng Tai, c.*1920–*c.*1930   *116*
7.7   Characters and Costumes in the Classical Play *Hamlet*,
      *c.*1920–*c.*1930   *117*
7.8   Characters and Costumes in the Hindustani Play *Gul
      Bakawali, c.*1920–*c.*1930   *118*
7.9   Characters and Costumes in the Javanese Play *Panji
      Semerang, c.*1920–*c.*1930   *119*
7.10 Characters and Costumes in the Thai Play *Raja
      Bersiong, c.*1920–*c.*1930   *120*
7.11 The *Dayang, Inang, Sultan*, and *Permaisuri* and Their
      Costumes in the Malay Play *Laksamana Bentan*,
      *c.*1920–*c.*1930   *121*
7.12 The *Laksamana di Bahtera, Laksamana di Istana*, and
      Orang Kampung and Their Costumes in the Malay Play
      *Laksamana Bentan, c.*1920–*c.*1930   *122*
7.13 The *Puteri* and Her Costumes in the Malay Play
      Laksamana Bentan and the Heroine and Her Costumes
      in the Modern Malay Play *Bawang Merah Bawang
      Puteh, c.*1920–*c.*1930   *123*
8.1   Title-page of Songbook *Penghiboran Hati*   *157*
9.1   *Bangsawan* Handbill of 1950, Featuring *Thief of Bagdad*   *171*
9.2   *Bangsawan* Handbill of 1952, Featuring *Sampek Engtair*   *172*
9.3   *Bangsawan* Handbill of the 1950s, Featuring *Putri
      Gunong Ledang*   *173*
9.4   *Bangsawan* Handbill of 1980, Featuring *Megat Teraweh*   *180*

Map

2.1   Popular Theatre in South-East Asia in the Late
      Nineteenth and Early Twentieth Centuries   *19*

Plates

Between pages 72 and 73

1 Laksamana's greeting (*siku di lutut*), Bangsawan Workshop, 1985.
2 Tengku Halijah's greeting, Bangsawan Workshop, 1985.
3 Queen in *kebaya labuh*, Bangsawan Workshop, 1985.
4 Maid-in-waiting in *baju kurung*, *panglima* in *baju Melayu*, Bangsawan Workshop, 1985.
5 Painting the side-wings of the garden scene, Bangsawan Workshop, 1985.
6 Painting the side-wings of the palace scene, Bangsawan Workshop, 1985.
7 Learning *silat* with Alias Manan (*left*), Bangsawan Workshop, 1985.
8 Setting up the stage for the performance on the last night of the Bangsawan Workshop, 1985.
9 Minah Alias distributing costumes, Bangsawan Workshop, 1985.
10 *Ronggeng* ensemble accompanying the *bangsawan* performance, Bangsawan Workshop, 1985. (*From left to right*) Pak Wan (violin), Ahmad (*rebana*), and Pak Mat Hashim (accordion).
11 Raden Mas advising Tengku Halijah and her maids, Bangsawan Workshop, 1985.
12 Minah Alias singing in the extra turn, Bangsawan Workshop, 1985.
13 Columbia record, 1950s, manufactured by the Columbia Graphophone Co. Ltd., England.
14 His Master's Voice record, 1940s, manufactured by the Gramophone Co. Ltd., Calcutta.
15 Pathe record, 1950s, made in India.
16 Grand record, 1950s, manufactured by the Gramophone Co. Ltd., Dum Dum, India.
17 Chap Kuching record, 1940s, manufactured by the Gramophone Co. Ltd., Dum Dum, India.
18 Parlophone record jacket, 1950s, record made in India.
19 *Bangsawan* stage and performers, 1940s.
20 *Bangsawan* performance with Chinese, Indian, and Malay characters, 1941, held to collect money for the Police War Fund.
21 Javanese play, 1940s.
22 Javanese play, 1950s.

23 Only performance of *Hamlet* in the 1970s; scene where the murder of the King is re-enacted, with Hamlet, Gertrude, Claudius, and guests looking on.

24 Play with characters wearing Malay, Javanese, and Middle Eastern costumes, 1950s.

25 Performance of *Jula Juli Bintang Tiga*, 1960s. The three sisters appear behind the paper stars while the fairies dance in the clouds.

26 Performance of *Jula Juli Bintang Tiga*, 1960s. Jula Juli rides a goose in the sea.

27 Characters in a Middle Eastern play, 1970s.

28 Extra turn, 1940s.

29 Extra turn, 1940s.

30 Tok Wan, 1985.

31 Pak Mat Arab and Mak Ainon Chik, 1970s.

32 Mak Menah Yem singing and dancing in an extra turn, 1940s.

33 Pak Rahman B. in Malay costume, 1960s.

34 Pak Rahim B. in Roman costume, 1960s.

35 Mak Minah Alias (*extreme right*) teaching a group of students the *asli* dance, 1985.

36 *Bangsawan* band consisting of drum, saxophone, accordian, and trumpet, 1950s.

37 *Rebana ibu* and *anak*.

38 Pak Wan playing the violin and Pak Aziz playing the *rebana ibu*, 1986.

39 *Kroncong* ensemble consisting of flute, violin, guitar, gong, and accordion, 1980s.

40 Pak Mat's *ronggeng* ensemble and *ronggeng* dancers, 1986.

41 Orkestra Dungun, 1950s.

42 Extra turn from *Raden Mas*, Som Kenangan Sandiwara, 1960s.

43 Hindustani play *Patangga*, Som Kenangan Sandiwara, 1960s.

44 Malay play *Aboo Jenaka*, Som Kenangan Sandiwara, 1960s.

45 Performance of *Laksamana Bentan*, 1986; court scene.

46 Performance of *Laksamana Bentan*, 1986; scene in the pirates' den.

47 Performance of *Laksamana Bentan*, 1986; garden scene.

48 Performance of *Laksamana Mati Dibunuh*, 1986; death scene.

Musical Examples

6.1a Typical Piano Bass and *Rebana Rentak* Pattern of
Lagu Asli   85
6.1b *Patahan Lagu* Played by the Violin   85
6.1c *Bunga* (Ornaments)   86
6.1d The Use of Pitches 3 and 5 with Pitch 2 in a Typical
Chinese Pentatonic Scale   87
6.1e The Use of Pitches 5 and 3 with Pitches 6 and 1 in a
Typical Chinese Pentatonic Scale   87
6.2a Rhythmic Pattern of the Melody Played by the Cane
Flute in *Beledi* Dancing in Iran   88
6.2b Masmūdī Kabīr Rhythm   89
6.2c Mode of Hicaz   89
6.2d Mode of 'Telek Ternang'   89
6.2e A Melodic Pattern of Hicaz   89
6.2f Voice Melody of 'Telek Ternang'   90
6.3a Intervallic Structure of Zengüle   90
6.3b Intervallic Structure of 'Gambos Sri Makam'   90
6.3c Repetition of Vocal Phrase   91
6.3d Intervals and Repeated Notes in 'Gambos Sri Makam'   91
6.3e *Patahan Lagu Padang Pasir*   92
6.3f Trill and Turn (Violin)   92
6.4a Intervallic Succession Resembling the Javanese *Pélog*
Pathet Nem   93
6.4b *Asli* Rhythmic Pattern of the *Rebana*   93
6.4c *Irama Dua* Pattern of the *Rebana*   93
6.6a Vibrato at Melismatic Phrases   94
6.6b Ascending Pattern Common in Bhairavī   95
6.6c Ascending Pattern in 'Mostikowi'   95
6.6d *Kaharvā Tāla* Played on Harmonium in 'Mostikowi'   95
6.7a Musical Emphasis of Text   96
6.8a Syncopated Melody against a Straightforward Bass   97
6.8b Typical Chinese Pentatonic Scale   97
8.1 Waltz Rhythm   132
8.2 A 1930s Score of 'Donou Walen'   133
8.3 Slow Waltz (*Lagu Nasib*): 'Penceraian Jula Juli dengan
Sultan'   134

8.4	Slow Waltz (*Lagu Taman*): 'Teribet Jula Juli'	*135*
8.5	A 1930s Score of 'Teribet Jula Juli'	*136*
8.6	Fast Waltz (*Lagu Taman/Kayangan*): 'Telesmat Bintang Satu dan Dua'	*136*
8.7	Fanfare and Section of Tune of 'Colonel Bogey'	*137*
8.8	Tango Accompanimental Patterns	*137*
8.9	A 1933 Score of a Tango Piece, 'La Femme Qui Tue'	*138*
8.10	'Maple Leaf Rag' (1899) by Scott Joplin	*139*
8.11	Ragtime (*Lagu Strit*): 'Shanghai Street'	*140*
8.12	Quickstep (*Lagu Taman/Kayangan*): 'Telesmat Bintang Satu dan Dua'	*142*
8.13	*Asli* Rhythmic Pattern	*143*
8.14	Variations of *Asli* Rhythmic Pattern	*143*
8.15	Left-hand Improvisations of *Asli* Rhythmic Pattern	*144*
8.16	Slow-paced *Asli* (*Lagu Sedih/Nasib*); 'Puja Kamati Darsha Alam'	*145*
8.17	Fast-paced *Asli* (*Lagu Pengasoh/Inang*): 'Che Wan Gayah'	*146*
8.18	*Inang* Rhythmic Pattern	*147*
8.19	Left-hand Improvisation of *Inang* Rhythmic Pattern	*147*
8.20	*Inang* (*Lagu Cakap*): 'Baginda Yam Tuan Melaka'	*148*
8.21	*Joget* Rhythmic Pattern	*148*
8.22	Left-hand Improvisation of *Joget* Rhythmic Pattern	*149*
8.23	*Joget* (*Lagu Silat*)	*149*
8.24	*Masri* Rhythmic Pattern	*150*
8.25	Left-hand Improvisation of *Masri* Rhythmic Pattern	*150*
8.26	Slow *Masri* (*Lagu Nasib*): 'Nasib Pandan'	*151*
8.27	Fast *Masri* (*Lagu Telek*): 'Telek Ternang'	*152*
8.28	*Zapin* Rhythmic Pattern	*152*
8.29	*Gambos* (*Lagu Nasib*): 'Bercerai Kasih'	*154*
8.30	Strummed Chords of *Kroncong*	*156*
8.31	Banjo and Ukelele Alternating	*156*
8.32	Rhythmic Movement of the Guitar	*156*
8.33	Pizzicato Cello	*156*
8.34	*Stambul*: 'Stambol Satoe'	*158*
8.35	*Stambul* (*Lagu Asli*): 'Boenga Tandjung'	*158*
8.36	*Stambul* with *Kroncong* Accompaniment: 'Anak Koe'	*159*
8.37	*Barshat* Played on the *Rebana*	*160*
8.38	*Dādra Tāla*	*160*
8.39	*Irama Hindustan*: Variation of *Dādrā Tāla* in 'Paraber'	*160*
8.40	*Kaharvā Tāla* in 'Mostikowi'	*161*
9.1	'Lagu Sambut Kekasih'	*182*
9.2	'Lagu Sambut Kekasih'	*182*
9.3	'Bunga Tanjung' ·	*184*
9.4	'Boenga Tandjung'	*185*

Musical Transcriptions

6.1   *Lagu Melayu*: 'Hiburan Raja Ahmad Beradu'   *196*
6.2   *Lagu Padang Pasir/Arab*: 'Telek Ternang'   *198*
6.3   *Lagu Padang Pasir/Arab*: 'Gambos Sri Makam'   *198*
6.4   *Lagu Jawa*: 'Sinandung Jawa'   *200*
6.5   *Lagu Hindustan*: 'Paraber'   *203*
6.6   *Lagu Hindustan*: 'Mostikowi'   *204*
6.7   *Lagu Klasik/Opera*: 'Penceraian Jula Juli dengan Sultan'   *205*
6.8   *Lagu Cina*: 'Shanghai Street'   *208*

1
Bangsawan in the 1980s

This workshop is aimed at reviving the *traditional theatre* [*emphasis added*], bangsawan. The Ministry hopes to increase the number of people trained in it by exposing the participants to all aspects of bangsawan. The workshop is part of the Ministry's five-year plan to set up bangsawan associations in five states: Perak, Penang, Melaka, Kuala Lumpur and Sarawak.
(Puan Siti Aishah bt. Yahya)

THE Deputy Director of the Ministry of Culture, Youth and Sports (now known as the Ministry of Culture, Arts and Tourism) in Penang, Puan Siti Aishah bt. Yahya, declared the above at the opening of a one-week *bangsawan* workshop organized by the Ministry and Universiti Sains Malaysia (USM) in Penang in December 1985.

The workshop was conducted by USM lecturer, Dr Ghulam Sarwar, and veteran *bangsawan* performers, Alias Manan and his wife Minah Alias. The twenty-six participants included factory workers, typists, clerks, telephone operators, technicians, students, and this researcher. Except for two Chinese, the other participants were Malays. The workshop marked the beginning of my research on *bangsawan*.

For one week, we listened to lectures on the characteristics of *bangsawan*. We were told that as traditional Malay theatre, *bangsawan* stories were set in Malay courts and used Malay costumes, dances, and music. Elaborating upon the acting style used in *bangsawan*, Alias emphasized that it followed traditional Malay court etiquette. He said that 'when the warrior pays respects to the Malay Sultan, he must sit bending his knees at an angle (*siku di lutut*) and be ready to draw his *keris*' (Plate 1). Minah added that 'women must bend their backs and their knees with hands on either side when they walk in front of the Sultan' and that 'they should kneel on one knee when they pay respect to him' (Plate 2). Following a string of do's and don't's in performing *bangsawan*, Alias and Minah amused the participants with anecdotes of mistakes they made in the past and how they were subsequently punished. But their point was clear: the *bangsawan* traditions must be learned and reproduced.

Alias emphasized that the costumes followed closely those of the Malay royalty then as well as now. According to him, 'The Sultan wears yellow pants (*seluar*), inner shirt with collar (*baju dalam dengan leher tutup*), outer coat (*baju luar*), head-dress (*tanjak*), sarong (*kain samping*), sash (*selampit*), state kris (*keris kerajaan*), and an ornamental medallion for royalty (*aguk kebesaran*) [see Chapter 7]. The ministers' costumes are similar to the Sultan's except that they are not allowed to wear yellow.' The participants were in turn told by Minah that 'the attire of the queen consists of the knee-length blouse (*kebaya labuh*) and a crown' (Plate 3), and that 'the maids-in-waiting put on the Malay traditional dress (*baju kurung*) and decorate their hair with flowers' (Plate 4).

Scripts of the play *Raden Mas*, a traditional Malay classic, were then circulated and auditions were held to choose the main characters. Following this, we rehearsed the story of *Raden Mas* daily. Minah and Alias demonstrated and played different character types for the participants to imitate.

We constructed props and sets used in *Raden Mas*, and painted backdrops and flats depicting the Malay palace garden (Plate 5), the palace hall (Plate 6), and the forest for the respective scenes. We made flower stands, as well as the yellow throne for the Sultan, and decorated the Sultan's yellow umbrella.

The women rehearsed the Malay *inang* (nursemaid) dance, while the men practised *silat*, the Malay art of self-defence (Plate 7). We learnt the *lagu taman* (garden song) and the *lagu kahwin* (marriage song) in *Raden Mas* from Mat Hashim, a veteran musician who came daily. I had the opportunity to study the *rebana* (Malay frame drum) and the bossed gong with him. He also showed me the rhythmic patterns for the *lagu silat* (*silat* song) and the *lagu buka tirai* (curtain-opening song).

The workshop culminated in the performance of *Raden Mas* to a live audience on the last night. Excited about the performance, we got up extremely early that morning. Everyone helped to load the props, sets, costumes, and instruments into the bus which breezed through the winding roads by the sea to Telok Bahang, the site of the performance. When we reached our destination, the smell of dried fish greeted us as our bus stopped in front of the makeshift stage.

With fifty years of experience as a *bangsawan* performer, Alias directed the boys to unload the sets and props and to set up the stage (Plate 8). The technician brought ten microphones, four speakers, and two amplifiers. The women were sent to the house of a family to rest. Minah stressed that this was in line with *bangsawan* custom. 'Women actresses especially the *sri panggung* (heroine) cannot go out during the daytime in case their faces become too familiar to the public,' she clarified.

After a quick meal at 7 p.m., we made our way to the stage which had already been lighted up. Soon the place was bustling with activity. Minah distributed costumes to the individual actors and actresses (Plate 9). According to *bangsawan* custom, one side of the stage had been partitioned for the women to change. The performers put on their glittering and colourful costumes and their make-up.

Following the instructions of Alias, a few volunteers stuck real flowers and branches into wooden stands and made ornamental eggs for the enactment of a Malay wedding. At 8 p.m., Alias announced: 'No spectacles and no watches are allowed on stage. No one is allowed to go down after they have changed.'

The musicians had a quick run-through of the songs to be performed that night. The practice was for my benefit as this was the first time I was playing in the *ronggeng asli* ensemble which usually accompanies social dancing at Malay weddings, festivals, and other functions. Mat Hashim was playing the harmonium, Wan Pekak the violin (*biola*), and Ahmad the *rebana* (Plate 10). The women rehearsed the opening garden scene with us.

Alias then called the performers together for prayers. '*Raden Mas* is a true story and we do not want anything untoward to occur. Raden Mas and Pengeran Agung (her father) were both buried in Telok Belanga and Malays in Singapore still offer incense at their graves till today,' he explained.

By 8.30 p.m., the chairs set up in front of the stage were filled. The audience was predominantly Malay. The guest of honour was Haji Yahaya Ahmad, a Penang State Assemblyman. Also in attendance were the Director and Deputy Director of the Ministry of Culture, Youth and Sports, Penang, who acted as judges for the best actor, best actress, and best participant awards. The guest of honour gave a speech and handed out certificates to all participants.

At 9.15 p.m., the audience was told that although the performance of *Raden Mas* that night was the product of a workshop, it was a traditional *bangsawan* story and would be performed in the 'authentic' *bangsawan* style. The show proper then started. I had to play the gong three times to signal that the show was about to begin. As only five scenes were to be acted out that night, Alias announced the story-line to the audience:

There once lived in Java a king named Ratu Kediri. His brother, Pengeran Agung, married Ayu, a commoner who was a dancer. They had a daughter named Raden Mas. Afraid that Raden Mas might one day take over the throne, Ratu Kediri planned to kill Ayu and her daughter. One day, when Pengeran Agung was out hunting, Ratu Kediri burnt Pengeran Agung's palace and killed Ayu. Fortunately, Pengeran Agung managed to save Raden Mas. They escaped to Kerimun in Sumatra. Pengeran Agung lived there as a fisherman.

To the accompaniment of *lagu buka tirai*, the curtain opened. Scene 1 was set in the palace garden. Tengku Halijah, the daughter of the Sultan of Kerimun, and her maids-in-waiting were dancing and singing the song 'Suriram'. The lyrics were in Malay *pantun* form with an *a b a b* rhyme scheme and the first couplet alluding to the meaning of the verse:

Seludang mayang cempaka sari
Suntingan puteri bukit siguntang
Cantik molek wajah berseri
Seperti bulan di pagar bintang

Palm blossom frangipani flower
Posy of the princess hill of sigun trees
Beautiful pretty glistening face
Like the moon encircled by stars (Author's translation)

Just as the maids were praising Tengku Halijah for her beauty, Raden Mas entered and, through song, advised Tengku Halijah to pray instead (Plate 11). She used the Malay *syair* form with *a a a a* rhyme scheme and the same idea conveyed throughout each verse.

Kalau hidup tidak sembahyang
Allah dan rasul tentu tak sayang
Waktu nyawa hendak melayang
Azab sengsara malam dan siang

If (you) live without praying
Allah and His apostle will definitely not love (you)
On your deathbed
(You) will suffer agony night and day (Author's translation)

Angry, Tengku Halijah ordered her warriors to beat Raden Mas.

Set in the forest, scene 2 opened with the entrance of Dandiar, a former warrior of Pengeran Agung in Java. He had been ordered by Ratu Kediri to look for Pengeran Agung. When Dandiar saw Tengku Halijah's soldiers beating Radin Mas, he and his warriors chased the Malay soldiers to the Kerimun palace to the rhythm of *lagu silat*.

This was followed by scene 3 at the palace hall. Dandiar refused to stop fighting until Pengeran Agung came. To average the blood spilled by Raden Mas, the Sultan of Kerimun ordered Tengku Halijah to marry Pengeran Agung although she protested vehemently. They were married and had a son, Tengku Cik, and an adopted daughter, Cik Nong.

Scene 4 was also set at the palace hall. The family of the Sultan of Kerimun had moved to Singapore or Temasek. Raden Mas was ill-treated by Tengku Halijah who made her sweep, clean, wash dishes, and do housework the whole day. Tengku Halijah broke a plate on Raden Mas's head. When Pengeran Agung heard about this incident, he attempted to kill Tengku Halijah with his kris but stabbed Tengku Cik instead. Luckily, the boy did not die. Pengeran Agung was sentenced to life imprisonment in a disused well. Before he was thrown into the well, he cried and sang the Malay *asli* (traditional) song, 'Sri Siantar', a *lagu nasib* (song of fate).

The last scene was a Malay wedding. Raja Bagus, the son of Raja Temenggong, had asked for the hand of Raden Mas as she no longer had a father to take care of her. On the day of the wedding, Dandiar brought money belonging to Pengeran Agung but was told that the latter had gone away on business. However, when the subject of guardian arose at the wedding, Tengku Cik declared that Raden Mas's father was still alive. Pengeran Agung was brought from the disused well. However, he was so weak that he died shortly after that. Raden Mas asked Allah to let her die with her father. She too collapsed. Suddenly, Tengku Halijah, who refused to ask for forgiveness, was struck by lightning and died. To show the effect of lightning, an arrow illuminated with fire at the sharp end was made to slide down a wire stretched across the stage. Pointing to Tengku Halijah, Dandiar proclaimed: 'This is what happens to those who are disloyal; disloyal to husband and Allah.' The performance ended with a tableau showing the cast frozen with their hands lifted in Muslim prayer.

In between the scenes, while the sets were being changed, the performers took turns to sing Malay songs mainly from the *ronggeng asli* repertoire. Some examples included 'Joget Hitam Manis' [Sweet and Black Joget], 'Siti Payung' [Umbrella Lady], and 'Cempaka Sari' [Frangipani Flower]. Alias and Minah entertained the audience with a *dondang sayang*, an elaborated form of Malay poetry singing (Plate 12). They tried to outwit each other by improvising witty verses. For many, seeing the veteran performers sing was the highlight of the evening.

The best actress award went to a typist, Zuraidah Ahmad (as Tengku Halijah); the best actor award to a student at USM, Mohd. Bahroodin Ahmad (as Pengeran Agung); and the best participant award to a technician, Ali Abdul Rahman (as Dandiar).

The show ended with a rendition of the Malay song, 'Alhamdulilah' by all the participants. This song was written in 1928 by Minah's father, Wak Nani bin Haji Omar, who was attached to Genani Opera then:

Alhamdulilah wajah laksana
Berkatlah wali nabi saidina
Persembahan bangsawan sudah sempurna
Dijauhkan Allah bala bencana

Alhamdulillah syukur nikmat
Budaya bangsa akan selamat
Di dalam hati biar tersemat
Persembahan bangsawan sudahlah tamat.

    Thanks to Allah (your) countenance is an example
    Blessings from the guardian Prophet Muhammad
    The bangsawan performance has ended successfully
    May Allah keep calamities and disaster away from (us).

    Thanks to Allah for His blessings
    The culture of the nation will be saved
    In (our) hearts let the culture be entrenched
    (The) bangsawan performance has ended. (Author's translation)

* * *

Involvement in the *bangsawan* workshop, as well as rehearsals, performances, and the study of musical instruments, made me quite sure that the Ministry, government officials, and academics such as Rahmah Bujang and Mustapha Kamil Yassin were right in asserting that *bangsawan* is traditional Malay theatre. After all, Malay stories set in Malay courts of the past with Malay music, songs, poetry, dances, costumes, and etiquette are the mainstay of present-day performances. This is certainly true of *Raden Mas*.

When I conducted my research in 1986, *Laksamana Bentan* [Admiral Bentan] and *Laksamana Mati Dibunuh* [The Murder of the Admiral], both set in the Malay court of Bentan, were two other popular stories performed by the Bangsawan Sri USM at the university and at the annual Penang Festival (Pesta Pulau Pinang). The group also staged *Laksamana Bentan* in Taiping to celebrate the coronation of the new King of Malaysia. The same plays were performed for the Pacific Asia Tourist Association (PATA) delegates by troupes in Kuala Lumpur. Other common Malay stories staged included *Mahsuri* and *Tengku Sulung Mati Digantung* [The Hanging of Tengku Sulung].

Furthermore, the Malay *ronggeng asli* ensemble comprising the knobbed gong, *rebana*, accordion, and *biola* accompanied the performances in which I took part in Penang and Taiping and which I watched in Kuala Lumpur. Malay songs and dances from the *ronggeng asli* repertoire were employed. *Pantun* and *syair* verses formed the lyrics. In all three cases, virtually all the performers involved were Malays.

Additionally, most of the characteristics of *bangsawan* performed in the 1980s were similar to those of other older or traditional Malay theatrical forms such as the shadow puppet theatre which developed in South-East Asia. As in Malay traditional theatre, *bangsawan* of the 1980s had plots which were episodic and didactic; integrated comedy, melodrama, and serious elements; and mixed dance, music, dialogue, narration, and drama (Brandon, 1967).

Like Malay traditional theatre, formulas (Lord, 1976), mnemonics (Ong, 1982), or schemata (Sweeney, 1980) which were known by the performers and audiences were used in the dialogue and plot building. Stock characters and scene types were employed. These formulas, stock characters, and scenes helped the audience to follow the story and assisted performers in organizing materials for recall (Sweeney, 1980).

Moreover, as in traditional theatre, the structure of the music of *bangsawan* of the 1980s was built on cycles. As Judith and Alton Becker wrote of the Javanese gamelan (which applies to Malay equivalents), the 'basic unit of ... music is an entity called a *gongan*, a melodic cycle which can be repeated as many times as one wishes and whose beginning (marked by a stroke on the largest gong) is simultaneously its ending' (Becker and Becker, 1981: 207; Matusky, 1980).

With all these similarities in mind, I was almost sure that I was investigating a traditional theatrical form even though it was not linked to community events such as the harvest festival and had no religious functions such as propitiating spirits. After all, the traditional *wayang kulit* and *makyong* are performed to entertain tourists and for state functions in contemporary situations as well. Workshops and classes are also held to train the young in the skills of *wayang kulit* and *makyong* today.

However, as I researched deeper into *bangsawan*, perusing old newspapers, travel books, photographs, and early notations of music and listening to 78 r.p.m. recordings, something seemed amiss. The *bangsawan* of the early twentieth century that I began to unearth and accumulate information on seemed to be quite different from that being promoted by the government and government institutions today. While retaining many elements of traditional Malay theatre, the earlier *bangsawan* seemed to be more commercial and heterogeneous. It incorporated non-Malay stories and Western and other non-Malay elements in its stage setting, music, and dances. Unlike traditional Malay theatre, the performers were promoted as stars. Moreover, some of these stars were even non-Malays. The earlier *bangsawan* was also constantly changing and adapting itself to audience preferences. As a result, it attracted a non-Malay following as well.

Somewhat confused, I queried Minah and Alias, who had conducted the Ministry of Culture, Youth and Sports–USM workshop. The same questions were raised with Mat Hashim, my music instructor. They confirmed the differences. Other veteran *bangsawan* performers who were interviewed in Penang, Alor Star, and Kuala Lumpur further attested to my observations and findings.

2
The Development of Urban Entertainment and Commercial Theatre, *c.*1880–*c.*1930

Changes in Malaya

BANGSAWAN was one of many new cultural forms which emerged in response to and in the wake of the rapid social, economic, and political changes caused by British colonial expansion into the Malay Peninsula in the late nineteenth and early twentieth centuries. Following British intervention in 1874, a new political system was set up, superimposed on the existing Malay one. British officers 'whose advice must be asked and acted upon in all questions, other than those touching Malay religion and custom' (Emerson, 1964: 121) were appointed in the Malay States.

In time, this new political system brought political stability to the Malay States which, when the British intervened, were undergoing one of their perennial episodes of succession conflicts. Beginning from the late nineteenth century, these states began to experience rapid economic development. Tin mines and rubber estates were opened, and to service them a modern system of communications was built.

Political stability and a fast-growing economy attracted many Chinese, Indian, and Indonesian immigrants to the peninsula. They provided labour for the tin mines and rubber estates and the construction of roads and railways. By 1931, the population of Malaya had increased from 376,000 in 1835/40 to 4,348,000 (Gullick, 1963: 231). Ethnic Malays who had formed the vast majority of the population during the nineteenth century comprised, by 1931, only 44.4 per cent of the population. Malaya had willy-nilly become a multi-ethnic society.

Urban settlements or towns with administrative offices (to maintain law and order and provide public services) began to develop on the west coast of the peninsula where most of the mines and estates were located. Government and missionary schools were established to produce personnel for the lower rungs of the administrative system.

The multi-ethnic character of colonial Malayan society was best exemplified by the social composition of the urban centres where

Europeans were engaged in government service, trade, finance, the mining industry, and the plantations; Chinese from China were employed in tin mining and commerce; locally born Chinese or Babas were interpreters and clerks for the British; South Indians worked in the rubber estates and constructed railways, and Sikhs formed the backbone of the police force. In addition, there were Jawi Peranakan or locally born offspring of Malay women and South Indian traders who also worked as clerks and interpreters for the British. In the towns could be found Arab traders and Malays who were engaged in the Civil Service, the teaching profession, journalism, or the police force (Roff, 1967: 48–9).

The Growth of Urban Entertainment

With the development of towns and the appearance of an urban multi-ethnic population, new cultural forms and recreational activities began to emerge. Social clubs appeared in the 1910s and 1920s. In 1913, there were no fewer than forty sports clubs in Singapore alone (Roff, 1967: 187). Outdoor games such as cricket, rugby, soccer, hockey, and badminton, and indoor games like billiards and card games were played in these clubs (*Straits Echo*, 18 December 1933).

Some of these clubs promoted interest in music and drama and staged plays. Chinese Peranakan clubs such as the Wales Minstrel Party of Singapore performed plays like *Greed, Repentance*, and *Nyai Dasima* in aid of charity (*Malaya Tribune*, 28 August 1934). Many of the clubs had their own musical ensembles which performed at club meetings, parties, and exhibitions (*Straits Times*, 23 January 1935). The Malays could participate in *kroncong* (popular music) and *boria* (popular theatre) groups (*Straits Times*, 28 January and 6 December 1935). Such cultural clubs drew their membership from different income-earning groups.

Silent movies were introduced into Malaya in the first decades of the twentieth century. Commercial companies like Matsuo's Japanese Cinematograph (*Times of Malaya*, 8 August 1906), the British Cinematograph (*Times of Malaya*, 1 June 1907), the French Cinematograph (*Times of Malaya*, 22 August 1907), and the Besan Bioscope Co. (*Times of Malaya*, 18 August 1910) toured the peninsula. The screenings were held in tents. Several film clippings were shown each time; for example, Matsuo's Japanese Cinematograph showed the following programme in Ipoh on 8 August 1906:

1. Bear and the Sentinel; 2. The Russo-Japanese War; 3. The Poachers; 4. The Life of Napoleon Bonaparte (lst part); 5. Beauty at the Dancing School (in colour); 6. The Russo-Japanese War; 7. The Great Excited Argument at the Russo-Japanese Peace Meeting at Portsmouth; 8. The Pleasure Trip; 9. Great Fire! Great Fire!; 10. The Russo-Japanese War; 11. Adventure of Hop-o-My-Thumb; 12. Scandal at the Staircase; 13. Sleeping Beauty in Colour; 14. The Owners' Up-to-date Burglars; 15. The Great Joculation Boy. (*Times of Malaya*, 18 August 1910.)

During intervals when reels were being changed, 'gramophone selections, consisting of favourite English, Chinese and Malay music' were
played (*Straits Echo*, 26 August 1905). Sometimes there would be a
band in attendance (*Straits Echo*, 20 October 1905). In the 1920s,
Chinese and Indian silent movies were imported. *Aw Chua Pek Chua* or
The Righteous Snake in 19 reels was reportedly screened in Ipoh in 1926
(*Times of Malaya*, 20 October 1926). *Ramayana*, a Hindu film depicting
the life of Sri Rama, was shown at the Choong Wah Cinema, Ipoh, from
19 January to 21 January 1929 (*Times of Malaya*, 19 January 1929).

The talkies came to Malaya in 1929. Some of those shown included
The Rainbow Man (*Times of Malaya*, 23 November 1929), *The Jazz
Singer* (*Times of Malaya*, 25 January 1930), the Indian talkie *Rajah
Harischandra* (*Times of Malaya*, 9 August 1932), the Chinese talkie
Romance of the Opera (*Times of Malaya*, 1 December 1931), and the
Indonesian talkie *Forbidden Romance* or *Terpaksa Menikah* (*Times of
Malaya*, 6 May 1932 and *Straits Times*, 6 May 1932).

In 1934, the first Malay film, *Laila Majnun*, was released (Figure 2.1).
Produced by an Indian film crew under the direction of B. S. Rajan and
sponsored by the Motilal Chemical Company, the film had 'an all-Malay
cast', contained many beautiful 'Egyptian and Arabian dances with
songs and witty dialogue', and boasted 'beautiful Malayan scenery'
(*Times of Malaya*, 24 August 1934). Subsequently, the Chinese
entrepreneurs, Run Me and Run Run Shaw, better known as the Shaw
Brothers, began producing the first of their Malay films like *Mutiara*
(*Sunday Gazette*, 4 August 1940), *Ibu Tiri*, *Bermadu* (*Times of Malaya*,
27 October 1940), and *Tiga Kekasih* in Singapore.[1]

As entertainment, the urban population could also listen to the gramophone and the radio. The Gramophone and Typewriter Ltd. and Beka
of Berlin had already made recording expeditions to Malaya in 1902 and
1906 respectively. Songs like 'Bloemenlied (Opera Zang)' (10621),
'Kampak Besar Marsch' (10623), and 'Souvenir Singapoer' (10624)
were recorded by the Gramophone and Typewriter Ltd. in 1902
(Gramophone and Typewriter Ltd., 1903).[2] Some of the records of the
Gramophone and Typewriter Ltd. were advertised for sale in the *Times
of Malaya* (13 July 1904). These songs included 'Lagu Jalak Lanting'
(12893), 'Timang Burong' (12909), and 'Gambos Bunga Tanjong'
(12919). The Beka of Berlin visited Singapore on 11 January 1906 and
made a 22-hour stop at Penang. It was reported that 'they recorded a
number of so-called "stamboul" [popular Javanese theatre] songs and a
series of Javanese songs' (Want, 1976). These two companies and
others like Columbia, Pathe, Victor Talking Machine Co., and Carl
Lindstrom also recorded and disseminated the indigenous music of Asia,
Russia, North Africa, and Latin America (Gronow, 1981: 251–82). By
the 1920s and 1930s, gramophone recordings had become quite
widespread in the towns and accessible to the urban inhabitants of
Malaya (Figures 2.2 and 2.3; Plates 13–18).

The wireless or radio was also an important source of entertainment.

FIGURE 2.1

Advertisement for the First Malay Film Made in Malaya

WINDSOR CINEMA—*Opening To-morrow*

GALA MATINEES TO-MORROW & SUNDAY AT 2.45 P.M.

NIGHTLY AT 6-15 & 9-30

The Most Spectacular Malay Talkie Ever Brought To The Screen!

'LEILA MAJNUN'

Feast your eyes on the enchanting Egyptian and Arabian Dances!

SEE the Gorgeous Settings unmatched for their grandeur!

SEE the Glittering Beauty of the Natural Scenes of Malaya never before Filmed!

Hear the Lilting Song Hits in Classical Malay!

STARRING

Miss Fatima Benti Jasman of H.M.V. Records Fame.

Mr. Suki Bin Noordin, Eminent Malay Actor.

Mr. Syed Ali Bin Mansoor (the Renowned Artiste of the Bangsawan Stage).

and a Combination of Reputed Stars.

Entirely Produced in Singapore at a Cost of $50,000.

PRICES OF ADMISSION:—UPSTAIRS $1.50 and $1.00. DOWNSTAIRS—70, 40 and 20 cts. CHILDREN—HALF PRICE

Come Early To Avoid The Rush! Downstairs Tickets On Sale One Hour Before Start of Performance.

Source: Straits Echo, 20 April 1934.

FIGURE 2.2
Advertisement for Pagoda Records

Source: Malaya Tribune, 26 April 1935.

By the 1930s, British amateur wireless associations had sprung up in Johore (1923), Penang (1925), Ipoh (1926), Kuala Lumpur (1928), and Singapore (1931) (Wan Kadir, 1988: 196–8). These private radio stations played recorded Western popular music, as well as selections of popular music of the other ethnic groups in Malaya, in addition to hosting 'live' programmes. Among those who presented 'live' concerts through this new medium were musical groups like the Royal Ruby Opera, Penang Concert Orchestra, Hu Yew Seah Orchestra, Gaylads Musical Party, Frank Oriental Melodians, Rezels Troupe, Penang Lichi Seah Orchestra, Sri Majlis Kronchong Party, Evergreen Kronchong

FIGURE 2.3
Advertisement for Chap Kuching Records

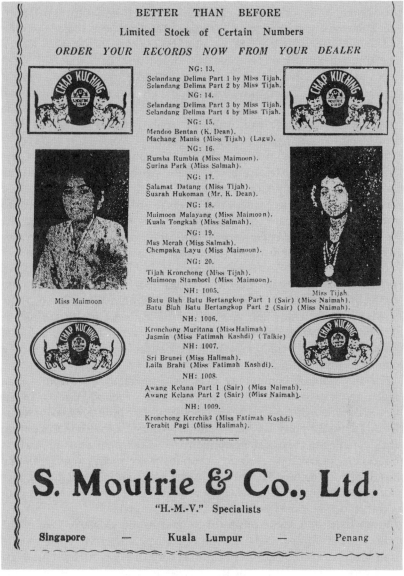

Source: *Malaya Tribune*, 17 October 1934.

Party, Jawi Peranakan Party, Hindu Sabah Tamil School, Tai Sun Cantonese Musical Party, and Beach Combers (*Straits Echo*, 13 November 1936).

Amusement parks, the first of which were set up in the late 1920s and 1930s, provided entertainment as well (Wan Kadir, 1983: 96–102). By 1933, the Hollywood Park, Great Eastern Park, and Fairyland had been

established in Kuala Lumpur (*Straits Times*, 23 February 1933), while
the Fun and Frolic Park and Wembley Park had been set up in Penang
(*Straits Times*, 13 April 1933) (Figure 2.4). The amusement park was a
place where different types of entertainment such as theatrical performances, movies, gambling stalls, *ronggeng* (Malay social dance) parties,
and joyride cars were available to all (*Straits Echo*, 16 February 1932).
The amusement park was also famous for its dance halls which included
stages for cabaret and *joget* (popular Malay dance) that catered to members of the working class, invariably men.[3] For a dance, the single man
gave a ticket (costing 10 cents) to the dance hostess he fancied. The
latest dances like the foxtrot, waltz, or rumba were performed in these
dance halls (*Straits Times*, 14 October 1933).

The urban inhabitant could also attend commercial theatrical performances during his leisure hours. These performances catered to the
varied tastes of the multiracial society. Operas, plays, and revues were
performed by touring professional theatre groups from the West to
entertain the Europeans. Some of the troupes that came included the
Willard Opera Co. (*Pinang Gazette and Straits Chronicle*, 22 September
1894), Williamson and Maher's Chicago Tourist Minstrel and Variety
Co. (*Pinang Gazette and Straits Chronicle*, 7 August 1895), Cordelier
Hicks Company's Theatre Parisien (*Straits Echo*, 21 October 1903), and
Mr M. B. Leavitts Elite Anglo-American Troubadors (*Straits Echo*,
23 March 1904). Although these theatrical troupes were 'never plentiful', they came 'at fairly regular intervals ... and at least half a dozen
musical celebrities would embark on an Eastern tour in the course of a
season' (*Straits Times*, 2 July 1930).[4]

For the Chinese community in towns, opera troupes from China
staged epics in the Cantonese, Hokkien, and Teochew dialects. In his
book, *Manners and Customs of the Chinese of the Straits Settlements*, written in 1879, Vaughan (1975: 85) observed that at the time there were
already Chinese theatrical performances, which consisted of 'endless
processions of soldiers, relieved occasionally by single combats of the
most ludicrous nature. The dresses [were] gorgeous long silk gowns covered with designs of dragons, flowers and quaint devices worked with
gold thread. Their dresses cost a great deal of money.'[5]

From India, too, came theatrical troupes to tour Malaya. One of the
most popular forms was the semi-operatic commercial Parsi theatre
from Gujerat. In the late nineteenth century, troupes such as the New
Elphinstone Theatrical Co. of Bombay performed in Hindustani to the
Indian community, who comprised mainly traders in the towns as well
as their children of mixed Indian–Malay parentage. Malays and Arabs
were also attracted to the form.

Local Indian stories, adaptations of Shakespeare, and Arabic fairy-
tales were performed. The calendar of the New Elphinstone Theatrical
Co. of Bombay at the King Street Parsee Theatre, Penang, included:

5 February—Aladdin and the Wonderful Lamp; 8 February—Ali Baba and the
Forty Thieves; 10 February—A Trip to Fairyland or Hawai Majlis; 12 February—
Fasani Ajaib alias Janealum and Anjoomanara; 15 February—Aladdin or The

FIGURE 2.4
Amusement Park and Radio Advertisements

RADIO SAIGON.

The following programme of Concerts by the "Radio-Saigon" Orchestra under the direction of M. André Soyer, will be transmitted over the Radio from Saigon daily.

Wednesday, Feb. 10—9.15 p.m. To 10.15 p.m.
1. Semiramis. Overture. (Rossini)
2. Snegourotchka. (Rimsky-Korsakov)
3. Arioso. (Cassado)
   Violoncello Solo by Mme. Simone Chefnay.
4. Burlesque Serenade. (Schmitt)
5. Procession of Bacchantes. (Taëyr)
6. The Inn of Virtue. Selection. (Verdun)

Thursday, February 11—9.15 p.m. To 10.15 p.m.
1. The Vampire. (Marschner)
2. The Georgians. (Offenbach)
3. Romance. (Bruneau)
   Flute Solo by Jean Chefnay.
4. Impressions of Provence. (Brun)
5. The New Spring. (Vidal)
6. Lips to Lips, Selection. (Yvain)

Friday, February 12—9.15 p.m. To 10.15 p.m.
1. The Two Battles. (Cherubini)
2. Etienne Marcel. (Saint-Saëns)
3. Violin Concerto, Final Movement.
                              (d'Ambrosio)
   Violin Solo by Robert Barras.
4. Morning, (Chaminade)
5. Serenade. (Widor)
6. Mannequins, Selection. (Szule)

RADIO BANGKOK.

Wednesday, February 10:
7.00 p.m. Atmospheric report, commercial news, etc.
7.30   ,,   A paper on "Weights and Measures."
7.35   ,,   A paper on "Flax" by Phya Bhojakara.
8.00   ,,   Siamese Music.
9.00   ,,   Time Signal: News.
9.20   ,,   Teochew music.

Thursday, February 11:
7.00 p.m. Atmospheric report, commercial news, etc.
7.30   ,,   A paper on "Personality" by Luang Vichitr Vadakar.
8.00   ,,   Siamese Music by Royal Pi-pat.
9.00   ,,   Time Signal: News.

Friday, February 12:
7.00 p.m. Atmospheric report, commercial news, etc.
7.30   ,,   Dhanyavan Tales.
8.00   ,,   Siamese Music by Pi-pat.
9.00   ,,   Time Signal: News.
9.20   ,,   European Music by Marine Orchestra, relayed from the Grand Palace.

The following selections will be played:—
1. March. "Cadiz Chueca," Y. Valverde.
2. Overture, "Cleopatro," L. Mancinelli.
3. Selection, "Stradella," Flotow.
4. Selection, "Sullivan's Melodies," Charles Godfrey Junr.
5. Invitation, a la valse, Beber.
6. March, "Indian blood," Albert Mattausch.

Saturday, February 13:
11.55 a.m. Siamese Records.
12.00   ,,   Stories for school children by Khun Sarngabhudad.

FUN & FROLIC LIMITED

USUAL 10 CENTS ADMISSION ONLY.

THE GREAT TOLONI TRIO MYSTICS and MAGICIANS will be giving extra turns NIGHTLY from 5th February 1932, and will mystify you with their latest illusions
1. HAND-CUFF ESCAPES
2. SAWING THRO A WOMAN
3. SLEEP IN MID-AIR
4. and other Magical illusions and thrills.
   So come and be convinced.

The Ritz Cantonese Opera Co., will also show you the modern Chinese wayang and you will see all that should be seen.

Open-air Cinema, side shows and other amusements.

Commencing from February 9, 1932, we are having special Krontjong Stambocls and dances, accompanied with latest songs and hits. This is by a Malay troupe of talented artists and will show nightly for a short season.

The Darulazuan Opera Co., will be staging their show at Fun & Frolic as from 11th February, 1932, (Thursday Night).

On Saturday Night, February 13th 1932, there will be exhibitions of Feats of Strength by a troupe of local artists.

The Bintang Dua Blas Krontjong Party will also give their latest pieces of special Kronchongs, and Stambocls. Watch for date of Announcement.

NO EXTRA CHARGE.

KUALA LUMPUR.

Amateur Radio Society.

Kuala Lumpur regular broadcasts are until further notice:—
Daily on 55.5 Metres 10.30 to 11 a.m. Petaling Hill Testing.
(Except Sundays and Public Holidays).
Tuesday on 75 Metres from 7.30 p.m. to 8.30 p.m.
Friday on 75 Metres from the Studio.
6.30 p.m. Krontchong Music.
7.00 p.m. English.
7.15 p.m. British Official Wireless News.
7.25 p.m. Recital of H.M.V. Record Music
8.30 p.m Close down.
Sunday on 75 Metres Orchestral Concert from the Selangor Club.

Source: *Straits Echo*, 10 February 1932.

Wonderful Lamp in real Chinese costumes; 17 February—Chatra Bakavli; 18 February—Pakdaman Dilaran; and 24 February—Gulzar-e-Nekey. (*Pinang Gazette and Straits Chronicle*, 5–24 February 1896.)

Spectacular tricks, thrills, and suspense were highlighted, and songs and dances accompanied the performances (Balwant Gargi, 1962: 130; Mulk Raj Anand, 1951: 45–6; Shri Chandravadan Mehta, 1956: 94).

The Development of *Bangsawan*

It was in the midst of socio-political changes and the unprecedented exposure of the local population to a wide range of non-indigenous cultural activities that the new form of theatre called *bangsawan* emerged. *Bangsawan* literally means 'of the aristocratic class', the term referring to the plays and characters about royalty (not necessarily Malay) which are the mainstay of the form.

Bangsawan performers say that the Parsi theatre triggered off the development of *bangsawan*. By the 1880s, the Parsi theatre had become so popular in Penang that its Hindustani songs were sung by Indians, Indian Muslims, Arabs, and Malays. These songs, with Malay lyrics in place of the original Hindi, were also performed during weddings (Edrus, 1960: 50–1). Singing troupes which presented such songs were formed, one of the most well known of which belonged to an Arab-Malay, Mamat Mashor of Penang. Mamat Mashor added plays like *Indera Saba* to the performances. His troupe became so well known that the Sultan of Deli in Sumatra invited the group to perform at his palace, and for the first time two women actresses were included. After his return to Penang, Mamat Mashor formed a professional troupe (Edrus, 1960: 52). In 1885, Mamat Pushi, a rich Parsi who lived in Penang, was so attracted to this new theatre that he formed his own troupe, Pushi Indera Bangsawan of Penang, the first troupe to call itself *bangsawan*. The troupe travelled as far as Singapore (Edrus, 1960: 52).

From the 1890s on, other troupes which called themselves variously *wayang Parsi* (Parsi theatre), *tiruan wayang Parsi* (imitation Parsi theatre), *komedi Melayu* (Malay comedy), or *bangsawan* (Figure 2.5) were formed (Camoens, 1982).[6] At the turn of the century, however, 'opera' was the term commonly used for what is now known as *bangsawan*; this was probably because many of the Western vaudeville and operetta troupes, which toured Malaya and which influenced *bangsawan*, were called opera. Some of the opera troupes formed included the Wayang Yap Chow Thong (*Straits Echo*, 12 May 1904), the Straits Opera (*Straits Echo*, 21 March 1912), and the Grand Opera Co. (*Straits Echo*, 5 January 1914).

Bangsawan attracted multi-ethnic participation at all levels. Proprietors included Chinese like Yap Chow Thong (owner of Wayang Yap Chow Thong) (*Straits Echo*, 14 May 1904) and Tay Boon Teck (owner of Opera Stamboul and the Empire Theatrical Co.) (*Straits Echo*, 22 November 1904). Managers of the troupes were also of various ethnic origins. Opera Stamboul was managed by a European, H. Housen

FIGURE 2.5
Advertisement for the Empress Victoria Jawi Peranakkan
Theatrical Company, Indra Bangsawan

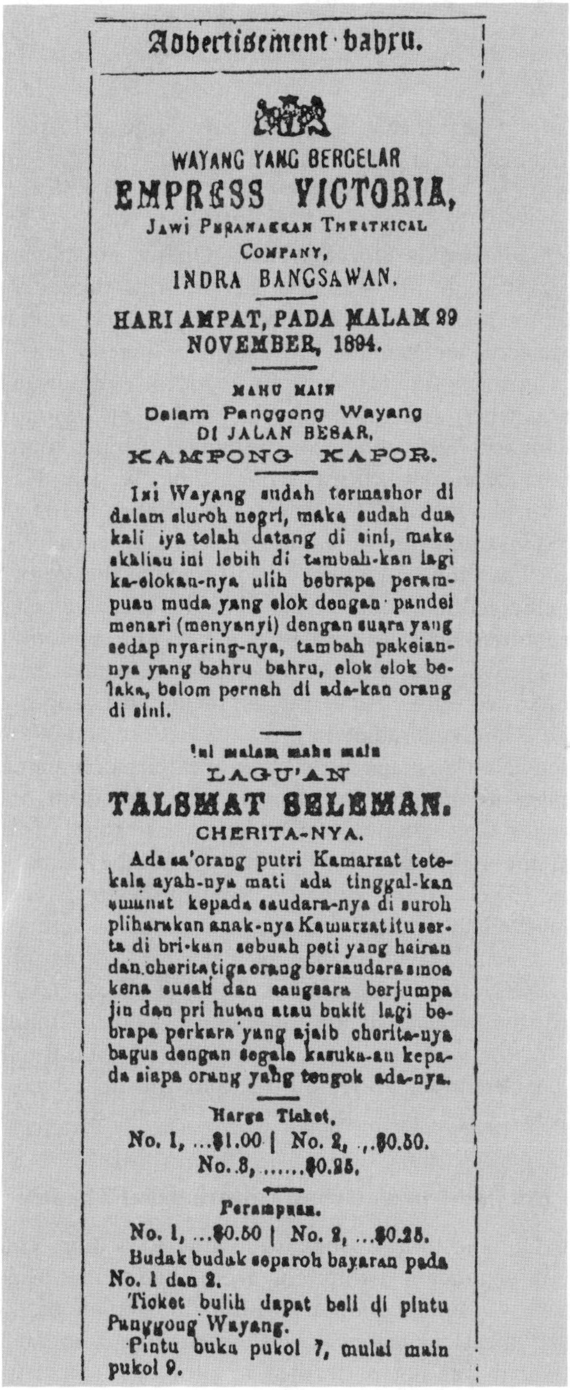

Aobertisement babru.

WAYANG YANG BERGELAR
EMPRESS VICTORIA,
Jawi Peranakkan Theatrical
Company,
INDRA BANGSAWAN.

**HARI AMPAT, PADA MALAM 29
NOVEMBER, 1894.**

MAHU MAIN
Dalam Panggong Wayang
DI JALAN BESAR,
KAMPONG KAPOR.

Ini Wayang sudah termashor di
dalam sluroh negri, maka sudah dua
kali iya telah datang di sini, maka
skaliau ini lebih di tambah-kan lagi
ka-elokan-nya ulih bebrapa perampuan muda yang elok dengan pandei
menari (menyanyi) dengan suara yang
sedap nyaring-nya, tambah pakeian-
nya yang bahru bahru, elok elok be-
laka, belom pernah di ada-kan orang
di sini.

Ini malam mahu main
LAGU'AN
TALSMAT SELEMAN,
CHERITA-NYA.

Ada sa'orang putri Kamarzat tete-
kala ayah-nya mati ada tinggal-kan
amanat kepada saudara-nya di suroh
pliharakan anak-nya Kamarzat itu ser-
ta di bri-kan sebuah peti yang hairan
dan cherita tiga orang bersaudara smoa
kena susah dan sangsara berjumpa
jin dan pri hutan atau bukit lagi bebrapa perkara yang ajaib cherita-nya
bagus dengan segala kasuka-an kepada siapa orang yang tengok ada-nya.

Harga Ticket.
No. 1, ...$1.00 | No. 2, ...$0.50.
No. 3, ...$0.25.

Perampuan.
No. 1, ...$0.50 | No. 2, ...$0.25.
Budak budak separoh bayaran pada
No. 1 dan 2.
Ticket bulih dapat beli di pintu
Punggong Wayang.
Pintu buka pukol 7, mulai main
pukol 9.

Source: Bintang Timor, 29 November 1894.

(*Straits Echo*, 11 November 1904); Wayang Aishah by a Malay or Indian Muslim, Omar bin Osman (*Straits Echo*, 26 April 1905); Star Opera Co. by a Chinese, Y. L. Tan (*Straits Echo*, 26 August 1912); and Britania Opera Co. by an Indian, A. Babjee (*Straits Echo*, 18 March 1918). The performers were also 'generally mixed', comprising 'Malays, Eurasians and sometimes Chinese players' (*Straits Echo*, 20 October 1928) (cf. Chapter 4).

By the early twentieth century, then, many large and small *bangsawan* troupes had emerged and were active in Malaya. Some of the well-known ones included Wayang Kassim or the Zanibar Royal Theatrical Co. of Singapore, Wayang Yap Chow Thong, Wayang Inche Puteh, Dean's Opera, Peninsula Opera, Malaya Opera, and Nooran's Opera. These troupes were, by any standard, adventurous; they took *bangsawan* to the major town centres and rural districts in Malaya and across the Straits of Malacca; for example, the Empress Victoria Jawi Peranakkan Theatrical Company or Comedy Pusi Indra Bangsawan played in Palembang, northern Sumatra, for two and a half months (*Bintang Timor*, 24 January 1895). Some of the bigger troupes toured as far as Burma, Thailand, and Java. It was reported that Wayang Kassim played in Bangkok for two months (*Straits Echo*, 5 October 1910) while Dean's Opera toured Java and Burma (*Idaran Zaman*, 24 February 1933).

Bangsawan was similar to other types of popular theatre of South-East Asia which emerged and toured Malaya in the late nineteenth and early twentieth centuries—not least in its appeal. The *komedi stambul*, for example, which was created by A. Mahieu in Surabaya in 1891,[7] drew audiences of varied ethnic backgrounds, including Europeans, Chinese, and Javanese. Mahieu combined aspects of Eastern and Western theatre but used the Malay language in dialogue and lyrics. He named the form *komedi stambul* as most of the stories originated from Stambul (the Malay name for Constantinople or Istanbul, the capital of Turkey) and actors wore the red fez and white turban of the Turks and Arabs (Manusama, 1922). Other forms of popular theatre which resembled *bangsawan* in the late nineteenth and early twentieth century include the *ketoprak* of Central Java (Hatley, 1985), the *ludruk* of East Java (Peacock, 1968), the *sandiwara* or *tonil* of West Java (Brandon, 1967: 50–3), the *zarzuela* of the Philippines (Lapena-Bonifacio, 1972; Larkin, 1978), the *likay* of Thailand (Smithies, 1971), the *lakon bassac* of Cambodia (Brandon, 1967: 60–1), and the *cai luong* of Vietnam (Brandon, 1967: 75) (Map 2.1).

Bangsawan as Urban Commercial Theatre

As a product of the times, *bangsawan* came to acquire characteristics that made it significantly different from traditional Malay theatre, although there was some continuity with its indigenous past. Unlike traditional Malay theatre, *bangsawan* was entertainment-oriented and highly commercial. It was not performed to propitiate spirits which might

19

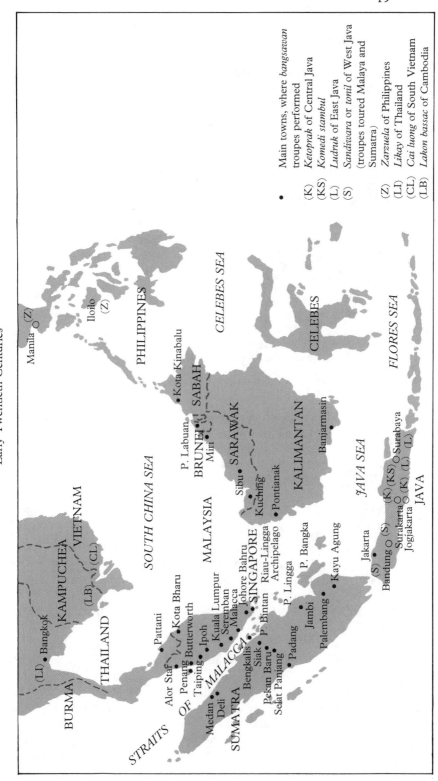

MAP 2.1
Popular Theatre in South-East Asia in the Late Nineteenth and
Early Twentieth Centuries

• Main towns, where *bangsawan* troupes performed

(K)   *Ketoprak* of Central Java
(KS) *Komedi stambul*
(L)   *Ludruk* of East Java
(S)   *Sandiwara* or *tonil* of West Java (troupes toured Malaya and Sumatra)
(Z)   *Zarzuela* of Philippines
(LI) *Likay* of Thailand
(CL) *Cai luong* of South Vietnam
(LB) *Lakon bassac* of Cambodia

bring disease to humans and crops, or to thank the gods for a good harvest; rather it was performed to entertain, and as a corollary of this, to
make money for its proprietors and performers.

Like Western commercial theatre, the performances were publicized
through advertisements and leaflets or handbills. Stage hands and young
boys were despatched to nearby kampongs and through the streets of
the town to hand out leaflets before the show. Billboard paintings were
put up in front of the theatre. Sometimes the shows were announced
across town by vans fitted with loudspeakers. These advertisements
emphasized the commercial nature of *bangsawan* by inviting the public
to visit the theatre and enjoy a good evening's entertainment and to forget one's worries:

Why leave your house after dinner without a fixed destination? Go to Tek
Soon's Hall where the Straits Opera Coy. is performing to crowded houses and
enjoy a good evening's entertainment. (*Straits Echo*, 8 January 1912.)

Moonlight Opera's advertisement said:

After 6 days of hard work
after 6 nights of unrest, thinking of your business, be sure, that you'll choose
your weekend to enjoy and forget your worries
You should make your Saturday night thoroughly enjoyable and bright—make it
a night of bliss with Eddie's Crystal Follies. (*Straits Echo*, 17 June 1933.)

The Oriental Malay Opera lured the audience with the following advertisement:

If the evenings hang heavily on your shoulders, and if you have no special
engagements, your time will assuredly be well spent by paying the show a visit.
    You may conveniently shed your business and worries for 3 solid hours; you
can rest your congested brains and ease your torpid minds with comfort.
    The show guarantees to remove your fits of the blues by the bushel and infuse
mirth and laughs by meteorological consistency. (*Times of Malaya*, 2 February
1926.)

The performances were also scheduled to fit the general recreational
calendar of the wage-earner. Special performances were staged on
Saturday and Sunday nights and on holidays. To attract as many as possible, vaudeville performances comprising songs, dances, and comic
sketches were performed on these occasions (cf. Chapter 3).

Bangsawan was not performed all night as in traditional theatre; it
usually began at 8 or 9 p.m. and ended at midnight or 1 a.m. Although
prayers would be said and holy water sprinkled when the troupe first
arrived at a new place and while the stage was being set up, unlike traditional theatre the *buka panggung* (literally 'opening the stage') ceremony
for propitiating spirits before each performance was shortened or left
out completely. Instead, crackers would be fired, the orchestra would
play a few overtures, and a chorus would sing and dance before the start
of each performance. According to articles in the *Straits Echo*
(21 September 1906 and 12 December 1932), crackers were also fired

after every scene 'to remind the scene shifters when to pull'. Instead of sending the spirits off after the show, a *bangsawan* performance would end with the rendering of 'God Save the King', the national anthem of the colonial power (*Straits Echo*, 12 December 1932).

Nevertheless, as in traditional theatre, the atmosphere was informal and conducive to relaxation and socialization. Food and drinks were available. Audiences brought their own snacks or bought from hawkers walking up and down the aisles. There was always a 'refreshment bar or trestle' in the theatre where 'Burma cherrots [cheroots], "cycle" cigarettes and drink[s] of bright colour' were displayed and sold (*Straits Echo*, 14 November 1908). Sometimes troupes distributed food to the audiences as well: both Dean's Opera (*Straits Echo*, 4 November 1932) and Kiah Opera (*Straits Echo*, 12 and 17 January 1935) gave out *bunga telur* (eggs distributed during weddings) and *nasi kunyit* (yellow rice) to their patrons after the play *Dan Dan Stia* was presented. People talked, laughed, cried, and exclaimed while children ran around. It was not considered a disturbance to hear 'running comments during the progress of the play on the players and the turn of events' by members of the audience. On the contrary, according to a writer of the *Straits Echo*, such comments 'caused much merriment' and were 'almost as interesting as the play itself' (*Straits Echo*, 20 August 1906). On this particular occasion, the lady who was making the comments apparently was so worried that one of the actors, 'who was dancing, should fall over the stage' that the writer and other members of the audience felt pity for the former. Therefore not only was the theatre a venue to relax and socialize but it also gave audiences a sense of participation in the shaping of the evening. Audiences interacted not only with one another but with the performers as well.

These performances were held in closed-door rented theatres which were roofed and walled instead of the open-air platforms of traditional theatre. Makeshift tents were used when theatres were not available. When Comedy Pusi Indra Bangsawan played in Palembang in 1895, a 'big godown-like tent' (*khemah gedung besar*) was built. The tent was 'very wide' (*luas betul*), and it had a 'tiled roof' (*atap genting*) and 'wooden walls' (*dinding papan*) (*Bintang Timor*, 2 February 1895). At other times, the theatre was a 'palm-thatched barn' (*Straits Echo*, 14 November 1908).

At first, the halls were lighted with kitson lamps (*Straits Echo*, 11 May 1904), but by 1905 theatres in big towns were fitted with electric fans and electric light. House lights would be left on during the play (*Straits Echo*, 24 January 1905).

At one end of the hall or tent was a proscenium stage. As in Western theatre, the stage setting consisted of the drop and wing variety—painted cloth backdrops (*tirai*), curtains ('drop sin', *jalar*), crown (*mahkota*) where the name of the troupe was shown, and painted flats facing the audience on the sides (*kota bam*, 'said wing') between which performers entered and exited (Figures 2.6 and 2.7). As *bangsawan* was

22

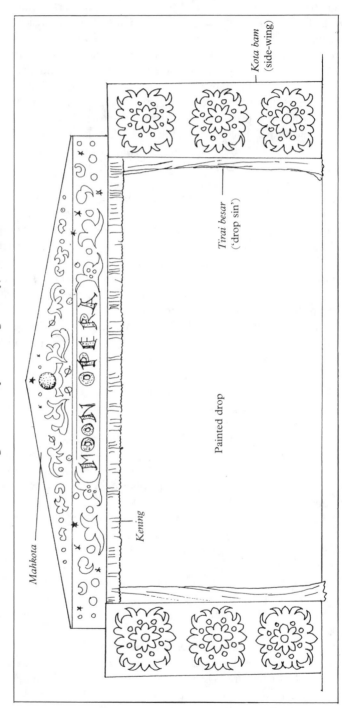

FIGURE 2.6

Proscenium Stage of the Drop and Wing Variety, c.1920–c.1930

Mahkota

Kening

MOON OPERA

Painted drop

Tirai besar
('drop sin')

Kota bam
(side–wing)

Source: Drawing by Mohd. Bahroodin Ahmad.

FIGURE 2.7
Three Types of Side-wings for Different Scenes, *c*.1920–*c*.1930

Hutan	*Taman*	*Istana*

Source: Drawing by Mohd. Bahroodin Ahmad.

influenced by Western theatre, English terms spelt the Malay style were often used to describe these sets. Sometimes 'cold-clay winged figures' adorned the wings (*Straits Echo*, 14 November 1908).

With the proscenium stage, the audience no longer watched the performances from three sides of the platform as they used to in the past. Nor could they sit wherever they liked. The audience was separated from the performers, seats were divided into different classes according to admission prices, and sometimes ushers led the audience to their seats (*Chahaya Pulau Pinang*, 9 July 1904). The expensive seats were in front 'facing the stage' and 'consisted of boxes, like old-fashioned square family pews' (*Straits Echo*, 4 June 1923). The less expensive seats were often plain wooden benches (Figures 2.8 and 2.9).[8]

To attend an ordinary performance by well-known troupes like the Wayang Kassim or Wayang Yap Chow Thong, one had to pay 25 cents for third-class seats, 50 cents for second-class seats, $1.00 for first-class seats, and $2.00 for reserved seats. Ladies who sat upstairs paid 25 cents for second-class seats and 50 cents for first-class seats (*Straits Echo*, 7 September 1903 and 16 April 1904). If the performance was held at the Town Hall, which meant it catered mainly for the Europeans and the richer Asians, prices were raised to $1.00 for unreserved seats and

FIGURE 2.8
Opera Tent Showing First-, Second-, and Third-class Seats, *c.*1920–*c.*1930

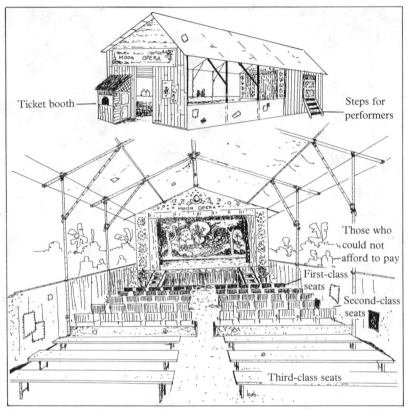

Source: Drawing by Mohd. Bahroodin Ahmad.
Note: Those who could not afford to pay were allowed to watch from outside.

FIGURE 2.9
Bangsawan Theatre in the Amusement Park, *c.*1930–*c.*1940

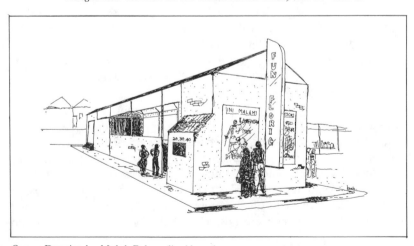

Source: Drawing by Mohd. Bahroodin Ahmad.

$2.00 for reserved seats (*Straits Echo*, 2 November 1903). Lesser-known troupes like the Wayang Aishah Indra Mahkota Theatrical Co. of Penang charged less ($1.00, 50 cents, 25 cents; ladies, upstairs: 50 cents, 25 cents, and 15 cents). During difficult economic times, as in the Great Depression of the 1930s, seat prices were lowered accordingly, and people who could not afford to pay were allowed to watch from outside.

Popularity of *Bangsawan*

Bangsawan had already become popular[9] in Malaya and Indonesia by the 1890s and early 1900s but it reached its peak in the 1920s and 1930s. Its popularity was indicated in many newspaper reports. When a new troupe, the Sree Penang Theatrical Co., was formed in 1895, 'hundreds of people went to see it and there was not even one empty seat' (*Bintang Timor*, 24 January 1895).[10] When Comedy Pusi Indra Bangsawan performed in Palembang, the '*wayang* hall was so full some had to stand for lack of places' (*Bintang Timor*, 13 February 1895).[11] And when the Palembang correspondent questioned a Muslim why he attended every night, he replied, 'If I don't see the show for even one night, I cannot sleep because I am not satisfied.... My heart feels like it is being sucked and yearns to see it.' (*Bintang Timor*, 12 March 1895.)[12] In 1904, even though there were five *wayang* in Penang (*Straits Echo*, 16 May 1904), the Wayang Yap Chow Thong in Penang drew 'crowds' which 'attended in full force and late comers had to be refused admittance' (*Straits Echo*, 30 May 1904). Another correspondent reported that 'inside the theatre hall the air was simply stifling and seats were so much huddled up together that it was simply impossible to move one's own elbow without touching one's neighbour. Tickets were sold over and over again when it was quite apparent there was no more room' (*Straits Echo*, 24 June 1907). These descriptions testify to the great popularity of *bangsawan* in the late nineteenth and early twentieth centuries. Indeed, 'the visit of a *bangsawan* or opera company' was 'an attraction' that never failed 'to draw the crowds in any town either of Malaya or the Dutch East Indies' (*Straits Echo*, 20 October 1928).

In the 1930s, there continued to be 'constant fights for seating accommodation'. In the case of Nooran Opera, 'additional chairs had to be brought in each night' (*Straits Echo*, 5 June 1933) during its performance in Penang. Such was the public reception of Dean's Opera during its entire season in Penang 'that night after night, it was the case of standing room only' (*Straits Times*, 9 January 1932). Opera fans requested troupes to stay longer or to come back for a second season. A certain Mat wrote to the *Straits Echo* requesting that the Normah Amateur Dramatic Party of Penang should 'extend [its] season to another three weeks or so in order to allow all the Penang Opera Fans a chance to see this wonderful show' (*Straits Echo*, 12 September 1935). And when Dean's Opera toured Sumatra in 1933, the troupe was 'recalled ... to give a second season in Medan' after an initial offering of three weeks (*Straits Echo*, 6 June 1933).

Although the main language used was Malay, *bangsawan* performances attracted a multi-ethnic audience. Besides Malays, locally born Babas and Nonyas (Chinese men and women born locally), Jawi Peranakan, Chinese, Indians, Arabs, and Europeans were drawn to it. When the Comedy Pusi Indra Bangsawan performed in Palembang, there were many people in the audience—'more aristocratic Malays and fewer Chinese, Arabs, Dutch and Indians' (*Bintang Timor*, 12 March 1895).[13] On another occasion, the *Chahaya Pulau Pinang* reported that 'since the wayang [Yap Chow Thong] played in Penang, every night ... the big theatre was full with European men, European women, Baba, Nonya, Malays, [and] Jawi Peranakan'(*Chahaya Pulau Pinang*, 11 May 1904).[14]

In fact, the 'Babas and Nonyas who spoke and understood Malay' were such great fans of *bangsawan* that they were motivated to set up their own amateur *bangsawan* groups. When the Chinese Babas of Penang performed a Malay *bangsawan* play called *Princess Nilam Chahaya* to collect money for the China Flood Fund at the Anglo-Chinese School Union Building in May 1918, a review article commented that even 'the Malay professionals present' admitted that 'the piece ... was fairly well performed' (*Straits Echo*, 28 May 1918). In 1919, the same group staged *Nyai Dasima* (*Straits Echo*, 12 October 1919) and in 1920, *Ginufifah* or *Herto Brabant* (*Straits Echo*, 13 July 1920). In 1926, a party of Chinese ladies calling themselves Penang Nyo Nya Bangsawan presented *Jula Juli Bintang Tiga* [The Third Star Jula Juli], *Nyai Dasima*, and *A Merchant of Bagdad* (*Straits Echo*, 21 December 1926) (Figure 2.10).

Audiences were composed of various social strata although the people were seated according to the rates of payment. *Bangsawan* also had a keen following among members of the Malay royal houses. The Sultan of Perak and his children were observed to be in the audience watching Wayang Yap Chow Thong in 1904 (*Chahaya Pulau Pinang*, 17 September 1904), while the Sultan of Kelantan graced the Straits Opera's performance in Singapore and requested to see the play *Jalil Shah* (*Straits Echo*, 20 June 1912). When Dean's Opera was touring Sumatra, 'royalty patronised the shows almost nightly, including the Sultan of Deli and the Sultan of Langkat' (*Straits Echo*, 6 June 1933). The Grand Nooran Opera of Singapore was invited to perform for eight nights by the royal family of Trengganu (*Malacca Guardian*, 7 September 1934). Royalty were given special seats in front (sometimes called box seats); according to Menah Yem, wife of the owner of Nooran Opera of Malacca, the Sultan of Kedah was such an ardent fan that a front-row seat covered with yellow cloth was reserved for him every night.

Box seats were also reserved for the British officials who were often invited to be the patrons of performances. The Grand Opera Co. performed under the patronage of the Honourable W. Evans, the British

FIGURE 2.10
Advertisement for Nyo Nya Bangsawan

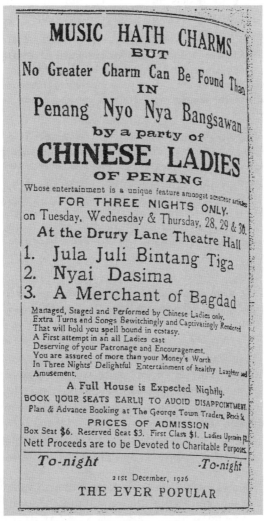

Source: Straits Echo, 21 December 1926.

Resident Councillor in 1909 (*Straits Echo*, 22 December 1909), while the British Resident of Selangor patronized the performance of Nooran Opera in 1933 (*Straits Echo*, 6 June 1933). Other box seats were reserved by the socially prominent—rich Chinese and Indian business-men and Malay professionals (*Straits Echo*, 1 September 1924).

The first-class seating area was usually occupied by middle-income earners—Chinese shopkeepers, Malay schoolteachers, Indian traders and clerks—while second-class seats were taken by the less well-off; labourers, peasants, and the servants of those seated in boxes watched from outside. Ladies and their little children sat upstairs (if there was one) for the sake of privacy and to maintain a kind of social decorum.

To show their appreciation, socially prominent members of the audience would give gold medals or silver and gold cups to the actors and actresses and the managers of the troupes. Newspaper reports like the following were common:

The Straits born Chinese of Kuala Lumpur presented Abu Bakar, manager of Wayang Yap Chow Thong, with a gold medal on the night of the first inst. during the performance of 'Rossini' ... the presentation was made in recognition of Abu Bakar's successful management and his marked ability as a comedian. (*Straits Echo*, 3 September 1904.)

On 17 Sept [1910], [Wayang Kassim] played before HM the King of Siam ... [who] presented Mr E. Thomas, the manager, with a silver and gold cup bearing the king's monogram. (*Straits Echo*, 5 October 1910.)

A gold medal set with diamond stars ... [was] presented by the Sabrul Jamil Football Club to the Star Opera. (*Straits Echo*, 27 September 1912.)

Mr Lim Choon Sim ... awarded a gold medal to Miss Jacoba [of the Rose Opera] for being the best Kronchong singer he had ever come across. Miss Jacoba was also given a medal by the management of the park. (*Straits Echo*, 9 November 1932.)

All roads led to the Wembley Amusement Park ... when a huge crowd ... visited the Moonlight Opera Co., the occasion being the presentation of a silver cup to the co. by the Happy Go-Lucky Party of Penang, in appreciation of the enjoyable performances they had been giving to the theatre loving public. (*Straits Echo*, 22 May 1933.)

Certificates of merit and letters of praise were also awarded to opera troupes by royalty (*Straits Echo*, 6 June 1933; *Saudara*, 18 July 1936).

It was commonly reported that individuals in the audience would fall in love with the performers and shower gifts on them. 'Lovesick youths' were known to 'pass their photographs up to their favourite actress' and to throw 'a good deal of money ... to her on stage' (*Malacca Guardian*, 9 May 1932).

Why was *bangsawan* so popular? First, even though various new forms of entertainment had emerged at the same time, the local people could not identify with many of them. The Malays preferred *bangsawan* to the silent movie or the talkie; they used to call the silent movie *wayang mati* (literally 'dead theatre'). To Pak Suki, a veteran *bangsawan* performer, the silent movie was not a 'live' performance. As he put it, '... after a screening the reel was rolled back into a box'.

The Malays could not really understand the Western talkie, while local talkies were few—and alien to them for other reasons. When Indonesian talkies like *Terpaksa Menikah* (*Times of Malaya*, 6 May 1932), *Nyai Dasima* (*Sunday Gazette*, 30 June 1935), *Anak Kecil Merah* (*Sunday Gazette*, 20 June 1937), and *Terang Bulan* (*Times of Malaya*, 17 June 1938) were screened, the Malays were not attracted to them. As a Kuala Lumpur correspondent reported in the *Straits Times* (20 February 1932), the Malays were critical of the first Malay talkie—

Terpaksa Menikah—when it was shown in the capital city:

The bazaar Malay, the rather harsh Javanese accent of the actors, and the air of reality which the cinema gives to domestic scenes which the orthodox Malay thinks should only be enacted in strict privacy, prejudiced them against the picture ... the heroine, a Malay girl of about 18 years of age, was seen sitting on the knees of her lover and caressing him—a sight calculated to give any Malay except the sophisticated townie type a very severe shock....

The picture revealed interesting differences between the customs of Malaya and Java. The girl referred to above was seen wheeling a bicycle, whereas in this country, girls of the more advanced communities rarely ride bicycles, let alone the Malays. In another scene, a number of Malay women were seated on chairs, whereas in Malaya, they would have squatted on the floor.

Technically, the picture was not very satisfactory. The photography was not first class and the Javanese Malay grated on the ear. The background of Javanese scenery was attractive, however, and there were some good dancing scenes.

What annoyed the Kuala Lumpur audience more than anything was that the Malay spoken by the actors was not the high Malay which is heard in the bangsawan entertainments in this country but the bazaar variety.[15]

The comment of a local motor-car driver was significant. He applied to the picture the adjective *kasar*, which means rough, vulgar or coarse.

Likewise, the locally born Chinese or Babas and Jawi Peranakan preferred *bangsawan* to the Chinese opera and Parsi theatre as, being Malay speakers, they understood it better. In fact, the Jawi Peranakan were the first to promote *bangsawan* while the Babas (as mentioned earlier) started their own groups in the early twentieth century.

The Europeans, on the other hand, went to *bangsawan* performances, not because they thought the performances were good, but because there was a paucity of entertainment. As a European reporter wrote, 'we have not the least doubt that many were, like ourselves, not a little disappointed; and yet, perhaps, they would patronise the wayang again.... Penang is a small place with few amusements and, like a drowning man, we clutch even at straws.' (*Straits Echo*, 24 June 1907.) As noted earlier, touring Western theatrical troupes were 'never plentiful'; by 1930, the 'supply of such entertainment had ceased almost entirely' (*Straits Times*, 2 July 1930).

Secondly, *bangsawan* became very popular because the mass media played an important role in promoting and disseminating it. By the 1920s and 1930s, recording companies like His Master's Voice, Beka, Columbia, Pathe, Parlophone, Odeon, Grand, and Chap Kuching had recorded songs from the *bangsawan* repertoire. Popular *bangsawan* artistes like Mr Khairuddin (or Dean), Miss Tijah, Miss Salmah, Miss Maimoon, Mr S. Abdullah, Miss Norlia, and Miss Riboet, and conductors like A. Soliano, C. Martinez, Zubir Said, Ahmad Jaafar, Mr Jaar, and S. Albar recorded with these companies (*Malaya Tribune*, 11 July 1934; A. Samad Hassan, 1977). Some *bangsawan* plays such as *Jula Juli Bintang Tiga* (Chap Kuching), *Laila Majnun* (His Master's Voice), *Noor-E-Islam* [The Light of Islam] (Chap Singa), and *Puteri Gunong Ledang* [The Princess of Gunong Ledang] (His Master's Voice) were also recorded. First made in Singapore, the wax mould was sent to India to be pressed, a process which usually took one to two months (*Straits Echo*, 24 May 1934).[16] Often, after release, the records were publicized at *bangsawan* performances. It was reported that 'Messrs S. Moutrie and Co. introduced the Chap Kuching Records ... at the Dean's Grand Opera at the Great World [Amusement Park] in 1934' (*Malaya Tribune*, 11 July 1934). Through the gramophone, *bangsawan* enthusiasts could listen to the latest *bangsawan* songs and their favourite stories at home.

The wireless helped to popularize *bangsawan* music as well. Local transmitting stations played *bangsawan* music from gramophone records and featured 'live' *bangsawan* programmes. Artistes of the Royal Ruby Opera gave a studio concert from the local Penang transmitting station (ZHJ), with the following programme (*Straits Echo*, 13 November 1936):

March: Durch che Lufte by Ruby's Orchestra
Kronchong: Stormy Weather by Miss Ainon
Extra Malay: Menahan Hati by Jahara
Stambul Dua by Idris
Manila Song: Pana Ginip by Miss Quinie
Leave Solo: Waltz Sorry Now by Mr Basco
Atjeh Song: Mabok Lanang by Mary Tan
Rumba by Miss Ainon
English: Alone by Miss Quinie
Extra Malay: Kurus Kiring by Jahara
Selection by Ruby's Orchestra (if time permits)

Bangsawan performances were also advertised in the newspapers. By the late nineteenth century, a number of lithograph presses had been set up in the Straits Settlements by the British and by the Jawi Peranakan. They published English and Malay newspapers respectively (Roff, 1972; Za'aba, 1939: 145–7), which carried advertisements of *bangsawan* troupes, announced the arrival and departure of troupes, and featured reviews and previews of performances.

Moreover, the newly developed communication routes (railways and roads) enabled troupes to travel to rural areas and parts of the peninsula which would have been impossible to visit in earlier decades. People living in rural areas could also now travel easily to nearby towns to watch *bangsawan* performances.

Thirdly, the introduction of amusement parks in big towns made certain that 'live' performances would become easily accessible to the public. For a charge of 10 cents, the wage-earner could enter the park. If he could afford it, he could pay another 10 cents to $3.00 to sit in the hall where *bangsawan* was performed; if he could not, he could still stand outside and watch through the doors. He could listen to *bangsawan* hits played over the air in the parks. He could himself attempt the latest dances like the foxtrot, waltz, or rumba (performed during *bangsawan* interludes) at the cabaret in the park.

In addition, entrepreneurs who owned amusement parks (like the Shaw Brothers) actively promoted *bangsawan* and helped to start troupes by extending loans to *bangsawan* performers. For example, Menah Yem, a veteran performer, informed me that her husband, Pak Yem, borrowed $5,000 from Shaw Brothers to start the Nooran Opera in the 1930s (Menah Yem, pers. com., 1986). In an advertisement in the *Malacca Guardian* (23 January 1933), the Malacca City Park announced that it had engaged the same Nooran Opera at 'enormous expense and under guarantee of $5,000'. In return, the troupe signed a contract with Shaw Brothers and performed in all their parks throughout Malaya. The troupe was given the gate money and 50 per cent of each night's collection. Rental of halls, printing of tickets and posters, and housing for performers were taken care of by Shaw Brothers. Amusement-park owners therefore helped not only to start troupes but to reduce the cost of maintaining them.

Fourthly, *bangsawan* was popular because it was the non-Europeans' version of Western theatre modified and adapted to suit local tastes. As in other colonial countries, it was thought to be prestigious to imitate facets of Western culture which were allegedly 'modern'. At the same time, however, Western cultural activities were not within the reach of non-Europeans. With the British being concerned to maintain their prestige based on racial exclusiveness and a European standard of living, the last thing they wanted was to share their leisure activities with the locals. Theatrical performances and other cultural activities in British clubs[17] were exclusive to club members (Butcher, 1979: 147–57, 170). Although the richer non-Europeans could attend performances of the latest Western plays staged in town halls and dances in hotel cabarets, the tickets for such entertainment were too expensive for the majority of wage-earners.[18] Besides, insistence on certain modes of dress kept the audience exclusive; as Alias Manan, a veteran *bangsawan* performer commented, 'one had to wear suits and ties to such performances. Where were we to find such clothes?'

Consequently, clubs with Western rules of organization and constitution resembling British clubs were set up by the non-Europeans for 'study and recreation' and for 'sports' (Roff, 1967: 181–3). Non-Europeans also began to create their own theatrical entertainment; *bangsawan* was a good example. Unlike Western theatre, though, this non-European theatre was open to all and sundry—rich, poor, Malay, Chinese, Indian, Arab, even European. *Bangsawan* was, moreover, a place and a social occasion where married as well as single women could be present without being looked down upon—at a time when women rarely ventured outside the home. A considerable section of the working population could afford to pay for *bangsawan* entertainment, and even those who could not could watch from outside.

Finally, *bangsawan* provided the opportunity for members of the urban community who happened to be away from their families to celebrate festivals. It was a substitute for older, customary festivals which were celebrated communally. Special *bangsawan* performances were staged during festivals of the various ethnic groups, such as Chinese New Year, Hari Raya, and Deepavali, which were open to all.

Just as cyclical rituals had historically promoted charity within the various communities (where the rich in freely distributing food and money benefited the poor), *bangsawan* performances were held to aid certain causes or to collect funds for associations, fairly regardless of ethnic affiliation. These performances were organized by the troupes themselves. Wayang Kassim, for instance, gave a performance in aid of the Penang Band Fund (*Straits Echo*, 16 November 1903); Wayang Yap Chow Thong for the orphans of the Convent (*Chahaya Pulau Pinang*, 9 July 1904); Genani Star Opera Co. of Malacca for the Kinta Malay Club Fund (*Times of Malaya*, 12 October 1925); Nooran Opera for the Young Muslims Union of Malacca (*Malacca Guardian*, 5 November 1934); and the Royal Zainab Opera of Selangor for the Straits Peranakan Club Fund (*Times of Malaya*, 11 August 1934). *Bangsawan* therefore promoted, in the Malaya of its time, a degree of social concern and assistance for the poor and needy across ethnic lines in the urban areas.

* * *

Although *bangsawan* of the late nineteenth and early twentieth centuries possessed many characteristics similar to traditional Malay theatre, it was not the same in crucial respects. *Bangsawan* was popular urban commercial theatre. It was performed solely for entertainment, not for spiritual purposes. It was promoted through advertisements in the press, radio, and handbills. For the first time, a proscenium stage was used and audiences had to pay to watch *bangsawan*.

Bangsawan gained popularity across a wide spectrum of society. The audience derived from various ethnic and class backgrounds. By the 1920s and 1930s, *bangsawan* had become so popular that its 'culture' was widespread. Much of the content found its way to homes through the wireless and gramophone. *Bangsawan* songs became the 'hits' of the day. Dances were imitated by the young at dance halls and cabarets. Sometimes, costumes and hair-styles worn by *bangsawan* performers became part of the fashion of the day. Troupes called on audiences to see their 'new fashions in costumes' (*fesyen pakaian yang baru*) (*Saudara*, 10 February and 10 October 1934). For a significant proportion of the urban Malayan population, *bangsawan* had come to provide the basis for cultural expression in a new milieu.

1. Because of the lack of skilled Malay film makers, Indian expertise was used. As a result, Malay films of the 1930s tended to resemble Indian ones of the period. It was only after World War II that Malay films which portrayed the social realities of the times were produced. For example, *Singapura di Waktu Malam* and *Chempaka*, both of which were produced by B. S. Rajan after the war, depicted the problems faced by Malay youths who

went to the cities to seek better job opportunities or to escape the constraints of village life.

2. See also Perkins, Kelly, and Ward (1976) for the dating of Gramophone Records.

3. Cabarets were started in hotels in the early twentieth century by the British. However, these cabarets were usually too expensive and formal for the common wage-earner to afford to attend.

4. According to this article, by 1930 the 'supply of such entertainment had ceased almost entirely'. This was because of 'higher steamer and hotel rates, political unrest and not too enthusiastic audiences'. Chronic social unrest in India and civil wars in China made the ventures of professional troupes dangerous. The talking picture which had arrived two years ago 'had taken the public by storm in all parts of the world'. Theatres which had presented drama or vaudeville began to screen talkies instead.

5. For descriptions of the Chinese opera and puppet theatre in Malaysia, see Tan (1980) and (1984b).

6. For a discussion of the terms *wayang Parsi*, *tiruan wayang Parsi*, *komedi Melayu*, and *bangsawan*, see Camoens (1982: 1, 16, 17), an article which is based on a survey of vernacular Malay newspapers (in particular the *Jawi Peranakan*, *Bintang Timor*, *Sekolah Melayu*, and *Bintang Timur*) from 1887 to 1900.

7. It has been said that the first professional *bangsawan* troupe, Pushi Indera Bangsawan, was brought to Betawi (now Java) and influenced the creation of *komedi stambul*. According to this story, Pushi had sold all his properties to Jaafar Turki or 'the Turk' as he was commonly known. Jaafar Turki then started the *wayang stambul* (Edrus, 1960: 54 and Rahmah Bujang, 1975).

8. As an estimate of the value of money at that time, a kati of beef or pork cost 36 cents, chickens cost 30 cents each while eggs cost 3 cents each (*Straits Echo*, 12 July 1904).

9. The term 'popular' is used in this section to mean *bangsawan* drew crowds of different ethnic origins to its performances. Both rich and poor were also attracted. See the Preface for a wider definition of the term 'popular'.

10. 'Orang beratus-ratus ada pergi tengok bangsawan itu, dan tiada satu tempat dudok kosong pun.' (*Bintang Timur*, 24 January 1895.)

11. 'Banyak sekali orang-orang ... datang tengok sampei penoh tempat wayang itu sahingga ada yang berdiri kerana kurang tempat.' (*Bintang Timor*, 13 February 1895.)

12. 'Kalau tida tengok barang satu malam sahya tida bulih tidor sebab belom puas ... hati sahya perti kena di isap mahu jalan pergi tengok sahja.' (*Bintang Timor*, 12 March 1895.)

13. '... bangsawan Melayu yang banyak tengok, bangsa China, Arab, Blanda dan Tambi sedikit....' (*Bintang Timor*, 12 March 1895.)

14. '... semenjak wayang ini datang bermain di Pulau Pinang pada tiap-tiap malam ... panggung besar itu penuh dengan orang-orang puteh, mem-mem dan baba-baba dan nonya-nonya, Melayu, jawi peranakan....' (*Chahaya Pulau Pinang*, 11 May 1904.)

15. On the other hand, to Indonesians like Mr T. D. Tio, the husband of the famous actress, Miss Riboet, the Malay used in Indonesian films like *Terang Bulan* was too 'high-brow' for Malays in this country, particularly those in cities and towns who speak 'bazaar Malay'. Consequently, in the production of a new film, *Kambing Hitam*, each word had to be 'considered from the point of view of its general use or otherwise in Malaya and the Netherlands Indies'. 'Regional variations in pronunciation' were also taken note of. A 'universal Malay dialect' had to be used. Thus, in the new film, *omony* [*omong*?]—meaning 'to speak' in both countries—was used instead of *chukup* [*cakap*?] in Malayan Malay or *bitjara* in Indonesian Malay (*Times of Malaya*, 16 August 1938).

16. This was written by a reporter who visited the Gramophone Co. recording studio at 96 Cairnhill Road, Singapore. He saw the 'Big Four' (Mr K. Dean, Miss Tijah, Miss Salmah, and Miss Maimoon) at work. 'Mr Martinez and his excellent orchestra, and Mr Ahmat Pochu, were also in attendance to supply the music.' (*Straits Echo*, 24 May 1934.)

17. Since the late nineteenth century, the British had social clubs built where they played golf, bridge, tennis, and other games, and listened to musical bands (Gullick, 1978: 39) and held parties away from the locals. The social clubs were places where the British

entertained, amused themselves, and relaxed. Western plays were performed by touring professional theatre groups from the West and local amateur British groups. For example, the Teluk Anson Amateurs staged *The Country Mouse* at the Ipoh Club on 17 June 1911. The charge was $2.50 (*Times of Malaya*).

18. Entry tickets to Western theatrical performances usually ranged from $1 to $3. This was considered to be expensive as one could already buy an egg for 3 cents, a chicken for 30 cents, and a kati of beef for 36 cents. (Market prices printed in *Straits Echo*, 12 July 1904.)

3
Variety, Adaptability, Novelty, and the Spectacular, *c.*1880–*c.*1930

Variety

ANY theatre that was as commercial as *bangsawan* and that hoped to survive, financially and as a form, had to take into account the cultural background and social composition of its audience. The audience in the towns of Malaya was multi-ethnic and stratified. To cater to as wide an audience as possible, *bangsawan* necessarily had to include many different types of entertainment. A 'typical' performance featured not only a full-length play (or three or four shorter plays) with instrumentally accompanied songs and instrumental music, but also interludes called *extra turns*[1] in between acts while the stage was being rearranged. On the one hand, *bangsawan* was like traditional Malay theatre in that performances offered music, dance, and comedy. On the other hand, in featuring interludes of music, song, dance, comedy, and novelty acts during scene changes, *bangsawan* was influenced by the Western theatrical and vaudeville groups which toured Malaya.

Both play and extra turns emphasized variety. In order to cater to as wide an audience as possible, stories of different national and ethnic origins were performed (Plates 19–27). Sometimes within a week, a theatrical company might offer as the evening's feature play a Hindustani or Arabic fairy-tale, a Shakespearian tragedy, a Chinese romance, and an English or Dutch play.[2] As the veteran *bangsawan* performer Pak Suki once told me, '*Bangsawan* was like a car workshop where different types of cars could be seen. Likewise, various types of plays— German, Italian, American, Malay, English, Roman, and Spanish—were staged in *bangsawan*.' However, performers always spoke in Malay, the language commonly understood by the multi-ethnic audience.

In the selection of stories, the type of audience to be attracted was always taken into consideration. When the troupe performed in a predominantly Chinese locale, popular Chinese opera plays were performed (Figure 3.1). During their seasons in Penang, Wayang Kassim performed *Sam Pek Eng Tai* or 'A Chinese Honeymoon' (*Straits Echo*, 15 December 1909), and *Lo Fen Koie* (*Straits Echo*, 19 December 1909), while the Grand Opera Co. staged *Boo Siong* (*Straits Echo*,

FIGURE 3.1
Advertisement for a Chinese Play

BAD NEWS
for late comers

BAD NEWS
for late comers

Wembley
THE FAIR AND AMUSEMENT PARK
MAGAZINE ROAD

BIG CROWDS UNABLE TO OBTAIN SEATS LAST NIGHT.

At Solar Hall Where

DEAN'S OPERA OF SINGAPORE

Will Stage To-night At 8.30 p.m.

The Great Chinese Dramatic Play Entitled

"Boo Siong Sat Soh"

Come and see "KOON THOW" and "PHAK BOO" in a great Chinese Play which will be presented to-night with appropriate Costumes and Stage Settings. Inche K. Dean has received several Scrolls from the Chinese Community of Malaya in token of their sincere appreciation of the unique merits of his performance in this Dramatic Story.

Supported by the Funniest Clowns in Malaya—Md. Noor (Sr. and Jr.).
· DEAN'S FOLLIES.

Misses Kluh, Boon, Aminah, Puteh, Baby Mas and Muna

Acclaimed The Most Beautiful and Jazziest Chorus appear in the latest songs and dances.

TO AVOID DISAPPOINTMENT KINDLY MAKE EARLY RESERVATIONS.

BOOKINGS:—13 Church St. or 'Phone 1015 from 10 a.m. to 4 p.m.
or 'Phone 1117 from 7 p.m. to 8 pm.

Popular Prices of Admission—60, 40 and 20 cents only.

"THE BETTER WE SERVE THE BIGGER WE GROW."
THE BIGGER WE GROW THE BETTER WE SERVE."

28 January 1914) and *Pow Kong Un* (*Straits Echo*, 29 January 1914). In Singapore, Dean's Opera performed at least one Chinese story a week when it was playing there in 1934. The troupe staged the different parts of the epic, *Seet Jin Kwee*, every Thursday from 31 May to 26 July 1934 at the Great World Park. This was followed by *Seet Teng Sun* (from 16 August to 27 September 1934), *Seet Kong* (from 28 September to 5 October 1934), and *Teik Cheng* (from 25 October to 16 November 1934). The last two epics were performed every Thursday and Friday of the week (*Malaya Tribune*, 16 August–27 September, 25 October–16 November 1934). Similarly, when the intention was to attract Indians, stories of Indian origin were staged. Dean's Opera performed *Soubhagaya Sundaree* when it was collecting money for the Indian Sanatan Dharam Sabha Building Fund (*Times of Malaya*, 26 July 1933).

To attract a multi-ethnic audience, a variety of plays was usually offered on farewell nights. It was reported that, on the last night of its season in Penang in 1910, Wayang Kassim performed five plays each of different ethnic origins: '1. Srie Kandie 2. The Golden Star 3. Monte Carlo 4. Rossina and 5. The Fancy Bazaar' (*Straits Echo*, 8 January, 1910). Dean's Opera performed a 'Pot Pourri' of three plays as its farewell performance in 1932: '1. The Devils' Door—A Tragic Oriental Drama 2. Soordas or Bilwal Mangal—A Hindustani Romance and 3. Hang Tuah—A well known Malay legend' (*Straits Echo*, 3 September 1932).

When patrons requested to see certain stories, the *bangsawan* troupe normally obliged. For instance, Nooran Opera staged 'a specially selected play entitled *Black Mask* at the request of its numerous Penang Baba patrons' at Wembley Park (*Straits Echo*, 1 May 1936).

The musical and dance selections were as varied. As reported in the newspapers, 'Dutch and English tunes' (*Straits Echo*, 1 October 1903; *Malacca Guardian*, 5 November 1928), 'special concertina and violin selections' (*Straits Echo*, 2 November 1903), or 'light classical music' (*Straits Echo*, 23 August 1913; *Malacca Guardian*, 2 November 1936) were performed before and after the play as well as during intervals. For instance, the Wayang Inche Baba Orchestra played the following items at a performance on 11 July 1914 (*Times of Malaya*): '"Violin Solo"—Ave Maria by Pondo, played by Mr O. B. Osman and J. Torio, conducted by Mr A. Leo; "Concert Solo"—The Rosary by Nerim, played by Mr Leo Faundi; and "Piano Solo"—That is a Fussy Rag by Smalloy, played by Mr R. Soliano.' The orchestra often 'tendered selections of music for an hour preceding the performance' (*Straits Echo*, 9 February 1910). It also accompanied singers and dancers during the play. These songs were sung to 'Malay tunes' or to the 'livelier strains' of pieces taken from English comic operas like *The Country Girl* or *The Geisha* or to the tune of 'Daisy Belle' (*Straits Echo*, 14 November 1908 and 12 December 1932).

To draw those who had a liking for singing and dancing and to fill in the time between acts, 'extra singing and dancing of different European,

Masri [Arabic?], Hindustan and Malay songs and dances' were performed (*Idaran Zaman,* 12 December 1925).[3] Appeal was extended to a
wide-ranging audience through ensuring variety in songs and dances.
Malay song–dance sequences like 'Jong Kina' and 'Track-tack-tack'
were performed by many groups in the early 1900s. The 'Jong Kina'
was first performed by Wayang Yap Chow Thong (*Straits Echo,*
18 May 1904). It apparently was so popular that other troupes like
Opera Indra Permata (*Straits Echo,* 11 February 1907) and Wayang
Aishah copied it (*Straits Echo,* 11 February 1907 and 14 August 1909).
'Track-tack-tack', made famous by Miss Atimah of Wayang Kassim,
was subsequently included in the repertoire of other troupes like
Wayang Komedi India Ratoe, Opera Indra Permata, Wayang Aishah,
Star Opera Co., and Penang Baba Bangsawan (*Straits Echo,*
4 September 1906, 11 February 1907, 14 August 1909, 31 August
1912, and 16 August 1920).

As one contributor to the *Straits Echo,* Ann Nacter, wrote in 1910,
'English Music Hall numbers ... such as songs, cake-walks, national
dances, sketches and the like ... were soon introduced' (*Straits Echo,*
2 July 1910). Wayang Kassim presented the latest European songs and
dances like the 'coon songs' in their performances. Some of these songs
included 'Scandal's Eye', 'The White Man Working for Me', 'Rainbow
Coon', 'Dixie', and 'Goodbye, Clorine [Irene?], bye' (*Straits Echo,* 19
and 25 September 1906). According to the reviewer of the *Times of
Malaya* (11 October 1906), the 'coon songs' were 'the hits' of the
evening and were loudly encored each time.

'Exotic' songs from other parts of the world were also adopted. It was
reported that 'Lolita, the graceful and charming Spanish dancer' of
Wayang Kassim sang and danced 'La Faida de Percal Plancia',
'Espanita Tambourine Dance and Song', 'La Paloma', and 'Ohi'
(*Straits Echo,* 15, 18, and 22 June 1907). Cakewalks (*Straits Echo,*
4 September 1906 and 12 January 1909), Hungarian dances (*Straits
Echo,* 4 December 1909), Cossack dances (*Straits Echo,* 15 December
1909), and Sailor dances (*Straits Echo,* 17 December 1909) were also
performed by Wayang Kassim. Even Hawaiian songs and dances were
staged (*Times of Malaya,* 13 December 1924). The following two advertisements illustrate the variety of songs and dances presented in just
one night.

The Kinta Opera Co.:

Miss Meda, our famous Prima Donna will sing Che Mamat War Wear and Arab
song (Yamallah)
Miss Anong, our beautiful actress the Nightingale of the Opera World will sing
nightly the popular Bercherai Kasih and the latest Egyptian song and dance.
Miss Soadah will sing Mak Enang Sayang and the latest best songs.
Miss Rowna will sing new Slendang Mayang and the latest Siamese dance.
Our famous actresses, Miss Meda, Miss Chik, and Miss Itam, will dance the
latest (Japanese) Kapary Dance.
Our latest Spanish Dance with handling umbrellas and the latest Gambus,

Miss Meda, Miss Anong, Miss Soadah and Miss Itam.... (*Straits Echo*, 27 January 1925.)

The Alfred Theatrical Co.:

Special Extra turns for Saturday.
'Serbt-Susu' by Miss: Haseah.
'Seram-Sejuk' by Misses: Halimah and Amah.
'Barcilona' by Mr: Ali Jago and Misses: Halimah, Amah, Ramla and Patimah.
'Titna' by Misses: Amanah (9 year old child actress)
'Ati-tak-sabar' by Misses: Halimah, Amah, Ramla Patimah.
'Stamboul Dua' by Misses: Puasa and Haseah and Mr Ali Jago.
'Then I will be Happy' by Miss: Amanah.
'Gambus' by Misses: Halimah, Amah, Ramla and Fatimah.
'I Want to be Happy' by Mr: Wansen and Misses: Halimah, Amah, Ramla and Fatimah.
'Mayong, Manurah and Chinese Wayang' etc. by Messrs: Aman Baloon and Mek China.
'Honolulu Blues' by Mr Ali Jago and Misses: Halimah, Amah, Ramla and Fatimah.
'Slendang Daik' Miss: Ramla
'Cherai Kaseh' Miss: Aisha
'Scout Drill' Misses: Halimah, Amah, Ramla, Aisha, Fatimah and Another.
(*Straits Echo*, 17 March 1928.)

Often, guest items were presented to add to the variety. 'The Town Band was in attendance and played selections at intervals' during the performance of Wayang Komedi India Ratoe in Penang in 1909 (*Straits Echo*, 9 July 1909). While they were touring Malaya, the 'celebrated Australian singers and dancers' of the Frank J. Sidney Co. performed with the International Dramatic Co. in Penang in 1910 (*Straits Echo*, 6 June 1910). In 1921 the Malayan Opera of Selangor invited Miss Mignon and Mr Williams 'to perform their latest serio comic musical entertainment ... the musical cigar boxes'. Part of their act included the 'imitation of an express train; the strange violin polka on the tuberphone; music on flower pots', and 'the one-stringed instrument' (*Straits Echo*, 11 October 1921). Other examples include 'a special entertainment by Alexis Pitroff's dashing troupe of Serbians' who performed 'national songs, ballet, folk dances and musical items' with the Oriental Malay Opera Company (*Times of Malaya*, 27 March 1926); and 'a series of Kronchong and Stamboul Duets' by the Gaylads Kronchong Party (*Straits Echo*, 1 May 1936) during a Nooran Opera performance.

Besides music, song, and dance, *bangsawan* accommodated itself to comic sketches and pantomimes. Encik K. Dean for instance, supported by Mat Noor (sen. and jun.) of Dean's Opera, appeared 'in various comical extracts' which kept 'the whole house roaring with laughter till 1 am' (*Straits Echo*, 10 December 1932).

Circus clown acts were especially popular. On its tour of Penang in 1907, Wayang Kassim engaged the clowns Guillaume, Baby, and

August, formerly from Harmston's Circus, to perform a 'burlesque
Spanish bull-fight' and a 'musical turn on all sorts of imaginable and
unimaginable instruments' (*Straits Echo*, 15 June 1907). The company's
performance on 22 June 1907 began with 'The General and the
Recruit', a 'screamingly funny entree by the inimitable clowns, August,
Guillaume and Baby'. There was also a 'comic parody' called 'Mr Boum
Boum and Madam Pam-Pam' by the clowns during the show. The same
performance concluded with the 'hilarious French pantomime', 'The
Living Statue' (*Straits Echo*, 22 June 1907).

On another visit to Penang in 1909, Wayang Kassim employed
'white' clowns including Adolf Klimanoff 'who used to be with Ott's
Circus' (*Straits Echo*, 12 January 1909). These clowns performed a
Spanish pantomime called 'Caesar Borgia' consisting of '2 acts, 16
scenes and 20 characters' after the play *Merchant of Venice* ended
(*Straits Echo*, 16 January 1909). When the company returned to Penang
at the end of the year (*Straits Echo*, 8 December 1909), the clown Adolf
'promised to make a photo in five minutes ... and [then] present [it] to
the public for inspection'. If any person found it unsatisfactory, Adolf
promised a payment of $100. According to the reviewer, this turn was a
joke:

A. Klimanoff adjusted the camera as if he were taking a snap-shot of the whole
house. In five minutes time, he came down the stage, with a number of packets
done up in paper, and distributed them among the audience. The eager recipi-
ent opened the packet to have a look at his photo—he saw a reflection of his face
in a small looking glass. (*Straits Echo*, 11 December 1909.)

In the same performance, Klimanoff also staged the pantomime 'The
Life of Peking or the Grand Celebration of the Mandarins' which he
had performed 'in the palace of China before the Empress Dowager of
China in the year 1903' (*Straits Echo*, 8 December 1909). 'New Chinese
dresses, Chinese songs, Chinese dances, acrobats, gymnasts, jugglers
etc.' were presented.[4]

Novelty and Spectacle

The audience's fascination with novelty on stage prompted stage managers and directors to constantly produce new acts and different spectacular scenic effects and settings for each performance. Playbills
repeated nightly: 'Don't forget! Great Novelty!' (*Straits Echo*,
8 December 1909).

To keep to their promise of presenting novelty on stage, troupes gave
exhibitions of 'conjuring and juggling tricks after the performance of the
play' (*Straits Echo*, 4 June 1904). Actresses 'made torn up paper turn
into flames and produced silk handkerchiefs from their empty fingers'
(*Straits Echo*, 8 October 1906). Men and lady 'illusionists puzzled' the
audience with their tricks. It was advertised that a 'lady illusionist' entertained the audience on 11 October 1906 (*Times of Malaya*), while

'Professor Balcombe, the world's wonder illusionist' performed for the Wayang Inche Puteh Theatrical Co. of the Federated Malay States on 25 March 1911 (*Straits Echo*). 'Great jumper[s]', 'whirlwind tumbler[s]', and 'trick cyclist[s]' of foreign troupes were invited to perform turns (Figure 3.2). Such members of the Frank J. Sidney Co. from Australia took part in the productions of the International Dramatic Co. in 1910 (*Straits Echo*, 7 and 10 June 1910).

Even boxing matches were held on stage. As a reviewer wrote: 'At about 10 o'clock, the play was interrupted by [an] exhibition of boxing by the scouts of the First Malacca (High School) Troop. There were four events of three one-minute rounds each.' (*Malacca Guardian*, 5 November 1928.)

On another occasion, Dean's Opera staged a 'wonderful display of feats and strength' by a famous Indian stage and film actress, Miss Anarkali. She 'support[ed] a big stone on her chest and allow[ed] another stone to be broken on the top'. A dance by 'a live snake' was also featured (*Straits Echo*, 26 November 1932). Nooran Opera showed 'a woman floating in the air' during one of its performances. 'A reward of $500' was promised to anyone who could 'prove that either rope or wire' was used (*Straits Echo*, 21 July 1933).

Novelty was also introduced into *bangsawan* stories through scenic effects, spectacles, transformation scenes, tricks, realistic props, and stunts. Such spectacles were performed to catch the audience's eye in an era where stage lighting was as yet unsophisticated. The audience was also kept fascinated by the technology used to stage tricks and trans-formation scenes. Wayang Aishah tempted the audience to the play *Lakuan Inder Sabah* with the following advertisement about its 'splendid scenes':

Come and see our splendid scenes.
The breaking of Clouds and the appearance of the Sun
The appearance of a Gigantic Lotus from the clouds
The breaking of the flower ...
Come and see the wonderful lotus and birds from it
Every petal opens, when you will see a flock of birds
The stem of the flower breaks and there comes out an
Elephant and seated amidst grandeur is King Indra.
(*Straits Echo*, 11 February 1905.)

Wayang Kassim showed, in the play *Wonders of the Deep*, 'the view of the bottom of the sea with mermaids swimming about' (*Straits Echo*, 19 June 1911). A Dean's Star Opera advertisement publicized that the play *The Desert Thief of Baghdad* included 'spectacular scenes' such as 'The Stormy Desert' with 'Rain and Lightning', 'The Flying Horse', and 'The Enchanted Dragon'. Preparation for such scenes, it was claimed, 'took more than three months' (*Straits Echo*, 10 December 1931).

On 30 July 1934, Nooran Opera of Malacca announced that 'a super stupendous sensational spectacular production ... that cost ... $500'

FIGURE 3.2
Advertisement for Guest Artists Frank J. Sidney and Company,
the Great Jumper and Whirlwind Tumbler, and the Philips Sisters
Performing with the International Dramatic Company

KING STREET THEATRE HALL

TO-NIGHT !   TO-NIGHT !!

Friday, 10th June, 1910,
" ROSSINA "

FAREWELL BENEFIT

TO

Frank J. Sidney & Company, the Great Jumper
and Whirlwind Tumbler,

AND

The Philips Sisters, the Celebrated Australian
Singers and Dancers,

AND

Grand Change of Programme.

New. **?La Poupee?** New.

In the Artist's Studio.

NEW. The Sisters' Philips in their Sketch, NEW.

" On the Sands."

Song and Dance " Splashing in the Briny."

IN CONJUNCTION WITH THE

International Dramatic Company.

PRICES OF ADMISSION.

Reserved Seats	...	... $ 1.50	Second Class	... 50 cts.
First Class ...	...	... ı. 1.00	Third	... 20 ..

Ladies, 1st Class, 50 cts.   2nd Class, 20 cts.

Source: *Straits Echo*, 10 June 1910.

was being prepared and urged the Malacca public to witness the following transformation scenes:

See—How a huge cave infested with poisonous reptiles, such as snakes, scorpions, centipedes and also rats, frogs etc., transform[s] into a beautiful fairyland with fairies appearing at the same time.

See—How a ragged clothing transforms into a beautiful costume before the eyes of the public.

See—How a palace flies into the clouds with the princess in it without the use of rope or wire. (*Malacca Guardian*, 30 July 1934.)

As described above, the principles of realism and pictorialism were applied to all stage settings and props regardless of the type or period of the play performed: the sun appeared from behind the clouds, petals of flowers opened, mermaids swam at the bottom of the sea, caves were filled with snakes, scorpions, and the like. *Bangsawan* troupes promised 'real waves', 'real boats that made sounds' (*Chahaya Pulau Pinang*, 27 February 1904), 'motor-cars' (*Straits Echo*, 17 June 1907), 'railway trains' (*Straits Echo*, 17 June 1907), and 'aeroplanes' (*Straits Echo*, 25 December 1931), 'actual rain and lightning' (*Straits Echo*, 20 July 1933), and 'moving clouds' (*Straits Echo*, 30 July 1934).

Tricks were also introduced to attract the audience. A 1935 advertisement of Nooran Opera went like this:

Last Monday, you have seen how Raja Bersiong severed the head of a child, picked it up and laid it on the table before your very eyes.... Now in 'Sri Sambas' we present another thrilling episode just as mysterious as the head on the table.

Here you will see a woman being led into the forest, placed on a pile of wood and burnt until you see the skeleton.

She will not leave the stack of fire but will remain there until burnt away.

Then amidst burning charcoals her bones will be gathered. What happens next we will have you to see for yourself. (*Malacca Guardian*, 11 July 1935.)

Most of these effects and tricks were the work of the set-designer known as the *mistri* who devised elaborate trapdoor and pulley systems. 'Famous painters' like Mr Bartholomeuz were sometimes hired to design 'special sceneries' (*Straits Echo*, 20 June 1914).

Impressive jumping and flying feats were accomplished in order to further lure the audience. In 1933, Nooran Opera called upon the people of Malacca to see 'how Sipendek' could fly 'across the stage in all directions and then descend ... to complete her dance' (*Straits Echo*, 6 June 1933). In the same performance, the audience would also see 'a bodiless head flying after its execution and then singing a farewell song' (*Straits Echo*, 28 July 1933). Another troupe invited the audience to 'see the Malayan Douglas Fairbanks doing stunts on the stage . . . stunts that no other opera ... had ... ever attempted' (*Straits Echo*, 9 January 1929).

Adaptability

As commercial theatre, *bangsawan* was extremely responsive to audience preferences. Dependent as they were on their performances' popular appeal for survival, opera companies were known 'carefully' to study 'the likes and dislikes of the *bangsawan* enthusiasts' (*Times of Malaya*, 26 January 1926).

To draw those who were familiar with the vaudeville shows performed by touring companies from the West, chorus dancing was introduced in between acts in the early twentieth century. In 1903, the *Straits Echo* reported that a new feature in Wayang Kassim's performance was a 'set of dances by eight of the company' (*Straits Echo*, 15 October 1903). Wayang Yap Chow Thong's performance on 14 May 1904 began with an 'opening chorus in which thirteen actresses took part' (*Straits Echo*, 14 May 1904). In 1906, 'can-can dances' with 'high-kicking' were so popular that 'there were some among the audience who were disappointed with the dancing' by Wayang Kassim when they 'got no high kicking' (*Straits Echo*, 19 September 1906).

By the 1920s and 1930s, 'chorus girls dressed in low-cut blouses and short skirts of velveteen' (*Straits Echo*, 20 October 1928) known as the Crystal Follies, Salomme Revue, and Eddie's High Steppers performing the latest dances had become a regular feature in *bangsawan* (*Straits Echo*, 10 June 1923; *Times of Malaya*, 14 October 1932; *Bumiputra*, 25 September 1933). The dances which were prominent during the 1930s included the tango, blues, charleston, foxtrot, quickstep, waltz, slow foxtrot, English waltz, paso doble, and rumba (*Straits Times*, 6 February 1932; *Straits Echo*, 13 December 1932). According to the *Sunday Gazette* (11 December 1938), 'get-together dances' like the 'Lambeth Walk' and 'Blackpool Walk' introduced by the Eastern and Oriental Hotel Dance Hall, 'Palais Stroll' presented at the Elysee Cabaret, and the 'Maney Twinkle' performed at the Wembley Cabaret had become popular. 'Even Malay Opera Girls' were 'tripping the steps ... of the Lambeth Walk' with loud 'Oi's and Oyez' (Plates 28 and 29), it was reported (*Sunday Gazette*, 27 November 1938).

Bangsawan actors and actresses learnt the latest dances from talkies. 'Miss Kiah, Dean's "IT" girl ... will lead her Beauty Chorus in the pick of the latest Talkie Numbers', which included 'hi-kicking, dancing and singing', declared an advertisement in *Straits Echo* (10 December 1932). Filipino choreographers were also employed to teach the chorus girls the latest dances.

Indeed the 'vaudeville turns' (as the song–dance interludes were called) attracted the audience even more than the plays. In a review of a performance by the Rose Opera of Singapore on 12 October 1932, it was reported that:

While the play itself 'The Rose of Paris' could not have been better acted it was the vaudeville turns that took the house by storm. Miss Jacoba, the foremost kronchong singer of Java who sings exclusively for His Master's Voice, could not have put more expression and technique into her singing and 'Zonne Bloem' Kronchong gives her sweet and caressing voice full scope; neither could she have put more grace and charm into her ballet dancing. Eddie Mendietta and his Beauty Chorus gave an outstanding performance in between the scenes and Eddie's high stepping alone is worth going a long way to see. His singing of the latest song hits evoked much applause.... (*Straits Echo*, 12 October 1932.)

These vaudeville turns became so popular that vaudeville nights, where only dancing, singing, and comic sketches were performed, were soon introduced (Figure 3.3).[5] As the following review indicates, the vaudeville nights drew the crowds: 'For the last six weeks, each vaudeville night—the great night from the manager's point of view—has seen the bangsawan hall of the Fun and Frolic Park filled to its utmost capacity, never mind the inclement weather and what other counter-attractions of the town might be.' (*Straits Echo*, 2 December 1932.)

The introduction of vaudeville turns and vaudeville nights was inevitable. As a commercial form of theatre, *bangsawan* had to adapt to the fancies of the multiracial audiences who were attracted to the variety shows performed by touring companies from the West. These turns were advertised as 'modern' (*moden*) (*Saudara*, 11 April 1936), 'modelled to suit the modern taste' (*Straits Echo*, 12 October 1932), and suitable for 'all nationalities' (*Times of Malaya*, 14 July 1933).

The types of stories and themes performed by *bangsawan* troupes were adapted to audience preferences. From the late nineteenth century, the majority of the stories performed in *bangsawan*, regardless of ethnic origin, were tales of fantasy and mystery with the aristocracy as the main characters. The ogre or the antagonist, often cast in the role of an evil spirit called *jin afrit*, was a regular feature. *Bangsawan* thus dealt with themes familiar to the audience. As one writer reported in the *Straits Echo* (10 December 1931):

Ninety per-cent of the themes are [about] the doings of the people of 'Kayangan' or Fairy-land where love reigns supreme, and where beauty, virtue and valour go hand in hand. But the people of 'Kayangan' love to roam in this world of struggle, revealing themselves to the eyes of human beings in different shapes, to punish evildoers and help the good attain victory in any strife whether of love or war. Thus the story is enacted on earth as well as in the heavens....

Even though some contemporary plays which were not based on mythical kings and princes were adapted, these were in a minority. Only a few troupes would stage them. Some of these plays included *Rossina*, based on a sketch by Dr Kramer of Batavia (*Straits Echo*, 2 November 1903 and 27 August 1906); *Nyai Dasimah* or *Edward William* (*Straits Echo*, 21 May 1904 and 1 February 1907); *East Lynne*, translated from Mr Henry Wood's novel (*Straits Echo*, 25 August 1904); *Doctor Faust*, translated from an original Dutch play (*Straits Echo*, 16 October 1903); and *Marysan* or *A European Geisha*, adapted from the English comic opera depicting the real life of geishas and scenes in Japan (*Straits Echo*, 9 May 1906 and 10 September 1906).

FIGURE 3.3
Advertisement for Vaudeville Night

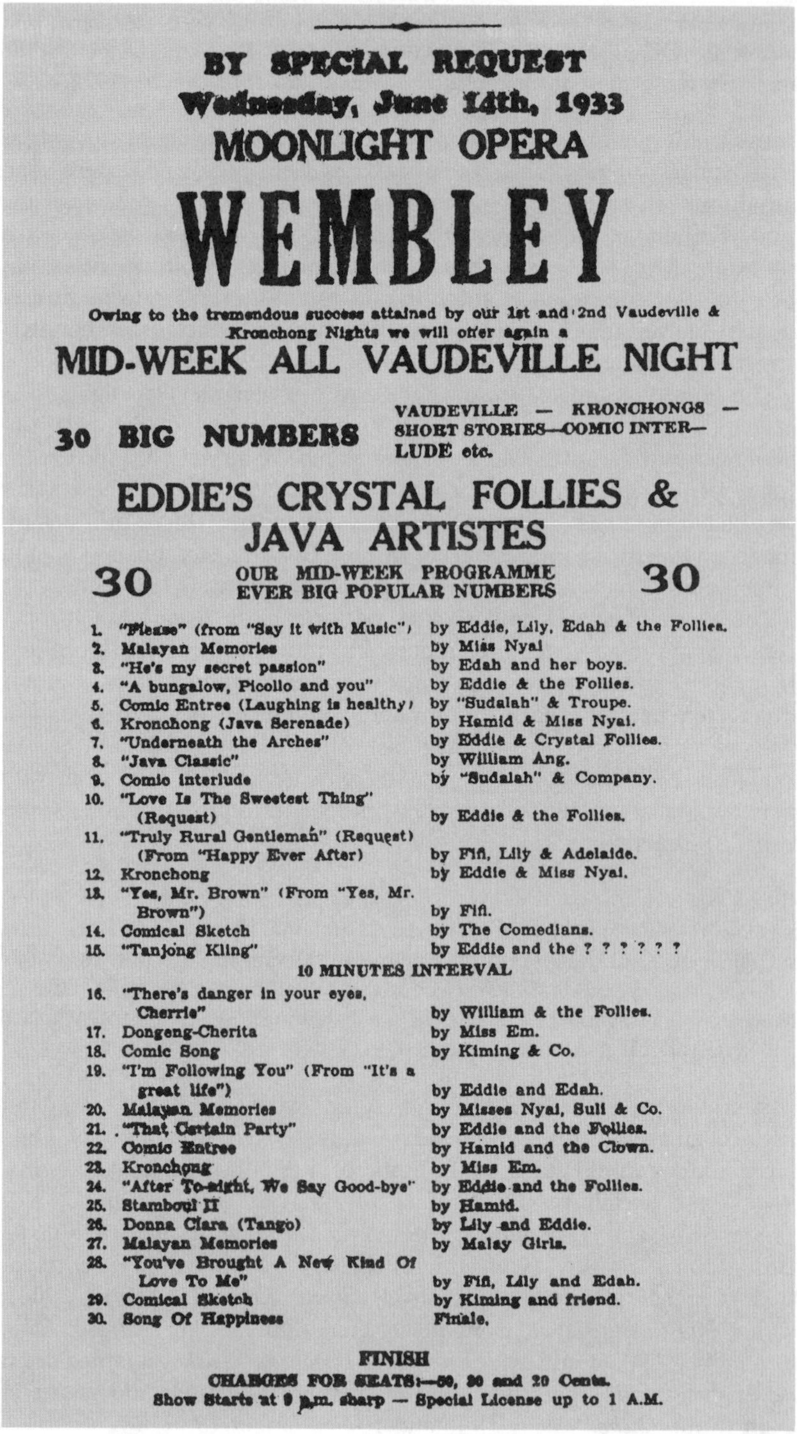

BY SPECIAL REQUEST
Wednesday, June 14th, 1933
MOONLIGHT OPERA

WEMBLEY

Owing to the tremendous success attained by our 1st and 2nd Vaudeville &
Kronchong Nights we will offer again a

MID-WEEK ALL VAUDEVILLE NIGHT

30 BIG NUMBERS   VAUDEVILLE — KRONCHONGS — SHORT STORIES—COMIC INTER—LUDE etc.

EDDIE'S CRYSTAL FOLLIES & JAVA ARTISTES

30   OUR MID-WEEK PROGRAMME EVER BIG POPULAR NUMBERS   **30**

1. "Please" (from "Say it with Music") — by Eddie, Lily, Edah & the Follies.
2. Malayan Memories — by Miss Nyai
3. "He's my secret passion" — by Edah and her boys.
4. "A bungalow, Picollo and you" — by Eddie & the Follies.
5. Comic Entree (Laughing is healthy) — by "Sudalah" & Troupe.
6. Kronchong (Java Serenade) — by Hamid & Miss Nyai.
7. "Underneath the Arches" — by Eddie & Crystal Follies.
8. "Java Classic" — by William Ang.
9. Comic interlude — by "Sudalah" & Company.
10. "Love Is The Sweetest Thing" (Request) — by Eddie & the Follies.
11. "Truly Rural Gentleman" (Request) (From "Happy Ever After) — by Fifi, Lily & Adelaide.
12. Kronchong — by Eddie & Miss Nyai.
13. "Yes, Mr. Brown" (From "Yes, Mr. Brown") — by Fifi.
14. Comical Sketch — by The Comedians.
15. "Tanjong Kling" — by Eddie and the ? ? ? ? ? ?

10 MINUTES INTERVAL

16. "There's danger in your eyes, Cherrie" — by William & the Follies.
17. Dongeng-Cherita — by Miss Em.
18. Comic Song — by Kiming & Co.
19. "I'm Following You" (From "It's a great life") — by Eddie and Edah.
20. Malayan Memories — by Misses Nyai, Suli & Co.
21. "That Certain Party" — by Eddie and the Follies.
22. Comic Entree — by Hamid and the Clown.
23. Kronchong — by Miss Em.
24. "After To-night, We Say Good-bye" — by Eddie and the Follies.
25. Stamboul II — by Hamid.
26. Donna Clara (Tango) — by Lily and Eddie.
27. Malayan Memories — by Malay Girls.
28. "You've Brought A New Kind Of Love To Me" — by Fifi, Lily and Edah.
29. Comical Sketch — by Kiming and friend.
30. Song Of Happiness — Finale,

FINISH

CHARGES FOR SEATS:—50, 30 and 20 Cents.
Show Starts at 9 p.m. sharp — Special License up to 1 A.M.

Source: *Straits Echo*, 14 June 1933.

In the late 1920s and 1930s, however, new types of stories began to appear. *Bangsawan* troupes started to perform Malay historical tales (*cerita sejarah Melayu*) such as *Laksamana Bentan* (*Straits Echo*, 1 August 1930 and 9 December 1931), *Laksemana Hang Tuah* (*Straits Echo*, 29 October 1929 and 30 December 1931), *Datuk Laksamana Sekam* (*Straits Echo*, 16 December 1931), and *Kris Melayu* (*Straits Echo*, 2 June 1932), which they borrowed from the *Hikayat* (Figures 3.4 and 3.5). These plays focused on the exploits of legendary Malay heroes, sultans, and aristocrats who were no longer shown along with mythical gods. Stories were also adapted from a number of *syair* written and published by lithographic firms in Singapore in the late nineteenth century (Za'aba, 1939: 145–7).[6] Three such examples included the 'Syaer Siti Zabidah' (*Straits Echo*, 13 December 1926), an epic about the wars of Sultan Zain al-'Abidin of Kembayat and his bride Siti Zabidah with the seven princesses of China, 'Syaer Dan Dan Setia' (*Straits Echo*, 4 November 1932), and the 'Syaer Selendang Delima' (*Straits Echo*, 15 December 1925).

Besides Malay historical tales, stories with contemporary settings were also introduced into *bangsawan* in the late 1920s and 1930s. In these, common people rather than kings, princes, and gods were depicted as heroes. *Bangsawan* troupes began to publicize their plays as 'comedy-dramas', 'real-life dramas', and 'modern stories'. The Madame HMV troupe, comprising 'a combination of well-known Malayan and Dutch East Indies artistes, many of whom [sang] 'for HMV records', was a good example. On 1 April 1935 the troupe arranged for the following to be published in the *Malaya Tribune*: 'A new company of Malay artistes will perform in a comedy-drama.' On 3 April 1935, it placed the following advertisement in the same newspaper:

Madame HMV
In a real life story 'The Order of Release'
An insoluble problem of Friendship vs. Duty
How the grim struggle affects them, striking at the heart of their normal round existence severing life-long ties and stirring to birth both family and racial animosities. The story is told with a tender simplicity and directness which should appeal to all who love a real life drama.

On 8 and 13 April, the same troupe called on readers to 'come and see modern Malay stage attractions' and 'new comedy-drama[s] (not fairy-tale[s])' (*Malaya Tribune*, 8 and 13 April 1935).

On another occasion, Moonlight Opera introduced its play, *The Price of a Woman's Honour* as a 'Modern Story depicting the life of a famous dancer and singer Ramon Rinaldo, from "Rinaldo Follies" with his three beautiful sisters Rita, Carmelia and Aida' (*Straits Echo*, 10 June 1933). 'Dean's United Opera strongly combined with Maimoon Opera' advertised itself as 'a modernised theatrical company' (*Malaya Tribune*, 25 March 1935).

Modern Western plays like *Topeng Hitam* or *Black Mask* by Alexandre Dumas were adapted. (This play was translated into Malay and published by the Malay Translation Bureau established at Sultan Idris

FIGURE 3.4
Advertisement for the Malay Play *Laksemana Hang Tuah*

FIRST VISIT TO PENANG.

THE FAMOUS

Dean's Union Opera

OF SINGAPORE

FOR A SHORT SEASON ONLY

AT THE

Drury Lane Theatre Hall

TO-NIGHT!   *TO-NIGHT!*

Tuesday, 29th October 1929

which puts on its boards nightly not only attractive selections of

VAUDEVILLE EXTRA TURNS

BUT ALSO A SERIES OF

Educational and Moral Plays

That will reveal to you the different phases of life as a guide to you for your welfare.

Come and see our new set of Sceneries, Costumes, Customs and etc., and our Galaxy of Stars, Miss Tijah and K. Dean, Md. Noor, the King of Clowns and famous comedian of Penang including our famous actors and actresses, Md. Kassim Wan Hussin, Abdul Rahman and Misses Saritnah, Chik, Sa'diah, with Misses Nancy, Zaitoon, Kiah & Bon specially trained in all the latest Vaudeville Extra Turns, Hindustani and English Songs and Dances. Music conducted by Messrs. C. Marteniz and A. Rahman. Harmonium by Professor A. Manan of Calcutta.

The management presents an all-star cast in

" *Laksemana Hang Tuah* "

with Ancient Malay Costume.

PRICES OF ADMISSION.

Special Seat $8; Reserved $2; First Class $1; Second Class 50 cts. Third Class 30

ADVANCE BOOKINGS AT 10, CHURCH STREET.

K. DEAN, President.   S. ALLY & MD. NOOR, Joint Secretaries.

THEATRE ROYAL

Monday, 28th to Wednesday, 30th.

Source: *Straits Echo*, 29 October 1929.

FIGURE 3.5
Advertisement for the Malay Play *Hang Tuah and Tun Tijah*,
and the Hindustani Play *Noor-E-Islam*

Dean's & Maimoon Opera

GRAND BENEFICIAL PERFORMANCE

IN AID OF

THE SINGAPORE BOY SCOUTS JAMBOREE

FUND

TO AUSTRALIA

Mr. Lee Choon Eng, the managing director of the Great World
and Messrs. Ong Boon Tat, J.P. and Ong Peng Hock of the New
World have kindly consented to co-operate with the Dean's
Grand Opera with the Maimoon Opera to stage   Special Selected
Plays for the above Fund.

Under the distinguished patronage of

H.H. THE SULTAN OF PERAK, G.C.M.G., Etc. & H.E. THE
G.O.C. COMMANDING THE TROOPS OF MALAYA

AT THE

GREAT WORLD SHOW HALL No. 3

ON SATURDAY, THE 8TH & SUNDAY, THE 9TH SEPT., 1934.
SATURDAY, 8TH SEPTEMBER, WILL STAGE
A WELL-KNOWN MALAY HISTORICAL PLAY

"HANG TUAH & TUN TIJAH."

All in Malay SONGS, DANCES, COSTUMES & CUSTOM.
SUNDAY, THE 9TH SEPTEMBER, WILL STAGE
A WELL-KNOWN HINDUSTANI PLAY

"NOOR-E-ISLAM"

VIEW THE DATE OPEN FOR SPECIAL PERFORMANCE.
BOOKING AT CHEONG KOON SENG & CO., LTD., ESTATE
DEPT. OR AT THE GREAT WORLD SHOW.

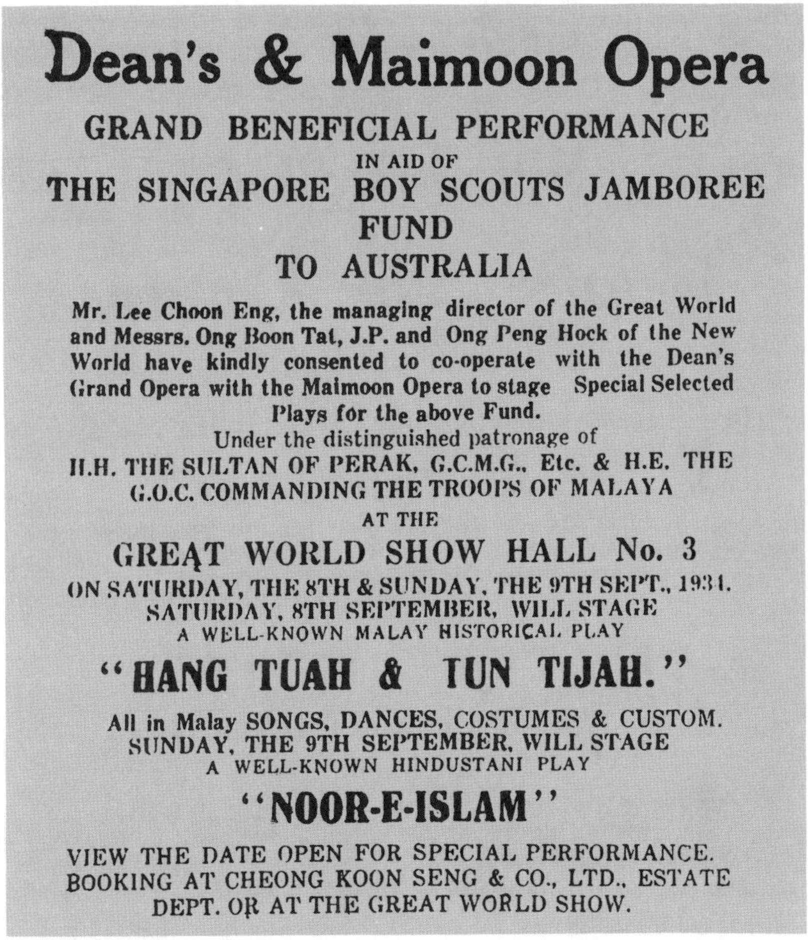

Source: *Malaya Tribune*, 6 September 1934.

Training College in 1924.) Plays derived from films were also performed. *The Silver Mask* (Figure 3.6), adapted from the screen version
of *The Mark of Zorro* (*Straits Echo*, 23 December 1931, 14 November
1932, and 23 July 1933), and *Only an Actress*, adapted from the film *The
Secret of Madame Blanche* (*Straits Echo*, 1 July 1933), were popular. *The
Forced Marriage* or *Terpaksa Menikah* (*Malaya Tribune*, 29 April 1935)
was also borrowed from the Indonesian talkie by Madame HMV. Plays
like *A Dutiful Son* (*Malaya Tribune*, 7 May 1935) and *Faridah Hanim*
(*Saudara*, 25 January 1929) were taken from Malay novels of the
period.

For the first time, directors, producers, and writers of these 'modern'
and 'real-life' dramas were advertised. It was recorded that the play

FIGURE 3.6
Advertisement for *The Silver Mask*, a *Bangsawan* Adaptation
of the Film *The Mark of Zorro*

Source: *Straits Echo*, 23 December 1931.

Punjab Mail was 'produced and conducted by Prof. A. Manan (Harmonium Master of India) and directed and controlled by Mr K. Dean, President [of] Dean's Union Opera' (*Straits Echo*, 4 November 1929). *Reward of Virtue* performed by Rose Opera was publicized as the 'master production of Mr K. C. Tan, the well-known and able organiser of Malay operas' (*Straits Echo*, 17 November 1932). *Amazah Damnah* staged by Madame HMV and *Faridah Hanim* by the Opera of Singapore were said to be written by well-known 'playwrights' Encik Noonmim Ainmim (*Malaya Tribune*, 1 April 1935) and Encik Nani bin Al. Hj. Osman (*Saudara*, 25 January 1929) respectively.

There were two main reasons for these changes in the direction of greater realism. In the first place, by the 1920s, 1930s, and 1940s the Malay intelligentsia had grown in number as a result of increasing opportunities in education, and it began to criticize *bangsawan*. As Za'aba (1941a: 18), a well-known Malay writer and teacher of the times, wrote:

In spite of the popularity of the Bangsawan shows among Malays of the less cultured classes ... the standard language of the bangsawan has been much criticised ... by the more educated section of their audience. Such expressions as 'Saya empunya diri pergi di mana ayahanda empunya istana' [I myself go to my father's palace] have provoked smiles and good-natured jokes among the better informed students of Malay speech. Then there are the many ridiculous anachronisms in costumes and scenes, the strong bias for magic elements and fairy tales in the stories enacted, and the hybrid, often dull song interludes between scenes!

These criticisms arose at a time when nationalist sentiments began to be expressed among the Malays, especially the intelligentsia. They began to feel threatened by the immigrant Chinese who had arrived in great numbers. While most Malays remained peasants, the urban economy was increasingly dominated by the Chinese. The situation was made worse by the Depression of the 1930s when many Malay farmers experienced hard times (Roff, 1967: 205). In addition, the Malays were anxious about the growing political strength of the non-Malays. In particular, the Straits Chinese whose families had resided in the Straits Settlements for more than a century began to demand equal rights with the Malays. They wanted a 'greater share in government and administration than they had hitherto enjoyed, and quite simply ... the right to regard Malaya as their home and not simply their halting place' (Roff, 1967: 208). With the rise of nationalist consciousness, the Malay intelligentsia felt that Malay identity and nationalistic feelings should be expressed through theatre. To them, the fairy-tale stories dwelt far too much on fantasy and could not convey adequately the ideas of Malay nationalism. The Malay intelligentsia also stressed that *bangsawan* stories should portray the 'living conditions of the [Malay] race' (*hal-ehwal kehidupan bangsa*) and should 'educate' (*memberi pelajaran*) (*Tantuan Muda*, October 1926).

The Malay intelligentsia also began to judge *bangsawan* according to

Western standards. Those of its members educated in English schools had become used to Western drama and literary works. Dramatic activities were encouraged in schools and colleges. *Macbeth, Julius Caesar, Black Mask*, and *A Midsummer Night's Dream* (*Times of Malaya*, 3 December 1924) were translated into Malay and acted out by Sultan Idris Training College trainees. Western concepts of drama and realism were introduced. As a consequence, the educated Malays were moved to criticize the colloquial language (*bahasa pasar*), stories, costumes, scenes, magical elements, and interludes of *bangsawan* (Za'aba, 1941a: 18). They also argued that the 'movements' (*pergerakan*), 'manner of speech' (*gaya pertuturan*), and 'backdrops' (*tirai*) used were often not 'consistent with the period and country' (*tidak munasabah dengan masa dan negeri*) that the stories were supposed to portray (*Tantuan Muda*, October 1926).

Not surprisingly, the Malay intelligentsia created a new form of theatre called *sandiwara* (theatrical production), in which, unlike *bangsawan*, the emphasis was put on fully scripted plays with sets depicting details of a particular place and time. Mortal human beings were the main characters. Learned and literate Malay was used. Philosophical and nationalistic themes were stressed (Camoens, 1981: Chapter 4).[7] Both Malay historical and contemporary plays were promoted. Shakespeare and Greek tragedies became important sources of inspiration for *sandiwara* playwrights. The performers were amateurs who relied on written scripts and the skills of a director (Nanney, 1983: Chapter 3), not professionals who were accustomed to improvisation on stage.

In response to these criticisms of the Malay intelligentsia and the development of *sandiwara*, *bangsawan* troupes began to perform Malay historical plays. Accordingly, in comparison with previous decades where the majority of *bangsawan* performances comprised European, Indian, Chinese, and Arabian fantasy tales, by the 1930s Malay historical stories were common too. In the main, these historical stories sought to depict the glory of the old Malay kingdoms and to evoke in the Malay audience a sense of pride and solidarity. In part, then, they corresponded with the emergence of a new nationalist consciousness in Malay society. *Bangsawan* was, however, not an active instrument of social change. Although a few troupes like the Bolero Opera (led by Bakhtiar Effendi from Sumatra) were overtly political and urged the audience to stand up against the colonialists (*Berita Minggu*, 21 May 1970), most of the *bangsawan* troupes in Malaya at that time were not known to have done so.[8]

Secondly, new types of stories were introduced into *bangsawan* as performers were influenced by Indonesian *tonil* (the Dutch term for 'play') groups which toured the peninsula during the late 1920s and 1930s.[9] *Tonil* troupes like Dja's Dardanella (A. Piedro), Orion (Miss Riboet), Tchaya Timoer (Andjar Asmara), and Bolero (Bakhtiar Effendi) brought to Malaya plays with contemporary settings and dramas based on everyday life. Events, sets, and props were more realistic than in *bangsawan.* Plays were scripted (Boen Oemarjati, 1971: 21, 24; Krishen Jit, 1979). Songs, dances, and tricks on stage were no longer more important than acting. There was a minimum number of acts though entertainment was still provided during act changes. The role of the director became very important (Boen Oemarjati, 1971: 24–31). Of Miss Riboet's troupe, the following comments were made:

The arrangements are quite different from other shows of this nature that have visited Penang before. It [the production] is conducted on modern lines and is exceptionally well managed. The plot is given ... in acts and during the intervals extra turns are given in English and other languages. (*Straits Echo,* 13 January 1930.)

The play staged was 'Nyai Dasima', an old favourite, but the manner of presentation was entirely different. The present company treated the play purely as a drama whereas previous bangsawans have been in the habit of turning the play half into an opera and half into a drama.... (*Times of Malaya,* 10 February 1930.)

Special mention must be made of the scene of a portion of 'Singapore After Midnight'. Rikishas [rickshaws] and bicycles made their appearance on the stage and gave the audience a real street scene in Singapore. (*Sunday Gazette,* 13 August 1933.)

From the reviews, some of which are reproduced below, it can be surmised that the Indonesian troupes were indeed very popular among the Malay audiences in Malaya. 'Even though the Javanese Malay spoken made it difficult to follow the speech', the performances drew large crowds (*Straits Echo,* 28 September 1935).

Miss Riboet's Maleisch Tooneel Gezelschap 'Orion', which opened its season in Penang on January 10 at the Drury Lane Theatre Hall, has been crowded the last three nights. On Saturday night, many had to be satisfied with standing room. (*Straits Echo,* 13 January 1930.)

On Wednesday night, all the roads appeared to lead to the theatre hall in Tranquerah Road. All Malacca and his wife and even his family were there. (*Malacca Guardian,* 24 March 1930.)

Complaints were made by 'Disgusted Topan' and 'Fair Play' to the editor of the *Malacca Guardian* about how they had booked front row seats but were made to sit at the back instead. The explanation given was that the 'crowd was enormous on Friday night and in order to please the public, the management had to place extra $3.00 seats which resulted in $2.00 seats being pushed back' (*Malacca Guardian,* 24 March 1930). The Indonesian *tonil* troupe called Dardanella also 'played to capacity crowds everywhere', and was the 'cause of a huge uproar in the Malay-speaking world' (*Malacca Guardian,* 24 June and 3 July 1935) (Figures 3.7 and 3.8).

Given the popularity of the Indonesian troupes and the new plays they presented, it was not surprising that local *bangsawan* troupes began

FIGURE 3.7
Advertisement for Dja's Dardanella's *Fatimma*

Source: *Straits Echo*, 21 September 1935.

FIGURE 3.8
Advertisement for the 'Exotic' Plays of Dja's Dardanella

Source: Straits Echo, 20 August 1936.

FIGURE 3.9
Advertisement for the Indonesian Troupe, Miss Riboet's Opera

Source: *Straits Echo*, 11 March 1933.

to introduce contemporary stories into their performances. *Bangsawan*
troupes staged plays which were first performed by Indonesian *tonil*
troupes that toured Malaya. For example, Kiah Opera performed
Hunchback (*Straits Echo*, 30 November 1935) and *Devil's Island of Digol*
(*Straits Echo*, 28 July 1936) which were first staged by Dardanella in
1935 (*Straits Times*, 1 June, 4 June, and 5 June 1935). As Dardanella
brought the audience 'around the Orient' with stories set in Bali, Tibet,
Shanghai, Hawaii, and Bombay, so did local troupes start to do likewise
(Figures 3.9–3.10). Madame HMV, for example, premiered *Batak or
Dayang Si-Natdong* (A Sumatran Savage Drama), *The Slave Market* (A
Thrilling Romance in Central Africa), *The Desert Tragedy* (Strife in
Arabia), and *Zanzibar Prince* (*Malaya Tribune*, 4, 5, 10, and
12 April 1935). Kiah Opera took the Penang audience around the East
with the following plays: *Kraton Solo—A Javanese Story*, *Istri Kedua di
Burma*, *Spear of Stamboul*, *Prince of Morocco*, *Raja Laksamana Bentan*,
and *Devil's Island of Degol* (*Straits Echo*, 18–28 July 1936).

FIGURE 3.10
Advertisement for a Malayan Opera's Performance of an
'Exotic' Play from Hawaii

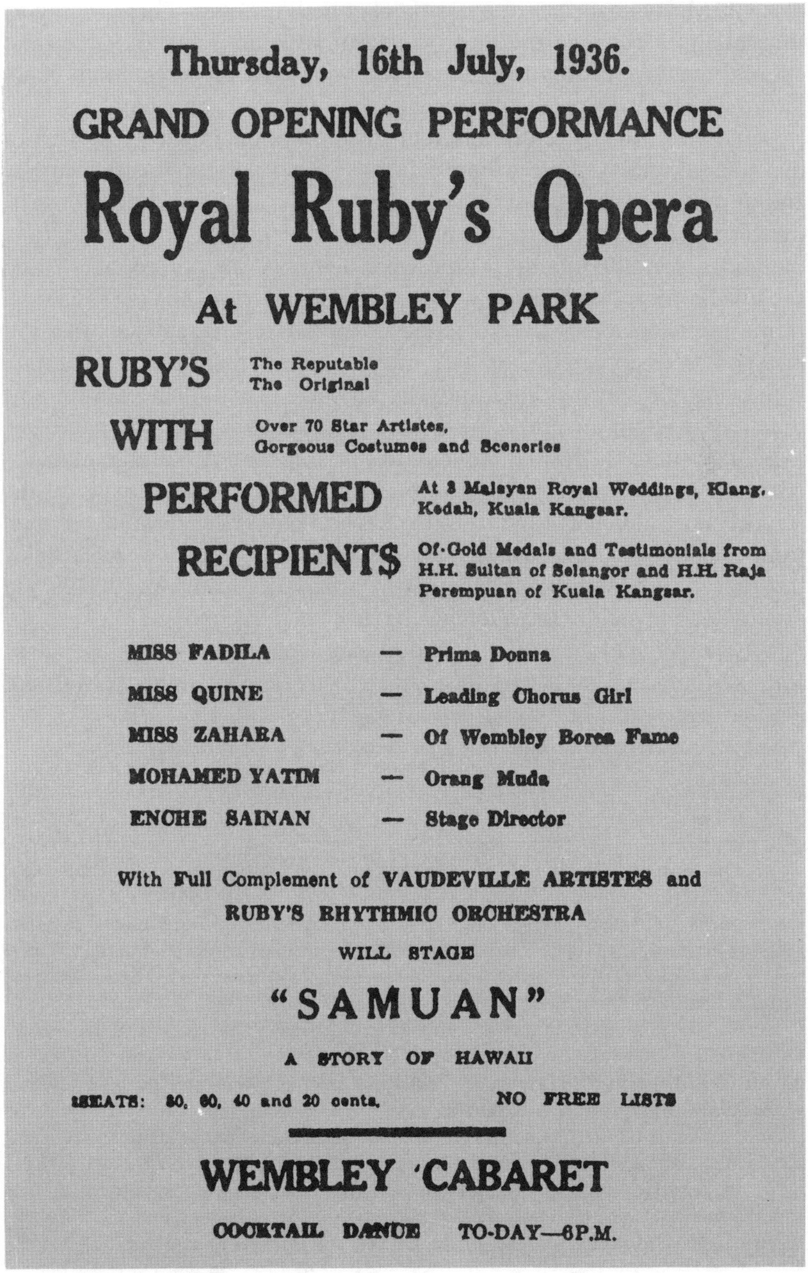

Thursday, 16th July, 1936.

GRAND OPENING PERFORMANCE

Royal Ruby's Opera

At WEMBLEY PARK

RUBY'S   The Reputable
           The Original

WITH   Over 70 Star Artistes,
      Gorgeous Costumes and Sceneries

PERFORMED   At 3 Malayan Royal Weddings, Klang,
               Kedah, Kuala Kangsar.

RECIPIENTS   Of-Gold Medals and Testimonials from
               H.H. Sultan of Selangor and H.H. Raja
               Perempuan of Kuala Kangsar.

MISS FADILA   —   Prima Donna

MISS QUINE   —   Leading Chorus Girl

MISS ZAHARA   —   Of Wembley Borea Fame

MOHAMED YATIM   —   Orang Muda

ENCHE SAINAN   —   Stage Director

With Full Complement of **VAUDEVILLE ARTISTES** and
RUBY'S RHYTHMIC ORCHESTRA

WILL STAGE

"SAMUAN"

A STORY OF HAWAII

SEATS: 80, 60, 40 and 20 cents.   NO FREE LISTS

WEMBLEY 'CABARET

COCKTAIL DANCE   TO-DAY—6P.M.

Source: Straits Echo, 16 July 1936.

* * *

As a product of the times, *bangsawan* articulated the changes taking place in Malayan society in the early twentieth century. There were correspondences between the theatrical form and the political, social, and cultural changes of the time. As a mode of visual representation, *bangsawan* was heterogeneous, innovative, and constantly changing.

Bangsawan was therefore different from traditional theatre. As part of the nascent multi-ethnic urban culture, *bangsawan* emphasized variety and novelty in its stories, themes, and interludes. Spectacular tricks, transformation scenes, and stunts were performed to attract and hold the audience's attention at a time when lighting was not yet able to do so. Furthermore, *bangsawan* with its stories and extra turns originating from 'exotic' places attracted audiences who were fascinated with but had no direct experience of the 'modern' and foreign world. Through witnessing the spectacles and novelty on stage, the audiences were able to fantasize about a world more enchanted than their own mundane one.

As commercial theatre, *bangsawan* was innovative and constantly adapting to the times. *Bangsawan* performers incorporated many of the songs, chorus dances, and comic sketches of vaudeville and operetta troupes which toured Malaya. The introduction of stories with Malay historical and contemporary themes in *bangsawan* in the late 1920s and 1930s was inevitable, the audience having been exposed by them to the new type of *tonil* performed by Indonesian troupes as well as the *sandiwara* scripted and staged by local amateur ones. The audience was also getting bigger and becoming better educated (Loh, 1975: 13–14). This changing audience increasingly preferred reality to fantasy.[10]

1. This term was used in *bangsawan* advertisements to describe entertainment between acts. See advertisements by Wayang Kassim (*Straits Echo*, 15 June 1907), Wayang Aishah (*Straits Echo*, 14 August 1909), and Opera Indra Permata (*Straits Echo*, 11 February 1907). The term is still used today by *bangsawan* performers. According to Tok Wan, a veteran b*angsawan* performer who is now in his eighties, the term *extra* is an English term meaning items that are 'temporary only' (*sementara sahaja*).

2. See, for example, Wayang Kassim's season in Penang (*Straits Echo*, 8 September–18 November 1903); the Star Opera Co. of Singapore's season in Penang (*Straits Echo*, 29 August–18 October 1912); or the Malayan Opera of Selangor's season in Penang (*Straits Echo*, 27 September–1 November 1921).

3. '... nyanyi dan tari menari ekstra daripada bermacam-macam lagu dan tari orang puteh, Masri, Hindustan dan Melayu' (*Idaran Zaman*, 12 December 1925).

4. The variety found in the stories and extra turns may suggest that there are no real limits to both the form and substance of *bangsawan*, but as Chapters 6 and 7 will show, performers have to adhere to standard scene types, character types, and musical pieces.

5. It is important to note here that 'variety performances' in which 'songs, dances, music and comedy' were already performed by troupes in the early 1900s. These variety shows, however, were staged as farewell performances by troupes. See *Straits Echo*, 16 November 1903 (last performance of Wayang Kassim in Penang) and 6 March 1910 (farewell performance of Wayang Inche Puteh). These shows were sometimes known as *Chow Chow Maraba* or *Rampai Rampaian* (variety show) (*Straits Echo*, 6 March 1910 and

12 April 1911). The Wayang Parsi used the same terms to describe their farewell performances (see, for example, *Straits Echo*, 23 July 1912).

It was only in the late 1920s that the term 'vaudeville' was used. (See, for example, the City Opera of Singapore's advertisement (*Straits Echo*, 13 December 1928).) These variety performances or vaudeville nights were also held at least once or twice a week instead of only on the occasion of the last performance.

6. A number of lithograph presses had been set up in the Straits Settlements from the late nineteenth century, mainly by the Jawi Peranakan. They published Malay newspapers as well as Malay translations of romances, Arabic and Persian legends, traditional folk-tales and poetry (*syair*) and some news adapted from the English language press or Egyptian and Arabic presses. Between 1876 and 1941, there were no fewer than 197 Malay and Arabic periodicals published in the Malay States and the Straits Settlements. They served as agents of social change. See Roff (1972).

7. Teachers and students of the Sultan Idris Training College began to write their own Malay plays. As an illustration, Said Haji Hussain wrote a play called *Laksamana Mati Dibunuh* which was performed by the Dramatic Society of the College in 1938. The students who graduated from the college as teachers continued their dramatic activities in the smaller towns and kampongs to which they were posted. Popular legends were scripted and new contemporary plays based on 'real life' were created. One famous teacher-playwright of the 1930s was Shahrom Hussain who wrote and published many plays, such as *Belot*, *Nasib Si-Puteh*, and *Anak Setia*. By the 1950s, both professional and amateur groups were performing throughout Malaya (Camoens, 1981: Chapter 4).

8. The main aim of local *bangsawan* troupes was to make money. It was the *sandiwara* rather than the *bangsawan* that was used by nationalists in post-war Malaya to evoke national consciousness. In the 1950s, however, *bangsawan* troupes helped to raise funds for the United Malays National Organization (UMNO) and provided an occasion for UMNO members to deliver speeches (see Chapter 9).

9. Significant changes were introduced into the *komedi stambul* after 1906. Among the changes was a new emphasis on realism. Contemporary plays like *Nyai Dasima*, *Oey Tam Bah Sia*, and *Si Tjonet* were also added (Boen Oemarjati, 1971: 21–4; Knaap, 1903).

10. Similarly, new literary forms like the novel and short story which presented real-life characters set against contemporary backgrounds appeared at this time. Literature was used as a 'platform to discuss and moralize on current problems, particularly those arising from the situation of social change'. See Mohd. Taib Osman (1984: 86) and Za'aba (1941a) for a description of novels of this period. Although the novels and short stories were mainly love stories, they were didactic and corresponded with the socio-cultural changes in society. Their themes typically centred on 'forced marriages', 'sufferings of women because their husbands took other wives', and 'moral traps' in the cities (Mohd. Taib Osman, 1984: 89).

4
The Promotion of Stars,
c.1880–*c*.1930

Stars

BEING commercial theatre, *bangsawan* depicted its performers not just as actors and actresses but as stars (*bintang*), that is, they were professionals who worked as entertainers. Unlike performers of the traditional *wayang kulit* or *makyong* who usually had other sources of income such as farming, for the *bangsawan* performer, particularly the stars viewed, acting was a full-time occupation. The *sri panggung* (heroine) and *orang muda* (hero) were the key members of the troupe; they were its stars. As the *Malacca Guardian* (9 May 1932) reported, 'the whole company gives way to the star, who gets a liberal sum of about forty pounds per week'. It was the stars which established a company's reputation.

The following announcements that 'the most famous actors, actresses and clowns from Medan, Batavia and Singapore' had arrived to tour Malaya (*Times of Malaya*, 22 January 1926) were typical:

The Starlight Opera Co. beg to announce the appearance of their young, beautiful, charming, attractive and famous new actress Miss Fatimah of Singapore who has never played in the FMS and is specialized in Extra Turns. Her songs in different languages are so numerous that they will not be repeated until she has sung the whole series. It will be delightful to see how pretty she looks, how clever she dances, how sweet she sings. (*Times of Malaya*, 29 December 1925.)

Several new artistes have arrived by the S. S. Denver Van Tuves yesterday to augment the troupe of the Rose Opera. Misses Paulino and Gina with Bob and Kasban, the well-known and popular Kronchong singers of Medan, and Haji Hassan, the famous Gambus Player and singer are amongst the arrivals to join force with the Sri Rose Opera. (*Straits Echo*, 10 December 1932.)

Performers of varied ethnic backgrounds were recruited and promoted as stars. Miss Van Cantarfischer and Miss Dora van Smith were important European prima donnas of the Indra Permata Theatrical Co. Their 'acting and singing' were reportedly so fine that they 'elicited loud applause from the audience' (*Straits Echo*, 19 May 1904). Mr Tan Tjeng Bok was a well-known Chinese actor. Born in Java, he was also known as the 'Douglas Fairbanks of Java' and he acted in the famous Dardanella and Miss Riboet's Orion. In 1933, Tan Tjeng Bok joined the

Moonlight Opera Co. of Penang and captivated the audience with his 'singing of the kroncong' (*Straits Echo*, 1 May 1933). In yet another performance by the same company, an Arab performer, 'Sheik Omar ... was applauded for his excellent singing' (*Straits Echo*, 22 May 1933).

Child stars were promoted as novelties. The audience at a Wayang Kassim performance was invited to see 'the youngest clown in the world' who was 'only five years old' (*Straits Echo*, 8 August 1908). The Kinta Opera Co. had its Miss Echon, a 'nine-year-old actress' who sang English songs (*Straits Echo*, 3 January 1925), while Genani Star Opera boasted of 'Baby Star Miss Nani' (*Straits Echo*, 7 November 1925).

Recruits of Various Ethnic Backgrounds

What attracted young people of various ethnic origins to join the *bangsawan* troupes? The stories related to me told of motives which were not very different from those of young men and women aspiring to be actors and actresses in the film world of today. Young boys from the kampong were lured to the town to earn a living, many no longer contented with a life of farming. Others came from poor or broken homes; they saw the *bangsawan* as a way to earn a living (*cari makan*) or to see the world (*merantau tempat*). All who joined *bangsawan* were tempted by the glamour of stardom and fame which the touring companies—and the urban areas, seen as places of adventure, excitement, and drama—offered.

In his late eighties when I met him, Wan (Plate 30), a former *orang muda*, manager of Starlight Opera, and proprietor of Wan Man Sri Bangsawan, remembered that as a young boy he had always wanted to see the world. After completing four years of schooling in Penang, Wan decided to become independent of his parents and to earn money so that he could travel. His father, a schoolteacher, could not do anything to change his mind. Wan left school and found himself a job as a delivery boy for the Fraser & Neave Aerated Water Company, delivering bottles of aerated water to shops on his three-wheel bicycle for $12 a month. However, he still could not afford to travel to the places he had heard of. Disheartened, he looked up a Bengali friend, a *bangsawan* performer by the name of Babjan. Wan recalled the advice of Babjan: 'Wan, Wan, if you want to travel but do not have money, join the *bangsawan*. Food and shelter will be provided, and you will get to go places.' He was about fourteen or fifteen years old then.

Many recruits came from impoverished or broken homes. The 70-year-old veteran *orang muda*, Mahmud Jun, was born the son of a poor farmer. Leaving his family and village at the age of fourteen with $3 in his pocket, he took the train from Alor Star to Ipoh. There, he helped a porter to carry baggage at the railway station in return for some pocket money. Then he set up a stall selling noodles in a park. It was there, two or three months later, that a *bangsawan* troupe, the Grand Jubilee Opera owned by Shaw Brothers, happened to pitch its tent. The general manager was a Kedah man who used to live in Mahmud Jun's village. 'He knew my father and my uncle but he was richer than we were,' Mahmud Jun said. The manager told Mahmud, 'Follow me and work in the *bangsawan*. If I see your father, he would be angry with me if I did not take care of you.' 'That was how I joined the *bangsawan* and became like his son,' according to Mahmud Jun.

In his late eighties, Suki, a former *orang muda*, film star and owner of Dian Sandiwara, gave me the following account of why he went into *bangsawan* acting. Born in Padang, Sumatra, Suki joined the *bangsawan* because he wanted to look for his father who had left home to manage the estate of the Sultan of Negeri Sembilan. Suki's father was the chief police ranger of Padang but had quit the police force because he disliked the Dutch colonialists. By then, he had already divorced Suki's mother. After his mother died, Suki stayed with his grandmother for a while. But he wanted to meet his father again. 'I thought that if I joined the opera, I would have the opportunity to go to Singapore and then to the mainland to look for my father,' he said. So when the Royal Opera came to Padang, Suki offered his services. 'The manager took me in as I had the looks and could sing and act.'

Ainon Chik (Plate 31), a 70-year-old veteran *sri panggung*, recalled that she followed her sister and brother-in-law who joined Genani Star Opera after the death of both her parents in Singapore. The sisters had no relatives to turn to. Ainon's mother was a Sarawakian Chinese while her father was a Bugis who had migrated to Sarawak. Ainon's parents eloped to Singapore because her grandparents did not approve of the mixed marriage. Ainon was eight years old then. 'My brother-in-law could earn twice as much as an electrician and stage hand in the *bangsawan* than as an electrician in a private firm,' she said.

Menah Yem (Plate 32), a well known dancer and *sri panggung* of her time, started performing in the *bangsawan* at the age of nine. That was almost eighty years ago. Menah Yem's mother joined the City Opera (owned by Ong Peng Hock) after she separated from her husband. So Menah grew up with *bangsawan* performers as her larger family. She sang in the chorus and replaced other, more experienced child actors when they fell ill.

Mat Arab (Plate 31), a famous comedian, now in his seventies, claimed that he was left to fend for himself at an early age after both his parents died. His father was an Arab who worked in the police force while his mother was a Malay woman from the kampong. With no brothers or sisters to take care of him, Mat Arab followed a *bangsawan* man by the name of Haji Pokar, or 'Ging', as he was commonly known. Ging adopted Mat Arab as his son and brought him to Singapore where he joined the City Opera. 'I went because I had no one to turn to. Besides, Ging said that it would be enjoyable,' added Mat Arab.

Other performers grew up in the midst of *bangsawan* activity. Their parents were performers or proprietors of famous *bangsawan* companies. Rahman B.'s father, Bakar M., was the proprietor of Rahman Star Opera, which was named after Rahman B. (Plate 33), the eldest son.

His brother Rahim B. (Plate 34) and sister Rohani B. also performed in the troupe.

Minah Alias (Plate 35), a former heroine who is in her seventies and who instructs the Bangsawan Sri USM today, came from a family of actors and performers. Her grandfather was a shadow puppeteer (*dalang*) in Java. Her father, Nani bin Haji Omar, started off as a *dalang* and an actor in the *wayang wong* (*orang*) but joined the opera upon the invitation of a Chinese opera owner. Nani soon became a hero and a star in *bangsawan* and was sought after by women of all ethnic backgrounds. Minah's mother, Catharine de Brish, a foreigner, was one of these women. After watching Nani's performance, Catharine de Brish fell in love with him, attending his performances every night, making eyes at Nani and throwing flowers to him after the performances. When Catharine's brother forbade her to see Nani, she fell ill. Nani and Catharine finally got married and she joined the *bangsawan*. It was inevitable that Minah, coming from such a family, was to take up acting as well.

The late Alfonso Soliano, pianist and band leader of *bangsawan*, and later conductor of the Orkes Radio Malaya, was a Filipino who came from a family of musicians. His parents were among the sixty-four musicians engaged by the British government to form the Selangor State Band. When the Band disbanded in 1927, all the musicians except one stayed on in Malaya. These musicians played in night-clubs, hotels, cabarets, funeral bands, and in the *bangsawan*. Soliano's father, Rupino, a string bass player, performed with the Lake Band which accompanied silent movies, and subsequently joined the *bangsawan*.

That was how Alfonso's whole family became involved in the *bangsawan*. Soliano's mother, Pacita, became a *bangsawan* singer, his two sisters were dancers and singers, and his brother Jerry played the violin and later became a band leader. Alfonso himself studied under his father and brother and became a *bangsawan* pianist.

Yahya Sulong, a well-known comedian today, was literally born on the *bangsawan* stage of the New World Park about sixty years ago. 'My mother began to have labour pains when she was performing the story "Panglima Alam Yahya". That is why I was named Yahya,' he said.

There were others who were so attracted to the *bangsawan* that they ran away from their homes to join it. Abdullah Abdul Rahman's father had been a chief surveyor and wanted him to finish his Senior Cambridge so that he could get a good job. But Abdullah had been interested in acting since he was a child, having become familiar with *bangsawan* performances whenever they were staged at the park. 'After I finished my Junior Cambridge examinations, I decided to quit school to join the *bangsawan*. I did not dare tell my father. He did not know where I was till he saw me on stage many years later!' Abdullah declared.

My *bangsawan* music teacher, Mat Hashim (Plate 10), also joined a *bangsawan* troupe without his parents' knowledge. 'I used to go to the performances of the Oriental Opera of Selangor every night when it was playing in Butterworth,' recalled the sixty-year-old Mat. 'I made friends with the child actors and played with them after school. When the troupe left, I followed them.' Realizing that he would be punished for doing so, Mat did not dare go home for the next four years. The opera troupe fed and clothed him.

Finally, there were some who were recruited by *bangsawan* troupes because of their skills as tailors or football players. (*Bangsawan* troupes competed with each other in football.) Such was the case of Alias Manan (Plate 7), who also instructs the Bangsawan Sri USM today. After finishing his Standard Five, Alias left home to earn a living in the town of Nibong Tebal, becoming a tailor's apprentice. Shortly after that, some performers from Ruby's Grand Opera came to order football clothes. They invited Alias, who was known to be a good football player, to play a match with them as the troupe was short of players. After winning the game, Ruby's Grand Opera members invited Alias to join their troupe, telling him that 'you can tour Malaya with us without having to pay a cent'. So Alias became their football player, selling tickets, and doing odd jobs for the troupe. He also began to learn singing and dancing and played small roles.

Learning to be Stars

Typically, the newcomer was drawn gradually into the life of the troupe, initially playing small, undemanding roles. Young children were given children's or other minor parts. Minah Alias remembered her less-than-propitious-though edifying debut as an actress very clearly:

It was a performance staged by Genani Star Opera, owned by Tan Kam Choon and managed by my father, Nani. I was eight years old and was very excited when I was called upon to replace Ainon Chik who was sick. I was to be a 'jungle child' in the play 'Ginufifa'. To my dismay, the leaves with which I was covered were full of ants. I was feeling so itchy that I forgot my part. Instead of pulling the antelope's tail, I pulled his horns. The head came off and I fell. (*Star*, 15 December 1984.)

If the young recruits proved themselves to be good, they could sing or dance in the extra turns. Minah Alias was praised for her efforts in the turns at a performance in 1925 (*Times of Malaya*, 13 October 1925): 'Miss Nani [Minah Alias], the four year old daughter of the stage director [Nani], was the first to give an extra turn. Her song and dance were charmingly performed. Later she gave another turn during which she forgot a part of the words but achieved a triumph with her winsome smile.'

Ainon Chik also started her career performing as a singer and dancer in the extra turns. She recalled singing songs like 'I Wanna Go Where You Go' and 'You Were Meant for Me'. She also acted children's parts in plays like *Musalma* and *Jambatan Patah*.

Most apprentices had to play the role of court attendants which was often referred to as '*pegang tombak* (holding the spear)'. As Abdullah

Abdul Rahman recalled, 'I had to hold the spear for three years and the only words I was allowed to say were *ampun tuanku* (forgive me your highness), *bermohon patik tuanku* (I request your highness), and *kembali patik tuanku* (I leave your highness).'

The apprentice learnt that to make it in the world of *bangsawan*, he had to win recognition as a star; the rewards were substantial. Stars earned more money—sometimes as much as $50 a month. They were often presented with gifts or large tips by wealthy admirers. As Mat Arab said, 'When I became a star, I did not face financial difficulties. I had enough to eat and clothes to wear. I could always find a job.' Stars also became household names. If the performers were good, special honorary titles were bestowed upon them. Yem was known as the Roman Nevaro of the East; Menah Yem, the Queen of Dance; Suki, the King of Bangsawan; Ainon Chik, the Greta Garbo of Malaya; Aman Belon, the Charlie Chaplin of the East; and Purita Clarino, the Jazz Queen.

Consequently, the apprentices had every reason to persevere, observe, and learn from the side-wings every night. They had to diversify their interests and familiarize themselves with all the roles, songs, and dances. According to Wan, he used to sit by the side and observe the more experienced performers. Although as a chorus boy he could actually go down stage to the cabaret or wherever he wished and return to the stage at a designated time, he chose to watch the other performers instead. During the day, he studied Malay, Western, Chinese, Hindustani, and Arabic songs, *silat Melayu*, and *kuntau* (Chinese art of self-defence using sticks), and *adat istiadat* (rituals) of the Malay court from the other performers. He learnt the different ways of paying respect to royalty.

Rahman B. confirmed that for the *bangsawan* performers learning was through *latih-pandang* (rehearse-watch): 'We sat by the side-wings and watched the other performers. If we were interested to become an *orang muda*, we looked at what the *orang muda* did. We observed all the characters so that if we were called to play any character, we knew what to do.'

Wan made clear that *bangsawan* roles were committed to memory, there being no scripts to study. Before any new or major play was performed, the director would call all the actors and actresses together, narrate the story to the cast, and then assign each role. It was left to the performers to improvise the dialogue and the accompanying actions, relying only on their skills (*kebijaksanaan*).

The performers were thus compelled to think before they spoke anything on stage. As Rahman B. emphasized to me, 'The correct language used was important. If the conversation was centred around the palace, palace language must be used. If the scene was centered around the village, market Malay (*bahasa pasar*) had to be employed.' Alias added that the performers had to keep their wits sharp by improvising Malay poetry (*pantun*) on the spot; the person who could not reply with a *pantun* was the loser.

Strict discipline was the rule. Mahmud Jun remembered that he had to rise at eight in the morning to jog and exercise for two hours in the park where he was performing. It was only after ten o'clock that the apprentices were allowed to have breakfast. After the meal, they were expected to perform their daily chores. In the Grand Jubilee Opera, Mahmud Jun had to sweep the floor and put up posters. Abdullah Abdul Rahman recalled that the apprentices had to carry and fix props as well. They often had to distribute flyers and posters in the villages too.

Typically, after lunch the apprentices would practise dancing and singing with the other leading actors and actresses till about five o'clock. After a short rest, a bath, and a meal, they would prepare for the evening's performance.

Some of the more fortunate or promising ones were sent to Indonesia for their apprenticeship. Minah Alias, for example, lived in Java and studied dance, music, and acting with the famous Miss Riboet for ten years. The training was demanding and rigorous. Waking up at five in the morning to jog, she was also required to attend to some household chores. At one o'clock, the practice sessions at which Minah Alias learnt Balinese dances, folk dances, and dances of the *kraton* (palace) would begin. At night, she performed with the Miss Riboet Orient Opera.

Training for apprentice musicians was also long and arduous. Alfonso Soliano studied the piano, violin, and other instruments with his father and brother for many years. The family had joined the *bangsawan* when Soliano was four years old, but he was not allowed to perform in public till he had mastered the piano, by which time he was twelve.

Despite the long hours and hard work, payment for apprentices was upredictable. According to Mahmud Jun, sometimes he received 30 cents, at other times 50 cents. 'Sometimes we only got free food. This happened when audiences did not turn up because of heavy rain,' recalled Abdullah Abdul Rahman.

Promotion for the apprentice came after learning all the parts that he was exposed to. Rahman B. started as a court attendant, one of those holding the spear. He was then given the opportunity to play 'bad' characters as he knew *silat*, and he also understudied the clown character. Only after he had become expert in these roles was he promoted to second or third hero, and only if the main hero was absent could Rahman B. get to play in his stead.

For the child apprentice, formal schooling was an irregular matter. As the troupes were always on the move, there was scarce opportunity for the children to register in any school. It was pointless anyway, for they would move in a matter of weeks to another town. Rahman B. studied up to Standard Five only. For him, schooling was irrelevant to making his way in life: 'I could survive in the *bangsawan*; I used my acting abilities, initiative, and worked hard.' *Bangsawan* was, in this respect, both school and life for those who came to it as children and young people.

Maintaining Star Status

It was no easy matter to maintain one's star status. The stars were prodded on by competition and rivalry. Minah Alias remembered her mother telling her that 'if you want to be good, you must have the ambition to be better than your friends'.

Further, stars had to keep up with the changing tastes of audiences. Menah Yem, known to her admirers as the Queen of Dance, learnt the latest vaudeville dances from dancers who were brought over from the Philippines, and she and her Filipino dance partner, Henry, would study dances like the rumba and samba at screenings of foreign films, later including these in their acts. Demonstrating the rumba to me, Menah Yem remembered with pride that she and her partner were up-to-date in their knowledge of dances, executing them faithfully. 'As a result, we were so popular that if we did not appear at least three times in a performance, the audience would shout '*pendek-panjang, pendek-panjang* [short-tall, short-tall].' (This referred to the fact that Henry, her partner, was tall and she was short.)

Performers who had acquired star status felt that they owed it to themselves to constantly improve their skills in singing, dancing, and the art of self-defence. Minah Alias recalled studying *kuntau* from a Chinese opera actress even after becoming a star, and in return, she taught *silat* to the opera actress.

As professional actors, *bangsawan* performers had to learn to forget themselves on stage. Performers had to cry during sad scenes, Menah Yem said, and if real tears did not flow, they had to dab oil on their faces. Menah Yem herself was particularly convincing in the role of a wicked stepmother: 'Once, someone in the audience became so worked up when I beat my stepdaughter with a broom and broke a plate on her head that she shouted, "Are you an animal?".' Males sometimes had to masquerade as women. Suki recalled that he had to learn to play female roles—not without initial embarrassment—as the opera did not have enough women.

Stars, being stars, had to be aware of their conduct and personal behaviour on stage and off. Minah Alias remembered having to follow many rules which curbed her personal freedom. 'I could not go out during the daytime or go near a window lest I was seen by outsiders. I was told that if people could see my face during the daytime, they would not come and see me at night when I performed.' So much importance was placed on maintaining their image as public figures that 'even men were not allowed to wander aimlessly in town', Mahmud Jun declared. If they wanted to see a film, he recalled, they had to go as a group.

There were also a number of *pantang larang* (prohibitions) on stage which had to be observed by all. This was as much a matter of custom as a move to ensure propriety and professional conduct. 'We were not allowed to go up or down the stage by the front. To go up the front meant we were stepping on our own face; it would bring disaster,' said Abdullah Abdul Rahman. 'We were also not allowed to eat nuts or drink on stage in case we fought or quarrelled with each other.'

Prayers (*doa*) were said before each show as the performers feared accidents. 'After all, our livelihood depended on the success of each show,' Mat Arab said. 'When we played stories of legendary heroes such as Hang Tuah, Mahsuri, and Raden Mas, we had to prepare special feasts (*kenduri*) so that nothing untoward would happen,' according to Wan.

Above all, however, the rationale for the observance of custom, ritual, and strict discipline was pragmatic in nature: performers, especially stars, in conducting themselves with propriety and dignity on and off the stage, maintained their professional image status as public figures, which in turn ensured their continuing appeal and the attraction of *bangsawan* as commercial theatre.

Changing Troupes

As *bangsawan* troupes proliferated, performers, especially the stars became increasingly entrepreneurial. Depending on *bangsawan* as a means of earning a living, they tended not to be loyal to any particular troupe and aspired to join the bigger and better-known ones. When the opportunity to join such troupes arose, or when another troupe offered them more important roles and higher salaries, they would move. This was particularly true of the stars, who had their own following.

Wan, for example, first joined the Grand Nooran Opera as a chorus boy but was lured to join the Dean Tijah Opera after five years. Dean, the manager of Dean Tijah Opera told Wan that he had the looks and talent to become an *orang muda* or hero and invited him to join. Wan was thus promoted from chorus boy to the 'number two' hero, and whenever the 'number one' was not available, he would play the leading role.

Three years later, Wan was given the opportunity to manage the 63-member Starlight Opera. The high point of his career as manager was when the troupe toured Brunei, Sarawak, Labuan, and Sabah by boat. The collection at the shows was so good that they performed two shows a day. After this stint, Wan performed with the Arah Bangsawan till World War II broke out.

Suki recounted that when he landed in Singapore with the Royal Opera in 1921, he was approached by Ong Peng Hock, the manager of the City Opera of Singapore, to join the troupe. City Opera took him to Penang, Taiping, Ipoh, Klang, and Kuala Lumpur. In the City Opera, Suki graduated from court attendant to the 'number three' or 'number four' hero.

He moved again when Saadiah, one of four *sri panggung* recruited by City Opera from Medan to perform the latest charleston and vaudeville dances, fell in love with him. 'The Komet Opera invited her to join with the promise of a lot of money, but she would not go without me!' according to Suki. 'So I was stolen in the middle of the night from the City Opera which was playing in Singapore!' Saadiah and Suki were married in Batu Pahat, where the Komet Opera was performing. There was no happy ending to the marriage, though. At Batu Pahat, one important local official apparently adored Saadiah so much that he wanted to see her on stage all the time. 'When I appeared, he tried to chase me off the stage and took a shot at me with his pistol,' Suki said.

Suki fled to Singapore where he joined the Genani Star Opera owned by Tan Kam Choon of Malacca and managed by Nani. After this, Suki followed the Wayang Jupiter to Sumatra again. Upon his return in 1929, he rejoined the City Opera when it presented the first performance of *Laksamana Bentan* where Malay costumes with the *tanjak* (head-dress) and other Malay accessories were worn for the first time.

The performers were required by the troupes' managers and owners to return jewellery and costumes they had borrowed before they could join another troupe, or risk being taken to court. When she left the Wayang Komedi India Ratoe to join Wayang Kassim, Miss Jahara, it was reported:

... was charged at the instance of Syed Ali with criminal Breach of Trust in respect of one American gold coin with silver chain attached and two gowns amounting altogether to $35.60.... The defendant was employed in the company at the salary of $40 a month. Upon joining she received an advance of $120 which she agreed to pay off by monthly instalments of $6. (*Straits Echo*, 4 December 1906.)

Similarly, if a performer received an advance from a company and did not fulfil his contract, he could be brought to court. It was reported in the newspapers that:

Hasan Kechi, a well known Malay actor, was charged with cheating by dishonestly inducing one Cheah Chin Keong, manager of the International Dramatic Co. of King Street, to deliver him an advance of $12 ... and failing to perform on the following night as promised.... After meeting the advance, the accused disappeared ... until he surrendered himself to the Pitt St. Station after a warrant had been issued for his arrest. It was then learnt that he had from the time he received the advance been acting in a rival company—the Indra Bangsawan at the Kuala Kangsar Road Theatre. (*Straits Echo*, 24 June 1910.)

Community Integration

Although the *bangsawan* performers moved from troupe to troupe, a camaraderie was fostered among themselves as they were dependent on one another for survival. Mutual help and fellow-feeling arose because they were away from their families in the kampong. Having to travel long and sometimes hazardous journeys by sea also brought them close to one another.

Not surprisingly, therefore, *bangsawan* performers came to regard the

troupe of which they were members as a substitute family. Living in a
rumah kongsi (shared house), they cooked and ate together and shared
food, water, and other facilities. They addressed each other as *mak*
(mother), *pak* (father), *kak* (sister), *abang* (brother), or *adik* (younger
brother or sister), as they would in their kampong. They gave one
another nicknames which captured the individual's specific characteristic
qualities. Menah Yem was nicknamed 'Menah Ketot' (Short Menah)
because she was short. Alias Manan was called 'Cikgu' (Teacher) as he
used to teach the children in the troupe to read.

New recruits were adopted as *anak angkat* (adopted children). The
practice of adoption–parenthood ensured that the children were taken
care of. This was important because many of the recruits were young
and living away from their immediate families and kampong for the first
time. Ainon Chik recalled fondly that her adopted father (who happened
to be Minah Alias's real father) treated her like his own daughter.

Moreover, the *bangsawan* family was an extended family that
embraced members of all races. Children of different ethnic groups grew
up together. Rahman B., Yahya Sulong, and Alfonso Soliano were like
brothers when they were growing up, playing marbles and hopscotch
and sharing secrets with one another. 'Alfonso was our chief, our gang
leader,' Yahya Sulong said, amused at the memory of their childhood
games.

As members of an adoptive multi-ethnic family, *bangsawan* performers regularly celebrated festivities like Chinese New Year, Hari Raya,
and marriages together. These shared celebrations were occasions for
expressing communal solidarity.

The performers comforted each other in times of trouble, especially
when there were deaths. The death rate among babies was particularly
high. This was because there was often no proper medication available,
especially during long tours overseas. In addition, it was common for
women to perform right till the day they gave birth—with deleterious
consequences for the health of their babies. Ainon Chik, for instance,
had sixteen children, eight of whom died in infancy.

The performers had only each other to turn to when allegations of low
morals were thrown at them. Wan claimed that many village elders
looked down on *bangsawan* performers and accused them of impiety,
not praying, and not reading the Koran. 'This was all untrue,' Wan
asserted. 'We prayed five times a day. There was a religious teacher living with us. Our children studied the Koran when they were not acting.
Those who were good entered Koran reading competitions.'

Performers endured hardships together. 'When the rain came, the
roof would leak, the stage would leak, we had to run hither and thither.
Still, we were satisfied with our life,' Rahman B. said.

Outside of performances, sports such as football helped to reinforce
solidarity and to inculcate the team spirit among them. The football
teams of different troupes used to compete with each other and sometimes women performers too were invited to play. When I interviewed

her, Ainon Chik still had in her possession the medals and cups which she won in football competitions in her days as a *bangsawan* actress.

The manager took care of the members of his troupe as he would his own family. He would pay for the medication if his performers fell ill. For example, when Ainon Chik's husband contracted tuberculosis, the manager gave him $100 to return to Indonesia for medical help. Wan paid his performers *ex gratia* and even their fare home, when his troupe Wan Man Sri Bangsawan had to close down.

Bonuses reinforced the ties of sentiment between manager and performers, besides serving as incentives. After the Starlight Opera's tour of Sabah, Sarawak, and Labuan, Wan, its manager, rewarded individual performers with bonuses of $50–70.

For Menah Yem, the memories of her early years are fond ones. It was, she recalled, 'enjoyable' (*seronok*), a time when she was happy. 'We were like one big happy family.'

Women in *Bangsawan*

Through *bangsawan*, women came to prominence in cultural life for the first time ever. This was a radical departure from traditional folk theatre wherein men often played the roles of women. Although women danced the leading roles in the *makyong* theatre (Ghulam, 1976), this was an exception. In outlook the *makyong* actresses were not entrepreneurial; nor were they professional dancers. The *makyong* was in fact often performed for spiritual purposes.

Through *bangsawan*, however, women performers were afforded the unprecedented opportunity to gain self-expression in public. In Malay village society of the early twentieth century, a young woman's movements outside the home was limited. She had to assist in the cooking and washing, take care of her younger brothers and sisters, and help in the rice fields (Manderson, 1980: 15, 16). Although women *bangsawan* performers still cooked, sewed, and took care of the children during the day, they were not at all confined to household chores and childbearing. As Menah Yem put it, 'During the day, I cooked, washed clothes, and took care of the children. At night, I was free to work (*cari duit*).'

Courtship and marriage within the *bangsawan* community differed from that in Malay village society where a young woman had no right to choose her husband (Manderson, 1980: 16). On the contrary, *bangsawan* actresses often married fellow *bangsawan* actors or musicians. Menah Yem fell in love with a *bangsawan* hero named Yem, married him when she was twelve or thirteen years old, and followed him on an acting tour of Sumatra and Java. Minah Alias married another *bangsawan* performer, Alias Manan, who saved her from the advances of a Japanese official.

Bangsawan women were independent in that they were able to support themselves and their children financially should the men in their lives desert them or die. Indeed, they themselves were in a position to initiate divorce or separation. According to Ainon Chik, if a relationship soured, the couple usually separated by mutual agreement. *Bangsawan* stars, according to Wan, had no problems remarrying as they were much sought after as spouses. After the breakup of her marriage with Ahmad Kassim, a pianist from Bandung, Ainon Chik married Abdul Wahab, an Indonesian actor.

The women were, however, viewed by some sectors of Malayan society, especially the religious and socially conservative, as women of loose morals. They bore the stigma of women who dressed up to be ogled by men, who worked at night, and who seemed to be changing spouses ever so often; but it was a stigma which, on the evidence of their personal testimony, they bore remarkably well considering the times and the society they lived in.

* * *

The lives of the performers indicate that in the Malaya of the early twentieth century, *bangsawan* was indeed different in form and function from Malay traditional theatre. Performers, including women, were promoted as stars. These stars were professionals who worked solely as entertainers, who were known for the specific roles in which they specialized, who were entrepreneurial and competitive in their outlook, and who were sensitive to the changing tastes of employers and audiences. *Bangsawan*, it can be claimed, was the vehicle for a career as we would understand it today.

Even though *bangsawan* stars tended not to place a premium on loyalty to any particular troupe and competed individually with each other, they were dependent on one another for survival. Out of these circumstances they came to regard their troupe members as their family. As family, they perforce observed an informal set of rules, the function of which was to minimize conflict and enable the troupe to cohere as a social unit. This family-like unit was able to socialize younger members, cushioning the new recruits' transition from an agricultural to an urban setting and yet guaranteeing that they were not alienated from their cultural roots.

Most significantly, *bangsawan* departed from Malay traditional theatre in that performers of different ethnic origins were recruited. These performers lived together, learning elements of one another's culture. This contributed directly and obviously to cultural and musical interaction, absorption, and synthesis. The evidence for this is to be found in the content of the theatrical performances as well as the musical compositions which emphasized variety and adaptability.

1 Laksamana's greeting (*siku di luut*), Bangsawan Workshop, 1985. (Photograph by S. B. Tan)

2 Tengku Halijah's greeting, Bangsawan Workshop, 1985. (Photograph by S. B. Tan)

3 Queen in *kebaya labuh*, Bangsawan Workshop, 1985. (Photograph by S. B. Tan)

4 Maid-in-waiting in *baju kurung*, *panglima* in *baju Melayu*, Bangsawan Workshop, 1985. (Photograph by S. B. Tan)

5 Painting the side-wings of the garden scene, Bangsawan Workshop, 1985. (Photograph by S. B. Tan)

6 Painting the side-wings of the palace scene, Bangsawan Workshop, 1985. (Photograph by S. B. Tan)

7 Learning *silat* with Alias Manan (*left*), Bangsawan Workshop, 1985. (Photograph by S. B. Tan)

8 Setting up the stage for the performance on the last night of the Bangsawan Workshop, 1985. (Photograph by S. B. Tan)

9 Minah Alias distributing costumes, Bangsawan Workshop, 1985. (Photograph by S. B. Tan)

10 *Ronggeng* ensemble accompanying the *bangsawan* performance, Bangsawan Workshop, 1985. (*From left to right*) Pak Wan (violin), Ahmad (*rebana*), and Pak Mat Hashim (accordion). (Photograph by S. B. Tan)

11 Raden Mas advising Tengku Halijah and her maids,
Bangsawan Workshop,
1985. (Photograph by
S. B. Tan)

12 Minah Alias singing in the
extra turn, Bangsawan
Workshop, 1985. (Photo-
graph by S. B. Tan)

13 Columbia record, 1950s, manufactured by the Columbia Graphophone Co. Ltd., England. (Photograph by S. B. Tan)

14 His Master's Voice record, 1940s, manufactured by the Gramophone Co. Ltd., Calcutta. (Photograph by S. B. Tan)

15 Pathe record, 1950s, made in India. (Photograph by S. B. Tan)

16 Grand record, 1950s, manufactured by the Gramophone Co. Ltd., Dum Dum, India.
(Photograph by S. B. Tan)

17 Chap Kuching record, 1940s, manufactured by the Gramophone Co. Ltd., Dum Dum, India. (Photograph by S. B. Tan)

18 Parlophone record jacket, 1950s, record made in India. (Photograph by S. B. Tan)

19 *Bangsawan* stage and performers, 1940s. (Courtesy of Kementerian Kebudayaan, Belia dan Sukan Malaysia)

20 *Bangsawan* performance with Chinese, Indian, and Malay characters, 1941, held to collect money for the Police War Fund. (Courtesy of Mak Ainon Chik [*second from left*]).

21 Javanese play, 1940s. (Courtesy of Kementerian Kebudayaan, Belia dan Sukan Malaysia)

22 Javanese play, 1950s. (Courtesy of Pak Rahman B.)

23 Only performance of *Hamlet* in the 1970s; scene where the murder of the King is re-enacted, with Hamlet, Gertrude, Claudius, and guests looking on. (Courtesy of Pak Rahman B.)

24 Play with characters wearing Malay, Javanese, and Middle Eastern costumes, 1950s. (Courtesy of Pak Mat Hashim)

25 Performance of *Jula Juli Bintang Tiga*, 1960s. The three sisters appear behind the paper stars while the fairies dance in the clouds. (Courtesy of Pak Rahman B.)

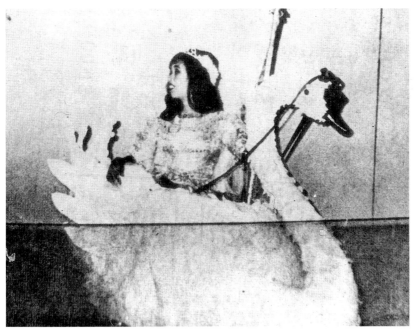

26 Performance of *Jula Juli Bintang Tiga*, 1960s. Jula Juli rides a goose in the sea. (Courtesy of Pak Rahman B.)

27 Characters in a Middle Eastern play, 1970s. (Courtesy of Kementerian Kebudayaan, Belia dan Sukan Malaysia)

28 Extra turn, 1940s. (Courtesy of Kementerian Kebudayaan, Belia dan Sukan Malaysia)

29 Extra turn, 1940s. (Courtesy of Kementerian Kebudayaan, Belia dan Sukan Malaysia)

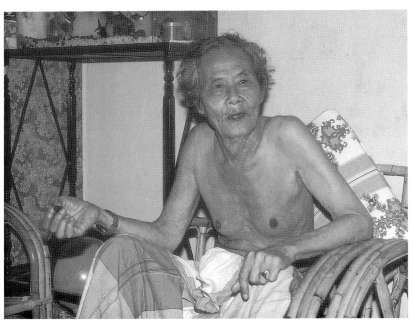

30 Tok Wan, 1985. (Photograph by S. B. Tan)

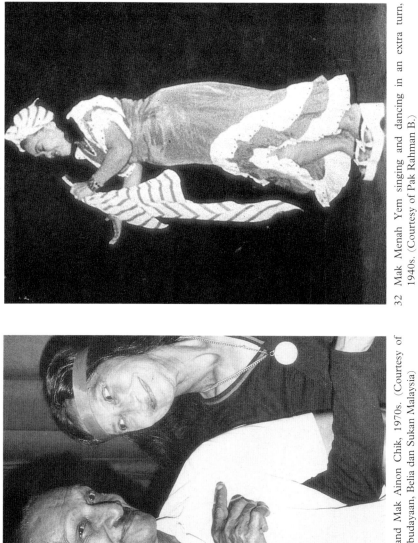

31 Pak Mat Arab and Mak Ainon Chik, 1970s. (Courtesy of Kementerian Kebudayaan, Belia dan Sukan Malaysia)

32 Mak Menah Yem singing and dancing in an extra turn, 1940s. (Courtesy of Pak Rahman B.)

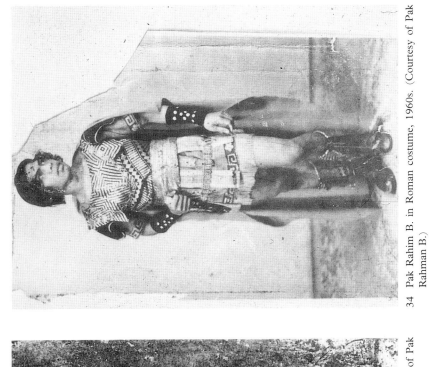

34 Pak Rahim B. in Roman costume, 1960s. (Courtesy of Pak Rahman B.)

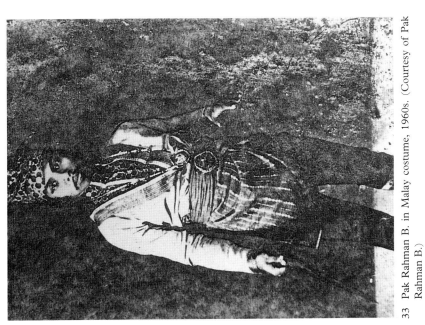

33 Pak Rahman B. in Malay costume, 1960s. (Courtesy of Pak Rahman B.)

35 Mak Minah Alias (*extreme right*) teaching a group of students the *asli* dance, 1985.
(Photograph by S. B. Tan)

36 *Bangsawan* band consisting of drum, saxophone, accordion, and trumpet, 1950s.
(Courtesy of Pak Mat Hashim)

37 *Rebana ibu* and *anak*. (Photograph by S. B. Tan)

38 Pak Wan playing the violin and Pak Aziz playing the *rebana ibu*, 1986. (Photograph by S. B. Tan)

39 *Kroncong* ensemble consisting of flute, violin, guitar, gong, and accordion, 1980s. (Photograph by S. B. Tan)

40 Pak Mat Hashim's *ronggeng* ensemble and *ronggeng* dancers, 1986. (Photograph by S. B. Tan)

41 Orkestra Dungun, 1950s. (Courtesy of Pak Mat Hashim)

42 Extra turn from *Raden Mas*, Som Kenangan Sandiwara, 1960s. (Courtesy of Pak Mat Hashim)

43 Hindustani play *Patangga*, Som Kenangan Sandiwara, 1960s. (Courtesy of Pak Mat Hashim)

44 Malay play *Aboo Jenaka*, Som Kenangan Sandiwara, 1960s. (Courtesy of Pak Mat Hashim)

45 Performance of *Laksamana Bentan*, 1986; court scene. (Photograph by S. B. Tan)

46 Performance of *Laksamana Bentan*, 1986; scene in the pirates' den. (Photograph by S. B. Tan)

47 Performance of *Laksamana Bentan*, 1986; garden scene. (Photograph by S. B. Tan)

48 Performance of *Laksamana Mati Dibunuh*, 1986; death scene. (Photograph by
    S. B. Tan)

5
Development of the
Orkestra Melayu, c.1880–c.1930

IT was through *bangsawan* that the first *orkestra Melayu* (Malay orchestra) was formed in Malaya. Similar to the dance orchestras of the West, the *orkestra Melayu* consisted of Western instruments such as the violin, trumpet, trombone, saxophone, flute, clarinet, piano, guitar, drums, and maracas (a pair of gourd rattles). The *orkestra Melayu* also included non-Western instruments such as the Indian tabla. It accompanied singing and dancing in cabarets and hotels in Malaya, and till the 1950s, popular music recorded by gramophone companies were also accompanied by the *orkestra Melayu*. The *bangsawan* orchestra was in fact the direct forerunner of the Orkes RTM (Radio and Television Malaysia Orchestra), the main ensemble which performs instrumental music and plays with singers on television and radio in Malaysia today.

Development of the *Orkestra*
or Band: The Incorporation of New Instruments

The first known *bangsawan* ensemble consisted of the harmonium and tabla which were used in the Wayang Parsi from which *bangsawan* originated (Edrus, 1960: 63). The harmonium was a small reed organ set in a box which was introduced by missionaries to India around the middle of the nineteenth century. The player fingered the keyboard with one hand and pumped a bellows at the back with the other (Owen and Dick, 1984: 131). The tabla was a treble drum whose body consisted of a tapering wooden cylinder. The tabla was played together with a bass drum or *baya*, which had a hemispherical body of clay or chromed copper. The heads of the two drums consisted of two membranes of goat skin which were laced with thongs. The thongs were tightened with cylindrical wooden dowels. The heads were treated with black tuning paste (Dick and Sen, 1984: 492–6).

Soon after *bangsawan* made its debut in Malaya, new instruments were added. By the turn of the century, the piano, the flute, the violin, the cornet, and the drum had joined the ensemble, although the number and type of instruments used was not fixed. The Malay newspaper *Chahaya Pulau Pinang* (11 May 1904) reported that the Wayang Yap

Chow Thong ensemble was 'complete with piano, flute, harmonium, violin and tabla'. Sometimes a concertina· was added. During one of Wayang Kassim's performances, 'Mr. Hurley, the company's talented pianist, displayed his musical skill on a concertina' (*Straits Echo*, 22 September 1903). Winstedt described the ensemble accompanying the performance of *Hamlet* which he reviewed in 1908 as comprising 'a couple of fiddles, a drum and a small harmonium only' (*Straits Echo*, 14 November 1908). A review of Wayang Komedi India Ratoe praised the flute, first violin, and cornet players (*Straits Echo*, 8 October 1906). Big troupes had as many as sixteen musicians.

It is interesting to note that the orchestra of the *komedi stambul* of the late nineteenth century was quite similar to that of *bangsawan*. The orchestra that Manusama (1922: 15–16) witnessed in 1894 consisted of one piano, three violins, one flute, one clarinet, one cornet, one trombone, and one double bass. Knaap (1903), a music critic and friend of August Mahieu (creator of *komedi stambul*), wrote that when Mahieu first started his troupe, he formed an orchestra consisting of violin, guitar, and flute.

Terms like 'band' (*Straits Echo*, 15 November 1904),[1] 'string [band] with an extra brass band' (*Straits Echo*, 14 November 1904), 'orchestra' (*Straits Echo*, 19 September 1906), or 'string orchestra' (*Straits Echo*, 19 November 1904) were used to describe the ensemble or group of musical performers in *bangsawan*. String and brass bands or orchestras were differentiated from one another. Often, Indian instruments used were named separately. For instance, a *wayang stambul* advertisement called on the audience to listen to their 'special string orchestra' and their 'extra Harmonium, Doll [dol], Turblar [tabla] and Siperinggy' (*Straits Echo*, 19 November 1904).

New instruments (especially Western ones) were added to the *bangsawan* ensemble for various reasons. The musical stage, like many other Malayan cultural forms at the turn of the century, developed at least partly in imitation of European styles and genres, as these symbolized 'modernization' and prestige. Malayans developed their own styles through regular comparison and competition with foreign works. The introduction of Western instruments was one way of adapting to the world of Western music.

In addition, as commercial theatre, *bangsawan* had to compete with the bands and orchestras with which the town dwellers were already familiar, including the musical bands which were established in the towns by the British. The Selangor State Band was formed in 1894 (Gullick, 1978: 39) while the Penang Band was set up in the early part of the twentieth century. It was announced in the *Straits Echo* (9 July 1903 and 16 November 1903) that the Penang Amateur Dramatic Society and Wayang Kassim gave performances to collect money for the Penang Band Fund.

The Malayan bands were organized along the lines of the British ones. Woodwinds (flutes, oboes, clarinets, bassoons), brass (saxophones, cornets, horns, trombones, euphoniums, tubas), and percussion instruments (side drums and bass drums) were used (Robinson, 1984: 129–34). These bands maintained the morale of British regiments, entertained the British at their exclusive clubs, and performed at bandstands in parks (*Straits Echo*, 22 November 1904) to entertain the public. The Penang Band was also known to play at garden parties, dinners, dances, and even at Chinese funerals. This is shown in the following advertisement which appeared in the *Straits Echo* (30 August 1906):

Notice is hereby given that charges for the services of the Band will be as
    follows:-
Dances 9 pm to 2 am $60
Chinese funerals 11 am to 4 pm $60
    after the above hours $15 per hour or part of an hour
Dinner 8 pm to 11 pm $30
Garden parties 5 pm to 7 pm $30
    after the above hours $10 per hour or part of an hour
Transport extra
Subscribers now entitled to engage band at half price
LA Coutier Biggs
Sec. to the Municipal Commissioner
Municipal Office
Pg. 28 July 1906.

In addition, bands performed at big hotels. As advertised in the *Times of Malaya* (17 May 1905), a 'fine Band of HMS Vengeance' played 'frequently' at the Hotel de l'Europe. Some of these bands even 'played selections at intervals' during *bangsawan* performances (*Times of Malaya*, 9 July 1909).[2]

More importantly, new foreign instruments were added to the *bangsawan* ensemble as *bangsawan* adapted to the orchestras of professional theatre troupes from Europe and America which toured the peninsula in the late nineteenth and early twentieth centuries. Troupes like the Willard Opera Co. (*Pinang Gazette and Straits Chronicle*, 22 September 1894), Williamson and Maher's Chicago Tourist Minstrel Variety Co. (*Penang Gazette and Straits Chronicle*, 7 August 1895), the Cordelier Hicks Co.'s Theatre Parisien (*Straits Echo*, 21 October 1903), Mr M. B. Leavitts Elite Anglo-American Troubadors (*Straits Echo*, 23 March 1904), the Gaiety Stars Polite Vaudeville and Specialty Co. (*Straits Echo*, 30 October 1905), and the Henry Dallas Musical Comedy Co. (*Straits Echo*, 6 June 1904) brought the opera, minstrel show, vaudeville, musical comedy, and musical play to Malayan towns. The orchestras of such troupes usually consisted of two violins, viola, bass (or cello), flute, clarinet, cornet, and trombone (Root, 1977: 48, 126). The piano was also a very important instrument in the touring theatrical troupes.[3]

It was not surprising, then, that the *bangsawan* orchestra incorporated instruments used in such bands and orchestras. The addition of such instruments meant (both to *bangsawan* performers and audiences) not only that the orchestra was 'up-to-date', but that the ensemble could also be hired for other purposes when the troupe was not performing. *Bangsawan* troupes began to advertise both string and brass bands for weddings, funerals, and parties (*Times of Malaya*, 11 July 1914). Such 'string bands' also entertained the audience before silent films were featured. The Straits Cinematography Co. tried to attract the audience to listen to its 'String Band, with an up-to-date repertoire under the direction of Prof. Oemar whose musical abilities ... [were] ... well known locally ...' (*Straits Echo*, 22 August 1912).

By the 1920s, the standard orchestra or band used by *bangsawan* troupes was very similar to the orchestras of visiting foreign theatrical troupes. For example, the Grand Bangsawan, a troupe consisting of amateur Baba and Nonya amateur artistes, was accompanied by an orchestra which consisted of four first violins, two second violins, three flutes, two cornets, two cellos, one drum, and one piano (*Straits Echo*, 23 November 1920).

The original Wayang Parsi ensemble consisting of harmonium and tabla was maintained. Big troupes like the City Opera usually had 'two sets of musicians, an English orchestra which played at intervals and accompanied singers, and also harmonium music which accompanied, so it seemed, when the finer refrains were sung' (*Straits Echo*, 1 September 1924). It was also reported that the audience of the Peninsula Opera Company was 'entertained with orchestral and harmonium music' (*dihiburkan dengan bunyi-bunyian muzik (orkestra) dan harmonium*) (*Idaran Zaman*, 2 April and 12 December 1925).

The *bangsawan* orchestra was flexible and continued to incorporate new instruments. With the popularity of Hawaiian-style dance music brought by visiting troupes like Kaai's Royal Hawaiian Troubadors (*Straits Echo*, 28 November 1921) and Antido Vod-a-Vil Coy (*Straits Echo*, 6 June 1922), the Hawaiian guitar was added to the *bangsawan* orchestra in the 1920s. *Bangsawan* troupes like the Peninsula Opera Co. publicized the fact that a 'newly arrived troupe of Malay Hawaiian Troubadors from Batavia' was performing with them and that the troupe used the 'Hawaiian guitar' (*Straits Echo*, 24 April 1925). This guitar was developed in Hawaii in the second half of the nineteenth century. The strings were stopped with a 'steel metal bar forming a moveable nut going right across all strings. The particular intervals of the tuning could be reproduced at any pitch by sliding the steel' (Jacobs, 1977).

By the 1920s, the saxophone too was added to the *bangsawan* orchestra. The orchestra of Baba Bangsawan was a good example. It consisted of six first violins, two second violins, two saxophones, one cornet, one cello, one clarinet, one flute, one bass, and one piano (*Straits Echo*, 26 February 1923).

The introduction of the saxophone accompanied the prelude of new jazz and ragtime sounds in Malaya (Plate 36). Dance bands which had absorbed the instrumental characteristics of ragtime and jazz ensembles were among the highlights of the gramophone and radio programmes.

These dance bands usually consisted of saxophones (doubling clarinets), trumpets, trombones, double bass, piano, guitar, drums, and vocalists.[4]

Jazz ensembles and sounds were also introduced through the talkies. The talkie *The Jazz Singer*, starring Al Jolson, was shown in Malaya in 1930 (*Times of Malaya*, 25 January 1930). This talkie featured jazz music which was accompanied by the jazz ensemble.

As a matter of interest, opera troupes from Java incorporated the saxophone and jazz sounds as well. A review of the International Opera of Java reported that 'the several songs in the play and the extra items were accompanied by a fine orchestra, European members of the Co. taking turns at the piano, jazz and drum, violin and saxophone' (Straits Echo, 4 January 1928). The term 'jazz' could mean trumpets and trombones. It also implied that jazz was already popular then.

In the 1930s, *bangsawan* orchestras began to incorporate percussion instruments used in Latin American dance orchestras, such as the maracas and woodblocks (rectangular blocks of wood with one or two slotted longitudinal cavities played with wooden drum sticks).[5] This followed popular interest in Europe and elsewhere in Latin American dancing (specifically the rumba) to the accompaniment of a band whose rhythm section included these instruments (Blades, 1984b: Appendix 2). According to the veteran actress and owner of Nooran Opera, Menah Yem, 'the rumba which was popular in the 1930s had to be accompanied by the maracas'. The maracas were used in the song 'Lagu Telesmat Bintang Satu dan Dua' in the classical play *Jula Juli Bintang Tiga* (see Chapter 8: Example 8.6) while the woodblock was used in the song 'Nasib Pandan' in the Arabic story *Laila Majnun* (see Chapter 8: Example 8.26). Both songs were recorded by the Gramophone Co. Ltd. and produced in Dum Dum, India (78 r.p.m record). The former was distributed under the label of Chap Kuching (NG 31) while the latter was distributed under His Master's Voice (P 12804).

Finally, some orchestras started to use the Malay *rebana* (Plate 37) to accompany the slow and sad Malay *asli* songs used in stories of Malay origin. Manusama (1922) also mentioned the use of the *rebana* in *komedi stambul* to accompany pieces which came from Malaya in 1922. These pieces were called *dendang*. Examples of *asli* pieces accompanied by *rebana* in *bangsawan* can be found in the 78 r.p.m. recordings of the Malay play *Puteri Gunong Ledang* manufactured by the Gramophone Co. Ltd., Dum Dum, India, under the label of His Master's Voice (P 12760–P 12766) in the 1930s.

Although the *rebana* is said to have originated in the Middle East,[6] it is considered by *bangsawan* musicians to be a Malay instrument. This Malay frame drum has a 'goat skin head, laced with leather and pinned to a wooden frame, and is tautened by pressing a piece of rattan into its inner rim and heating near a flame' (Dobbs, 1984: 200). The incorporation of the Malay instrument into the *bangsawan* orchestra coincided with the introduction of Malay historical stories into the *bangsawan* repertoire.

In summary, the *bangsawan* orchestra of the 1930s was a mix of

Indian, Western, Latin American, and indigenous Malay instruments. The majority of the instruments, however, were Western in origin. As Menah Yem clarified, 'although the kinds and number of instruments used differed from troupe to troupe and from story to story, the piano, violin, trumpet, and drum had to be employed'. The orchestra was innovative and adapted to the latest trends in the West, India, and Malaya. In the 1930s, big orchestras became the norm. This followed the advent of recordings of the big swing bands of Benny Goodman, Glen Miller, and others playing 'sweet' style jazz (compared to a more Black-derived variety of jazz). These bands usually consisted of five brass, four saxophones, and four rhythm instruments. String sections appeared regularly as a concession to popular taste (Robinson, 1984: 139). Veteran musician Alfonso Soliano added that 'before the war, bigger bands' were used because 'classical music ... such as Light Cavalry ... was played'.

Classification of *Bangsawan* Instruments in the 1930s

As shown in Table 5.1, the musical instruments were classified by *bangsawan* performers and musicians according to their country of origin: Western (*alat orang putih*), Indian (*alat à la Hindustan*), or Malay (*alat*

TABLE 5.1
Classification of Instruments in the 1930s

Western Instruments (Alat Orang Putih)	Indian Instruments (Alat à la Hindustan)	Malay Instruments (Alat Melayu)
String instruments (*alat tali*)	*Melodic instrument* (*alat melodi*)	*Rhythmic instrument* (*alat rentak*)
Violin	Harmonium	Rebana
Guitar		
Hawaiian guitar	*Rhythmic instrument*	
Bass	(*alat rentak*)	
Cello	Tabla	
Wind instruments (*alat tiup*)		
Cornet		
Trumpet		
Trombone		
Saxophone		
Clarinet		
Percussion		
Drum set		
Maracas		
Woodblock (characteristic of Latin American dance music)		

Melayu). These instruments were further categorized according to the classification used by the various ethnic communities. Western instruments were subdivided into stringed instruments (*alat tali*), wind instruments (*alat tiupan*), and percussion instruments (*alat percussion*).[7] Many of the *bangsawan* performers including Alias Manan considered both brass and woodwind instruments as *alat tiupan*. Indian and Malay instruments were classified as melodic or rhythmic instruments.

The classification of instruments according to their country of origin showed that the performers were aware of the origin of the instruments they were using. They were also conscious of the way the various instruments were further subclassified and the roles each of these instruments played in the ensembles of the different communities. This suggested that the *bangsawan* musicians were consciously integrating instruments of the West with instruments of the various ethnic groups living in Malaya.

Instrumental Combinations in the 1930s

How were these musical instruments combined? Different instrumental combinations were used to accompany Western, Malay, Hindustani, Arabic, Chinese, Javanese, and other foreign music. Characteristic sounds of the music of these various countries were emulated through these combinations.

Four different instrumental combinations were used in *bangsawan*. One combination was the Western orchestra (comprising violins, piano, Hawaiian guitar, cornet or trumpet, trombone, saxophone, drum set, maracas, woodblock, and tambourine), which was used to accompany the songs in classical and Middle Eastern stories. This orchestra also 'tender[ed] selections of music for an hour preceding [the] ... performance' or during intervals (*Straits Echo*, 27 April 1905). Mahmud Jun emphasized that the Western orchestra would also entertain the audience with overtures before the show proper began. The number and types of instruments employed varied from troupe to troupe.

The instruments were used in the same way as in a Western dance orchestra of the 1930s. The first violin, treble section of the piano, Hawaiian guitar, cornet or trumpet, and saxophone usually played in heterophony[8] with the voice; the second violin and trombone harmonized with the main melody in thirds and sixths; the drum, piano bass, maracas, woodblock, and tambourine marked the main accents of the metre or played the rhythmic pattern. The piano also provided the harmony by playing triads or chords. The songs in the play *Jula Juli Bintang Tiga* were accompanied by such a Western orchestra. The songs were recorded in the 1930s by the Gramophone Co. Ltd. and produced in Dum Dum, India under the label of Chap Kuching (NG 29–NG 32) (see Appendix 1: Transcription 6.7).

Another combination was a smaller ensemble consisting of the violin, piano, and drum or *rebana*, which accompanied Malay songs mainly in Malay and Javanese plays as well as during extra turns (Plates 38–40). This ensemble resembled the traditional *ronggeng* ensemble which accompanied 'social dancing in mixed sex couples in which couples dance[d] and exchange[d] verses in the accompaniment of a violin, 1 or 2 frame drums and a gong' (Goldsworthy, 1979: 334). *Bangsawan* troupes altered the ensemble by replacing the accordion with the piano. The Western drum set was often used in place of the frame drum. The Malay songs in the play *Puteri Gunong Ledang* were accompanied by the violin, piano, and *rebana* (or the Western drum for some pieces). The songs were recorded by the Gramophone Co. Ltd. in the 1930s under the label of His Master's Voice (P 12760–P 12766).

The *ronggeng* ensemble could be enlarged and supplemented with a plucked bass or trumpet. The plucked bass was used to accompany the song 'Lagu Sambut Kekasih' in the 78 r.p.m. recording of *Laila Majnun* (His Master's Voice, P 12801) (see Chapter 9: Example 9.2). The song 'Sinandung Jawa' had a part for trombone (Chap Kuching, NG 73) (see Appendix 1: Transcription 6.4). Sometimes, as in the song 'Seri Serdang' (His Master's Voice, P 7433), the harmonium was used.

Although new instruments were added to the traditional *ronggeng* ensemble, the *ronggeng* sound was maintained. Extra violins, trumpet, treble part of the piano, or harmonium still played in heterophony with the voice, while the bass part of the piano, plucked bass, and drum produced characteristic rhythmic patterns of *ronggeng* songs.

A third ensemble comprised the harmonium and tabla, which accompanied Hindustani songs in performances of Hindustani stories and in extra turns. As in Hindustani popular songs, the harmonium played in heterophony with the voice as well as provided the drone. The tabla played the rhythmic patterns. Some of the songs of the Hindustani play *Noor-E-Islam* were performed to the accompaniment of this ensemble (Chap Singa or Lion Label, QF 34–QF 37).

Finally, the piano provided background music for most stories. It was used to accompany pieces in ragtime style as well as for Chinese stories. Minah Alias once told me that 'if for some reason the musicians were not available, the piano alone could be used'. The musical piece 'Shanghai Street', for example, was accompanied by the piano (His Master's Voice, P 15978) (see Appendix 1: Transcription 6.8).

As she had studied the piano and accompanied performers in the past, Minah Alias demonstrated some guidelines that the *bangsawan* pianist had to adhere to. The treble part of the piano was often played in heterophony with the voice or the melody (if there was no singing) while the bass part contributed characteristic rhythmic patterns as well as provided the harmony. It played the dance rhythms of the waltz, foxtrot, quickstep, *asli*, and so on. For pieces at slower tempos, arpeggios were used. In non-metric parts, it accompanied the singers by rolled chords.

In order to produce music for and to play the music of the different ensembles, it was necessary for *bangsawan* troupes to employ musicians who were well-versed in the music of the different ensembles. The Union City Opera of Singapore, for example, had two different conductors— 'Sheik Abdullah—Prof. of Hindustani Music and Inche Nut—[a] ... well known ancient Malay music conductor'. Minah Alias and Mat Hashim both insisted that 'Chinese musicians from Chinese opera troupes were invited to accompany songs sung in Chinese stories'.[9]

Alfonso Soliano stressed that Filipino musicians who could read Western notation and could play the new Western instruments introduced into *bangsawan* were favoured for employment in *bangsawan* troupes. Many of the musicians of the orchestras performing in British hotels and clubs like the Solianos, D'Cruzes,[10] and Martinezes[11] were in fact Filipinos who had originally been brought in by the British to form the Selangor State Band (Gullick, 1988: 118). Having had the benefit of a Western musical training, they played Western instruments as well as wrote the musical scores and conducted many of the *bangsawan* performances.

* * *

From its inception, the *bangsawan* orchestra was innovative in style and was constantly incorporating new instruments, so that by the 1930s the *bangsawan* orchestra had become quite different from that of Malay traditional theatre. It was a mix of Indian, Western, Latin American, and indigenous Malay instruments. Most of the new essential instruments added were, however, Western ones. Big ensembles were the norm. Adaptation of Western instruments and the large Western orchestra or band was one way to show that *bangsawan* was 'up-to-date' and 'modern'.

Besides the Western orchestra, *bangsawan* performers used traditional instruments of the various ethnic communities and employed specific instrumental combinations to produce the sound ideals and styles of the music of different cultures. Troupes often had experts in Hindustani, Malay, Chinese, and jazz music to conduct and compose for the respective ensembles.

The *bangsawan* orchestra was a venue for the interaction of the musical instruments of the West with those of the various ethnic groups in Malaya. As such, it was also a vehicle for musical change.

1. According to H. M. Brown (1980: 106), the term 'band' is defined as 'an instrumental ensemble larger than a chamber ensemble. By extension, "band" came to mean an orchestra in colloquial British usage. More particularly, the word refers to a combination of brass and percussion or woodwind, brass and percussion instruments as in Brass Band, Military Band and Symphonic band.' In Malaya at the turn of the century the term 'band' was used interchangeably with the term 'orchestra' to mean a group of musical performers.

2. Private bands were also set up by musicians. Such bands played at parties, dinners, dances, and Chinese funerals (*Times of Malaya*, 10 April 1907). Similar bands were used by circuses which toured Malaya at that time. As an example, see the advertisement of Harmston's Circus (*Pinang Gazette and Straits Chronicle*, 15 October 1895).

3. The British also had amateur theatre groups set up in Malaya. In their performances of comic operas, minstrel shows, and musical comedies, the piano played an important part. For descriptions of amateur theatricals and music in Singapore, see Makepeace, Brooke, and Braddell (1921: Chapter XIX).

4. These dance bands provided a popular image of jazz. Dance bands were probably the closest experience which the general public had of jazz. Paul Whiteman, a widely known band leader of the 1920s, achieved the popular title of 'King of Jazz'. His band toured Europe in 1923 and the dance band sound that made use of syncopated rhythms and jazz instrumentation flourished between the wars and provided a popular image of jazz. As he was a violinist, his dance band included the violin at the beginning. The instrument was later dropped.

Earlier, at the end of World War I, American military bands like James Reese had already displayed jazz in Europe with the instrumental combination of cornet, trombone, clarinet, two violins, banjos, piano, and percussion. The Original Dixieland Band had also created a sensation with their combination of trumpet or cornet, clarinet, trombone, piano, and drum (Lamb, 1980b: 94).

5. See (Blades, 1984a: 861). Today, the term 'woodblock' is generally used to signify a Western orchestral instrument. The instrument is closely related to temple blocks of China, Japan, and Korea. The instrument is said to have entered the West by way of early ragtime and jazz.

6. Kartomi (1988) has suggested that one route by which the violin and frame drum came to South-East Asia was via Portugal. She states that 'the use of the two instruments together and the popularity and variety of frame drums found in Portugal (which was under Moorish domination for many centuries) suggest that they came with the Portuguese' (Kartomi, 1988: 360).

7. Performers do not use any Malay term for percussion instruments but refer to them as 'percussion'.

8. The term 'heterophony' is used here to mean 'the simultaneous use of slightly or elaborately modified versions of the same melody by two (or more) performers' (Randel, 1978).

9. I was not, however, able to find any 78 r.p.m. recordings using traditional Chinese instruments.

10. Ruby's Rhythmic Orchestra was under the direction of Mr Santiago D'Cruz (*Straits Echo*, 2 November 1936).

11. The Baba *bangsawan* orchestra was under the direction of Mr C. Martinez (*Straits Echo*, 26 February 1923).

6
An Arena for Musical Interaction in the 1920s and 1930s

A mix of Malay and Western elements formed the basic musical idiom of *bangsawan*, but Chinese, Indian, Middle Eastern, Javanese, and other foreign elements were also incorporated;[1] and it was the performance of a variety of music and musical instruments within a single theatrical form in the early twentieth century which provided the opportunity for some of them to interact.

To show that musical interaction occurred in *bangsawan*, eight musical examples of the 1930s following six classificatory categories used by *bangsawan* performers will be examined: (1) *lagu Melayu* (Malay song), (2) *lagu Padang Pasir/Arab* (Middle Eastern/Arabic song), (3) *lagu Jawa* (Javanese song), (4) *lagu Hindustan* (Hindustani song), (5) *lagu klasik* (classical or Western song), and (6) *lagu Cina* (Chinese song). *Lagu* is the Malay term used for both instrumentally accompanied songs and instrumental music in *bangsawan*.

The detailed analyses presented here are based on transcriptions of the eight musical examples. According to the veteran performers, these examples are representative of the six categories of *bangsawan* songs and were commonly performed in the early twentieth century. My conclusions have been verified by aural studies of other 78 r.p.m recordings of *bangsawan* songs of the 1930s, performance studies of the *rebana* and gong parts with Mat Hashim (a veteran musician who still performs with the Bangsawan Sri USM troupe today), and my own performances with the USM troupe as a *rebana* and gong player. It should be noted that the musical examples used are drawn from gramophone records of the 1930s when gramophone technology first became widely available in Malaya. It is not possible to establish what the music was like before then as no musical examples can be found in the country.

Examples of Musical Interaction*

Transcription 6.1—Lagu Melayu: 'Hiburan Raja Ahmad Beradu'
[Song of Entertainment for Raja Ahmad While He Rests]

This is one of the songs from the Malay historical play *Puteri Gunong Ledang* adapted from *Sejarah Melayu (Malay Annals)*. In this story, Sultan Mansur Shah of Malacca wishes to marry the Princess of Gunong Ledang and sends his warriors to climb the mountain to ask for her hand in marriage. After a very difficult and dangerous climb, they finally meet the Princess's nursemaid who says that the Princess will accept the offer of marriage if the Sultan can fulfil seven conditions. Because the Sultan cannot fulfil the last condition, which is to provide a bowl of his own son's blood, the wedding is eventually called off. The following analysis is based on the transcription of the song recorded in the 1930s by the Gramophone Co. Ltd. in Malaya. The record was manufactured in Dum Dum, India, under the label of His Master's Voice (P 12761).

This song serves to entertain Raja Ahmad, the son of Sultan Mansur Shah, as he prepares to wake up in the morning. He calls his maids-in-waiting to sing for him. Although this song is considered to be a *lagu Melayu* and is used mainly in Malay plays, it is in fact a combination of Malay, Western, and Chinese elements in terms of its instrumentation, texture, formal structure, metric structure, tonal system, and singing style.

INSTRUMENTATION

The ensemble which consists of the violin, piano, and *rebana* resembles the *ronggeng asli* ensemble. However, in this *bangsawan* ensemble, the accordion has been replaced by the piano and the gong left out. While the violin and piano are Western instruments, the *rebana* is said to have originated from the Middle East but is regarded as a Malay instrument by *bangsawan* musicians.

TEXTURE

The texture also combines features of Malay and Western music. As in traditional Malay music, this song consists of several fairly independent melodic and rhythmic lines (that of the voice, melodic instruments, and *rebana* [and piano bass]). First, the lower register of the piano and the frame drum play the basic 8-beat rhythmic pattern (*rentak*) associated with the Malay *lagu asli* (meaning 'traditional' or 'original') of the *ronggeng asli* repertoire. This pattern is repeated throughout the song (Example 6.1a).[2]

*Transcriptions are to be found in Appendix 1.

EXAMPLE 6.1a
Typical Piano Bass and *Rebana Rentak* Pattern of *Lagu Asli* (Bars 2–3)

rebana   d   t   t   t | t t t.d d d   ⅜ |

Note: d = drum syllable 'dung', undamped stroke played by the right hand, striking drum towards the centre of drum head producing a deep, resonant sound; t = drum syllable 'tak', light, sharp stroke striking drum near the rim.

The drum rhythmic pattern establishes the metre, determines the tempo for other members of the ensemble, provides cues for the vocalist's entry, and identifies the dramatic situation. The low bass notes on 1 and 5 (as in bars 2 and 6 respectively) played by the piano and the 'dung' of the drum perform the same function as the gong which has been left out (see 'Metric Structure' below).

Secondly, although the violin and upper register of the piano occasionally play exactly the same melody as the voice, they often take off on their own, improvising with embellishments or ornaments (*bunga*) but with the melody implied and coinciding at the end of phrases. These embellishments include trills (bars 5 and 7) and turns (bar 4) (Transcription 6.1).

In addition, melodic patterns called *patahan lagu*, associated with Malay *asli* songs, are also played. According to musician, composer, and conductor Abdul Fatah Karim, 'these *patahan lagu* are so closely associated with *asli* that when one hears them, one feels that the *lagu* is a *lagu Melayu Asli*' (Abdul Fatah, 1980: 7) (Example 6.1b).

EXAMPLE 6.1b
Patahan Lagu Played by the Violin (Bar 7)

Thirdly, the vocal line is fairly independent of the violin and piano lines. The performer improvises the vocal line rhythmically and melodically. As shown in Transcription 6.1, variants between the vocal lines of stanzas 1 and 2 of 'Hiburan Raja Ahmad Beradu' are a matter of course.

The singer also improvises the melody with ornaments (*bunga*) characteristic of Malay *asli* singing (Example 6.1c). These *bunga* include (i) glides from one tone to another—sometimes continuous glides occur over a succession of notes (a) and vocal phrases often begin with a glide (b); (ii) vibrato on sustained notes; (iii) trill; (iv) single appoggiatura; and (v) mordents.

EXAMPLE 6.1c
Bunga (Ornaments)

At the same time, however, even though this piece is a combination of three fairly independent horizontal melodic and rhythmic lines, these lines coincide vertically at certain parts to form triads,[3] usually on tones 1 and 5 (bars 1–2) (Transcription 6.1). Vertical triads are also played by the piano on tones 1 and 5.

FORMAL STRUCTURE

The structure also combines Malay and Western elements. The song is in strophic form. Although the four-phrase melodic structure setting lyrics in quatrain verse form might have been derived from Portuguese folk-songs in the sixteenth century (Goldsworthy, 1979: 768; Kartomi, 1988: 361; Kornhauser, 1978: 112–15), there are strong Malay features present in the structure. For instance, as in *ronggeng asli* songs, each stanza is sung to a modified rendition of the similar melody. Additionally, each stanza is a quatrain in Malay *syair* verse form. The *syair* verse has an *a a a a* rhyme scheme. The same idea is conveyed continuously throughout each verse and throughout all the verses.[4] As in bars 3–4 (Transcription 6.1), each line of the *syair* text corresponds to one cycle of the drum rhythmic pattern. In 'Hiburan Raja Ahmad Beradu', the two *syair* verses are:

Bersiram bersalin pakaian dah sama
Makanan disantap rasanya nikmat
Datangnya ma'a cucuran rahmat
Beta ucapkan syukur selamat

Ayohai mak pengasoh yang berbudi
Panggil kemari dayang-dayang tadi
Menyanyi ramai jangan tak sudi
Beta beradu supaya jadi.

Bathing and changing clothes have been completed
The food [I am] eating tastes wonderful
God's mercy has flown like water
I am grateful for God's blessings

Oh nursemaid who is wise
Call the maids-in-waiting to come
Sing together let none be unwilling [to join in]
So that I may rest.

METRIC STRUCTURE

Since pre-World War II days, *bangsawan* songs have been notated by musicians using the Western metre with bar lines placed before stressed beats. Although this notation is borrowed from the West, the metric structure of traditional Malay music is still maintained. As in traditional Malay music (where the stressed beats fall at the end of the gong cycle or rhythmic cycle), the stress is placed at the end of the phrase rather than at the beginning. The singer often begins singing only after the first beat of the phrase. Also, the singer's phrase ends on the same pitch as the violin and piano and at the same beat as the 'dung' of the *rebana*. As shown in bars 3–4 (Transcription 6.1), the singer aims toward this 'dung' (which signals the end of the rhythmic cycle and plays a punctuating role like a gong in traditional Malay music). Bass notes 1 and 5 replace the gong punctuating points in 'traditional' Malay music, thereby stressing the end of a phrase rather than its beginning.

TONAL SYSTEM

As far as the tonal system is concerned, *bangsawan* performers say that the melody of 'Hiburan Raja Ahmad Beradu' (played by the violin and piano) has some Chinese characteristics (Abdul Fatah, 1980). Chinese elements could have been added as this song is sung antiphonally between Raja Ahmad and his Chinese maid-in-waiting Che Wan Gayah. In particular, although the song is in the diatonic major mode, the melodic interludes or cadential phrases (*patahan lagu*) use pitches 3 and 5 together with pitch 2 (Example 6.1d) and pitches 5 and 3 with pitches 6 and 1 (Example 6.1e).

EXAMPLE 6.1d
The Use of Pitches 3 and 5 with Pitch 2 in a Typical
Chinese Pentatonic Scale

EXAMPLE 6.1e
The Use of Pitches 5 and 3 with Pitches 6 and 1 in a Typical
Chinese Pentatonic Scale

These cadences suggest the intervallic structure of the typical Chinese anhemitonic pentatonic scale (which can be represented as pitches 1 2 3 5 6 from the diatonic major scale).[5] The above phrases emphasize the minor third intervals (between notes 3 and 5 and 6 and i) character- istic of the Chinese pentatonic scale.[6] The melodic patterns or contours shown above are also similar to those found in Chinese folk-songs (see Transcription 6.8).

SINGING STYLE

The singer uses the traditional Malay style of singing characterized by a nasal quality and a fairly narrow and tense vocal width.[7] The female singer, in particular, sings in the upper register of her voice.[8]

'Hiburan Raja Ahmad Beradu' is therefore a combination of Malay, Western, and Chinese elements. On the one hand, the four-phrase melodic structure set to lyrics in quatrain verse form is characteristic of popular and folk Western music. On the other hand, the cyclic nature of the drum rhythmic pattern, the varied renditions of the melody, the strong linearity of the song, the singer's emphasis on the last beat of the musical phrase, and the singing style are characteristics of Malay tradi- tional music as a whole. The occasional use of triads shows the Malay variation of Western harmony. At the same time, some melodic patterns characteristic of Chinese folk-songs suggesting the intervallic structure of the pentatonic scale are introduced.

Transcription 6.2—Lagu Padang Pasir/Arab: 'Telek Ternang'
[Song for Going into Trance using a Water Jar][9]

Like Transcription 6.1, this song has been transcribed from the same set of 78 r.p.m. recordings of the Malay play *Puteri Gunong Ledang* (P 12763). In this song, two shamans—Tok Ngah and his wife Mek Ngah—go into trance. They are supposed to look for a suitable princess who is worthy to become the Sultan's wife. As in the first ex- ample, this song combines Malay and Western elements especially in the instrumentation, singing style, and texture; however, as the spirits that the shamans are consulting are of Middle Eastern origin, a song with Middle Eastern characteristics is chosen. Accordingly, this is considered to be a *lagu Padang Pasir* (Middle Eastern song).

These Middle Eastern characteristics include the *rebana* and piano playing the following *masri* rhythmic pattern: ‖ : d̲ t t̲ d t : ‖. As illus- trated in Example 6.2a and as expressed by *bangsawan* musicians, the

EXAMPLE 6.2a
Rhythmic Pattern of the Melody Played by the Cane Flute
in *Beledi* Dancing in Iran

Nai

masri rhythmic pattern resembles the rhythmic pattern which accompanies *beledi* (belly) dancing in Iran (Nettl, 1972: 237).

The *masri* rhythmic pattern also resembles one of the common rhythmic patterns (Masmūdī Kabīr) in the Middle East. This rhythmic pattern is repeated throughout the entire piece (Pacholczyk, 1980: 261) (Example 6.2b).

EXAMPLE 6.2b
Masmūdī Kabīr Rhythm

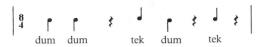

Note: 'dum' = primary beat, played in centre of membrane of drum; 'tek' = secondary beat played at edge of membrane.

Furthermore, this song is associated with one of the melodic modes[10] found in Middle Eastern music. 'Telek Ternang' uses a melodic mode similar in intervallic structure to that of the Hicaz (Signell, 1977: 35). However, in 'Telek Ternang', B♭ instead of B♮ is used (♮ lowers a note by approximately 90 cents) (Examples 6.2c and 6.2d).[11]

EXAMPLE 6.2c
Mode of Hicaz

EXAMPLE 6.2d
Mode of 'Telek Ternang'

The notes A and D are emphasized both in the mode of 'Telek Ternang' and the mode of Hicaz (Signell, 1977: 78–9) (Examples 6.2e and 6.2f).

EXAMPLE 6.2e
A Melodic Pattern of Hicaz

EXAMPLE 6.2f
Voice Melody of 'Telek Ternang'

Lastly, *masri* may well have Middle Eastern associations as the term could have been derived from the term '*Mesir*' which means Egypt.

Transcription 6.3—Lagu Padang Pasir/Arab: 'Gambos Sri Makam'
[Gambos Sung at the Grave]

'Gambos Sri Makam' has been transcribed from a 78 r.p.m. recording of the Middle Eastern play *Laila Majnun*. This play was recorded by the Gramophone Co. Ltd., India and produced under the label of His Master's Voice. *Laila Majnun* tells of the love of Majnun and Laila which is forbidden because of their different social backgrounds. Majnun is the son of a rich businessman while Laila is the daughter of a poor schoolteacher. In this song (P 12803), Majnun and Laila sing of their love for each other. They declare that they can only be together when they are dead.

Although this song uses the *asli* rhythmic pattern, it is identified as a *lagu Padang Pasir*. The characteristics that distinguish it from *lagu asli* are the mode, repeated phrase technique, ornamentation, and the style of accompaniment used. 'Gambos Sri Makam' uses a melodic mode similar in intervallic structure to the melodic mode Zengüle (Examples 6.3a and 6.3b) found in Middle Eastern music (Signell, 1977: 35). This mode is of the Hicaz family. It is made up of a combination of two Hicaz tetrachords.

EXAMPLE 6.3a
Intervallic Structure of Zengüle

EXAMPLE 6.3b
Intervallic Structure of 'Gambos Sri Makam'

In 'Gambos Sri Makam', B♮ is raised to B♭ and F♯ is lowered to F so that the Western principle of equal temperament is realized (♯ raises a note by one koma or 23 cents).[12] The notes A and E are emphasized (Signell, 1977: 34).

Resembling Middle Eastern folk and popular music (Nettl, 1972: 222–3; Zonis, 1973: 105–7), the vocal melody of 'Gambos Sri Makam' is constructed using repeated phrases and melodic sequences. For example, the first vocal phrase of 'Gambos Sri Makam' (bars 1–4) is repeated in bars 5–8 (Example 6.3c). Each couplet of the *syair* verse which corresponds with a vocal phrase is also repeated twice.

EXAMPLE 6.3c
Repetition of Vocal Phrase

bars 1–8

In addition, couplets with different texts are sung using different registers of the mode as in many Middle Eastern classical pieces (Zonis, 1973: 272). The first couplet of 'Gambos Sri Makam' (bars 1–8) is sung in a lower register while the second couplet (bars 8–16) is sung in the upper register (Transcription 6.3).[13]

Furthermore, the singing style resembles Koran cantillation. Melodic movement is characterized by stepwise movement, with small upward leaps most commonly involving an interval of a third or fourth (Al-Faruqi, 1987: 9).[14] Notes are frequently repeated (Example 6.3d).

EXAMPLE 6.3d
Intervals and Repeated Notes in 'Gambos Sri Makam'

bars 1–4

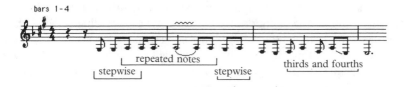

The style of accompaniment, which characterizes the *gambos* genre (see Chapter 8), also creates a Middle Eastern character in the song. The violin and piano play in heterophony with the voice modifying the basic vocal melody rhythmically and melodically with the addition of notes and ornaments (Transcription 6.3). The melodic instruments elaborate on the basic vocal melody with *patahan lagu Padang Pasir* (Example 6.3e).

EXAMPLE 6.3e
Patahan Lagu Padang Pasir

The melodic instruments frequently play ornaments which are characteristic of Middle Eastern art and music (Zonis, 1973: 108–9). As in
Koran reading, quick alternations between adjacent tones like trills
(bars 9 and 11) and turns (bars 3, 5, and 7) are common features of the
melodic line (Al-Faruqi, 1987) (Example 6.3f).

EXAMPLE 6.3f
Trill and Turn (Violin)

Rhythmic movement throughout 'Gambos Sri Makam' is kept constant by the violin and piano and it progresses in semiquaver or quaver
note values (Transcription 6.3). Perhaps this rhythmic movement is to
imitate the melisma characteristic of music of the Middle East (Zonis,
1973: 107).

Transcription 6.4—Lagu Jawa: 'Sinandung Jawa'
[Song of Melancholy Java][15]

This song is often used in street scenes (*lagu strit*) in Javanese plays.
This example is sung by a famous *bangsawan* actress, Miss Tijah, on a
78 r.p.m. record manufactured by the Gramophone Co. Ltd., India,
under the label of Chap Kuching (Cat Label, NG 73) in the 1930s. The
song resembles the first example in texture, structure, ensemble (except
for the addition of a trombone), and vocal style. According to *bangsawan*
performers whom I interviewed, this song is an adaptation of the *asli*
song called 'Siti Payong'. When this song is used in Javanese plays, even
though the *asli* rhythmic pattern is maintained, some Javanese characteristics similar to those of *langgam jawa* (Kornhauser, 1978: 160–4) of the
kroncong repertoire are incorporated. With the Javanese elements added,
the song becomes a *lagu Jawa* (Javanese song).

In the first instance, although a pitch set of the diatonic major scale is
used, a 'Javanese modal effect" (Kornhauser, 1978: 160) is created. As
shown in Example 6.4a, the intervallic succession similar to the Javanese
pélog pathet nem is produced. In this example, the sixth degree is completely left out while the second degree is used sparingly. The five tones

shown in Example 6.4a are reiterated throughout the piece by the voice, violin, and piano in a variety of patterns.[16]

EXAMPLE 6.4a
Intervallic Succession Resembling the Javanese *Pélog Pathet Nem*

Another characteristic borrowed from *langgam jawa* is *irama dua*.[17] (This concept was originally adapted from the Javanese gamelan by *kroncong* performers.) By using *irama dua*, which involves twice as many subdivisions per beat as the 'normal' *irama*, the rhythmic texture of the song is altered. For example, the *asli* rhythmic pattern of the *rebana* in bars 10–11 is notated as shown in Example 6.4b.

EXAMPLE 6.4b
Asli Rhythmic Pattern of the *Rebana*

| d   t t t   tt tt | · t t·d d d   ·t d d d |
                                        ⌣5⌣

In bars 12–13, the pattern is changed to that shown in Example 6.4c.

EXAMPLE 6.4c
Irama Dua Pattern of the *Rebana*

| d · t   ·t t. ·t . . | .t t t   d d t t d d ⅄ |

Transcription 6.5—Lagu Hindustan: 'Paraber' [Song of Prayer]

'Paraber' is an excerpt from the Hindustani play *Noor-E-Islam*. This story is about the conversion of the heathen King Nero to Islam by his brother Prince Tahir. Nero tells his brother that he will become a Muslim if Tahir's God can show him a few miracles. Nero asks Tahir to kill his own daughter. Even though Tahir's daughter miraculously survives the slashing of her throat, Nero is still not convinced. He asks Tahir, his wife, and his daughter to walk into a bonfire. Another miracle occurs. Not even a single hair is burnt. The fire transforms into a palace. Nero and his wife convert to Islam and are named 'Noor-E-Islam' by Tahir.

In 'Paraber', Tahir shows Nero how Muslims pray. He sings that God is pure and clean all day and night. He submits himself to God. This song was recorded under the label of Chap Singa (Lion Label) and distributed by M. E. and T. Hemsley in the 1930s (Cat. no. QF 35).

Known as *lagu Hindustan* (Hindustani song) by veteran *bangsawan* performers, this piece is an adaptation of a devotional song which was popular in India during the 1930s and 1940s. It combines Indian and Malay elements. The singer uses a mixture of Urdu, Hindustani, and Malay words. According to Minah Alias, the Urdu and Hindustani words are sometimes mispronounced as the singers often do not speak the languages but memorize the text.[18]

As in many Indian devotional songs, the voice is supported by a harmonium (Wade, 1980: 157). In addition, as in many religious songs where the text is emphasized, melodic repetition occurs (Wade, 1980: 156). 'Paraber' is in A A B A C B A form where A is repeated four times (Transcription 6.5). Futhermore, the tune moves in conjunct motion with few large leaps. Melodic intervals consisting of thirds occur occasionally while fourths are sometimes played between two melodic phrases (Tewari, 1974: 207).

The fast six-beat pattern (*dādrā tāla*)[19] common in 'light' Indian music (Manuel, 1988: 162) is used for accompaniment. Instead of being played on the tabla, however, this rhythmic pattern is played on the Malay frame drum with the following Malay *rebana* strokes and sounds: $\|: \underline{d\,t\,t} \quad \underline{d\,t\,t}: \|$. Finally, although the song is not based on any raga, the first two sections resemble the *āsthāyī* or *sthāyī* ('at home') and *antarā* ('interval') sections of some classical forms like *khyāl*. As in *āsthāyī*, notes of the lower tetrachord are played in the first section of the song. In the second section, notes of the upper tetrachord prevail as in the *antarā* (Kaufmann, 1968: 25–6).

Transcription 6.6—Lagu Hindustan: 'Mostikowi'

This song is also from *Noor-E-Islam* (QF 36). It is a *lagu nasib* (song of fate) sung by Tahir's wife, Shahirah. She is sad that all three of them have to walk into the fire, but accepts her fate. She asks God to give her strength. Tahir joins her at the end of the song.

According to Ashok Roy, a famous Indian performing artist, 'Mostikowi' is also an adaptation of a popular Indian religious song of the 1930s. As in 'Paraber', the voice is supported by a harmonium. The singer uses a mixture of Hindustani and Urdu words. There are few leaps in the melody. The singer first sings in the lower tetrachord and then in the higher one.

In addition, in order to achieve an Indian sound, the voice concentrates on ornaments which are used in Indian folk-singing. In particular, the singer uses vibrato at melismatic phrases (Example 6.6a).

EXAMPLE 6.6a
Vibrato at Melismatic Phrases

Na ho - - - gi

Although there is no clear raga, the tonal material is derived from Bhairavī (beginning on a different tonic). This raga is associated with devotional songs (Kaufmann, 1968: 25–6). As shown in Examples 6.6b and 6.6c, 'Mostikowi' uses an ascending pattern resembling that of Bhairavī (Kaufmann, 1968: 534), although a minor second instead of a major second is used.

EXAMPLE 6.6b
Ascending Pattern Common in Bhairavī

EXAMPLE 6.6c
Ascending Pattern in 'Mostikowi'

As in many Indian folk-songs, 'the melody maintains a looser structure for individual lines or phrases than a metre would allow. The number of counts in a line can be flexible to accommodate text changes from verse to verse.' (Wade, 1980: 157.) As shown in Transcription 6.6, the number of beats in the first, second, and third lines of 'Mostikowi' are 11, 15, and 6 respectively. Although the harmonium starts with the *Kaharvā tāla*[20] (8 beats—3 + 3 + 2) Example 6.6d, which is common in light Indian classical music (Manuel, 1988: 162), both the singer and the harmonium player alternate between 7 and 8 beats (Transcription 6.6). (This is probably because the *bangsawan* singer who made the recording was not a trained classical Indian singer.)[21]

EXAMPLE 6.6d
Kaharvā Tāla Played on Harmonium in 'Mostikowi'

count: 1 2 3 1   2   3 1 2

Transcription 6.7—Lagu Klasik/Opera: 'Penceraian Jula Juli dengan Sultan' [The Separation of Jula Juli from the Sultan]

This song is an adaptation of the Western popular song 'Ah Che La Morte'. It is a *lagu nasib* often sung in sad situations especially when the heroine has to leave the hero whom she loves. This example is an excerpt from a 78 r.p.m. recording of the play *Jula Juli Bintang Tiga*.

The recording was produced in the 1930s in India under the label of Chap Kuching (NG 30). Briefly, the story is about a princess who comes down from the heavens to look for a husband. She finds the Sultan of Zamin Tawaran's ring and agrees to return it if the Sultan marries her. But he must not ask for her name or her background. The Sultan agrees, they get married, and she bears him a son.

After a few years of marriage, the Sultan changes his mind and asks Jula Juli for her name so that he can introduce her to his guests. This song is about the separation of Jula Juli from the Sultan. She takes him to the garden by the sea where they first met, asks him not to have any regrets, bids him goodbye, and sits on her goose before revealing her name. She disappears. (The same song is also sung by Ophelia, in the *bangsawan* rendition of *Hamlet*, just before she falls into the sea or river.)

Although Malay elements such as the *syair* text and singing style (including vocal ornamentations) are used, this song is quite different from the previous examples. It is considered to be a Western song (*lagu klasik*)[22] and accordingly has many Western characteristics. For instance, the Malay *syair* text is sung to the melody of the Western song 'Ah Che La Morte' which is arranged as a two-part waltz. The singer also emphasizes the first beat of the phrase instead of the last beat (Transcription 6.7).

As in some Western theatrical music, there is a close relationship between the meaning of the text and the music. To show the effects of the words '*kali-kali*'(meaning 'repeatedly') the same note is repeated. To emphasize the word '*ya*' (meaning 'yes'), the note is made short and accented (Example 6.7a).

EXAMPLE 6.7a

Musical Emphasis of Text

In addition to the relationship between the meaning of the text and the music, a Western element also appears in the ensemble: violins, trumpet, trombone, piano, and Hawaiian guitar. For diversity, different combinations are used in different stanzas. In stanza 1, to accompany Jula Juli, the trumpet and piano play the main melody while the trombone harmonizes with this melody. When the Sultan sings, only violins and piano are used. In stanza 2, the Hawaiian guitars replace the trumpet, trombone, violins, and treble part of the piano. The whole orchestra plays in stanzas 3 and 4 (Transcription 6.7).

Finally, compared to the previous examples, this piece has a greater feel of harmony and harmonic texture. Melodic invention is governed by rules of harmony, and modulation occurs. The notes are restricted to the

Western scales of A minor in verses 1 and 2 and A major in verses 3 and 4 (although the sharpened fourth [D#] is used to emphasize the dominant note and the passing note [C#] is employed). Modulation to A major is introduced by raising the third note C to C#.

Vertical triads are more abundant than the previous examples. The piano bass plays the 'oom-pah-pah' or waltz rhythm on triads I, IV, and V throughout the piece. In stanza 1, the trombone and piano harmonize in thirds and sixths with the violin and voice, while in stanza 3, the trombone and piano harmonize with the muted trumpet, violin, and Hawaiian guitar, so that vertical triads are formed. Solo instruments end phrases with either an arpeggio or with chordal statements (Transcription 6.7).

Transcription 6.8—Lagu Cina: 'Shanghai Street'

This example is a *lagu Cina* (Chinese song) which is usually performed in street scenes in Chinese plays. It may also be sung by Chinese servants or clown characters in plays of other ethnic origins. This recording was sung by a well-known *bangsawan* actress, Che Norlia, and produced by the Gramophone Co. Ltd., India, under the label of His Master's Voice (P 15978). 'Shanghai Street' is in the style of ragtime, where a syncopated melody is sung and played against a straightforward bass (Example 6.8a).

EXAMPLE 6.8a
Syncopated Melody against a Straightforward Bass (Bars 1–3)

However, what differentiates it from other songs is its Chinese characteristics. These Chinese traits include the use of an intervallic structure which resembles the typical Chinese pentatonic scale (Example 6.8b) described in 'Hiburan Raja Ahmad Beradu'. Pitch 7 is completely omitted by the singer and pitch 4 is left out by the singer in the last seven bars.

EXAMPLE 6.8b
Typical Chinese Pentatonic Scale

'Shanghai Street' also uses syllables which have no 'meaning' and which are often found in Chinese folk-songs. For example, *'hai-lah'* and *'a-hai a-hai'* are sung in bars 8, 9, and 13 (Transcription 6.8).[23]

Summary of Musical Style

As shown in the above examples, the basic musical idiom of *bangsawan* in the 1930s was a fusion of Malay and Western elements. Malay elements included the singing style, the vocal ornamentation, the singer's emphasis on the last beat of the phrase, the linear texture, the cyclic drum rhythmic patterns, and the use of Malay *syair* texts. Western elements included the harmony or implied harmony in or between the instrumental and vocal parts (a factor which strongly influenced melodic invention), close relationship between the text and the music, and Western melodic instrumentation.

Sometimes the Western elements in this mix were not stressed while at other times they were omitted entirely, especially in songs associated with Malay stories, characters, or dramatic situations (*lagu Melayu*). For example, in 'Hiburan Raja Ahmad Beradu', Malay characteristics predominated while Western triads were used sparingly. (In this case, some cadential phrases resembling those of Chinese folk-songs were also added.) Likewise, in songs associated with Western stories (*lagu klasik*), for example, 'Penceraian Jula Juli dengan Sultan', Western characteristics prevailed; the *syair* text and the singing style were the only Malay elements used.

Bangsawan songs which were not Malay or Western in association— such as *Lagu Padang Pasir*, *lagu Cina*, *lagu Hindustan*, and *lagu Jawa*— usually had some other characteristics adapted to the basic Malay/ Western mix. For example, the Middle Eastern rhythmic pattern and mode were used in 'Telek Ternang', while the Middle Eastern mode, repeated phrase technique, ornamentation, and style of accompaniment were employed in 'Gambos Sri Makam'. A type of Chinese pentatonic scale and 'meaningless' syllables were added to 'Shanghai Street'. The Indian rhythmic pattern, melodic structure, and harmonium were employed in 'Paraber' while the Indian vocal style, rhythmic pattern, mode, melodic structure, and harmonium were used in 'Mostikowi'. A Javanese modal effect and rhythmic texture characterized 'Sinandung Jawa'. Depending on the musical skills of the performers and the type of story performed, appropriate changes could be made to the basic Malay/Western mix. In 'Paraber', for example, all Western elements were omitted.

The music of the *bangsawan* of the 1930s was therefore heterogenetic and innovative.

Reasons for Musical Interaction

Musical interaction took place in *bangsawan* due to a number of extra-musical factors. In the first place, as commercial theatre, *bangsawan* had to adapt to the changing popular tastes of the urban population. As described in Chapter 5, Western characteristics were adopted since listening to and performing the music of the colonialists were thought to be 'modern', 'up-to-date', and 'prestigious'. Playing the piano and other Western instruments, and using Western harmony and notation, were also associated with being 'modern'. Adopting the latest trends in Western music also implied that *bangsawan* could do anything that Western music was capable of.

Musical interaction could take place because *bangsawan* as well as non-*bangsawan* performers of different ethnic groups were remarkably open to and actively learnt from one another. Minah Alias recalls studying the Chinese art of self-defence (*kuntau*) from a Chinese opera actress; in exchange, she taught her the Malay art of self-defence (*silat*). They exchanged gifts at the end of each lesson: Chinese noodles (*mee suah*) for the Chinese actress and eggs for Minah Alias. As Rahman B. commented: 'At that time the Malay *bangsawan* [players] and Chinese *bangsawan* [players] ... were brothers. When we needed to perform a Chinese story, we asked them [Chinese opera performers] ... "please teach us the music". That's how it was that we sang Chinese songs.'[24]

Sometimes, Rahman B. added, musicians were borrowed from Chinese opera troupes when the *bangsawan* group performed Chinese stories. This underlined that *bangsawan* troupes were open to performers of all ethnic backgrounds. Malay performers worked, lived, and travelled with Filipinos, Eurasians, Indians, Chinese, Indonesians, and Arabs, while non-Malay musicians who were well-versed in Malay, Western, Indian, Arabic, and Chinese music were often employed. According to Alfonso Soliano, Filipino musicians who could read Western notation and who could play Western instruments were sought after by *bangsawan* troupes, for they not only played Western instruments but wrote the musical scores and conducted many of the *bangsawan* performances.

Technological innovations and the mass media also played important roles in promoting musical interaction. Through the gramophone and radio, *bangsawan* performers were exposed to and could follow closely developments in popular music in other parts of the world. By the turn of the century, recording companies like Columbia, Pathe, Victor Talking Machine Co., Gramophone, and Carl Lindstrom had already recorded the indigenous music of Asia, Russia, North Africa, and Latin America (Gronow, 1981: 251–82).[25]

Musical interaction was further made possible because the British authorities did not impose censorship or control over *bangsawan* as they did over the cinema. As Butcher (1979: 170) stated in his book *The British in Malaya, 1880–1941*:

Implicit in British thinking about their rule throughout the empire was the principle that their power was based on prestige rather than military might.... Since prestige was the basis of power, it was absolutely essential to do everything possible to maintain that prestige and to eliminate anything which threatened to undermine it.[26]

Film censorship was imposed to reduce the local population's exposure to 'the bare flesh of white women in films' and to the depiction of white men as 'criminals, tramps, clowns' or 'lustful lovers' (Butcher, 1979: 171; Stevenson, 1974: 209–16). But *bangsawan*, with its fairy-tale stories, was no threat at all to British prestige.

Bangsawan was allowed to take its own course so long as certain guidelines were followed. *Bangsawan* troupes were required to obtain licences from the Sanitary Board (Wan Kadir, 1988: 47). For theatrical performances in closed theatres or tents, non-Malay, non-Chinese, or non-Tamil producers had to pay $1.00 if there were more than 200 people, $1.50 for 200–400 people, and $2.00 for more than 400 people. Malay, Chinese, or Tamil producers paid less (50 cents for 200 people, 75 cents for 200–400 people, and $1.00 for more than 400 people a performance). If performances ran past midnight, payments were at double the rate.

* * *

Bangsawan thus provided the venue for the interaction of foreign and indigenous music. *Bangsawan* music was 'up-to-date' and was commonly referred to as 'modern' by the troupes, the audiences, and the media. Indeed, opera troupes called on the public to listen to their 'modern' (*Saudara*, 11 April 1936) and 'up-to-date' songs of 'different languages' (*Straits Echo*, 11 June 1926). *Bangsawan* in fact witnessed the development of the first popular music in Malaya to incorporate Malay, Western, and (sometimes) other foreign musical elements. *Bangsawan* music as popular music was changing rapidly even as it appeared on the scene, was promoted commercially by the stars, and was disseminated widely through records, radio, music books, theatrical performances, and dance halls.

1. Nettl (1978: 13) notes that urban music has a 'tendency to very rapidly combine material from a diversity of sources'.

2. The *rebana*'s part is shown here (and throughout this chapter) using letters that stand for 'drum syllables' (onomatopoeic representations of the 'drum strokes'). The drum syllables 'dung' and 'tak' were used by my teacher Pak Mat Hashim when he taught me to play the *rebana* when I was doing my fieldwork in 1985–6.

3. In the absence of Malay harmonic terms, I have used Western terms.

4. See Mohd. Taib Osman (1975) for details. Most *ronggeng asli* songs, however, use

the *pantun* instead of the *syair*. The *pantun* has an *a b a b* rhyme scheme with the first couplet alluding to the meaning of the verse. Perhaps one of the reasons why *syair* is preferred to *pantun* in *bangsawan* is that each line of the text conveys meaning and can portray the dramatic situation better. In the past, the *syair* had also been used to relate stories, information, praises, and advice (whereas *pantun* had been used mainly for expressing emotions).

5. The phrases illustrated here are also similar to phrases found in the Malay *joget gamelan* (D'Cruz, 1979: Appendix D). The Malay gamelan could have incorporated Chinese elements as it is believed that the development of the *joget gamelan* of Pahang was influenced by one of the wives of Sultan Ahmad (1863–1914), Che Zubedah, who was a Chinese. Later the gamelan was brought to Trengganu and further developed by Tengku Mariam, the daughter of Che Zubedah and Sultan Ahmad (D'Cruz, 1979: 11–13).

6. At the same time, other parts of the melody use tones 4 and 7 as in the Western diatonic scale. For example in bar 7, the use of notes 3 and 4 together within a single phrase produces the diatonic scale 1 2 3 4 5. Pitch 4 changes the intervallic relationships of the Chinese pentatonic scale by eliminating the position of the minor third interval. Furthermore, in the Chinese scale, the two tones 4 and 7 are always employed in descending motion if the motion is stepwise (Wiant, 1965: 3).

7. These terms are borrowed from Lomax (1968: 71–2). To produce a nasal quality, it needs to be clarified that it is actually the cheek-bone (and not the nose) that vibrates. Vocal width is defined by the distance from the outside of the lips to the back of the oral cavity, the width of the opening of the throat, the opening of the glottis, and the relative tension of the glottal region.

8. The other style of singing is often referred to as 'crooning' style. See, for example, Kornhauser (1978: 147). The voice quality has 'less clear enunciation of consonants and little or no nasalization'. *Kroncong* is sung using the crooning style.

9. This is not a direct translation of the terms. 'Telek Ternang' is a trance ritual.

10. The *maqam* or melodic mode is a 'set of compositional rules by which the melodic component of a piece of music is realized' (Signell, 1977: 16). Signell further explores five criteria (intervallic structure, sequence of tonal centres, modulation, stereotyped melodies, and tessitura) which can be used to explain the differences between two Turkish *maqamat*. According to Signell, the five criteria are often not all distinctive, but at least one of them should be (Signell, 1977: 149).

11. In this sense, the mode used in *bangsawan* is closer to the Hicaz used in night-club music in Turkey (Signell, 1977: 45).

12. The mode, however, does not make references to melodic fragments associated with the Middle Eastern mode.

13. However, the first couplet is based on the Hicaz tetrachord on E instead of the tetrachord on A as is customary although A is emphasized (Zonis, 1973: 137).

14. The cantillation of the Koran has had an impact on the rendition of popular songs by singers of the Middle East like Umm Khulthum of Cairo (Danielson, 1987: 35). The singing style of 'Gambos Sri Makam' resembles Egyptian recorded music of the 1930s. These recordings were sold in Malaya.

15. 'Sinandung' literally means 'melancholy'. It also denotes a genre of songs (Goldsworthy, 1979).

16. A similar mode is used in *kroncong* of the *langgam jawa* type (Kornhauser, 1978: 160).

17. *Irama dua* is described by Kornhauser as 'double density'. 'The term density refers to the number of notes per unit of time either performed in a single ensemble part or collectively in all simultaneous parts.' (Kornhauser, 1978: 141.)

18. Mak Minah (who was active during the pre-World War II days and who teaches the Bangsawan Sri USM troupe today) can still sing some of the songs in *Noor-E-Islam* . She does not know the meaning of the words though.

19. *Dādrā tāla* (fast):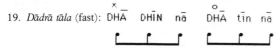

Notes: '(a) DHĀ and nā indicate the presence of a sharp clear pitch made by striking the forefinger on the edge of a tightly stretched and tuned right drum or drum head, half damping with the annular finger; (b) DHĪN indicates a deep undamped resonance from a lax left drum; (c) syllables in lower case shows that the left hand resonance is absent; (d) x = *tālī* (beat), o = *khālī* (empty).' (Powers, 1980: 124.)

20. *Kaharvā tāla*:

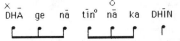

See Powers (1980: 123–4) for a clarification of the basic system of table strokes, syllables, sounds, contrasts, and signs used.

21. See Manuel (1988) and Arnold (1988) for discussions of popular music in India in the early twentieth century.

22. The term *lagu klasik* (classical song) is used by *bangsawan* performers for all popular as well as operatic songs of Western origin.

23. For a comparison, see the song 'The Haunts of Pleasure' (Van Aalst, 1966: 42). 'Shanghai Street' could have been borrowed from the Chinese opera as Western popular tunes were also used by Chinese operas in the 1920s and 1930s (Yung, 1989: 107). Both *bangsawan* and Chinese opera performers also learnt from one another in the 1930s.

24. 'Masa itu bangsawan Melayu dengan bangsawan Cina .... bersaudara. Bila kita perlu cerita Cina, kita panggil dia ... "tolong ajar muzik itu". Jadi kita menyanyilah lagu Cina.'

25. Between 1900 and 1910, the Gramophone Co. Ltd. alone produced about 4,400 recordings in India, 2,000 in Turkey, 1,200 in Egypt, 97 in Java, and 44 in Tibet (Gronow, 1981).

26. This prestige was based on racial exclusiveness supported by a 'European standard of living'. This high standard of living was characterized by exclusive clubs and resort areas, high salaries, and servants.

7
Scene Types, Plot Structure, and Stock Characters in the 1920s and 1930s

ALTHOUGH *bangsawan* emphasized variety, spectacle, and novelty, it also depended for its impact on conventions which were known to and accepted by both performers and audiences, conventions with which they were familiar. Scene types (*babak*) were used in plot building, stock characters (*watak*) with their stereotyped behaviour, costumes, facial expressions, and gestures were also featured, and even foreign plays were adapted using these prescribed patterns.

As in traditional theatre, scene types and stock characters were important in *bangsawan* for two reasons. First, although the audience was separated from the performer by the raised stage, among the audience the norms of daily behaviour prevailed, for theatre then was still considered very much an extension of the everyday life of the urban community, rather than a formal occasion. Members of the audience would inevitably be conversing freely with each other even as the performers performed, while children roamed about the seats and food was sold by roving vendors. Amidst these distractions, basic conventions on stage were necessary to help the audience make sense of the plot as it unfolded. A familiarity with the conventions also allowed the multi-ethnic audience, some members of which would not understand the language spoken on stage, to follow the story-line.

Secondly, scene types and stock characters were important for *bangsawan* was an oral form and there were no written texts in the early twentieth century. They helped the performer to arrange materials for easy recollection and helped him to create the story (Sweeney, 1980). Conventions were also relied upon because performers had constantly to put on new stories and create new sensations, novel acts, and tricks; there was little time to practise. Scene types and stock characters helped to keep both performer and audience on the right path.

The following analysis is based on six plays which were popular in the early twentieth century (synopses in Appendix 2): (1) *Jula Juli Bintang Tiga*, a classical or opera story (*cerita klasik* or *opera*); (2) *Puteri Bakawali* [The Princess Bakawali], a Hindustani story (*cerita Hindustan*); (3) *Laila Majnun*, an Arabic story (*cerita Arab*); (4) *Laksamana Bentan,* a Malay historical story (*cerita sejarah Melayu*); (5) *Sam Pek Eng Tai*, a Chinese story (*cerita Cina*); and (6) *Hamlet*, a classical or opera story. The categories used here are those employed by veteran *bangsawan* performers as well as those found in advertisements of *bangsawan* performances in the newspapers of the early twentieth century. The analysis of *Jula Juli Bintang Tiga* and *Laila Majnun* is based on 78 r.p.m. recordings of the plays. The former was produced by the Gramophone Co. Ltd. in Dum Dum, India in the 1930s under the label of Chap Kuching (NG 29–NG 32). The latter was also recorded by the Gramophone Co. Ltd. but under the label of His Master's Voice (P 12800–P 12805]. *Laksamana Bentan* and *Puteri Bakawali* were performed by the Bangsawan Sri USM troupe in December 1985 and July 1986 respectively. Scripts for these two plays were written by Alias Manan, one of the instructors of the troupe, and were based on performances of the 1930s. *Laksamana Bentan* was also staged by the Ministry of Culture, Youth and Sports in Kuala Lumpur in April 1986. *Sam Pek Eng Tai* and *Hamlet* were related to me by Minah Alias, who performed the roles of Eng Tai and Ophelia in the respective plays in the 1930s. I have also relied on reviews of *Hamlet* written by R. O. Winstedt, an officer in the Federated Malay States Civil Service and a Malay linguist, in the *Straits Echo* (14 November 1908), and three other anonymous writers in the *Times of Malaya* (11 January 1912) and the *Straits Echo* (20 October 1928 and 5 October 1932). It was not possible for me to establish the conventions used in *bangsawan* in the late nineteenth century for lack of resource materials.

Scene Types (*Babak*) and Plot Structure

In *bangsawan* plot building, the director or stage manager used conventions with which both the performers and the audience were familiar. As in traditional *wayang*, the director relied on situations which occurred again and again in all performances. These situations were called *babak*. Each scene type was restricted to one locale:[1] *istana* (palace) for court audience; *taman* (garden) for love scenes; *laut* (sea) for fighting and sailing scenes; *hutan* (forest) for hunting and fighting scenes; *kampung* (village) for ordinary village scenes; *kayangan* (heaven) for scenes in heaven; and *pasir* (sand landscape) for desert scenes (Figures 7.1–7.3).

Each *bangsawan* scene type was characterized by a different backdrop and sometimes by props. The backdrops and props signalled to the audience the type of scene being portrayed. The main backdrops consisted of *tirai strit* (street in the town or kampong), *tirai hall* (hall in the palace or house), *tirai hutan* (forest), *tirai taman* (garden), *tirai laut* (sea), *tirai awan* (clouds), *tirai gua batu* (cave), *tirai kain hitam* (black cloth), and *tirai extra* (unpainted backdrop for the interludes). Backdrops were painted to simulate the scenery of foreign countries. For example, during the performances of *Sam Pek Eng Tai* and *Laksamana Bentan*, two different types of *tirai hall* would be used: one resembling the interior of a Chinese house and the other depicting the interior of a

FIGURE 7.1

Backdrops of Malay/Javanese *Taman*, Arabic/Hindustani *Taman*, *Hutan Tebuk*, and *Hutan*, c.1920–c.1930

Arabic/Hindustani *taman*

Hutan

Malay/Javanese *taman*

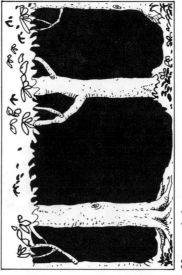

Hutan tebuk

Source: Drawings by Mohd. Bahroodin Ahmad.

FIGURE 7.2

Backdrops of *Gua Batu, Istana, Istana Tebuk,* and *Rumah Kampung,*
c.1920–c.1930

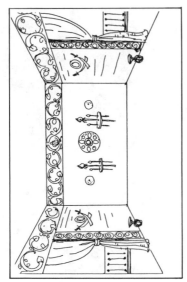

Istana

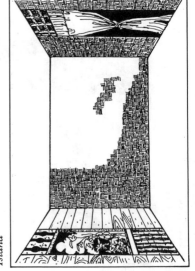

Rumah kampung

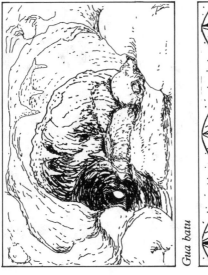

Gua batu

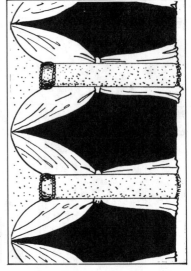

Istana tebuk

FIGURE 7.3

Backdrops of *Padang Pasir, Kayangan, Kampung,* and *Strit,*
*c.*1920–*c.*1930

Kayangan

Strit

Padang pasir

Kampung

Source: Drawings by Mohd. Bahroodin Ahmad.

Malay palace. Other stage properties which helped the audience identify the scene type were the throne for the sultan in the palace scene, plants and flowers for the garden scene, and a hut for the kampong scene. Performers stressed that the backdrops and props had to look 'real'. As Menah Yem said, 'The *tirai laut* must resemble the real sea; the rock must look like a real rock.'[2]

Before any production, a list of the scene types and their sequence were first drawn up and written on the blackboard by the director of the troupe. This list of scene types was the reference point for performers who knew the conventions which corresponded with each scene type. For instance, in *Jula Juli Bintang Tiga*, the sequence of the *babak* was outlined as follows:

Babak 1: *Takhta Kerajaan di Negeri Zamin Tawaran* (Throne or Reception Hall at the Palace at Zamin Tawaran); Babak 2: *Taman di Tepi Laut* (Garden by the Sea); Babak 3: *Takhta Kerajaan Istana* (Reception Hall of Palace); Babak 4: *Jalan* (road); Babak 5: *Taman di Tepi Laut*; Babak 6: *Kayangan*; Babak 7: *Istana Zamin Tawaran*.

Stories in which the aristocracy were the central characters usually began and ended with the court scene. (See the *babak* outlines of *Jula Juli Bintang Tiga*, *Puteri Bakawali*, and *Laksamana Bentan* in Appendix 2.) As a scene opener, the Sultan's first lines were always:

Saudara beta Raja Temenggong. Apa khabar saudara beta? Bagaimana keadaan rakyat dan negara kita?

My dear Raja Temenggong. How are you? How are my people and my Kingdom of Bentan?

The Temenggong's reply was always:

Ampun Tuanku beribu-ribu ampun, sembah patik harap diampun. Bagi pihak patik khabar baik, tuanku. Rakyat berada di dalam makmur, negara berada di dalam keadaan aman dan sejahtera.

I beg for your forgiveness, my King. I am well, my King. The people are prosperous, the kingdom is peaceful and secure.

Although the name of the official spoken to changed from play to play, the phrases used were invariably the same.

Unlike this first court scene, there were no set rules for the sequence of other scenes in *bangsawan*. In this sense, *bangsawan* was similar to *wayang Siam*, the sequence of scenes of which was also not fixed, except for the prologue (Sweeney, 1980: 52).[3] None the less, as shown in the six plays in Appendix 2, standard locations like *taman*, *jalan* or *strit*, and *kampung* appeared in almost every *bangsawan* performance. In addition, *perang* (battle), *lawak* (comedy), *cinta* (love), and *nasib* (literally meaning 'fate' but used in this context to mean sad scenes) were important and were usually included. Even though there were no clown scenes in the case of *Laksamana Bentan*, there were a few humorous episodes. In the last scene, Megat (the pirate chief) teases the Laksamana (admiral) who wants to kill himself because he thinks that Princess Wan Entah, his girl-friend, is dead. Megat says that the Laksamana is crying like a child thirsting for milk and that it is shameful for an admiral to cry in front of so many people. Megat further annoys the Laksamana by touching Wan Entah's forehead and hand. He then drinks some water which he has prayed over and spits the water all around, making sure that it hits the Laksamana.

Moreover, as in the *wayang*, there was often a return to the initial place (such as the palace scene of the first *babak*) at the end. Except for a few tragedies like *Laila Majnun* and *Sam Pek Eng Tai* (where both the hero and heroine died), virtue normally triumphed over vice at the end of a *bangsawan* story. Whatever the danger faced or misfortune experienced by the hero or heroine throughout the story, all was set right in the final scene. Order was restored. In *Jula Juli Bintang Tiga*, Baharom Alam brings his mother Jula Juli Bintang Tiga from heaven, and with the magical bow *panah pancawarna* resotres his father to life again. In *Laksamana Bentan*, Wan Entah recovers from her sickness, marries her lover, whereupon the couple are made king and queen of Bentan. In *Puteri Bakawali*, King Tajul Bahri regains his eyesight; his son Tajul Muluk marries the princess Nurul Asyikin; Puteri Bakawali is taken back to heaven by her father; and the magic flower Bunga Bakawali is planted on earth so that its healing powers are available to all on earth.

Just as the *wayang* usually ended with the *pohon beringin* (banyan tree), *bangsawan* would end with a tableau. As with the *pohon beringin*, the tableau not only symbolized the victory of virtue over vice and the forces of good over evil but also stressed the moral of the story and gave the audience time to reflect on it. In the last scene of *Laksamana Bentan*, for example, the cast stood frozen with their hands lifted in prayer in the Muslim fashion (*menadah tangan berdoa*).

However, unlike *wayang*, where simultaneous plots tended to occur (Becker, 1979), *bangsawan* performers usually had one main plot with a number of subplots. Compared to the *wayang*, the structural movement was more linear, sometimes leading towards a climax. In *Laksamana Bentan*, the climax occurred when the Laksamana and Megat's men fought, the heir to the throne of Bentan died, the Laksamana lamented, and the evil pirate Megat repented.

Nevertheless, the linearity of the plot was often obscured.[4] This was usually due to the interaction between the performer and the audience. Often, members of the audience passed their personal photographs to the stars on stage. On one such occasion, the performance stopped 'while the whole company inspected and discussed the picture ... [on stage]. Then, much to the youth's chagrin and the delight of the audience, the photos [were] ... torn up.' (*Malacca Guardian*, 9 May 1932.) Sometimes, bottles of beer were given to performers, who took time from the production to drink the beer (*Malacca Guardian*, 9 May 1932), again in the midst of the performance.

At other times, presentations of awards by admirers took place during the performance. For example, after receiving an award, a certain Mr Abdul Azziz 'returned thanks in song and then presented those in the reserved seats with bouquets' (*Malacca Guardian*, 2 February 1909). In addition, guests of honour might arrive late and in the middle of a performance. On one such occasion, the Resident Councillor (the Honourable W. C. Michelle) and his party arrived only at about 10 p.m. on the opening night of the Star Opera's performance on 31 August 1912 in Penang (*Straits Echo*, 31 August 1912). The show was interrupted for the prima donna to garland the Resident Councillor. The proprietor then gave a 'short address, thanked the Resident Councillor and his party for their honoured presence and asked the public to give their support to the company'.

Sometimes, extra turns were prolonged, especially if there were requests from the audience who, to encourage fulfilment, would throw cash on to the stage (*Malacca Guardian*, 9 May 1932). Furthermore, members of the audience would occasionally request special dances by performers whom they admired (*Straits Echo*, 14 January 1909). Clowns were also often urged on by the audience and consequently took longer than usual for their interludes (*Straits Echo*, 11 December 1909). During a performance by Wayang Kassim on 11 December 1909 of the Shakespearian play *The Merchant of Venice*, the comic turns took up so much of the time that 'the whole plot was not gone through' and the curtain 'timed to drop at 12 pm, did not do so till past 1 am'.

Where the plot was concerned, *bangsawan* showed the characteristics both of traditional Malay and modern Western theatre. Performers still organized the plot according to scene types. However, the movement of the plot was more linear. At the same time, this linearity was often obscured because of 'stoppages caused by unexpected or extraneous circumstances' (*Malacca Guardian*, 9 May 1932). In general, as in the musical comedies performed by foreign vaudeville troupes, plots remained less important than spectacular settings, songs, dances, and beautiful chorus girls.

Dramatis Personae (*Watak*)

After drawing up the scenes, the stage manager assigned the actors to their parts. This section focuses on the characters of stories which form the main repertoire of *bangsawan*, that is, stories set in the courts. As in the *wayang*, stock characters consisted of (1) *halus* (fine) characters— the hero (*orang muda*), heroine (*sri panggung*), and king (*raja*); and (2) *kasar* (coarse) ones—the villain, usually acting as a pirate or *jin* (spirit), and the clown (*pelawak*). Other minor characters included the queen, officials, warriors, maids, villagers, and *mambang* (a kind of spirit).[5]

Regardless of the origin of the plays, these stock characters had specific functions or roles in the plot. Each character wore a standard costume, though there was some variation in dress depending on the time period and geographical location of the specific play. Each character also had a repertoire of standard expressions and movements.

Roles

The hero was patriotic, faithful in love, heroic, and brave. His main function was to serve the king, present a picture of idealized virtue and patriotism, and rescue the princess if anything happened to her. Although he was portrayed as *halus*, he was expected to be strong looking as well as a good fighter as he had to struggle against the evil villain. Thus, he normally had a 'pleasing appearance' and a 'passable voice' (*Straits Echo*, 2 July 1910).

The heroine portrayed the ideal 'aristocratic' lady—one of fair delicate beauty, possessing the qualities of pristine goodness, meekness, humility, patience, and refinement. She had unequalled powers of resistance and an inflexible attitude to chastity. At some point or other, she had to undergo suffering and face trials and tribulations. Her role was to be faithful in love, and be totally devoted to father, lover, and husband. When faced with an open attack on her chastity, she preferred death to dishonour.

Sometimes, as in *Laksamana Bentan*, another type of heroine was portrayed. Wan Senari, the sister of Wan Entah, was a stronger and more assertive princess who was to take over the throne when her father died. Her role was to set up the conflict between the hero and heroine's love for each other and their duties to parent and king.

The king was father of either the hero or the heroine. As ruler of the kingdom, he was a person of dignity and elevated sentiment. He emphasized the moral of the story through bestowing good advice all around. He was just, benevolent, and forgiving. When Megat repented, the Sultan forgave him, made him headman, and gave him and his pirates land on which to found a kampong.

The villain (such as Megat in *Laksamana Bentan*) was able to raise fear in the audience. A thief and deceiver, he often pursued the heroine, showing great persistence in his attempt. He was a good fighter, and in line with the morality emphasized in *bangsawan*, villains too faced their fate with dignity. Their fate was to die or, as in the case of Megat, to repent and become virtuous. Megat was sometimes portrayed as a comic villain.

Comic figures were often the servants. Although they poked fun at the hero, who was sometimes portrayed as a callow youth, they would always be at hand to aid and support him in times of trouble. They were usually humble, lively, and light-hearted, having a quality of sensible forthrightness. These traits contrasted with the solemnity of the hero or heroine, who was always faced with problems. Although these stock comic figures were not portrayed in *Laksamana Bentan*, Kembang Cina (maidservant of the heroine) and Megat (villain) were comic in some instances. Both poked fun at the heroine and hero respectively.

The *jin* or giant was usually 'a very ugly specimen of humanity, with face bedaubed with black paint'. He delighted 'in carrying off other people's wives, almost invariably meeting his death at the hands of the orang muda' (*Straits Echo*, 2 July 1910). In *Puteri Bakawali*, the *jin* Gurda, although known to eat human beings, did not attempt to kill Tajul Muluk because he had a soft spot for him and wanted him to marry his daughter.

Other minor characters included the court officials and queen who were patriotic and willingly served the king. There were also women comic maids who served the princess. Ordinary village men and their nagging wives were portrayed in village scenes.

Characteristics of Stock Characters

The character types were easily identified by their costumes, make-up, movements, voices, and language. The acting style was stylized and depended on the type of scene portrayed (Figures 7.4 and 7.5). Each figure's tone of voice and language was appropriate to his function in a particular scene type.

Royal characters, ranging from the king to the court officials, were richly clad and adorned with head-dresses and royal accessories. The king wore yellow, which is the traditional colour of royalty in many parts of the Malay world. Royal faces were powdered white and rouged. Royal characters wore slippers.

In the court scene, characters of *halus* nature moved slowly and smoothly. This was in accordance with the dignity of the Sultan and the court. The scene was characterized by demonstrations of respect to the king: in greeting the king, one had to *sembah* (pay one's respect) by pressing ten fingers to the head.

The dialogue in the court scene always used *istana* speech. Regardless of the origin of the play, the term *patik* was employed for 'I' when speaking to the Sultan, who was addressed as *Tuanku*. When the king spoke, he used the term *beta* for 'I'. Speeches were made using dignified and calm voices. In love scenes, however, intimate terms like *abang* (brother) and *adinda* (sister) were used by the hero and heroine. Giggling was also allowed.[6] In the fighting scene, *halus* characters were allowed to display their strength and bravery.

In contrast to *halus* characters, villains invariably had black moustaches, long untidy hair, dark skins, and reddish faces, and they usually wore black. In the villain's domain (an island in *Laksamana Bentan*), the characters were rowdy, laughed loudly, and moved quickly and roughly. They used harsh gruff voices and were colloquial in speech.

Clowns wore patched clothes showing their humble position and low status. They were allowed to touch and slap each other. Clowns spoke in *bahasa pasar* (bazaar Malay) or conversational, colloquial Malay. They spoke loudly and created humour even in court scenes.

FIGURE 7.4

Movements of the Sultan, c.1920–c.1930

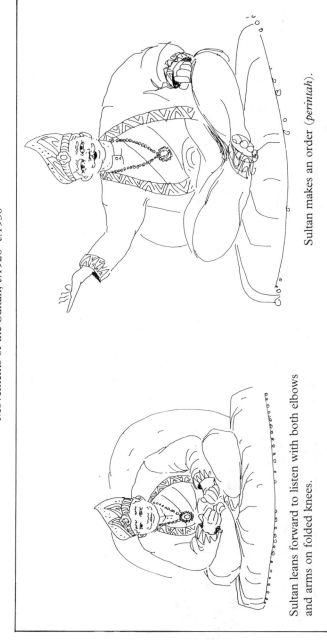

Sultan makes an order (*perintah*).

Sultan leans forward to listen with both elbows and arms on folded knees.

Source: Drawings by Mohd. Bahroodin Ahmad.

114

FIGURE 7.5
Hand Movements of the *Puteri* and the *Orang Muda*, c.1920–c.1930

The *puteri* (princess) sings of her love for the hero.

The *orang muda* (hero) sings of his love for the princess.

Source: Drawings by Mohd. Bahroodin Ahmad.

Similarities and Differences between Wayang and
Bangsawan Characters

It is clear that *bangsawan* characters had much in common with characters of the traditional *wayang*. Characters were divided into *halus* and
kasar types, and each character had specific functions, movements,
speeches, and voices. It was not so much what was said but the way it
was said that revealed the nature, motivation, and inner feelings of the
characters. In times of emotional crises, lengthy laments were made by
the heroine. She sang in sobbing fashion to arouse the sympathy of the
audience. It hardly mattered if the audience could not make out the
exact words sung.

Through the characters, the audience was familiarized with the
accepted mode of conduct and behaviour in Malay society. The characters indicated the proper way to address royalty; before addressing the
Sultan substantively, one begged for forgiveness: '*Ampun Tuanku beribu-
ribu ampun.*' In replying to an order, the court official would say '*titah
dijunjung di batu jemala patik*' [your orders are carried on the crown of
my skull]. Before dying or leaving the country, one asked the Sultan and
friends to forgive all one's sins. The behaviour of *bangsawan* characters
also indicated the correct way to treat one's elders: one had to obey
one's parents even in the selection of marriage partners.

Women in *bangsawan* stories were portrayed as refined princesses or
comic maids. They corresponded to stereotypes of women portrayed in
traditional *wayang*. As in *wayang*, the noble refined woman who was
totally devoted to her husband was idealized. Sometimes, an assertive
princess such as Wan Senari appeared in plays such as *Laksamana
Bentan*. However, she was not positively portrayed, and in fact was to
die at the end of the play. It was only occasionally in plays set outside
the courts such as *Sam Pek Eng Tai* that the woman dared to imperson-
ate a man so as to get an education.

Similar though *bangsawan* characters were in many respects to those
of the *wayang*, there were differences. In contrast to the characters of
traditional *wayang* which were stylized, characters in *bangsawan* signified
realism to the performers and audience. Costume style was determined
by the location and time period of the play. *Bangsawan* strove for
authenticity in costume (at least according to the imagination of the performers), and Chinese, Middle Eastern, Javanese, Indian, and Western
costumes were designed for the respective plays (Figures 7.6–7.13).
However, 'a great deal of imagination' was still required of the audience
when, for example, the actor came out in front of the street scene,
explaining that he had 'now arrived in a certain country', only to re-
appear five minutes later on the same scene, singing that he was 'now
one thousand miles away and so on' (*Straits Echo*, 2 July 1910).

The promotion of authenticity in costume (and as discussed earlier, in
setting and instrumental combinations) was part of a general tendency
towards realism[7] in Malay theatre. Realism was marked in *sandiwara*
which emphasized contemporary and nationalistic themes (see

116

FIGURE 7.6
Characters and Costumes in the Chinese Play *Sam Pek Eng Tai*,
c.1920–c.1930

Ordinary *samfu* for men

Men's costume for wedding (red)
and for ordinary occasions (blue)

Ordinary *samfu* for women

Wedding dress for women

Source: Drawings by Mohd. Bahroodin Ahmad.

FIGURE 7.7

Characters and Costumes in the Classical Play *Hamlet,*
*c.*1920–*c.*1930

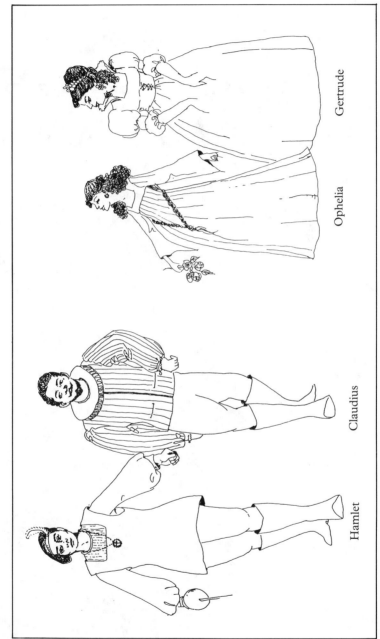

Hamlet   Claudius   Ophelia   Gertrude

Source: Drawings by Mohd. Bahroodin Ahmad.

FIGURE 7.8

Characters and Costumes in the Hindustani Play *Gul Bakawali,*
*c.*1920–*c.*1930

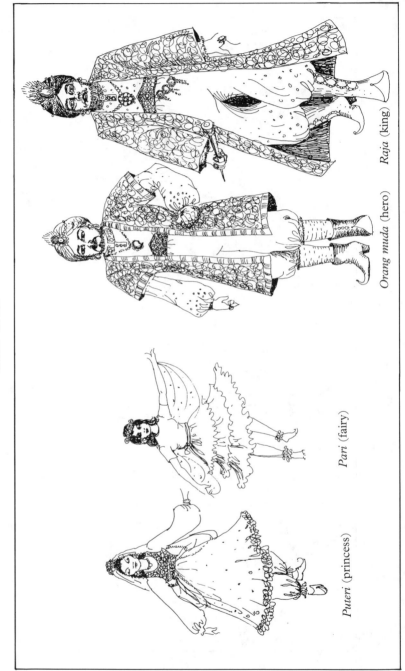

Puteri (princess)

Pari (fairy)

Orang muda (hero)

Raja (king)

Source: Drawings by Mohd. Bahroodin Ahmad.

FIGURE 7.9

Characters and Costumes in the Javanese Play *Panji Semerang*,
c.1920–c.1930

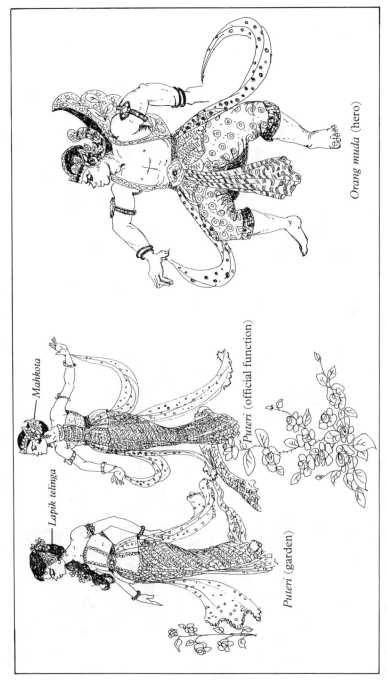

Orang muda (hero)

Mahkota

Puteri (official function)

Lapik telinga

Puteri (garden)

Source: Drawings by Mohd. Bahroodin Ahmad.

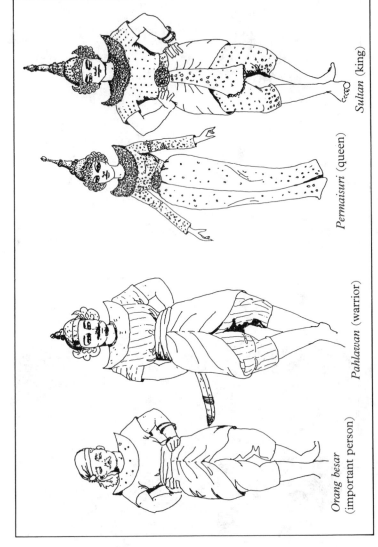

FIGURE 7.10

Characters and Costumes in the Thai Play *Raja Bersiong,*
*c.*1920–*c.*1930

Orang besar
(important person)

Pahlawan (warrior)

Permaisuri (queen)

Sultan (king)

Source: Drawings by Mohd. Bahroodin Ahmad.

FIGURE 7.11

The *Dayang, Inang, Sultan,* and *Permaisuri* and Their Costumes
in the Malay Play *Laksamana Bentan, c.*1920–*c.*1930

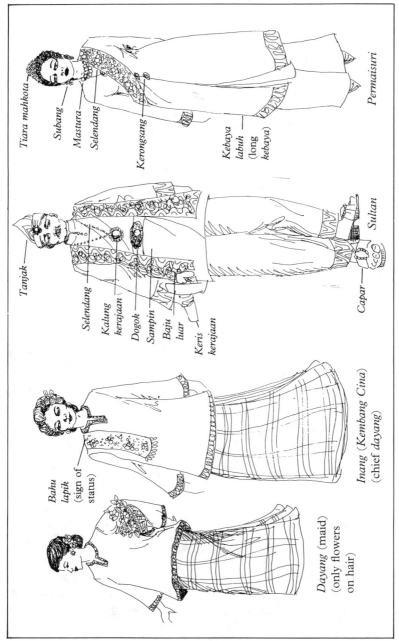

Source: Drawings by Mohd. Bahroodin Ahmad.

122

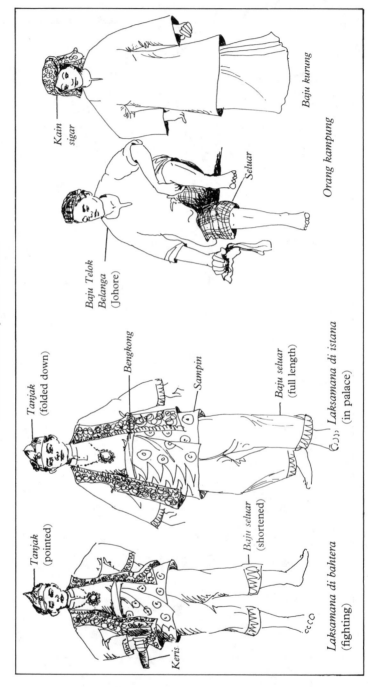

FIGURE 7.12

The *Laksamana di Bahtera*, *Laksamana di Istana*, and *Orang Kampung* and Their Costumes in the Malay Play *Laksamana Bentan*, c.1920–c.1930

Kain sigar

Baju kurung

Orang kampung

Baju Telok Belanga (Johore)

Seluar

Tanjak (folded down)

Bengkong

Sampin

Baju seluar (full length)

Laksamana di istana (in palace)

Tanjak (pointed)

Baju seluar (shortened)

Keris

Laksamana di bahtera (fighting)

Source: Drawings by Mohd. Bahroodin Ahmad.

FIGURE 7.13

The *Puteri* and Her Costumes in the Malay Play *Laksamana Bentan*
and the Heroine and Her Costumes in the Modern Malay Play
Bawang Merah Bawang Puteh, c.1920–c.1930

Heroine in *Bawang Merah Bawang Puteh*

Puteri in *Laksamana Bentan*

Source: Drawings by Mohd. Bahroodin Ahmad.

Chapter 3), culminating in the 1960s when realistic plays depicting everyday life and contemporary issues in closely observed detail were produced (Nanney, 1983: 48).

As part of the trend towards realism in *bangsawan*, there was a more open, though sometimes exaggerated, display of feeling in some scenes.[8] As expected, this melodramatic quality was adapted from Western theatre and film. In moments of emotional crisis, *halus* characters cried, sobbed, sang, or fainted. When, for example, the Laksamana heard that the princess was going to die, he cried and sang the *lagu nasib*. When the Sultan heard that his son was dead, he fainted in shock at the news. Villains, in contrast, would beat their chests and tear their clothes in an emotional crisis. As a reviewer once wrote of an actress's portrayal of emotion: 'Her portrayal of the elementary emotions is really great acting. In fear, for instance, she does not strike a grotesque attitude, with eyeballs rolling in a stage frenzy. No, she feels fear, and makes you feel that she is afraid.' (*Straits Echo*, 25 July 1908.)

Lovers in *bangsawan* showed more emotion than lovers in *wayang*, and were allowed to touch hands, giggle, and sit next to each other. If the hero disliked a woman, he could show it physically: during one performance, Hamlet not only refused to marry Ophelia but spat at her (*Straits Echo*, 14 November 1908). In another performance, Hamlet knocked Ophelia 'down eight times' (*Straits Echo*, 11 January 1912).

Even dying on stage was an energetic affair. There was groaning, gasping for breath, and stretching of the body (and often stage-blood oozed out from the dying character). For instance, when *Hamlet* was performed in 1912, it was reported that 'Laertes died with half a dozen convincing shudders and kicks' (*Times of Malaya*, 11 January 1912). On another occasion, King Claudius 'pranced about like a scalded cat' and 'delighted the little boys with some really superb face-pulling' before he was allowed to die (*Straits Echo*, 5 October 1932).

In contrast to the high degree of emotional control and restraint (except for the clowns) in traditional *wayang*, there was greater public expression of individual emotion in *bangsawan*. Conflicts within the individual, say between 'love' and 'duty', were openly expressed, especially in the new plays like *Sam Pek Eng Tai* and *Laila Majnun*. These conflicts were never really resolved, though; lovers who were not permitted by their parents to marry never disobeyed but died instead.

In line with the tendency towards realism, more realistic speech was employed in *bangsawan* than in traditional *wayang*, which used a 'heightened form of local dialect' and special *wayang* words (Sweeney, 1972: 63). The actual language employed in Malay courts was adopted whenever there were court scenes. Clowns and villagers employed *bahasa pasar*, the language spoken among all races in the urban marketplace, and Chinese and Indian characters would speak Malay with their characteristic distinctive accents. In love scenes, terms of endearment like *adinda* and *abang* were used.

Below is one example of how a foreign play *Hamlet* was altered using conventions familiar to both *bangsawan* audience and actor.

Adaptation of *Hamlet*

Bangsawan renditions of foreign works like *Hamlet* were not direct translations of the original script but adaptations. As a European writer once wrote (*Straits Echo*, 20 October 1928): 'A Shakespearean entertainment is particularly ludicrous to European spectators by reason of their familiarity with the original, but players and Oriental playgoers perpetrate and accept the wildest incongruities with intense gravity.' This, though, was for good reason. Foreign works like *Hamlet* were changed to suit the tastes of the audience and to facilitate communication. They were also altered because actors did not read the original scripts but were only told the outline of the plot before each performance. Indeed, the actors' only knowledge of Shakespeare was the sight of an occasional rendering of Shakespeare by a foreign troupe. As a result, performances of works like *Hamlet* were transformed using the scene types and stock characters which *bangsawan* performers and audiences were familiar with.[9]

Scenes

As in other *bangsawan* plays, the plot of *Hamlet* was built by deciding on the *babak* and their sequence. Minah Alias related that the following *babak* were played when she performed *Hamlet* in the 1930s. Variations occurred depending on the occasion, availability of performers, and the time available:

Babak 1: *Taman Istana* (Garden of the Palace—Queen Gertrude murders the King by putting a poisonous leaf in his ear while he is sleeping);
Babak 2: *Kubur* (Graveyard—Ghost of the King appears and tells the two clowns and Hamlet about the murder);
Babak 3: *Rumah Ophelia* (House of Ophelia—Hamlet invites everyone to a performance);
Babak 4: *Opera* (Opera—dumb-show re-enacting the murder is performed);
Babak 5: *Istana* (Palace—Laertes goes overseas);
Babak 6: *Istana* (Palace—Hamlet meets with Ophelia, rejects her, and kills her father);
Babak 7: *Sungai* (River—Ophelia commits suicide);
Babak 8: *Kubur* (Graveyard—Laertes declares that he will avenge Ophelia's death and fights Hamlet);
Babak 9: *Istana* (Palace—Hamlet shows his mother pictures of his father and Claudius and tries to make her feel guilty);
Babak 10: *Istana* (Palace—Hamlet, Gertrude, and Claudius die).

Compared to the Shakespearian script (Kean, 1859), fewer scenes were performed in *bangsawan*. The main story-line was, however, kept. Often, scenes in one act of the *Hamlet* script were combined to make one *babak* in *bangsawan* (see the comparison of four versions of *Hamlet* in Appendix 2). For example, Act 1 of Charles Kean's version of *Hamlet* comprised the following scenes: the ghost appears (a platform before the castle), Laertes asks for permission to depart for France (a room of state in the palace), Ophelia declares her love for Hamlet (a room in Polonius' house), the ghost appears again (the platform), and the ghost

speaks to Hamlet (more remote part of platform). In *bangsawan*, these
five scenes were combined into one or two: the ghost appears to some
clowns who report to Hamlet; Hamlet comes to the grave, and Hamlet's
father relates to Hamlet the story behind his death.

Scenes from different acts were also combined and changed. For
instance, the encounters between Ophelia and Hamlet were often combined into one to two scenes: Hamlet rejects Ophelia, knocks her, and
kills her father in one scene, and Ophelia kills herself by falling into the
pond, sea, or river in another. Whereas the death of Ophelia was
announced by the Queen in the Shakespearian script (Kean, 1859), in
bangsawan Ophelia was shown to fall into the sea. As one reviewer
wrote:

Hamlet was as mean as he could be to her [Opeelyer]. It was purely in mistake
that he slew her father, Tungku Polonius, but he was quite deliberate in
snatching back the diamond solitaire engagement ring he had given her and in
knocking her about. He knocked her down 8 times—we counted. Fortunately
she fell right on a soft part, each time, or she'd never be able to go on acting. As
it was, it made her real mad, and after announcing her intention in 19 verses to
the air of 'Ah che la morte', she plunged into the sea.... (*Times of Malaya*,
11 January 1912.)

Scenes were also often excluded due to time limitations or the fact
that performers thought them minor. As Winstedt commented in his
review of a performance of *Hamlet* (*Straits Echo*, 14 November 1908),
after the love scene between Hamlet and Ophelia the 'remaining scenes'
were 'slurred' till 'the last scene of indiscriminate slaughter'. Winstedt
further indicated that 'scenes that offend[ed] Malay taste or superstition
like the gravedigger scene or the scene where Hamlet upbraids his
mother' were excised altogether (*Straits Echo*, 14 November 1908).

Besides omitting and combining scenes, new scenes not found in
Shakespeare were added. *Bangsawan* performances of *Hamlet* often
began with an *istana* scene, as was conventional in other *bangsawan*
stories centred around the court. As shown below, an *istana* scene
opened a performance of *Hamlet* even though the Shakespearian script
began with the graveyard scene.

The curtain rises on a room in the palace, represented by a canvas back-ground
painted with yellow bricks, blue square-paved windows and red curtains. A high
dais serves for the throne and windsor chairs are placed [for] the queen and
councillors. The King of Denmark, arrayed in a costume which but for black
spectacles, would do credit to a circus performer, pulls terrific moustaches, signs
off his estate and degree and the incident of his recent marriage; then sinks into
prose and addresses the Queen, a half-caste Dutch girl, and Polonius, a bearded
vizier in turban, spangled velvet coat and carpet-slippers. She expresses fear for
Hamlet's sanity and Polonius with an obsequious shuffle of carpet-slippers and
due pulling of beard hurries off to enquire into the business. The curtain falls.
(*Straits Echo*, 14 November 1908.)

In addition, small subscenes were added to give the performance a
local flavour. As an illustration, a new subscene where people of

different ethnic backgrounds bought tickets to the dumb show to be staged by Hamlet was added to a 1912 production (*Times of Malaya*, 11 January 1912):

A towkay and his nonia had to pay. The ticket seller at the door said that *satu* [one] class was *satu ringgit* [one dollar], *dua* [two] class *dua ringgit* [two dollars] and so on. A Malay fisherman and an Indian lady got in for 20 cents each, but so far as we could understand, that was due to favouritism. The ticket seller, a handsome youth had a penchant for the Indian lady. The Malay seemed rather annoyed about it. Even a blind Sikh tapped his way in and the human ticket seller mocked his blindness....

Entertainment interludes were also included. In a 1932 performance of *Hamlet*, for instance,

after the love scene between Hamlet and Ophelia, a Court Lady glided in and sang: 'What are you waiting for now?' ... [Then the audience was given] ... a unique insight into life at the Danish Court; seven ladies of high degree came and gave exquisite shimmy; Ophelia sang appallingly in her private apartments, and Horatio with a few waves of his hands made a lady float in mid-air and passed a golden hoop round her to show that there was no deception. (*Straits Echo*, 5 October 1932.)

In another performance, it was reported that

after Hamlet leaves the court, he reappears in an admirable interlude of a white *tuan* (master) engaging a *dhobie* (washerman). His boy (servant) produces the *dhobie* and explains his qualifications, then the audience rocks with delight, as the master explains, in bad Malay, all that he expects in way of service. At that moment, a small child entertains the house with a song and dance—very demure and very decorous, but making her exit with a wave of her hands.... (*Straits Echo*, 4 June 1923; Wise, 1985: 201–2.)

As in other *bangsawan* stories, such entertainment interludes (as well as the extra turns included between *babak*) blurred the linearity of the plot.

Besides omitting, combining, and altering some scenes, other scenes not emphasized in an English performance were stressed and prolonged in *bangsawan*. In the Shakespearian script, when the King ordered Hamlet to leave for England after he had killed Polonius, Hamlet walked off the stage. The details of how he returned were not shown. In the next scene, Hamlet had already returned and indicated he wished to see the King the next day. In the *bangsawan* renditions of *Hamlet*, the details of Hamlet's trip and his return were portrayed. In the 1912 version, Hamlet jumped from one ship to another (*Times of Malaya*, 11 January 1912):

When in mid-ocean, on a one funnel steamer called 'The Star Line', he met a cruiser going back to Denmark, and just as they were passing, he jumped from one to the other. The scene was very realistic. The sea was rough, and the cruiser pitched and rolled so much that we could see her triple expansion engine. It had bare brown arms and a blue singlet. Hamlet turned up again at the Court, and Claudius and his mother pretended to be glad to see him. He shook hands with both. When he was telling the Sultana lies about all he had seen in England—he described England as a *negri banyak bagus* [very good country], though he hadn't got so far....

In the 1932 version (*Straits Echo*, 5 October 1932), to make it more exciting for the audience, a fighting scene was introduced: 'Hamlet booked two first-class railway tickets for his journey to England ... he was ambushed by bandits ... [but] ... he pacified them....'

Finally, to further add to the local flavour, backdrops used in the various scenes usually included paintings of some local building, tree, or plant. As one reviewer stated, 'stock sets' consisting of Western 'palatial halls' and gardens usually included 'a view of Singapore with St. Andrew's Cathedral looming large in the background' (*Times of Malaya*, 11 January 1912). In addition, Ophelia 'plunged into the sea ... on the shores of which coconut grew and marble mosques and things' (*Times of Malaya*, 11 January 1912).

Characters

As in the scene types, characters of foreign plays like *Hamlet* were also altered according to *bangsawan* conventions. Heroes and heroines were given the characteristics of heroes and heroines of *bangsawan*. The hero Hamlet, for example, was faithful to his murdered father and was determined to take revenge and see justice done. He was a good fighter, heroic, brave, 'easeful and majestic in his carriage and demeanour' (*Straits Echo*, 5 October 1932). Although he wore 'green plush breeches, pumps and a Cavalier hat' (*Straits Echo*, 14 November 1908), Hamlet was the typical hero of *bangsawan*.

The heroine Ophelia was delicate, good, meek and refined. As the *bangsawan* heroine, she suffered a great deal and was said to 'sob ... quite a lot' and 'imported a pathos into her parts' (*Times of Malaya*, 11 January 1912). She was knocked down and spat at (*Times of Malaya*, 11 January 1912; *Straits Echo*, 14 November 1908). Still, she was faithful in love, and devoted to father, brother, and lover.

The villains, King Claudius and Queen Gertrude, were evil. The Sultana Gertrude was described as 'tragically wicked' by a reviewer (*Times of Malaya*, 11 January 1912). According to *bangsawan* models, the evil king had a 'moustache' which he pulled (*Straits Echo*, 14 November 1908).

Polonius, the Prime Minister, was a 'bearded vizier in turban, spangled velvet coat and carpet-slippers' (*Straits Echo*, 14 November 1908) while Horatio, the friend of Hamlet, became 'a policeman dressed in sergeant's khaki uniform and football boots and brandishing a scimitar'.

The clowns were 'familiar beggar clowns who figure[d] in all Malay productions, with baggy pantaloons and face painted with vermilion streaks. Their banter was almost purely topical and was varied by such popular numbers as "Over there" and "Daisy, Daisy, give me your answer do".' (*Straits Echo*, 20 October 1928.)

Besides giving characters from foreign plays the characteristics of *bangsawan* characters, minor characters like the courtiers (Rosencrantz and Guildenstern) were often replaced by local *pahlawan* (warriors), or left out completely. Guards such as Marcellus and Bernado in *Hamlet* were sometimes substituted by humorous characters like PC 142 and his sergeant (*Straits Echo*, 18 February 1907) or by clowns named 'Sunday' and 'Monday'.

Furthermore, names of characters were Malayanized. Hamlet became H. H. Pramas Hamlet, Rajah of Denmark (*Times of Malaya*, 11 January 1912) or Tuan Omelet (*Straits Echo*, 20 October 1928); Queen Gertrude, Sultana Gertrude (*Times of Malaya*, 11 January 1912); King Claudius, Rajah Claudius; Ophelia, Opeelyer; and Polonius, Tungku Polonius.[10]

Lastly, the fates of characters were altered accordingly. As virtue had to win over vice in *bangsawan*, evil characters like King Claudius and Queen Gertrude always died. However, since Polonius and Hamlet were supposedly good characters, their fates were sometimes changed. On one occasion, Polonius did not die at the end but stood looking at the dead. On another occasion, after everyone had died, Hamlet went off to see a witch who gave him herbs to save his life.

* * *

Where scene types and stock characters were concerned, *bangsawan* restated the conventions already known to the multi-ethnic audience and to the actor. Even so, *bangsawan* was clearly influenced by trends in Western theatre and film, and a new tendency towards realism was evident in the stage setting, plot structure, and stock characters (though not fully articulated). What had in traditional theatre served primarily as a performing space with few signals of location became a more fully represented, real place outlined by realistically drawn scenic backdrops and stage props. Stories were increasingly set in known periods and in countries like China or Malacca, instead of some timeless fantasy world, for *bangsawan* performers were concerned with re-creating the setting of plays as they imagined them to be. Hence, gardens in Indian stories were made to look like gardens in India. Furthermore, there was greater realism in the portrayal of characters through emotions, costumes, language, speeches, and acting style. Plot became more linear, although the linearity was often obscured by the songs, dances, and novelty acts, and the interaction between the performers and the audience. Fairy-tales were still popular, but stories with tragic endings where conflicts between duty and love occurred were introduced. These stories and other Malay historical ones excluded supernatural intervention from the dramatic action, so that human action was played in human terms.

This tendency towards realism articulated the changes in the social relations between man and material environment in the new urban areas of Malaya where life was increasingly secular. A realization that the world was man-made, and that man, not supernatural beings, determined his own life pervaded the content of theatre. Yet, the belief that all man's activities had somehow to do with the supernatural world was not totally erased. Thus, spirits were appeased when the stage was set up, though the opening and closing ceremonies for propitiating spirits were shortened or even omitted (see Chapter 2).

Bangsawan in the 1920s and 1930s was, in short, a theatrical arena in which the elements of a society, economy, and culture undergoing change and subject to foreign influences were shown to be interacting; specifically in its stage setting, plot structure, and character types, it could be seen that *bangsawan* actively incorporated these new elements while retaining those which were familiar to both audience and per-formers and which derived from the traditional theatre that preceded it.

1. The *bangsawan* scene type was similar to the 'sub-scene' of the *wayang Siam* which also occurred in one locale. According to formal divisions discussed by Sweeney (1980: 53), a number of 'sub-scenes' made up a scene. Sweeney defines a scene in the *wayang Siam* as 'a section of continuous drama, opened and closed by formulas such as '*timbul royat*' and '*hilang royat*'. For him, a new scene in the *wayang* 'occurs when none of the characters appearing at the end of a section of repertoire appears at the beginning of the following sections, and there is thus no character able to carry over the action from one section to the next' (Sweeney, 1980: 52).

2. 'Kalau laut macam laut betul, kalau batu, betul-betul macam batu.'

3. For a comparison of the scene types in *ketoprak* and the *wayang* in Java, see Hatley (1979).

4. See Hatley (1985: Chapter 1) for a discussion of the plot structure of *ketoprak*. The linearity of the *ketoprak* plot structure is also often blurred.

5. For a detailed description of the characters, see Ghulam Sarwar (n.d.).

6. See Sweeney (1972: 54–6) for a comparison of character types in the Malay shadow play. The characteristics of *bangsawan* role types are similar to those of *ketoprak* (Hatley, 1985).

7. Brockett (1980: 184) states that an advocate of realism 'strive[s] to depict truthfully the real world ... since he can know the real world only through direct observation, he should write about the society around him and should be as objective as possible'. The sets are detailed representations of the surroundings.

8. There were parallels in *ketoprak* characters as well (Hatley, 1985).

9. In this, *bangsawan* merely perpetuated the tradition of foreign drama being con-stantly 'localized' in South-East Asia (Brandon, 1967: 113). The *Ramayana* which originated in India is adapted and presented in Thailand, Malaysia, and Java using a mixture of local and foreign elements.

10. Likewise, it is interesting to note that in a performance of *Dr. Faust* by Goethe, 'Marguerite' became 'Siti Merkaji'; 'Valentine', 'Felantain'; and 'Mephistopheles', 'Satan'.

8
Categories of *Lagu* and Their Dramatic Uses in the 1920s and 1930s

As the stage director relied on scene types and stock characters to build his story, the musical director or bandmaster had a repertoire of musical pieces or *lagu* to cover all eventualities. These *lagu* helped to evoke mood, establish characters, convey ideas, or accompany action in the plot of the story.

As in traditional *wayang*, specific musical pieces were used for specific dramatic situations in the *bangsawan* plot.[1] These pieces were either instrumentally accompanied songs, in which case they were simply called *lagu*, or they were purely instrumental music in which case they were called *lagu gad*. (None of the *bangsawan* performers could give me a literal translation of *gad*.) Each *lagu* had a specific rhythmic pattern, metre, and tempo associated with it. These musical elements helped the audience to identify the type of scene, character, or mood being portrayed.

As new urban commercial theatre, *lagu* in *bangsawan* were also quite different from *lagu* in traditional *wayang*. They mainly comprised popular musical genres which accompanied social dancing among the various ethnic groups in the urban areas of Malaya. To attract the multi-ethnic audience, new *lagu* which had been popularized by Western marching bands, touring theatrical groups, gramophone records, and radio were constantly incorporated. These *lagu* used rhythmic patterns and melodies from Malaya, Europe, America, Latin America, the Middle East, India, Java, and other parts of the world.

In order to define the relationship between *lagu* and dramatic situation and to specify the differences between the *lagu* of traditional theatre and of *bangsawan*, it is necessary first to define the musical forms used in *bangsawan*. The contexts of these musical forms will then be located in several stories. Musical examples of 78 r.p.m. recordings presented here are mainly those used in the plays described in Chapter 6: *Jula Juli Bintang Tiga* (*cerita klasik*), *Puteri Gunong Ledang* (*cerita Melayu*), *Laila Majnun* (*cerita Arab*), *Sam Pek Eng Tai* (*cerita Cina*), and *Noor-E-Islam* (*cerita Hindustan*). These recordings were made in the 1930s.

Rentak, *Irama*, and Dramatic Situation

Two basic criteria used by *bangsawan* performers for distinguishing *lagu* provide the bases for discussion. These criteria are *rentak* (rhythmic pattern) and *irama* (tempo).

1. *Rentak*. Each *lagu* had a characteristic rhythmic pattern associated with it which was played by the frame drum, Western drum, bass of the piano, or plucked bass.
2. *Irama*. Each *lagu* was also characterized by a certain speed at which it was performed, and this concept included metre and rhythm.

The discussion of *lagu* below will follow five broad categories used by *bangsawan* performers to classify them: (1) *Irama Orang Putih* (Western tempo, rhythm, and metre); (2) *Irama Melayu* (Malay tempo, rhythm, and metre); (3) *Irama Padang Pasir/Arab* (Middle Eastern/Arabic tempo, rhythm, and metre); and (4) *Irama Hindustan* (Hindustani tempo, rhythm, and metre); and (5) *Irama Jawa* (Javanese tempo, rhythm, and metre).

Irama Orang Putih

The *lagu* or musical genres in this category were usually accompanied by a Western orchestra consisting of some or all of the following instruments: violin, flute, clarinet, cornet or trumpet, trombone, saxophone, guitar, Hawaiian guitar, piano, and drum.

Waltz

The waltz is a dance in triple time which is characterized by an 'oom-pah-pah' rhythmic pattern (Example 8.1):

EXAMPLE 8.1
Waltz Rhythm

In Europe, the waltz had become the most popular ballroom dance of the nineteenth century. Large dance halls were opened in Vienna and composers of waltzes such as Johann Strauss and Joseph Lanner achieved popularity abroad (Lamb, 1980: 200–4). During the late nineteenth century, composers from other parts of the world began to compose waltzes as well. They included the Mexican Juventino Rosas, who wrote the famous 'Over the Waves' in 1891 (Behague, 1980a: 529).

Waltzes became important ingredients of operetta troupes in Europe (Lamb, 1980: 204). Some of these troupes toured Malaya in the late nineteenth and twentieth centuries, and brought waltzes with them. Waltzes were also performed by town bands and introduced to the urban population. The programmes of the Penang Band on 22 November 1904 included two waltzes: 'The Chorister' by Retford and 'Die Prager' by Andres (*Straits Echo*, 22 November 1904). Such waltzes as 'Toekang Kayoe Wals' and 'Bloemen Wals' which were recorded by the Gramophone and Typewriter Ltd. in 1903 also helped to popularize the form (Gramophone and Typewriter Ltd., 1903: Cat. nos. 2–12090 and 13515 respectively).

Waltzes were adopted into the *bangsawan* musical repertoire to attract the multi-ethnic audience. The waltz rhythmic pattern (played by the drum, piano bass, or plucked bass) and tempo ($\downarrow \simeq 144$) were used in classical, Arabic, and Hindustani stories when the king conversed with his queen, ministers, or children. 'Danube Waves' (known as 'Donou Walen' in *bangsawan*) was one such example. Example 8.2 is an old score of the piece which was given to me by Ahmad Shariff, a *bangsawan* musician who works in Radio and Television Malaysia today. Each character sang a section of the song. This musical piece was called *lagu cakap* (musical piece for dialogue).

It is interesting to note that the *komedi stambul* (created by A. Mahieu in 1891) of Java was said to have used 'dance music' comprising 'mainly popular marches, waltzes, polkas, polka mazurkas etc.'. Manusama mentioned the names of two waltzes played in a performance of *Djoela Djoeli Bintang Tiga* that he saw in 1894. These two waltzes were 'Donou Walen' and 'Eldorado' (a Spanish waltz) (Manusama, 1922: 3, 22–3).

EXAMPLE 8.2
A 1930s Score of 'Donou Walen'

Source: Courtesy of Pak Ahmad Shariff.

The relatively slow type of waltz known as 'English waltz', which became internationally popular[2] in the ballroom from about 1910, was also adopted in *bangsawan*. This slow waltz was derived from the 'Boston Waltz' which originated in the United States of America in the 1870s. Many such waltzes were adaptations of popular song hits such as 'Ramona' and 'Parlami d'Amore' (Lamb, 1980c: 206).

Such slow waltzes were frequently used in classical, Arabic, and Hindustani plays to express separation from a loved one or to bewail ill-luck. They were called *lagu nasib* (songs of fate). The rhythmic pattern was usually played on the piano. In the play *Jula Juli Bintang Tiga*, the song 'Penceraian Jula Juli dengan Sultan' (♩ = 74) was an adaptation of the Spanish slow waltz 'Ah Che La Morte' (Example 8.3; see Transcription 6.7 in Chapter 6). Jula Juli and the Sultan both sang this song in a garden scene by the sea as they said farewell to each other. Minah Alias emphasized that the same song was sung by Ophelia (in Shakespeare's *Hamlet*) just before the latter drowned herself.

EXAMPLE 8.3

Slow Waltz (*Lagu Nasib*): 'Penceraian Jula Juli dengan Sultan'

Source: 78 r.p.m. record (1930s), Chap Kuching (NG 30).

Both the slow and fast waltzes could also be used as *lagu taman* (song for the garden scene). Jula Juli sang a slow waltz 'Teribet Jula Juli' (♪ = 84) (Examples 8.4 and 8.5) when she was playing with her goose in the sea by the garden. (Pieces in 6/8 metre were considered to be waltzes by veteran performers.)

'Telesmat Bintang Satu dan Dua' (Example 8.6), on the other hand, was in fast waltz time (♩ = 152). This was sung by the three sisters (Jula Juli Satu, Dua, and Tiga) and their fairies when they were playing in the garden in heaven. The three sisters sat behind cardboard stars which were broken one at a time.

EXAMPLE 8.4
Slow Waltz (*Lagu Taman*): 'Teribet Jula Juli'

Source: 78 r.p.m. record (1930s), Chap Kuching (NG 29).

EXAMPLE 8.5
A 1930s Score of 'Teribet Jula Juli'

Source: Courtesy of Pak Ahmad Shariff.

EXAMPLE 8.6
Fast Waltz (*Lagu Taman/Kayangan*): 'Telesmat Bintang Satu dan Dua'

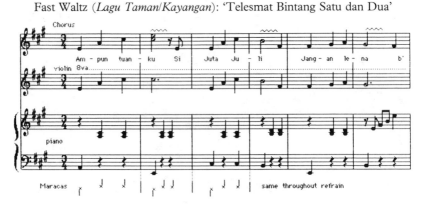

Source: 78 r.p.m. record (1930s), Chap Kuching (NG 31).

March

Marches are musical pieces written in common time with strong repetitive rhythms. They usually have 'introductory fanfares' which are 'followed by opening sections played by the whole band' featuring 'broad lyrical melodies' (Lamb, 1980a: 652).

In the nineteenth century, many different marches with lively rhythms were played to accompany popular dances. 'The Washington Post' by the famous American march composer John Philip Sousa, for instance, is 'linked to the two-step and is said to have led to the use of two step marches in the cakewalk' (Lamb, 1980a: 652).

Marches were introduced into Malaya by military and town bands as well as circus bands. The Penang Band's programme on 22 November 1904 (*Straits Echo*) included a march by Costa called 'A Frangesca' while the Town Band's programme on 30 August 1906 (*Straits Echo*) included a quick march by Rosy called 'Hurrah Boys'.

Marches were commonly used in *bangsawan*; they were sung by the *jin* (genie), a *kasar* character. Veteran performers emphasized that only *lagu garang-garang* (fierce songs) like the march could be used for the appearances of the *jin* character.

Marches were also used as background music (*lagu gad*) for fighting scenes in classical, Hindustani, and Arabic stories. 'Colonel Bogey' (1914) by K. J. Alford was a favourite march in *bangsawan* (Example 8.7). The 'Colonel Bogey' march was mentioned as one of the foreign songs (*lagu dagang*) used in *bangsawan* at the 'Forum on Bangsawan Music' which was organized by the Ministry of Culture, Youth and Sports on 4 June 1977 in Kuala Lumpur.

Other marches used in *bangsawan* included the 'Kampak Besar Marsche' by the Indra Zanibar Orchestra and the 'Songangan Marsche' by Jacobs (Gramophone and Typewriter Ltd., 1903: Cat. nos. 10621 and 2–12077 respectively). Manusama (1922) also wrote of the 'Monte-Carlo March' which was played during the *komedi stambul* performance of *Djoela Djoeli Bintang Tiga* in 1894.

EXAMPLE 8.7
Fanfare and Section of Tune of 'Colonel Bogey' (Whistled by Mat Arab)

Tango

The tango is a Latin American song and dance genre related to the Cuban contradanza, habanera, and Cuban tango.[3] All these dances are in duple metre (2/4) and use the following accompanimental patterns (Behague, 1980b: 563) (Example 8.8).

EXAMPLE 8.8
Tango Accompanimental Patterns

The internationalization of the tango took place during the first quarter of the twentieth century. This followed the modification of the movements, which were thought to be too abrupt for the ballroom, by a French dancer, Camille de Rhynal, in 1907 (Behague, 1980b: 564).

The tango became popular in England from 1912, when it was performed by the Gaiety Theatre in the play *The Sunshine Girl.* Following this, the tango was performed in dance halls, restaurants, and at tango parties or tango teas (Behague, 1980b: 564). Other stage shows such as the 'London Revue' featured the tango in their plays. *Hullo Tango* (1913) was one example (Lamb, 1980b: 94). In 1913, the *Times of Malaya* reported that the tango was 'danced in every drawing room' in England (*Times of Malaya,* 5 November 1913). Another article stated that the 'secret of its popularity' was its 'novelty' (*Straits Echo,* 8 December 1913). After World War I, the tango became the most popular ballroom dance and was featured in most dance competitions.

Town bands in Malaya were already performing tangos in the early twentieth century. The Penang Band performed 'La Paloma' by Balfour on 22 November 1904 (*Straits Echo*) while the Town Band performed 'Carmen' by Bizet on 30 August 1906 (*Straits Echo*).

The tango was soon adopted in *bangsawan.* Likewise, by 1922, the *komedi stambul* had incorporated 'modern art dances like the tango, foxtrot, one-step, cake-walk etc.' (Manusama, 1922: 10). The internationally popular tango 'La Cumparsita' by Gerardo Matos Rodriguez (1917) became associated with *keramaian* (celebration) scenes in classical, Arabic, and Hindustani *bangsawan* plays. It was often played as background music in such scenes. The rhythmic patterns were performed by the piano bass, plucked bass, or drum.

A tango melody entitled 'La Femme Qui Tue' played in Arabic plays (copied by Bai Kassim from Abdul Wahab of Cairo) in 1933 is shown in Example 8.9.

EXAMPLE 8.9
A 1933 Score of a Tango Piece, 'La Femme Qui Tue'

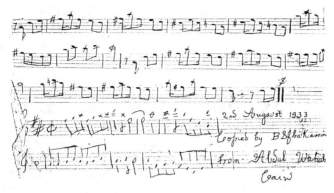

Source: Courtesy of Pak Ahmad Shariff.

Ragtime

Ragtime is a popular American style of piano playing. It is the effect created by a 'syncopated melodic line pitted against a rhythmically straightforward bass' (Talbot, 1980: 537) (Example 8.10).

EXAMPLE 8.10
'Maple Leaf Rag' (1899) by Scott Joplin

Source: Talbot (1980: 537).

Ragtime flourished between 1890 and World War I (1914–18) and was closely associated with dance. Two styles of ragtime emerged. One was led by Scott Joplin whose 'style of ragtime' was 'notable for its folklike, danceable character'. This 'classic' or 'Missouri Ragtime' accompanied the slow drag or cakewalk (Talbot, 1980: 537).

Another style called 'Eastern Ragtime' which developed in New York, Baltimore, and New Orleans was faster and more 'brilliant' in style. This style accompanied the 'animal dances' such as 'turkey trot' or 'chicken scratch' (Talbot, 1980: 537).

By the early twentieth century, commercial 'rags' were produced by mechanical pianos and piano rolls. Ragtime bands like the American Ragtime Octette introduced ragtime to Britain. Ragtime revues like 'Hullo, Rag-time' (1912) emerged. Ragtime dances which saw the foundation of a new era in social dance (Lamb, 1980b: 94) were performed in the dance halls of Europe.

Ragtime reached Malaya via the revues and variety shows which toured the country in the early twentieth century. Printed scores of ragtime pieces, widely disseminated throughout the world, were also sold in music stores of Malaya such as Barr and Co. (*Times of Malaya,* 1 July 1908). Ragtime was used to accompany cakewalk dances during the extra turns. The Wayang Komedi India Ratoe used to promise the audience 'many extra turns including a cakewalk' (*Straits Echo,* 1 December 1906).

As ragtime melodies were often strongly pentatonic, they were adapted to Malay texts and sung in Chinese plays. 'Shanghai Street' (Example 8.11; see Transcription 6.8 in Chapter 6) was a popular *lagu strit* with the ragtime syncopated melodic line played and sung against a straightforward bass played at ♪ = 132. As in many ragtime pieces, the piano was the only musical instrument used. In this piece, a servant who had been sent to look for a prince walked up and down the street looking for the house.

EXAMPLE 8.11
Ragtime (*Lagu Strit*): 'Shanghai Street'

Source: 78 r.p.m. record (1930s), His Master's Voice (P 15978).

Foxtrot

A social dance of the twentieth century, the foxtrot originated in the one-step, two-step, and syncopated ragtime dances (like turkey trot, grizzly bear, and bunny hug) of America after 1910 (Sadie, 1980: 738). 'The basis of the trot was a slow gliding walk at 2 beats per step and a fast trot at one beat per step. The tempo varied between 30 and 40 bars per minute and the dance could be done to almost any popular tune in simple duple metre with regular 4-bar phrases.' (Sadie, 1980: 738.)

During the 1920s, two distinct styles of foxtrot emerged: the slow foxtrot and the quickstep. The slow foxtrot was regarded as a response to nineteenth-century styles of social dance. 'It was danced at 30 bars per minute, with great attention to deportment using smooth gliding movements with feet pointing forward.' (Sadie, 1980: 738.)

The quickstep emerged as bands took up 'faster jazz-influenced' music in America. It became a hit in English social dance circles after Paul Whiteman's Band performed in England in 1923. It was danced at 50 or more bars per minute with simpler than foxtrot steps (Sadie, 1980: 738).

The foxtrot and quickstep soon made their way to Malaya through the 78 r.p.m. recordings, the gramophone, and vaudeville troupes visiting Malaya. There were descriptions about the new dances in the local newspapers. A correspondent, Maytum White, wrote in 1924 that 'the newest dance is a mixture of the one step and the foxtrot. It is called the quickstep.... The quickstep is played at a slower speed than the rather jaunty one-step rhythm, and yet it is quicker than the foxtrotting which has been universally recognized by dancers for the past few years.' (*Straits Echo*, 13 December 1924.)[4]

Soon after their advent, the quickstep and foxtrot were adopted by *bangsawan*.[5] The quickstep ($\downarrow$ = 94) was used in the song 'Telesmat Bintang Satu dan Dua' (Example 8.12) in the play *Jula Juli Bintang Tiga* to accompany the three sisters and their fairies as they sang and danced in heaven. 'Telesmat Bintang Satu dan Dua' could be considered as a *lagu taman* or *lagu kayangan*. In this song, Jula Juli Bintang Tiga asked her sisters and the fairies to go down to earth to give her son the magic bow and arrow.

EXAMPLE 8.12

Quickstep (*Lagu Taman/Kayangan*): 'Telesmat Bintang Satu dan Dua'

Source: 78 r.p.m. record (1930s), Chap Kuching (NG 31).

Irama Melayu

The musical genres in this category were usually accompanied by the *ronggeng asli*[6] ensemble (see Chapter 5) with Western instruments replacing some of the Malay instruments. The instruments usually consisted of the violin, piano (replacing the accordion or harmonium), and *rebana* (or the Western drum).

Asli

Asli (meaning 'traditional' or 'original') is the name of a slow, sad dance song with the following 8-beat rhythmic pattern played on a *rebana* (Example 8.13).[7]

EXAMPLE 8.13
Asli Rhythmic Pattern

Only the first beat of the first bar and the first, second, and third beats of the second bar are fixed. The other beats can be played differently, depending on the particular performer. Some examples of these variations are given in Example 8.14.

EXAMPLE 8.14
Variations of *Asli* Rhythmic Pattern

The above patterns are played by the right hand of the *rebana* player. The left hand often improvises 'tak' sounds in between the drum patterns as shown in Example 8.15.

EXAMPLE 8.15
Left-hand Improvisations of *Asli* Rhythmic Pattern

It has not been established when *asli* originated. But references to similar genres were made in Malay texts such as *Hikayat Hang Tuah* (Kassim Ahmad, 1973) and *Tuhfat al-Nafis* (Matheson and Andaya, 1982). *Hikayat Hang Tuah*, which dates from the seventeenth or eighteenth century, describes the singing of *pantun* to the accompaniment of the *rebana*, gong, and *kecapi* (a plucked string instrument). This ensemble resembled that of the *ronggeng asli* although the *kecapi* was used instead of the violin. As *asli* songs formed part of the *ronggeng* repertoire (Goldsworthy, 1979),[8] *asli* could have already existed in the seventeenth and eighteenth centuries.

Lagu asli had been sung during the extra turn sections of *bangsawan* since the beginning of the century. These songs were recorded by companies such as the Gramophone and Typewriter Ltd. Some examples which appeared in the Gramophone and Typewriter Co. Catalogue printed in 1903 included 'Het lied van de Tandjoengbloem' [The Song of Bunga Tanjung], commonly known as 'Bunga Tanjung', sung by Mohamad Hasan of Penang; and 'Boenga Mawar', sung by Gima of Samarang (Gramophone and Typewriter Ltd., 1903: Cat. nos. G. C. 12919 and 13526). *Lagu asli* also accompanied the slow *asli* dance during extra turns.

Musical pieces in *rentak asli* were performed in *bangsawan* only with the introduction of Malay stories into the *bangsawan* repertoire in the 1920s and 1930s. In fact, the majority of the musical pieces played and sung in Malay stories were in *rentak asli*. As shown in Appendix 3, most of the songs in the play *Puteri Gunong Ledang* (His Master's Voice, P 12760–P 12766) were *lagu asli*. After its introduction into the plots of Malay stories, *lagu asli* were gradually used to accompany several types of dramatic situations and characters in Javanese,[9] Arabic, Chinese,[10] and classical plays as well.

There were two types of *lagu asli*: slow-paced *asli* or *lagu sedih* (sad songs) and fast-paced *asli* or *lagu riang* (happy songs).[11] Slow-paced *asli* ($\downarrow$ = 60) or *lagu sedih* were sung during sad situations where separations or misfortune took place. These *lagu* helped to heighten emotions and evoke the appropriate mood. The slow tempo was associated with sadness.

For example, in the *cerita klasik Jula Juli Bintang Tiga*, the *asli* rhythmic pattern was used for the *lagu nasib* 'Puja Kamati Darsha Alam'

[Praying Over the Death of Darsha Alam] (Example 8.16). In this *lagu*, Baharom Alam wept and lamented that he had killed his own father. He wanted to commit suicide. His aunts and the fairies pitied him. From heaven, his mother begged him not to kill himself and promised to give him a bow and arrow that could make his father live again. The *asli* rhythmic pattern was played by the *rebana* while the piano bass interlocked with it. The 'dung' of the *rebana* and the low bass note of every 2 bars acted like the gong.

Asli played at a faster and livelier tempo ($\downarrow$ = 106) were used to accompany brighter and happier situations in Malay and Javanese plays. They could be employed when the king conversed with his ministers, queen, prince, or princess (*lagu cakap*); when the prince entertained himself (*lagu hiburan*); when the princess and her maids danced or when the prince met the princess in the garden (*lagu taman*); when the nursemaid wished to say something (*lagu pengasoh/inang*); and when there was a street scene (*lagu strit*).

EXAMPLE 8.16

Slow-paced *Asli* (*Lagu Sedih/Nasib*): 'Puja Kamati Darsha Alam'

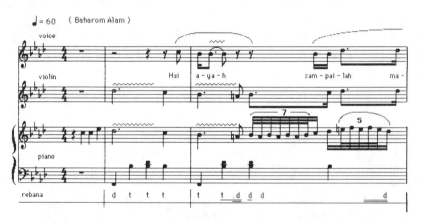

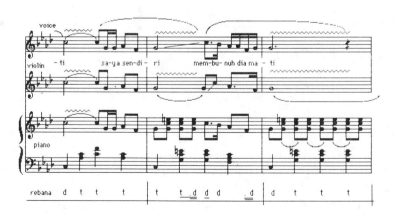

Source: 78 r.p.m. record (1930s), Chap Kuching (NG 32).

A *lagu riang* entitled 'Che Wan Gayah' from *Puteri Gunong Ledang* is given in Example 8.17. This *lagu* was sung by the nursemaid Che Wan Gayah as she summoned the palace maids and servants to get ready quickly so that they could take care of the prince. The 8-beat asli rhythmic pattern was played by the piano bass while the *rebana* interlocked with it. The low bass notes on the dominant and the tonic acted like the gong.

EXAMPLE 8.17

Fast-paced *Asli* (*Lagu Pengasoh/Inang*): 'Che Wan Gayah'

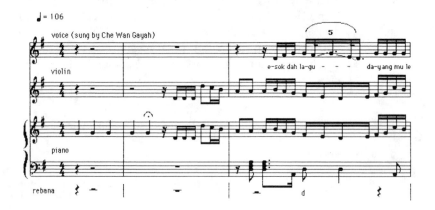

Source: 78 r.p.m. record (1930s), His Master's Voice (P 12760).

Inang

Inang (meaning 'wet nurse') is a lively, happy dance-song with a few rhythmic patterns associated with it. The most widely used one is shown in Example 8.18, which is played by the right hand of the *rebana* player. When the left hand improvises, the pattern usually becomes that shown in Example 8.19. *Inang* is normally played at a fast tempo ($\quarternote$ = 102).

EXAMPLE 8.18

Inang Rhythmic Pattern

EXAMPLE 8.19

Left-hand Improvisation of *Inang* Rhythmic Pattern

It is not known when exactly *inang* originated. However, since *inang* was accompanied by the *ronggeng asli* ensemble and formed part of the *ronggeng asli* repertoire, it could have been one of the musical genres described in the Malay classical texts of the seventeenth and eighteenth centuries.

Like *asli*, *inang* had been introduced into *bangsawan* as *lagu extra* by the turn of the century. For instance, the song 'Ma Inang' sung by Tambi Ketjik of Penang was recorded by the Gramophone and Typewriter Ltd. in 1903 (Cat. no. 2–12008).

It was only in the 1920s and 1930s, when Malay stories were performed by *bangsawan* troupes, that *inang* was used in *bangsawan* plots. Maids and princesses danced to *rentak inang* in the garden scene. The *inang* dance became the basis of other dances such as *tari piring* (saucer dance), *tari lilin* (candle dance), and *tari payung* (umbrella dance) which were commonly used in *bangsawan* (Mohd. Anis, 1990: 123).

Rentak inang became associated with lighter dramatic situations in Malay and Javanese stories. Like *lagu asli riang*, *inang* provided the accompaniment for lovers to sing of their love for each other in the garden (*lagu taman*). *Lagu inang* could be used for conversations between characters (*lagu cakap*). They also accompanied the nursemaid (*lagu pengasoh/inang*) and the common villager or clown (*lagu pelawak*). They could be used interchangeably with *lagu asli* played at a faster and livelier tempo.

The example shown here is a *lagu cakap* from the play *Puteri Gunong Ledang* entitled 'Baginda Yam Tuan Melaka' [His Highness, the Ruler of Malacca] (Example 8.20). In this song, Tun Mamat and Sang Stia informed the Sultan about Puteri Gunong Ledang's conditions for marriage. Tok Ngah and Mek Ngah concluded that the princess did not want to marry the Sultan.

The Western drum played the characteristic *inang* pattern while the piano bass interlocked with it. The 'dung' sound of the drum and the piano bass note acted like the gong. The use of the Western drum instead of the *rebana* reflected the livelier character of the piece. There was stronger emphasis on the beat than in *asli*.

EXAMPLE 8.20
Inang (Lagu Cakap): 'Baginda Yam Tuan Melaka'

Source: 78 r.p.m. record (1930s), His Master's Voice (P 12766).

Joget

Joget (meaning 'dance')[12] is a happy dance-song with the repeated rhythmic pattern shown in Example 8.21, played on the *rebana*.

EXAMPLE 8.21
Joget Rhythmic Pattern

The above pattern is played by the right hand of the *rebana* performer. The left hand usually improvises 'tak' sounds in between the pattern (Example 8.22).

EXAMPLE 8.22
Left-hand Improvisation of *Joget* Rhythmic Pattern

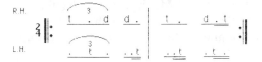

One of the characteristic features of this rhythmic pattern is the alternation of three notes against two. (The melody often alternates between 2/4 and 6/8.) The genre is usually played at ♩ = 150.

The genre is said to have developed after the Portuguese occupied Malacca in the sixteenth century (Daud Hamzah, 1973: 236). The use of alternating three notes against two and alternating 2/4 and 6/8, common in Spanish and Portuguese music (Goldsworthy, 1979: Chapter 6; Nettl, 1965: 112), lends weight to this claim. Furthermore, as the *joget* instrumental ensemble is similar to the one described in the classical Malay texts of the seventeenth and eighteenth centuries, the form could have been in existence since then.

Like *asli* and *inang*, *joget* songs and dances were performed in *bangsawan* during the extra turn sections at the turn of the century. The song 'Het Lied Van Tandjoeng Katoeng' in *rentak joget* (sung by Tambi Ketjik of Penang) was recorded by the Gramophone and Typewriter Ltd. in 1903 (Cat. no. 2–12035).

Joget was introduced into *bangsawan* plots only after the staging of Malay plays in the 1920s and 1930s. The song 'Lagu Silat' was commonly used as background music during *silat* or fighting scenes. It could also be played as an opening (*lagu pembuka*) or closing song (*lagu penutup*) in Malay stories with admirals or warriors as the main characters. The *joget* shown in Example 8.23 was played at the performance of

EXAMPLE 8.23
Joget (*Lagu Silat*)

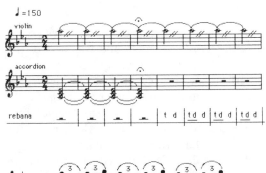

Source: 1985 recording played at the performance of *Laksamana Bentan*, Taiping.

Laksamana Bentan by the Bangsawan Sri USM in Taiping on 22 December 1985. The *lagu silat* accompanied the *silat* sequence between the Laksamana and Megat who were fighting because they both wanted to marry the princess, Wan Entah. (A recent recording is used here as I could not find a 78 r.p.m. recording of *lagu silat*.)

Irama Padang Pasir

Like *irama Melayu, irama Padang Pasir* was usually accompanied by the *ronggeng asli* ensemble. The piano, double bass, Western drum, and woodblock often replace the accordion and *rebana*. Sometimes the harmonium is used instead of the piano.

Masri

Masri is a dance-song with the recurring rhythmic pattern shown in Example 8.24, played by the right hand of the *rebana* performer.

EXAMPLE 8.24
Masri Rhythmic Pattern

The left-hand improvisation of the *masri* rhythmic pattern is shown in Example 8.25.

EXAMPLE 8.25
Left-hand Improvisation of the *Masri* Rhythmic Pattern

Again, it is not known when exactly *masri* developed. It was accompanied by the *ronggeng asli* ensemble and was part of the *ronggeng asli* repertoire.

Bangsawan performers stressed that *masri* shows Middle Eastern influence. In fact, as illustrated in Chapter 6, the *masri* rhythmic pattern resembles the rhythmic pattern which accompanies *beledi* dancing in Iran (see Example 6.2a).[13] *Masri* is also associated with some melodic modes found in Middle Eastern popular music.

As a result of the Middle Eastern characteristics, *masri* was used to accompany many *bangsawan* songs in plays of Middle Eastern origin. The *lagu nasib* 'Puja Kamati Darsha Alam' sung to *rentak asli* in *Jula Juli Bintang Tiga* was rendered in *rentak masri* in the Arabic play *Laila Majnun*, where its title was changed to 'Nasib Pandan' (Example 8.26). In this song Laila and Majnun sang of their forbidden love. *Bangsawan*

EXAMPLE 8.26
Slow *Masri* (*Lagu Nasib*): 'Nasib Pandan'

Source: 78 r.p.m. record (1930s), His Master's Voice (P 12804).

performers emphasized that the *masri* rhythmic pattern gave the *lagu nasib* a Middle Eastern character.

While slow-paced *masri* (♩ = 48) were used to accompany *lagu nasib*, fast-paced *masri* (♩ = 138) were played during lighter dramatic situations. According to veteran *bangsawan* performers, *inang* and *masri* rhythmic patterns could be used interchangeably in Malay and Javanese stories. The melody or tune could be played with either of the two different rhythmic patterns. Fast-paced *masri* patterns were sometimes referred to as *inang* (Chopyak, 1986: 123).[14]

The *masri* pattern was, however, preferred when a Middle Eastern atmosphere was required. In the Malay play *Puteri Gunong Ledang*, *rentak masri* was employed by the two shamans Tok Ngah and Mek Ngah as they prepared to go into trance (*lagu* 'Telek Ternang'). As the spirits that the shamans were praying to were of Arabic origin, the *masri* pattern was more appropriate than *inang* (Example 8.27).

EXAMPLE 8.27
Fast *Masri* (*Lagu Telek*): 'Telek Ternang'

Source: 78 r.p.m. record (1930s), His Master's Voice (P 12763).

Zapin

Zapin is a dance-song with the recurring rhythmic pattern shown in Example 8.28.

EXAMPLE 8.28
Zapin Rhythmic Pattern

Today, two forms of *zapin*—*zapin Arab* (Arab *zapin*) and *zapin Melayu* (Malay *zapin*)—are performed in Malaysia, specifically in Johore. It is said that the *zapin Melayu* is an adaptation of the *zapin Arab*. According to the Johore Malays, the *zapin* resembles a type of dance of the Arabs of Hadhramaut who settled in South-East Asia in large numbers at the beginning of the nineteenth century. The *zapin* was performed by men at Malay weddings and religious celebrations such as the Prophet Muhammad's birthday and the end of the Ramadan fasting month. Musical instruments included the *ud* or *gambos*, the *marwas* (hand drums), and the *dok* (Mohd. Anis, 1990: Chapter 2).

In the 1930s, *zapin* was introduced into *bangsawan* and dance halls in amusement parks. In *bangsawan*, women and men performed the dance. The *zapin* dance was popular in *bangsawan* because of its linear formation. Choreographers could produce the effect of dancers appearing and disappearing into the side-wings. The linear formation coupled with dancers having to face one another ensured that the latter never turned their backs to the audience or to the Sultan which would be considered disrespectful (Mohd. Anis, 1990: 125, 126).

The ensemble which accompanied the *zapin* dance was adapted in *bangsawan*. It consisted of a violin, a *gambos* (sometimes replaced by the guitar), a *gendang*, a harmonium, maracas, a *rebana*, and a tambourine (Chopyak, 1986: 120). Because the *gambos* was an important instrument, the term *gambos* was synonymously used to describe the dance-song.

The *zapin* or *gambos* was often used in *bangsawan* plays of Middle Eastern origin because of its Middle Eastern characteristics. Besides the use of the *gambos*, rhythmic movement was kept regular by the violin and *gambos* (or guitar) which played in semiquaver or quaver note values. *Zapin* or *gambos* songs also used Middle Eastern modes, ornamentation, and the repeated phrase technique (see Chapter 6).

Lagu gambos usually accompanied sad songs (*lagu nasib*) sung by lovers who were not allowed to marry. As shown in Chapter 6 (Transcription 6.3), the song 'Gambos Sri Makam' was sung by Laila and Majnun when they lamented their forbidden love at the graveyard.

Lagu gambos such as 'Bercerai Kasih' [Separation of Lovers] (Example 8.29) were also sung just before lovers parted with one another in Middle Eastern stories. In 'Bercerai Kasih', the violin, guitar (which replaces the *gambos*), and harmonium keep the rhythmic movement uniform by playing quaver and semiquaver note values (Example 8.29). In addition, the guitar and *rebana* play the *zapin* rhythmic pattern at the end of each vocal phrase (Example 8.29, bars 5 and 7).

EXAMPLE 8.29
Gambos (*Lagu Nasib*): 'Bercerai Kasih'

Source: 78 r.p.m. record (1930s), Chap Singa (QF 105).

Irama Jawa

The ensemble which played *irama Jawa* usually consisted of the violin, flute, guitar, piano, double bass, and *rebana*. It is interesting to note that in Manusama's writings, the *komedi stambul* orchestra which accompanied the performance of *Djoela Djoeli Bintang Tiga* in 1894 in Java consisted of one piano, three violins, one flute, one clarinet, one cornet à piston[s], one trombone, and one double bass. Manusama adds that when pieces which came from Malaya, British India, and Persia were played, the *rebana* was included in the European orchestra (Manusama, 1922: 12, 15–16).

Stambul and Kroncong

Kroncong is believed to have originated in the sixteenth-century music of the Portuguese colonies in the Moluccas and Batavia (Becker, 1976; Kornhauser, 1978). *Kroncong* consisted of Portuguese melodies sung to Dutch and Malay texts. These *kroncong* melodies were said to be used by August Mahieu to accompany the *komedi stambul* that he created in 1891 (Knaap, 1903).

Kroncong melodies employed in *stambul* became known as *stambul* melodies. Many of them did not have specific names but were known as 'Stambul Satoe' or 'Stambul Dua' (Kornhauser, 1978: 132). According to Knaap (1903), when Mahieu first started the *komedi stambul*, he used only six tunes. These tunes were repeated in different plays and sung to different improvised texts. He called the first two pieces 'fantasies', the third 'comedy drama', the fourth 'lyrical–philosophical', and the last 'tragic–sensual'.

Kroncong and *stambul* became 'almost interchangeable musical terms' (Knaap, 1903: 155) used to describe a specific style of performance or accompaniment style. An *asli* song could therefore become a *kroncong* or *stambul* piece according to whether the accompanying style was in *kroncong* or *stambul* (Example 8.35).

Originally, the accompaniment style consisted of continuous chords that were strummed on the guitar (or played on the piano) (Example 8.30).

EXAMPLE 8.30
Strummed Chords of *Kroncong*

In the 1930s, however, *kroncong* became more 'Javanized' (Knaap, 1903: 134). As a result, the banjo and ukelele replaced the guitar or piano as instruments playing the chords (Knaap, 1903: 137–9) (Example 8.31). The banjo and ukelele alternated with each other imitating the interlocking *saron* or *bonang* in the Javanese gamelan, while the guitar provided a uniform rhythmic motion improvising around the harmony of the song (Example 8.32). In addition, the pizzicato cello imitated the drum (Example 8.33). (Example 8.36 provides an illustration of how the parts come together as a unit.)

EXAMPLE 8.31
Banjo and Ukelele Alternating

EXAMPLE 8.32
Rhythmic Movement of the Guitar

EXAMPLE 8.33
Pizzicato Cello

Kroncong and *stambul* were introduced into the *bangsawan* performances in Malaya at the turn of the century. They were disseminated through 78 r.p.m. recordings of the day (Gramophone and Typewriter Ltd., 1903) as well as by visiting *komedi stambul* troupes.

These songs were first sung during the extra turn sections but were introduced into *bangsawan* plots in the 1920s and 1930s. According to the veteran *bangsawan* performer Mahmud Jun, *kroncong* and *stambul* were sung in the garden scenes in 'Javanese and classical stories especially if the stories were fairy-tales or modern ones'. Mahmud Jun went on to say that '*stambul* was used in classical stories because it sounded a bit Western'.

A few examples of *stambul* and *kroncong* used in *bangsawan* and *kome-di stambul* are given below. The first example is an extract from the book *Penghiboran Hati* (Figure 8.1) which is a collection of 'songs sung by the bangsawan world' (*Straits Echo*, 17 December 1924) put together by a certain H. S. L. and published by the Criterion Press Ltd., Penang, in 1924. The book has '16 pieces with selected musical notes for violin or mandolin and 16 more for guitar accompaniment'. Some of the pieces include 'Stambol Satoe' (Example 8.34), 'Stambol Dua', 'Kroncong Meritzkey', and 'Kronchong Pandan'. (The melody of 'Stambol Satoe' is the national anthem of Malaysia today.) The guitar accompaniment consisted of strummed chords.[15]

FIGURE 8.1

Title-page of Songbook *Penghiboran Hati*

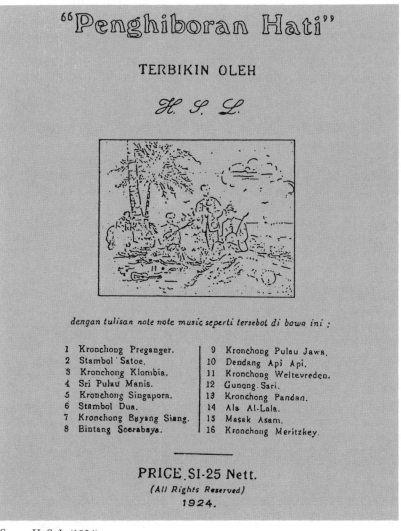

Source: H. S. L (1924).

EXAMPLE 8.34
Stambul: 'Stambol Satoe'

Source: H. S. L. (1924).

The second example is an excerpt from the *asli* song 'Boenga Tandjung' (sung to *stambul* style accompaniment) by Miss Riboet, the Javanese actress who owned the renowned Miss Riboet Opera (Example 8.35). This song was recorded by Beka Records in 1927 (Cat. no. 27801) and categorized as a 'stamboel' piece.

The musical accompaniment was provided by violin (one or more), flute, and piano. The piano bass played chords not unlike those shown in Example 8.34.[16]

EXAMPLE 8.35
Stambul (*Lagu Asli*): 'Boenga Tandjung'

Source: 78 r.p.m. record (1927), Beka Records (27801).

The last example is an excerpt of a *stambul* piece called 'Anak Koe'.[17] This song was sung by Ahmad C. B. and recorded by the Gramophone Co. Ltd. in India and distributed under the label of Chap Singa in the 1930s (QF 89). By the 1930s, the accompaniment style had become similar to the *kroncong* of today. Example 8.36 is a transcription of the rhythm section from the instrumental introduction of the song.

EXAMPLE 8.36
Stambul with *Kroncong* Accompaniment: 'Anak Koe'

Source: 78 r.p.m. record (1930s), Chap Singa (QF 89).

Irama Hindustan

The tabla and harmonium were used to accompany songs in *irama Hindustan*. However, if an opera troupe did not have the musicians to play these instruments, the *ronggeng asli* ensemble could be substituted.

Veteran musicians say that the rhythmic patterns of *irama Hindustan* were first used in the Parsi theatre which toured Malaya in the late nineteenth century. When *bangsawan* troupes were first formed, their ensembles consisted of harmonium and tabla, and songs in *irama*

Hindustan were played. Later, with the introduction of Western, Chinese, and Malay stories, *irama Hindustan* became associated with the plots of Hindustani stories only (although they were also performed during extra turns of other plays).

Two main types of *irama Hindustan* were used in *bangsawan*: one accompanied dances and happy situations while the other accompanied sad or dramatic occasions. The former played the same functions in Hindustani stories as fast-paced *asli* and *inang* in Malay stories. One of the common rhythmic patterns which was used to accompany dances and light dramatic situations was called *barshat* (Example 8.37).

EXAMPLE 8.37
Barshat Played on the *Rebana*

R.H. $\frac{6}{8}$ ‖: d d d   d d d :‖
L.H. $\frac{6}{8}$: . . t .   . . t . :

This rhythmic pattern was similar to the *dādrā tāla* which is used in light classical music of India (Powers, 1980: 124) (Example 8.38). (See Chapter 6, n. 19 for an explanation of the drum syllables used.)

EXAMPLE 8.38
Dādrā Tāla

‖: DHĀ   DHĪN   nā   DHĀ   tin   nā :‖

Source: Powers (1980: 124).

Variations of *barshat* were often played. The song 'Paraber' from the play *Noor-E-Islam* (see Transcription 6.5) in Chapter 6 used a slightly different rhythmic pattern which also resembled *dādrā tāla* (Example 8.39).

EXAMPLE 8.39
Irama Hindustan: Variation of *Dādrā Tāla* in 'Paraber'

Source: 78 r.p.m. record (1930s), Chap Singa (QF 35).

Although songs accompanying sad situations did not use any drumming, a *tāla* resembling *kaharvā*[18] was often implied. The harmonium played 8 beats (3 + 3 + 2) in 'Mostikowi' (also from *Noor-E-Islam*; see Transcription 6.6 in Chapter 6) (Example 8.40). However, as I have tried to explain in Chapter 6, the *tāla* is often not maintained throughout the song as the singers and performers are not trained in classical Indian singing.

EXAMPLE 8.40
Kaharvā Tāla in 'Mostikowi'

Source: 78 r.p.m. record (1930s), Chap Singa (QF 36).

It is important to note that *irama Cina* was not mentioned by *bangsawan* musicians and performers. This is possibly because Chinese opera aria types (music linked to specific dramatic situations) are not identified by specific rhythmic patterns but by the verse structure of the text, the syllable placement, cadential notes, mode, and instrumental accompaniment (Yung, 1983a: 32–4).

* * *

We have shown that as in traditional *wayang*, specific *lagu* were used for specific dramatic situations in the *bangsawan* plot. Each *lagu* had particular elements associated with it. These elements helped the audience to identify the type of scene, character, or mood being portrayed (Table 8.1).

However, there were fewer musical elements associated with a *lagu* in *bangsawan* than in traditional *wayang*. While the musical elements associated with each *lagu* in the *wayang* comprised its musical form, drum rhythmic pattern and, in some cases, *serunai* (or vocal) melody (Matusky, 1980: 207),[19] the major defining elements of a particular *lagu* in *bangsawan* were its rhythmic pattern and its tempo. Unlike traditional *wayang*, *lagu bangsawan* were usually not associated with particular melodies. One melody could be played with different accompanying rhythmic patterns. 'Puja Kamati Darsha Alam' (Example 8.16) was sung in *rentak asli* in *Jula Juli Bintang Tiga* and in *rentak masri* in *Laila Majnun* (Example 8.26). Even though the melodies used in both examples were the same, the former was identified as a *lagu asli* while the latter was called a *lagu masri*.

In *bangsawan*, new themes or melodies were constantly created using familiar or new rhythmic patterns. Influenced by film and Western theatre, new theme songs were composed for new plays. Some examples

TABLE 8.1

The Relationship between Dramatic Situation and Rhythmic Pattern

Dramatic Situation/ Character	Rhythmic Pattern		
	Classical Stories	Arabic Stories	Malay/Javanese Stories
Nasib	slow waltz, slow foxtrot	slow masri/ asli	slow asli
Taman	slow waltz, waltz, slow foxtrot, quickstep	inang, masri	inang, masri, fast asli
Cakap	waltz	waltz, masri	asli, inang
Strit	march, quickstep, foxtrot	march, quickstep, foxtrot, masri	fast asli/inang
Jin	march, quickstep	march, quickstep	(no such character in Malay stories)
Perang	march	march	joget/inang

included 'Mas Merah', 'Bungah Tanjung', and 'Seri Mersing'. The audience was able to identify what kind of story was playing by listening to the 'theme song'. There was emphasis on 'catchy' tunes which the audience could sing or whistle at home.

To attract the multiracial audience, new tunes popularized by Western marching bands, touring theatrical groups, gramophone records, and radio were constantly incorporated. As one reporter wrote in the *Straits Echo* (21 September 1906), *bangsawan* performers frequently took 'all the catchy tunes ... from an English comic opera' and sang 'them to different words for each play'.

In addition to melody, musical form too was not regarded by *bangsawan* performers as a criterion for distinguishing *lagu*. This was because the 16- or 32-bar song form popularized by theatrical troupes from the West and gramophone records became the standard song form used in *bangsawan*. Although *lagu asli, inang, masri,* and *joget* were traditionally built on gong units of specific structure (which defined the form of the *lagu*), the gong was often left out in *bangsawan*. It was replaced by the 'dung' of the *rebana* and by the bass note played by the piano or plucked bass.

Not only were there fewer musical elements associated with a *lagu* in *bangsawan* than in traditional *wayang*, but these musical elements in *bangsawan* were also not as rigidly prescribed. Unlike the traditional *wayang*, rhythmic patterns of a specific *lagu* in *bangsawan* did not need to be performed on specific drums. They could be played by the *rebana*, Western drum, piano, bass, or woodblock depending on the preferences of the musical conductor and the availability of particular musicians for the night.

The same rhythmic pattern could also be performed at different tempos, depending on the dramatic situation with which it was associated. Fast- or slow-paced *asli*, *masri*, waltzes, and foxtrots reflected different dramatic situations.

Furthermore, rhythmic patterns of popular musical genres from the West, Latin America, Middle East, India, and Malaya (which accompanied social dancing among the various ethnic groups in the urban areas of Malaya) were constantly incorporated. These included waltzes, marches, tangos, ragtime, and foxtrots (used mainly in classical, Arabic, Hindustani, and Chinese stories); and *asli*, *inang*, *joget*, and *masri* (employed in Malay, Javanese, and Arabic stories).

In general, innovation in music which was related to interest in variety, novelty, and spectacle on stage prevailed. As the late Malay *bangsawan* musician and violinist Daud Hamzah (1973: 234) wrote, this popular music was like '*lalang yang ditiup angin* [long grass blown by the wind].... To which direction it is blown, in that direction it will bend.'

As the audience began to prefer realism to fantasy, precise settings, costumes, characters, and musical sounds were required. To obtain these 'authentic' sounds, Western, Latin American, Malay, Indian, Arabic, and Javanese rhythmic patterns were adopted.

Finally, it must be emphasized that many of the rhythmic patterns used in *bangsawan* were adapted from Western and Latin American social dance music which was popular in the West and was introduced into Malaya via gramophone records, radio, film, and touring theatrical troupes. Adaptation of such dance music and, specifically, the rhythmic patterns associated with them enabled *bangsawan* to present itself as 'up-to-date' and 'modern' to its audience.

1. See Matusky (1980: 39 n. 1, 48) for definitions of *lagu* in traditional *wayang*.

2. The Viennese waltz declined rapidly after the destruction of the Austro-Hungarian Empire in World War I. After the war, Berlin became the centre of European light music. New dance styles emerged in the United States, a country which was not much affected by the war (Lamb, 1980c: 205).

3. The etymology of the term is still being debated (Behague, 1980b: 563).

4. See also *Times of Malaya*, 30 September 1929. The writer talks about dancing in Singapore. To him, the most fashionable dances then were the foxtrot, tango, and waltz.

5. According to Menah Yem, the rumba, samba, mambo, beguine, bolero, swing, cha cha, and conga were used in the extra turns. They were introduced in the 1940s and 1950s. But discussions of these dance forms are beyond the scope of this book.

6. *Ronggeng* troupes are invited to provide music and entertainment during weddings and parties in Malaysia today. These *ronggeng* troupes usually have a few female dancers who dance with guests at such functions. In Penang, *ronggeng* troupes also perform at the birthday celebrations of deities worshipped by the Chinese but considered to be of Malay origin (Tan, 1988a). In the 1930s and 1940s, *ronggeng* troupes were also popular in amusement parks.

7. For an in-depth analysis of *asli* songs and the frame drum, see Goldsworthy (1979: Chapters 4–6). The same type of dance is known as *sinandung* in Sumatra. See also

Chopyak (1986: 114–15). I have placed the gong beat at the beginning of the first bar as this was the way I was taught to play the frame drum and gong by my teacher Pak Mat. Chopyak, however, considers the second 4-beat pattern as the first. My method avoids having to put the gong beat in the middle of the rhythmic pattern.

8. Goldsworthy (1979) concludes that the *ronggeng* is a 'pre-Portuguese Southeast Asian art form' which has many 'post-Portuguese' features incorporated.

9. *Asli* songs were also sung by Indonesian troupes touring Malaya in the early twentieth century. For example, 'Boengah Tandjoeng', sung by Miss Riboet, the famous Javanese actress, was recorded by Beka Records (Carl Lindstrom A. G., Germany: Cat. no. 27801) in 1927. Although this song was categorized as a *stamboel*, it was played in *rentak asli*.

10. *Lagu asli* with Chinese characteristics like 'Tudung Periok', 'Seri Mersing', and 'Patah Hati' were used in Chinese stories.

11. In the 1940s and 1950s, *asli* tunes like 'Tudung Periok' and 'Seri Mersing' were sung to *rentak* cha cha and rumba respectively in the extra turns (Daud Hamzah, 1973: 234–42).

12. There is another type of *joget* called *joget gamelan* which flourished in the courts of Pahang and Trengganu in the eighteenth century (D'Cruz, 1979). The *joget* described here is different from the court *joget gamelan*. This *joget* was also known as *ronggeng* in the past but is generally referred to as *joget* today.

13. It is interesting to note that the *masri* rhythmic pattern is also similar to one of the characteristic rhythmic patterns associated with the tango (♫ ♩ ♫).

14. *Bangsawan* musicians such as Pak Mat and Pak Wan told me that there were other rhythmic patterns that were similar to *inang* which were used in plays of other origins. These rhythmic patterns were used in the same dramatic situations as *inang*. As we have seen, *masri* was used in Arabic plays. *Rentak ghazal* could also be substituted for *masri* in Arabic plays.

Rentak ghazal: 𝄴 ‖: d̲ t   t t   d̲ t   t :‖

If a Thai story was performed, the *rentak ramvong* was used:

𝄴 ‖: d .d   d .d   d d   t :‖

If a Hindustani story was performed, the following pattern was played:

𝄴 ‖: d̲ t   t t   t d   d :‖

15. Some of the pieces in the book (such as 'Kroncong Pulau Jawa') are accompanied by strummed guitar chords which are played with the *masri* rhythmic pattern:

‖: ♪♩ ♪   ♩   ♩ :‖

16. Other *stambul* songs sung by Miss Riboet and recorded by Beka Records in the 1920s (78 r.p.m.) which I found included 'Selendang Majang' (27751), 'Djoela Djoeli Bintang III' (27817), and 'Inang-Sarget' (27767). The first two were accompanied by piano chords with equal duration: ‖: ♩   ♩   ♩   ♩ :‖

while the last one had the piano chords played in the *masri* rhythmic pattern:

‖: ♪♩ ♪   ♩   ♩ :‖

17. In the 1940s and 1950s, different types of *kroncong* such as *kroncong rumba*, *kroncong masri*, and *kroncong* slow foxtrot were introduced into extra turn sections. A discussion of these styles is beyond the scope of this book.

18. Manuel (1988: 162) writes that the 8-beat *kaharvā* and 6-beat *dādrā* metres were the most common metres used in film music in the early twentieth century. One important source of film music was the music of the Parsi and Marathi theatres.

19. This definition applies to *lagu* with many functions. *Lagu* with only one function is defined by the musical form alone (Matusky, 1980: 207).

9

Decline of *Bangsawan* since World War II and Its Revival in the 1970s and 1980s

The Japanese Occupation

BANGSAWAN'S decline began after the outbreak of World War II and the Japanese Occupation of the Malay Peninsula in 1942. During this period, thousands of urban dwellers fled to the countryside to escape Japanese repression and food shortages in the towns. Many *bangsawan* troupes had to shut down because most of the *bangsawan* audience could no longer afford to buy tickets. The veteran performer Wan, who is now in his eighties, recalled that he performed with the Arah Bangsawan till the Japanese Occupation. 'Arah Bangsawan disbanded and I had to perform odd jobs here and there to earn some pocket money. Those were hard times,' he said. 'Sometimes, in the middle of performances, Japanese planes flew by and people screamed.'

During the war, *bangsawan* troupes faced many restrictions and had to seek permission from the Japanese to perform. As Wan recalled, after dabbling in odd jobs for a while, he felt the urge to perform *bangsawan* and with his friend, Aman Belon (a famous *bangsawan* comedian, now deceased), obtained permission from the Japanese to start a troupe in Singapore. 'We played Japanese propaganda stories at Japanese camps and travelled in a Japanese lorry. In return, we were given rice, salt, sugar and oil,' Wan added. The Japanese lorry stopped by all the towns on the west coast of the peninsula.

Likewise, Rahman B. recollected that his father's troupe, Rahman Star Opera, was playing in Kedah when the war broke out; his father, determined to carry on, sought the permission of the Japanese to continue performing. 'We had to change the name of our troupe to Ohaiyo Gozaimas Opera and had to perform Japanese propaganda stories that supported the Japanese,' he recalled. Elaborating on these propaganda stories, Rahman B. said that their troupe usually performed plays which consisted of a few scenes and the stories had to emphasize that the Japanese were the most powerful force in the country. *Bangsawan* scene types were used to portray how the Malayan communists and traitors were captured and punished by the Japanese soldiers. Between the scenes, the performers sang Japanese songs like 'Miyato Kaino'. The backdrop, resembling the Japanese flag, consisted of a white cloth with a red sun in the middle.

Another veteran actress, Ainon, said that *bangsawan* performers had to follow the orders of the Japanese soldiers. She herself had to change her stage name to Lei-ko. 'The Japanese drilled us and made us practise Japanese songs the whole day. At night, we performed for the Japanese troops.'

Even though the *bangsawan* performers staged Japanese propaganda stories, they were badly treated by the Japanese. Mat Arab, who used to play comic characters, remembered how the Japanese soldiers slapped and kicked him because he did not pay respect to them. 'Now I can laugh about it, but then we had to bow until our neck ached whenever we saw any of them,' he declared.

The women actresses were often harassed by Japanese officials. While the *sri panggung*, Minah Alias, was performing with the Grand Nooran Opera, she was saved from the advances of a Japanese official by another *bangsawan* performer, Alias Manan. Ever since that incident, Alias Manan had walked with a limp as his leg was injured during the struggle with the Japanese official. Minah and Alias were married in 1942.

Many women stopped performing altogether and went back to their villages. While her husband, Yem, continued to perform in Singapore, Menah Yem returned to her kampong in Batu Gajah. She did not act or dance in public again till after the war.

Movement for the performers was highly restricted. Mahmud Jun confirmed that *bangsawan* performers could only perform in designated areas such as Japanese camps. 'We could not move around as we liked or travel by ourselves. The Japanese would hit and torture us if we disappeared from the camps.'

The Immediate Post-war Period, the Emergency, and Independence

During the immediate post-war period, even though entertainment parks and cinemas were re-established, many *bangsawan* troupes were unable to start performing again as they did not have the necessary capital to buy costumes, equipment, and other properties (Camoens, 1981: 168).

Furthermore, *bangsawan* continued to decline as Malaya experienced a breakdown of political and economic stability due to food shortages, widespread unemployment, and labour unrest. In 1947 itself, there were three hundred major strikes (Bedlington, 1978: 76). Additionally, ethnic violence broke out between the surrender of the Japanese in mid-August and the return of British troops in early September 1945. Riots occurred after the Malayan People's Anti-Japanese Army (MPAJA), which comprised mainly Chinese, took control of many villages and towns and executed collaborators, the majority of whom were Malays (Bedlington, 1978: 63–5).

The Emergency, the euphemism used to describe the 12-year communist insurrection against the British, made the situation even less conducive to the survival of *bangsawan* troupes. In early 1948, the Malayan Communist Party (MCP) launched an attack on the colonial government as the party felt that the British were trying to curb its activities. In June 1948, following the murder of three European planters, a state of Emergency was declared and the MCP resorted to guerrilla warfare (Short, 1975).

During the Emergency, the British imposed censorship on all *bangsawan* performances. Before *bangsawan* could be staged, permission had first to be sought. In the early years, performances were sometimes stopped by the authorities because of fighting in nearby areas. Furthermore, performers and audiences were checked for weapons by the authorities before performances began. Abdullah Abdul Rahman, who used to be a *bangsawan* performer, described the period as follows:

They [The British] bring loudspeaker ... that time we are playing, Bidor, we are still on stage, at that time, they are shooting in town*lah*.... They come out, stop the show. Performers no heart to perform. *Dia tunggulah* [They wait]. Sometimes you are going in, all check*lah*. Sometimes these people come with hand grenade, they have to check everything ... [all the] audience coming in we check.

Although the Emergency did not officially come to an end until 1960, for all practical purposes the communists had been defeated by the mid-1950s. However, the return of more peaceful times did not see the revival of *bangsawan*. Instead, its decline continued into the late 1950s chiefly because of the expansion of the film industry in Malaya (Camoens, 1981: 164; Wan Abdul Kadir, 1988). In 1947, the Shaw Brothers (Run Run and Runme) set up Malay Film Productions which produced movies such as *Noor Asmara* [Light of Romance] and *Nasib* [Luck]. The company processed, produced, distributed, and screened its own movies. Another film company, Cathay-Keris Productions, was subsequently formed with the merger of Keris Film Productions (owned by Ho Ah Loke) and Cathay Productions (owned by Loke Wan Tho). In 1951, it made its first movie, *Buluh Perindu* [Aeolian Harp] (Baharudin Latif, 1989: 46).

According to Mahmud Jun, a *bangsawan* actor who later became a film star, *bangsawan* could not be revived because film companies like Shaw and Cathay recruited all the prominent *bangsawan* actors and actresses. As in the pre-war period, *bangsawan* performers became film heroes and heroines. *Bangsawan* dancers were employed as choreographers and *bangsawan* musicians as composers and performers. For their part, *bangsawan* performers were attracted to the film industry because it offered them and their families a chance to settle down in one town instead of having to travel every few days. More importantly, working for the film companies ensured regular monthly salaries, bonuses, social security, and annual leave. By comparison, their incomes as *bangsawan* performers depended on the evening's takings. Although the takings were high at times, more often than not they were low, and occasionally, as Mahmud Jun stressed, *bangsawan* performers were 'not paid at all', which had often been the case during the war and in the early 1950s. In addition, if *bangsawan* performers did not go on stage, they were not paid.

Shariff Medan, who joined Cathay-Keris Productions and performed in their first movie *Buluh Perindu*, said that he was attracted to the film industry because he could become a salaried staff. 'I was given a monthly salary of $300. After each film was completed, I was given a bonus. I could also apply for annual leave; I was entitled to two weeks' paid leave a year,' he reported.

Mahmud Jun, who also worked for Cathay-Keris Productions, said that Loke Wan Tho came personally to offer him the part of hero in Cathay-Keris films. Mahmud Jun could not resist the offer. He was given a monthly salary of $150, a rented house, free medical services, and a bonus of $350 after each film. 'Loke Wan Tho even hired a servant to take care of my three children,' he recalled.

Ironically, *bangsawan* further lost its following after *bangsawan* stories were filmed as audiences began to be more attracted to the cinemas than to live *bangsawan* performances. *Bangsawan* had lost its novelty. As another veteran *bangsawan* performer Ahmad B. pointed out, *bangsawan* stories shown in the cinema were perceived to be more realistic (*betul*). Mahmud Jun has stressed the same point. According to him, 'People liked to see films because the car was realistic, the river was realistic, the sea was realistic, everything was realistic.' On the other hand, these objects had to be drawn in *bangsawan*.

Bangsawan also declined in the 1950s because of the changing popular mood associated with the struggle for independence from Britain which was achieved in 1957. Coinciding with the temper of Malay mainstream nationalism, the audience began to prefer realistic and historical stories which depicted the glories of Malay kingdoms past. The spectacular tricks and fairy-tale characters of *bangsawan* were unable to compete with films and a new form of theatre, namely, *sandiwara* (see Chapter 3). The *sandiwara* plays contained realistic portrayals of humans instead of fairies. There was less emphasis on spectacle and novelty. Extra turns, which were the mainstay of *bangsawan*, were eliminated because they interrupted the plot. Music and dances were included in the drama itself. Historical, religious, nationalistic, and contemporary themes akin to the spirit of a mainstream Malay nationalism led by aristocrats and high-status administrators were emphasized. The *sandiwara* play *Burong Pipit Makan Jagong* [Sparrow Eats Maize] helped to raise national consciousness among Malays while *Semangat Pemuda* [Spirit of Youth] concerned itself with the themes of loyalty, race, and nation (Camoens, 1981: 210–11, 230–2). By the 1950s, both professional *sandiwara* troupes (such as Sandiwara Senang Hati and Sandiwara Cahaya Timor) and amateur troupes formed by youth groups, police organizations, and other associations had become the popular theatre in the towns of Malaya (Camoens, 1981: 232).

Audiences also began to prefer realistic stories as they were influenced by Indonesian *sandiwara* troupes which toured Malaya. These troupes had helped to raise the consciousness of the Indonesian people against the Dutch colonialists by performing stories with social messages (*tauladan*). Ahmad C. B., now in his eighties and living in Medan, Indonesia, used to spread anti-colonialist sentiments in Sumatra and Malaya through his s*andiwara* group Asmara Dana, which means 'loving to serve' (*kasih sayang untuk berbakti*). In 1947, the year of the Indonesian Revolution, his troupe came to Malaya to escape imprisonment by the Dutch. In Malaya, the name of the troupe was changed to Rayuan Asmara which means 'appealing for love' (*merayu kasih sayang*). 'Rayuan Asmara appealed for love to support the Indonesians who wanted to fight the Dutch,' he explained. Indeed, Ahmad C. B. was so aggressive towards the colonialists that his friends called him C. B., short for 'cas bara' or 'bekas bara', meaning 'receptacle which is hot like fire'.

Like other s*andiwara* troupes which toured Malaya in the 1950s, Ahmad C. B.'s Rayuan Asmara performed 'stories that could promote the development of people' (*betul-betul bisa kasi maju manusia*) and not stories that 'portrayed children turning into mountains' (*anak-anak jadi gunung*). 'I do not like mythical stories (*cerita mitos*),' Ahmad C. B. stated.

In Malaya, Rayuan Asmara staged modern stories (*cerita moden*) such as *Anak Derhaka* [Disloyal Child], *Gelombang Penghidupan* [Life of Waves], and *Bangun Anakku* [Arise My Child]. Malay legends such as *Laksamana Mati Dibunuh*, *Hang Tuah*, and *Siti Zubaidah* were also played. Sometimes, mythical stories with social messages—such as *Bawang Merah Bawang Puteh* (Red Onion, White Onion), the Malay version of Cinderella—were performed. To Ahmad C. B., *Bawang Merah Bawang Puteh* showed how stepmothers ill-treated their step-children. These *sandiwara* stories performed by Ahmad C. B.'s group were very popular among Malay audiences.

As the popularity of *bangsawan* faded, *bangsawan* performers who could not make it in the film world or make a living through *bangsawan* began to turn to other forms of entertainment which paid better. This, too, contributed to the decline of *bangsawan*. Many *bangsawan* performers joined *joget* and *ronggeng* groups in the 1950s. Wan Pekak, a *bangsawan* violinist, stopped performing *bangsawan* because the troupe he used to play with did not earn enough to give him cash. He was only given rice (*beras*) for his efforts. The *ronggeng* troupes Wan Pekak joined performed in amusement parks and at fun-fairs and Baba weddings.

Ainon quit *bangsawan* and joined the *joget moden* as a dancer and singer. The *joget moden* troupe paid her better. In addition, she could settle down in Kuala Lumpur with her daughter; however, whenever *bangsawan* troupes came to Kuala Lumpur, she sang and danced in the extra turns.

Accomplished musicians like Alfonso Soliano played in night-clubs, which paid even higher salaries. In 1948, Soliano became the leader of the Selangor Club Band. He was then engaged as a full-time conductor and composer with Radio Malaya in the 1950s.

Others were attracted to the mobile theatres (*pentas gerak*) set up by the government as salaried performers. For example, Mahmud Jun, before he entered the film industry, worked with the Department of Information (Jabatan Penerangan). He performed with the mobile theatre of the department which visited villages to advise the Malays against supplying food and clothes to the communists. He was paid a monthly salary of $150 and a daily food allowance of $3, an income that was higher and definitely more stable than in *bangsawan*.

Nevertheless, *bangsawan* did not die out completely in the 1950s. Despite hard times, groups like Yem's Grand Nooran, Seri Rani Opera, Kumpulan Dagang Bangsawan, Rahman Star Opera, Seri Kembangan Opera, and Royal Star Opera continued to perform (Camoens, 1981: 171–4) (Figures 9.1–9.3; Plate 41). Rahman B., after whom Rahman Star Opera was first named, said that his father changed the name of their troupe to Bintang Emas Malay Opera and later to Bintang Timur in the vain hope that the troupe would do better. 'Sometimes we did not even earn enough to feed our performers. Some older people who still liked to watch *bangsawan* would take pity on us and give us rice and dried fish,' Rahman B. recounted, adding that in the 1950s many troupes came to concentrate their efforts in the villages instead of in the urban areas where film and *sandiwara* performances were more readily available.

Some *bangsawan* performers renamed their troupes *sandiwara* instead of *bangsawan* (Plates 42–44) and performed more realistic modern-style Malay plays. Pak Suki called his troupe of *bangsawan* performers Dian Sandiwara. Another *bangsawan* actor, Baba Melaka, left the Nooran Opera to lead a *sandiwara* troupe (*Utusan Melayu*, 8 September 1956).

Like the *sandiwara*, many of the *bangsawan* troupes began to emphasize Malay historical tales. This shift coincided with the mood of Malay nationalism in the country and the struggle for independence in the 1950s. Prior to independence in 1957, the few existing *bangsawan* troupes joined *sandiwara* troupes in collecting funds for the United Malays National Organization (UMNO)'s campaign in the first national elections held in 1955. Malay *sejarah* tales which depicted the glory of the old Malay kingdoms became the subject-matter for most plays. These were performed to evoke in the Malay audience a sense of pride and of solidarity. Bakar M., the owner of Bintang Timur in the 1950s, stated that his troupe staged Malay *sejarah* stories like *Laksamana Bentan*, *Laksamana Mati Dibunuh*, *Hang Tuah*, and *Puteri Gunong Ledang* to support UMNO's campaign. According to his son Rahman B., 'Tengku Abdul Rahman [the UMNO leader later to become the first Prime Minister of Malaysia] would go on stage to campaign' in between acts.

FIGURE 9.1
Bangsawan Handbill of 1950, Featuring *Thief of Bagdad*

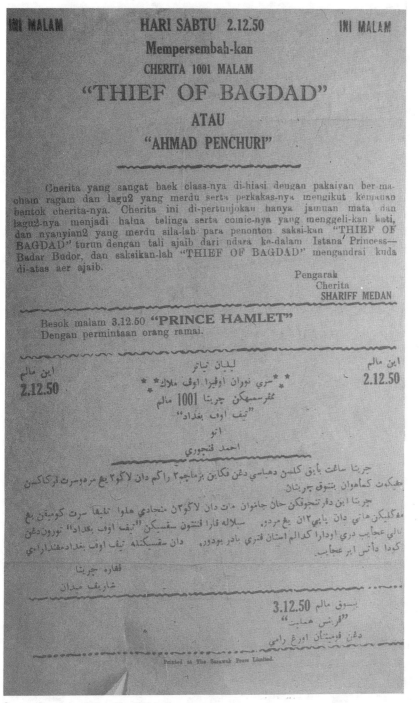

Source: Courtesy of Tok Shariff Medan.

FIGURE 9.2
Bangsawan Handbill of 1952, Featuring *Sampek Engtair*

Source: Courtesy of Tok Shariff Medan.

FIGURE 9.3
Bangsawan Handbill of the 1950s, Featuring *Putri Gunong Ledang*

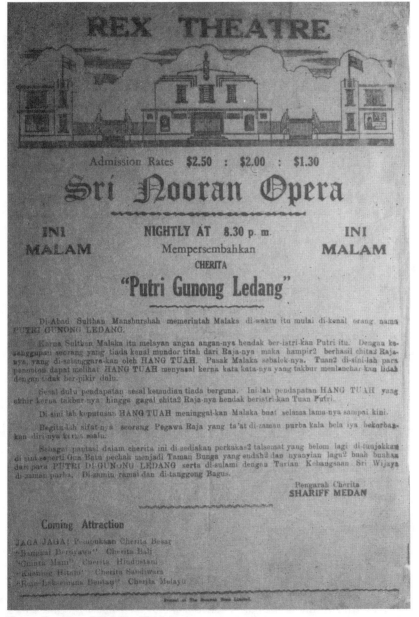

Source: Courtesy of Tok Shariff Medan.

Many of the theme songs of Ahmad C. B.'s plays were sung by *bangsawan* troupes during UMNO's campaign. 'Bangun Anakku' is an example:

Bangun anakku dari tidurmu
Sebelum sampainya menyerang pagi
Jikalau sudah segera berpakaian
Menuntut ilmu jangan-jangan dilupakan
Ini semua demi masa depan

> Arise my child from your sleep
> Before morning arrives and intrudes
> If you (have woken) dress quickly
> Do not forget to pursue knowledge
> All this is for the future.

The 1960s

Following the temporary boost given to it during UMNO's election campaign, *bangsawan* continued its decline in the 1960s. There were brief occasional announcements in the newspapers about *bangsawan* performances during the decade, but these performances were infrequent (*Utusan Zaman*, 20 October 1963; *Berita Minggu*, 25 October 1964, and 8 November 1964; *Berita Harian*, 23 July 1966; *Berita Minggu*, 4 September 1966). Bakar M.'s Bintang Timur, which had struggled through the 1950s, finally ceased to perform in the late 1960s.

For a short while in 1967, Radio Malaysia aired a few *bangsawan* plays performed by veteran performer Noor K. K. and his friends in a programme called 'Bangsawan di Udara' [Bangsawan on the Air]. Some of the plays included *Sitanggang* and *Puteri Gunong Ledang*. To many of the veteran performers, 'Bangsawan di Udara' was more like reading plays on the air: there were no stage or sets, no acting, no dancing, and no extra turns—the features which characterized *bangsawan*. The performers were usually allocated about an hour only, so the number of songs performed had to be reduced drastically. For example, in *Puteri Gunong Ledang*, aired on 4 October 1967, only three songs were rendered compared to the fourteen songs in the same story which was recorded by His Master's Voice (P 12760–P 12766) in the 1930s (Appendix 3). In the 'Bangsawan di Udara' version, instead of extra turns, short excerpts of different *asli* songs were played between the scenes.

Some comedians like H. M. Salim also experimented with a different form of *bangsawan* which they called *bangsawan jenaka* (comic *bangsawan*) in the 1960s. They performed *bangsawan* stories but included in them 'outrageous antics such as a *raja* riding a bicycle to the battle-field or speaking to somebody on the telephone' to make the audience laugh (Camoens, 1981: 181).

However, even this comic *bangsawan* failed to revive the popularity of the genre. Moreover, as Rahim B. stressed, the younger generation were easily more attracted to films and other types of entertainment which they thought of as modern. In the 1960s, a new type of Malay popular music called 'pop yeh yeh' became the rage. 'Pop yeh yeh' bands (*kugiran*) which took after the Beatles were formed all over the country. Bands such as 'The Hooks', 'The Siglap Five', and 'The Rhythm Boys' entertained youths with the 'twist', 'a-go-go', and 'soul' at open air concerts in towns and villages (Ismail Samaat, 1984). It is interesting to note that the *kugiran* marginalized the *orkestra Melayu* which had dominated *bangsawan* and popular music and accompanied social dancing during the pre-war and post-war periods.

Additionally, *bangsawan* declined in the 1960s as Malay theatre audiences in urban areas were attracted increasingly to a new form of theatre called *drama moden* (modern drama); Malay playwrights had begun to distance themselves even from *sandiwara*. Following Western playwrights like Shaw and Ibsen and Indonesians such as Usmar Ismail and Utuy Sontani, Malay playwrights of the early 1960s adopted an unambiguously realist mode in the belief that realism was a direct way for communicating ideas to the audience. Whereas both historical as well as contemporary plays with emphasis on nationalism were performed during the pre-independence era, predominantly realist plays dealing with contemporary social issues were written by *drama moden* playwrights in the post-independence era. Two examples of *drama moden* include *Buat Menyapu Si Air Mata* [For Wiping Away the Tears] by Awang Had Salleh and *Atap Genting Atap Rembia* [Tiled Roof, Thatched Roof] by Mustapha Kamil Yassin. The former portrayed corruption on a government land scheme while the latter compared urban life and values with village life and values. *Drama moden* playwrights constructed their plots more tightly and studiously avoided the elements of melodrama commonly found in *bangsawan* and *sandiwara* (Nanney, 1983: Chapter 4).

The Implementation of the National Culture Policy and the Revival of *Bangsawan* by the State, 1970s and 1980s

By the early 1970s, most *bangsawan* troupes had ceased to exist. Sporadic performances were staged by the Sri Timur Bangsawan (belonging to the husband and wife team of Alias Manan and Minah Alias) in Penang; the troupe performed yearly for the Penang Festival (Pesta Pulau Pinang). The Pertubuhan Seni Bangsawan Negara (PESBANA) (National Association of Bangsawan) from Kuala Lumpur also performed occasionally. In 1978, PESBANA gave performances in Kuala Lumpur, Penang, Kuala Trengganu, and Butterworth (*Berita Harian*, 6 July 1978). Set up in 1974 by the two brothers, Rahman B. and Rahim B., and other *bangsawan* performers, it was an attempt to bring the veteran *bangsawan* performers together.

Under the sponsorship of the Federal Land Development Authority or FELDA (a development scheme which opens jungle land and resettles the landless), another *bangsawan* performer, Noor K. K., set up a mobile troupe to entertain the FELDA settlers in various parts of the peninsula. It was reported that their performances of the *bangsawan* play *Sri Temiang* were enjoyed by audiences in the 'northern and east coast States of Perlis, Kedah, Kelantan and Trengganu' (*New Straits Times*, 1 April 1973). For Noor K. K., *bangsawan* helped to enrich the social life of the settlers. Besides *Sri Temiang*, his troupe played Syed Alwi's *Pak Hitam Dagang* [Pak Hitam, the Trader] and extra turns which included comedy, dancing, and singing (*New Straits Times*, 1 April 1973).

Bangsawan almost became extinct in the 1970s because it could not compete with television entertainment and other new types of popular music and theatre. Western television programmes, such as 'Hawaii Five-O' and 'Planet of the Apes', Malay and Indian films, and 'Bintang RTM' (featuring popular music) attracted both the young and old in urban and rural areas (Grenfell, 1979: Chapter 6). The young were also drawn to transnational music such as disco and the music of Michael Jackson and ABBA which were promoted by conglomerates like EMI, WEA, and CBS (Tan, 1988b). In addition, experimental plays, such as Noordin Hassan's *Bukan Lalang Ditiup Angin* [Not Blown by the Wind] (1970), attracted urban Malay theatre enthusiasts. This experimental theatre rejected realism, made greater use of symbolism, combined traditional theatre elements with modern Western ones, and addressed the problems in the country (Nanney, 1983: Chapter 5).

It was, however, in the 1970s that the first efforts were made by the government to revive *bangsawan*. This followed the development of a national culture policy by the State and its subsequent attempts to intervene in the performing arts following the 1969 racial riots when ethnic relations broke down in Malaysia.[1]

In the government's view, the root causes of the racial riots were Malay poverty and a 'crisis of values' resulting from the existence of divergent cultures (Ghazalie Shafie, 1979: 6–7). To eradicate Malay poverty, the New Economic Policy (NEP) was formulated in 1971. This had as its twin objectives the restructuring of society and the creation of a Malay commercial and industrial community in the expectation that Bumiputras (Malays and other indigenous groups) could thus become full partners in all aspects of Malaysian economic life (Jomo, 1984: 163). To achieve this, public corporations and statutory bodies were set up to implement policies favouring Bumiputras in employment, education, and business.

In addition, a common culture which would promote a national identity was deemed necessary to address the 'crisis of values'. Accordingly, at a nation-wide congress held in August 1971, three main principles of national culture were outlined (KKBS, 1973: vii):

1. The national culture of Malaysia must be based on the cultures of the people indigenous to the region;
2. Elements from other cultures which are suitable and reasonable may be incorporated into the national culture; and
3. Islam will be an important element in the national culture.

It was stipulated that the terms 'suitable' and 'reasonable' in the second principle must be seen in the context of (1) and (3).

Following the promulgation of these principles, an infrastructure to implement the national culture policy was created. The cultural division of the Ministry of Culture, Youth and Sports was reorganized into three sections: (1) research on indigenous culture; (2) promotion and training for organizing training programmes, festivals, and competitions; and (3) cultural production (Ismail Zain, 1977: 10–13). A network of district offices was established throughout the country.

State-run universities too were assigned and began to play an important role in the implementation of the national culture policy. Universiti Sains Malaysia (USM), Universiti Kebangsaan Malaysia (UKM), Institut Teknologi Mara (ITM), and Universiti Malaya (UM) introduced appropriate courses into their curriculum; these were confined to the Malay performing arts. Researches into the Malay folk arts and higher degree dissertations were encouraged. Besides offering courses on *wayang kulit*, USM made a decision to adopt and promote *bangsawan* while UKM chose the gamelan as its *anak angkat* (adopted child) (*New Straits Times*, 29 December 1985).

The government also took stronger measures to intervene directly in the arts. Laws were introduced or amended to give the police and other authorities greater control over both local and foreign arts. Under the Police Act (1967), which was amended in 1987, police permits had (and still have) to be obtained before any public gatherings, including theatre, music, or dance concerts, can be organized. An assembly of three or more persons without a police permit is deemed unlawful. To obtain a police permit for any theatrical, musical, or dance production, all scripts of productions and names of actors/actresses must be submitted to the police for censorship and approval beforehand. Licences are required to open theatres as well as to sell tickets (Malaysia, 1977).

Furthermore, domestic and foreign music programming for radio and television came under greater control. What is played on the radio and television must be passed by the censors and be in accordance with the objectives of Radio and Television Malaysia (Ministry of Information, 1975: 2). Only selected performing arts, opinions, and news can be aired.

The government also began to support those cultural activities which it deemed desirable. Competitions and festivals containing items of local culture were organized to promote what were identified as traditional Malay performing arts as well as to entertain tourists. Islam being an important component of the national culture policy, *nasyid* (a type of Arabic cantillation of poetry with noble and Islamic themes) was promoted. National *nasyid* contests were organized.

Seminars and workshops which brought performers, academics, and administrators together to deliberate on the documentation and preservation of the performing arts and to pass resolutions about their revival were regularly held. One such workshop was organized by the Ministry of Culture, Youth and Sports in 1977 to discuss the future of *bangsawan*. The workshop was attended by officials from the Ministry, veteran *bangsawan* performers, academics studying theatre, and other professional artists and film producers. The participants discussed the reasons for the gradual decline of *bangsawan* (since independence), which included competition from other types of entertainment like film and popular music. They concluded that *bangsawan* deserved to be revived and popularized because it 'manifested the culture of the Malays and a type of Malay theatre' (KKBS, 1977: 2). The revival of *bangsawan* then became part of the government's strategy to create a national, indigenously based culture.

Subsequently, another workshop—to which representatives from the different universities in the country were invited—was held at Port Dickson to discuss the preservation of traditional theatre. At the conclusion of this workshop a resolution was passed that each university should try to revive one art form. In 1978, Universiti Sains Malaysia introduced *bangsawan* as a course in the Arts Centre. Dr Ghulam Sarwar, Minah Alias, and Alias Manan were engaged as the main instructors (*Bintang Timur*, 17 September 1980). In 1980, with the encouragement of the Deputy Vice-Chancellor, Professor Datuk Sharom Ahmat, the '*bangsawan* preservation project' was launched and the Bangsawan Sri USM troupe was formed (*Star*, 17 November 1984). Factory workers, university staff, and students were invited to join the troupe.

In 1985, the Ministry of Culture, Youth and Sports launched a five-year plan for the development of *bangsawan* (Rancangan Lima Tahun untuk Pembangunan Teater Bangsawan) in the country. According to Aziz Deraman, the Director of Culture of the Ministry of Culture, Youth and Sports, five states (Perak, Penang, Kuala Lumpur, Malacca, and Sarawak) had been earmarked to form registered *bangsawan* associations. The director expressed the hope that these associations would ultimately be linked to form a national organization. Workshops where veteran performers could teach participants the skills of 'acting, characterization, speech, music, singing, and the rituals of the court' were to be organized (*Berita Harian*, 12 October 1985). Following the announcement, *bangsawan* workshops were held in Penang, Malacca, Kuching, Ipoh, and Kuala Lumpur. At the close of these workshops, the participants were afforded the opportunity to stage a *bangsawan* performance for a live audience. The workshop which I attended in Penang (described in Chapter 1) concluded with a performance of *Raden Mas* at the Telok Bahang fishing village.

The Malayization of *Bangsawan*

In line with the national cultural policy, the main *bangsawan* workshop organized by the Ministry of Culture, Youth and Sports in 1977 had stressed that 'Western elements (*unsur-unsur Barat*) have to be studied (*dikaji*) and considered (*dipertimbangkan*) carefully before they can be absorbed into *bangsawan* Malaysia' (KKBS, 1977: 2). Indeed, *bangsawan* should display the 'spirit and soul of nationalism and the culture of the nation in the aspects of language, literature, customs, ethics and so on' (KKBS, 1977: 2). What this meant, in effect, was that specifically Malay characteristics in *bangsawan* were to be emphasized. Consequently, *bangsawan* underwent national cultural streamlining based on the 1971 National Cultural Policy, which in practice meant Malayization. *Bangsawan* was to be one of the national styles of performing arts to be created and presented as the traditional arts of Malaysia. (Other examples include the *boria* (Rahmah Bujang, 1987).)

Accordingly, since the late 1970s specifically Malay stories have formed the mainstay of the repertoire of the State-sponsored *bangsawan* troupes (Figure 9.4). Thus the Universiti Sains Malaysia troupe performs mainly Malay stories, which include *Laksamana Bentan* (*Bintang Timur*, 17 September 1980; *Star*, 2 December 1985), *Laksamana Mati Dibunuh, Mahsuri* (*Bintang Timur*, 17 September 1980), *Tengku Sulung Mati Digantung* (*Utusan Malaysia*, 17 March 1983), and *Raden Mas* in 1985 (*New Straits Times*, 7 January 1986).[2] Only one Indian play *Gul Bakawali* [The Flower Bakawali] was performed in 1986. When the St George's Secondary School produced its first *bangsawan* play, it chose to stage the Malay story *Dandan Setia* [Loyal Dandan], under the direction of Cikgu Bahroodin Ahmad (*Mingguan Malaysia*, 1 May 1983). Likewise, the Bangsawan Seri Dagang Suria Jaya (under the leadership of veteran *bangsawan* performer Mohd. Nor Ismail) performed the Malay play *Perawan Kampung* [Village Virgin] in 1986 (*Utusan Malaysia*, 23 June 1986).

Performances on Malaysian television also comprise mainly Malay stories. *Alang Buana Tiga Bersaudara* [Three Brothers Cross the Universe], *Laksamana Bentan, Mahkota Berdarah* [The Crowned Prince Bleeds], *Keris Lok Tujuh* [Keris with Seven Curves], *Salim dan Hafsan* [Salim and Hafsan], and *Sultan Mahmud Mangkat Dijulang* [Sultan Mahmud Dies with Honour] were shown in 1983 (*Berita Harian*, 24 March 1983; *Mingguan Malaysia*, 1 May 1983). Television Malaysia also aired another series of Malay *bangsawan* stories by the Damisa Company in 1986. These included *Tudung Saji Terendak Bentan* [Dishcover as the Hat of Bentan], *Cinta Negeri Hang Tuah* [The Love of Hang Tuah for his Country], and *Keris Jalak Si-Ular Lidi* [Keris Jalak is a Lidi Snake] (*New Straits Times*, 27 May 1986).

As has been shown, there is virtually no place for Western, Chinese, and Indian stories in present-day performances. Veteran performers can recall only one performance of *Hamlet* in the 1970s (*New Sunday Times*, 20 April 1986). *Gul Bakawali* was staged by the Bangsawan Sri USM in 1986, while *Puteri Li Po* was produced by Rahmah Bujang in 1992. As Rahman B. (the owner of Rahman Star Opera today) stated: 'Today, I write many Malay scripts, Malay stories.... I know that even if I write other stories, they won't be developed.... In the past the selection of stories was wide.... We performed all kinds of stories.... Today the repertoire is limited to Malay stories.'[3] His brother Rahim B., who acts as a

FIGURE 9.4
Bangsawan Handbill of 1980, Featuring *Megat Teraweh*

Source: Courtesy of Pak Rahman B.

resource person in *bangsawan* workshops organized by the Ministry of Culture, Youth and Sports and freelances as an actor in *bangsawan* performances, added that in the past 'we combined all stories ... all kinds of stories because we know that Malaysia is made up of many races.... Bangsawan then was not like bangsawan today. Today bangsawan performs Malay stories only.'[4]

Accordingly, costumes used in the 1980s follow closely those of the

Malay royalty and villager; sets comprise flats and backdrops of the Malay palace hall and garden; and props consist of the Malay Sultan's yellow umbrella, throne, and kris and the Malay village *atap* house (Plates 45–48). Performers have to be versed in the rituals practised in the Malay court. Indeed, the costumes, sets, props, and rituals employed at the *bangsawan* workshop which I attended in Penang can be used interchangeably in all the Malay plays performed in the 1980s.

The musical ensemble and music of *bangsawan* have also been Malayized. The earlier *bangsawan* orchestra which was a mixture of Western, Malay, and other foreign instruments has now been replaced by the so-called traditional Malay *ronggeng* ensemble consisting of the violin, accordion, *rebana*, and gong. Sometimes, when a *rebana* is not available, a *kompang* (frame drum with goat skin tacked to the frame) is used. *Bangsawan* performers like Rahman B. say that it is difficult to get performers who can play Western instruments. At the same time, as Rahman B. points out, the anomaly is that the Ministry of Culture, Youth and Sports has a symphony orchestra yet insists that *bangsawan* performances be accompanied by its *asli* ensemble.

Furthermore, only a few Malay songs of the *ronggeng asli* repertoire in *asli*, *inang/masri*, and *joget* style are used to accompany the *bangsawan* plot today. For instance, in the story of *Raden Mas*, performed at the *bangsawan* workshop in which I participated in Penang, the following Malay songs were played: 'Suriram' (*inang/masri*) as *lagu taman*, 'Raden Mas' (*inang/masri*) as *lagu syair*, 'Anaklah Ikan' [Baby Fish] (*inang/masri*) as *lagu kahwin*, and 'Sri Siantar' (*asli*) as *lagu nasib*. The Kuala Lumpur production of *Laksamana Mati Dibunuh* in April 1986 used the following Malay songs: 'Mendam Brahi' [Head Over Heels in Love] (*inang/masri*) as *lagu taman*, 'Suriram' (*inang/masri*) as *lagu tarian*, 'Inang Pulau Bangka' [Bangka Island Inang] as *lagu tarian*, and *lagu silat* (*joget*) as opening and closing pieces. The varied musical repertoire of *bangsawan* of the early twentieth century, which consisted of songs of Western, Hindustani, Chinese, Malay, Javanese, and Arabic origins, has been narrowed down to Malay *ronggeng asli* songs.

Extra turns in the 1980s consist of mainly *asli*, *inang/masri*, or *joget* songs. In the *Raden Mas* performance in Penang, 'Joget Hitam Manis' [Sweet and Black Joget] (*joget*), 'Siti Payung' [Umbrella Lady] (*asli*), and 'Cempaka Sari' (Frangipani Flower) (*inang*) were sung as extra turns. In the Kuala Lumpur performance of *Laksamana Mati Dibunuh*, 'Kuala Deli' [Estuary of River Deli] (*asli*), 'Siti Payung' (*asli*), and 'Sri Kedah' (*asli*) were presented. Unlike in the early twentieth century, there were no chorus girls and boys who performed high-kicking and vaudeville items.

The few Malay songs used today have in turn been further Malayized. By way of example, two renditions of the piece 'Lagu Sambut Kekasih' [Song for Receiving Lovers] may be compared. Example 9.1 was recorded in the 1980s by Dr Ghulam Sarwar of Universiti Sains Malaysia and sung by Minah Alias while Example 9.2 is an excerpt from a 1930s recording of the play *Laila Majnun* by the Gramophone Co.

EXAMPLE 9.1
'Lagu Sambut Kekasih'

Source: Recording by Dr Ghulam Sarwar (1980s).

EXAMPLE 9.2
'Lagu Sambut Kekasih'

Source: 78 r.p.m. record (1930s), His Master's Voice (P 12801).

Ltd. under the label of His Master's Voice in Dum Dum, India (Cat. no. P 12801). The song is sung when two lovers (usually the hero and heroine) meet in the garden.

The 1980s example differs from the 1930s example in instrumentation, rhythmic pattern, and harmonic texture. In all these aspects, the 1980s example shows Malayization. In the first instance, the Western ensemble (consisting of the violin, piano, and double bass) of the 1930s has been replaced by the *ronggeng* ensemble (consisting of the violin, accordion, *rebana*, and gong) in the 1980s. While the 1930s example uses the double bass, piano bass, and woodblock to play the rhythmic pattern which is repeated throughout the song, in the 1980s example the *rebana* plays the rhythmic pattern while the gong marks the repetition of each rhythmic pattern.

In addition, although both examples use vertical triads sparingly (usually played at cadences by the accordion and piano respectively) and neither one modulates, the 1930s example shows a stronger presence of harmony because of the jumping bass played by the double bass and piano. This jumping bass alternates between notes from triads based on tones 1 and 5 (bars 1–3).

Although the *inang* rhythmic pattern ($\|: d\, \underline{.\, t}\, .\, \underline{d}\, d :\|$) is used in the 1980s example instead of the *masri* pattern, I am told by performers that the two rhythmic patterns can be used interchangeably in this piece today. The former is supposed to be Malay while the latter is associated with Middle Eastern *beledi* dancing.

Examples 9.3 and 9.4 are two versions of another song, 'Bunga Tanjung' [Flower of the Cape], which is commonly used in *bangsawan* today. Example 9.3 is also sung by Minah Alias while Example 9.4 was recorded in 1927 by Beka Records (27801). The song is an *asli* piece which is sung in garden scenes.

As in 'Lagu Sambut Kekasih', the 1980s example of 'Bunga Tanjung' shows Malayization. While the 1927 version uses Western instruments such as flute, violin, and piano as the ensemble, the 1980s recording employs the Malay *ronggeng* ensemble. Furthermore, the 1927 example

EXAMPLE 9.3
'Bunga Tanjung'

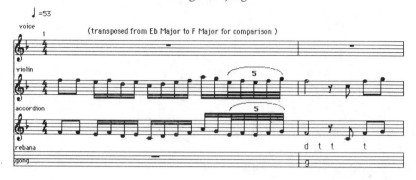

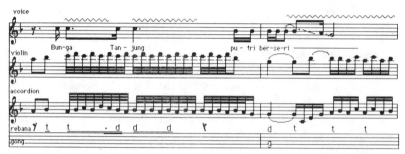

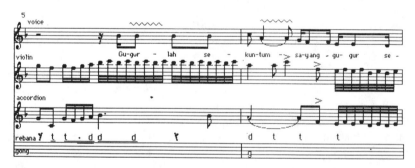

Source: Recording by Dr Ghulam Sarwar (1980s).

EXAMPLE 9.4
'Boenga Tandjung'

Source: 78 r.p.m. record (1927), Beka Records (27801).

portrays a greater feeling of harmony because of the chords played by the piano. Instead of piano chords, the 1980s example is accompanied by the Malay *asli* rhythm ($\|$: d t t t | .t t. d   d d ɼ: $\|$).

The 1980s version also shows Malayization in the instrumental lines. As in Malay *asli* music, the violin and accordion lines in Example 9.3 are highly ornamented (bars 3, 5, 6, and 7). By comparison, the flute and violin in Example 9.4 hardly play ornamentation except for a short trill in bar 7.

* * *

As a result of national cultural streamlining beginning in the 1970s, the innovative, heterogeneous, 'modern' (*Saudara*, 11 April 1936), and 'up-to-date' (*Straits Echo*, 11 June 1926) kind of *bangsawan* of the early twentieth century has become an increasingly traditional Malay theatrical form.

In this most recent form, *bangsawan* is no longer able to attract non-Malay audiences or performers.[5] Even Malays of the younger generation find it difficult to identify with this type of *bangsawan* which has distinctly failed to adapt to the times in terms of themes, music, dances, and setting, and which does not emphasize variety.

It is therefore not surprising that very few members of the audience stay till the end of a present-day *bangsawan* performance—a rough measure of any cultural form's capacity to resonate with the popular imagination. As Utih, a well-known theatre critic in Malaysia observed at a performance organized by the Ministry of Culture, Youth and Sports in 1986:

A standing-room-only audience greeted the bangsawan performance of *Laksamana Mati Dibunuh* last April 12 at Panggung Bandaraya, Kuala Lumpur. By the time the show was over, less than 50 remained in the hall which can house about 450 people.... [The night before] ... less than 10 enthusiasts stayed till the end.

The audience laughed ... at this strange anachronism called bangsawan. But only for a while, for soon they pushed off to the more exciting *pasar malam* [night market]. (*New Sunday Times*, 20 April 1986.)

Being one of the few who stayed till the end of these two *bangsawan* performances, I concur with Utih's observations. As in other present-day performances, the two shows were too 'fixed' and 'formal'. Performers relied excessively on scripts so that they hardly improvised. Although the sets and costumes were designed for historical fidelity and exhibited courtly extravagance, and rituals of the Malay court were observed in great detail, the Ministry of Culture's *bangsawan* did not cater to the audience's tastes. As Utih emphasizes, the 'soul of bangsawan was missing'. According to Utih, *bangsawan* can only attract audiences if it is done well and shows a sensitivity for the tastes of modern-day audiences.[6]

Even though—or perhaps because—*bangsawan* is promoted by the State, by State-sponsored universities, and by the State-sponsored television and radio, it is not 'alive' but etiolated. Society at large is more interested in soap operas, rock music, video, and other forms of modern entertainment. At the same time, the present *bangsawan* performances do not have popular appeal because they are artificially traditional and do not take into consideration audience preferences, as they used to in the early twentieth century. Rather, the official *bangsawan* of today is performed as cultural show-pieces at State functions, coronations of Sultans, cultural festivals to entertain tourists, and (occasionally) on television.

The predicament of *bangsawan* performers in the 1980s indicates the state of artificial survival of *bangsawan*. Except for a handful like Minah Alias and Alias Manan who are paid small salaries for instructing *bangsawan* at Universiti Sains Malaysia, most veteran performers are compelled to look for other types of employment in order to survive. A few of the younger performers who have some capital, like Ahmad B., Rahman B., and Rahim B., have started companies (like Damisa, Mash, and DHR) which produce videos of *bangsawan* and other modern Malay plays for sale to Television Malaysia. Others such as Mat Hashim, my *rebana* teacher, works as a security guard in a factory. His wife, a former *bangsawan* dancer, cooks and sells food at a coffee-shop. Wan Pekak, a former *bangsawan* violinist, plays the clarinet with a band which performs daily at funerals to pay for his rented room. He washes plates at another coffee-shop for his meals. All three of them perform occasionally with the *ronggeng* ensemble at weddings and other festivities and when there are *bangsawan* performances staged by Bangsawan Sri USM.

Many of the other veteran performers are unemployed. Every day, they gather at a coffee-shop in Kuala Lumpur to reminisce for hours on the days when they were stars and when fans chased after them. In their declining years, they nevertheless hope to be invited to perform again, when they can once more wear expensive costumes, stand under the spotlight, and forget momentarily about their poverty.

Though jobless, Wan, Menah Yem, and Mat Arab consider themselves fortunate, for they can stay with their children. Others, however, live alone and in poverty. In his eighties now, Suki stays in a rented room in a squatter area near Chow Kit Road in Kuala Lumpur. Ainon Chik, who is in her seventies, lives in a dilapidated hut full of dust and cobwebs in the backyard of her son's house. Even though her son's family has room enough for her in their brick bungalow, Ainon Chik has insisted on staying on her own with her cats, chickens, and ducks because she has been independent all her life.

1. Government intervention in the arts was part of an overall shift toward authoritarianism in Malaysia in the 1970s and 1980s. During this period, there was wider use of the Internal Security Act (1960) which allows detention without trial, the Sedition Act (amended in 1971) which prohibits the public debate of 'sensitive' issues such as Malay privileges, the Universities and University Colleges Act (1971) which reduces the autonomy of student organizations, and the Printing Presses and Publication Act (1988) which provides the government the power to ban all cassette tapes and books which it considers a 'threat to the security of the nation' (Kahn and Loh, 1992).

2. The instructors of the troupe, Minah Alias and Alias Manan, say that it is difficult to put up other types of stories because it is hard to find performers who will be able to sing *lagu klasik, lagu Hindustan, lagu Cina*, etc.

3. 'Sekarang pakcik banyak buat skrip Melayulah, cerita-cerita Melayu.... Pakcik tau, kalau pakcik buat pun tidak ada kembangan.... Dulu cerita luas dalam lakonan.... Keseluruh cerita kita dapat main.... Hari ini terhad, cerita Melayu, Melayu.'

4. 'Kita rangkumkan semua cerita ... semua corak cerita itu tadi kerana kita kena tau Malaysia berbagai-bagai bangsa.... Bangsawan tidak macam hari ini. Hari ini bangsawan tetapkan cerita Melayu sahaja.'

5. For the Chinese, the Chinese opera and new types of popular entertainment called *Ko-tai* [Song-stage], which present popular songs as well as sketches of contemporary life, have gained popularity. For discussions of Chinese opera and *Ko-tai*, see Tan (1980 and 1984a) respectively.

6. Unfortunately, the performance of *Laksamana Mati Dibunuh* was also 'technologically shabby. Audibility, for example suffered from poor sound technology.' (*New Sunday Times*, 20 April 1986.) As early as 1977, a well-known actor and director of modern plays, Hatta Azad Khan had already stressed that technical aspects should be emphasized in *bangsawan* (*Berita Harian*, 17 August 1970). He said that *bangsawan* would be able to attract audiences only if it followed the example of the Manohar Company of India which played to capacity crowds in Kuala Lumpur because the performances were technically well done. The company brought more than 100 tons of props.

10
Conclusion

THIS study, in tracing the social and stylistic history of *bangsawan* from the 1880s till the 1980s, has attempted to establish four main arguments. First, it has asserted that the *bangsawan* of the early twentieth century was commercial and innovative, that it emphasized variety, and that it contained characteristics that were modelled on Western productions. This goes against the claims of Mustapha Kamil Yassin, Rahmah Bujang, and the Malaysian government that *bangsawan* was traditional theatre. Unlike traditional theatre, *bangsawan* used the proscenium stage and stage setting of the drop and wing variety. It incorporated elements from pantomime, ballet, circus, and vaudeville from the West. At a time when lighting was not yet sophisticated in theatrical performances, emphasis was placed on spectacular tricks to attract the audience. Stage sets demanded the use of machinery and devices like trapdoors, sliding flats, and suspended, painted backdrops.

Bangsawan was a form of commercial theatre which was advertised through the mass media and its proponents were therefore conscious of stardom. Even women were allowed to appear on stage and were promoted as stars. Performers became professional artists who primarily earned their living by acting in *bangsawan*.

As commercial theatre, *bangsawan* was constantly adapting to audience preferences. Since patrons could choose from a wide variety of competing *bangsawan* troupes, the success of a troupe depended on its ability to attract large audiences. Indeed, opera troupes called on the audience to listen to their 'modern' and 'up-to-date songs of different languages'. With the rise of Malay nationalism, Malay stories with Malay costumes and sets were introduced. With greater exposure to Western film, theatre, and books, audiences began to prefer realism to fantasy, and *bangsawan* responded accordingly, moving gradually towards realism. Stories were increasingly set in specified places and periods. The stage became a 'real' place with backdrops and props to signal the location. Characters were more 'real' in that the emotions which they were given to feel were more intensely and openly expressed by the performers and, in addition, 'authentic' costumes were employed. (At least the audience imagined this to be so.) Characters of royal birth spoke in the language of the Malay courts but ordinary characters used colloquial speech. 'Authentic' music incorporating instruments and styles from foreign countries were introduced to accompany stories set in those countries.

Bangsawan also differed from traditional theatre in that it emphasized variety and heterogeneity. It became a receptacle for musical and cultural interaction and stimulated musical and cultural change. Compared to traditional theatre which catered specifically to the Malays, *bangsawan* brought people of different ethnic groups together. Its repertoire was stocked with Western, Malay, Indian, Chinese, Javanese, Spanish, Egyptian, Turkish, and other foreign stories, dances, and songs borrowed from touring operetta and vaudeville troupes from America and Europe, visiting opera troupes from China, and touring Parsi theatre groups from India. The orchestra was a mix of Western, Malay, Latin American, and Indian instruments. The basic idiom of *bangsawan* music was a fusion of Malay and Western elements. The Malay elements included the singing style, vocal ornamentation, the linear texture, the cyclic drum rhythmic patterns, and the use of Malay *syair* texts. Western elements included the use of harmony or implied harmony and close relationship between the text and the music. *Bangsawan* songs which were associated with Middle Eastern, Chinese, Hindustani, or Javanese stories, characters, or dramatic situations often had other characteristics added to the Malay/Western mix. Middle Eastern, Hindustani, or Javanese modes, ornamentation, vocal style, rhythmic patterns, and melodies were incorporated. The Chinese pentatonic scale and 'meaningless' syllables were also used.

This does not imply, however, that *bangsawan* was completely different from traditional theatre and that this new theatre was a form of Western theatre. Indeed, despite the variety, adaptability, and novelty of the form, *bangsawan* retained many conventions of traditional theatre with which the Malays in particular were familiar. Some of these characteristics included the emphasis on comedy, farce, and melodrama; the staging of fantasies where virtue was triumphant at the end; the combination of dance, music, and drama; and the use of stock characters, scene types, and specific *lagu* for given dramatic situations. Hence *bangsawan* did not represent a complete break with the past. Characteristics of traditional Malay theatre were manifested in the new form.

What this study rejects are those formulations which juxtapose the traditional and the modern as polar extremities, as forms transiting from one to the other in unilinear fashion. Instead, it maintains that traditions are continually changing. As has been shown, *bangsawan* acquired new characteristics while maintaining a continuity with the past. Although *bangsawan* did away with the *buka panggung* ceremony for propitiating spirits in traditional theatre, the practice of reciting short prayers before the stage was set up and the curtain opened was retained. There was a move towards realism, but this realism was not fully articulated. Although plots became more linear, this linearity was blurred by song and dance interludes, the performers' interaction with the audience, and the extended comedy, farce, melodrama, and fighting which were so typical of traditional theatre. Even though *bangsawan* drew heavily on the conventions of traditional theatre for scene types, stock characters, and specific musical elements associated with specific dramatic situations, the so-called conventions in *bangsawan* itself were flexible and subject to change. Stock characters began to show more emotion while conflict between 'love' and 'duty' was projected. Compared to the *lagu* of traditional theatre, the *lagu* of *bangsawan* operated on the basis of fewer stylistic regulations. (These regulations governed rhythmic pattern and tempo.) New themes and melodies from foreign popular songs were constantly adapted. The same *lagu* could be played at different tempos for different dramatic situations.

The second point this study wishes to highlight is that the emergence, development, decline, and revival of *bangsawan* have largely resulted from external social and political factors. *Bangsawan* emerged in the Malay Peninsula at a time when rapid socio-economic, political, cultural, and demographic changes were occurring as a result of British intervention. Colonialism saw the emergence of a multi-ethnic society, urbanization, the development of new communication systems, formal education, and the introduction of new foreign cultural activities in Malaya. As a product of the times, *bangsawan* articulated the changes taking place in colonial Malayan society. *Bangsawan* was heterogeneous, innovative, and constantly adapting to new situations and new audiences. Its conventions of plot structure, character types, costumes, speech, stage setting, and musical style corresponded with the new 'structure of feeling' that was emerging as a result of radical social changes.

The decline of *bangsawan* in the 1940s and early 1950s was a consequence of social hardships caused by World War II and the uncertainties and harsh living conditions of the immediate post-war and Emergency periods. The development of new forms of entertainment in the late 1950s further contributed to the decline of *bangsawan*. *Bangsawan* began to lose its novelty as the film industry took away its best actors and adapted its stories for the screen. Moreover, with rising Malay nationalism, the Malay intelligentsia had created a new form of theatre called *sandiwara* which could more readily express the current mood and spirit of anti-colonialism and the drive towards independence. Unlike in *bangsawan*, the emphasis in *sandiwara* was on scripted plays with realistic settings and costumes, real mortal characters who spoke proper (not colloquial) Malay, and texts which elaborated the economic, cultural, and political issues of current relevance to Malays.

The revival of *bangsawan* in the 1970s and 1980s, too, was a result of external political factors. In fact, *bangsawan* is still performed today largely because it is promoted and produced by the government and its institutions. Following the 1969 ethnic riots, the State began to intervene in the performing arts in an attempt to create a national art and culture and thereby contribute towards promoting national unity. This was in line with the newly adopted National Culture Policy. 'National' forms of the performing arts were thus created. In so doing, government officials and cultural experts often resorted to reshaping the past traditions. This is certainly true in the case of *bangsawan*.

However, it is inadequate to argue that government officials and cultural experts have created an artificial tradition for *bangsawan* to serve explicitly political ends. Rather, in reshaping *bangsawan*, State officials and experts are also responding to modernity. With the development of new types of communication such as radio, television, satellites, film, and books and their control by big corporations based in America, Europe, and Japan, a type of global consumer culture has spread all over the world and dominated most parts. By returning to the past and tradition, cultural producers often are looking for the roots which they have lost.

Indeed, the reshaping of *bangsawan* can be seen as part of a general revival of Malay tradition especially among 'a growing middle class of civil servants, educators and professionals' (Kahn, 1992). Besides *bangsawan*, other art forms such as *boria*, *dikir barat*, and *zapin* (Mohd. Anis, 1990) have been revived and re-created. There has been a revival of old songs and movies, and the promotion of cultural 'heroes' such as P. Ramlee and Saloma (*New Straits Times*, 11 September 1990). Dance-dramas based on Malay legendary tales such as *Putri Sa'Dong* (by Suasana Dance Co.) are also staged. Contemporary theatre groups have also incorporated *bangsawan* elements in their productions. *Pentas Opera* (by Zakaria Ariffin) depicted the trials and tribulations of a *bangsawan* troupe during the Japanese Occupation in Malaya; the musical *Nostalgia Laguku* (by Najib Nor) re-enacted the glamorous life and the set-backs of the *bangsawan* era; and *Hamba Allah* (by Syed Alwi) used *bangsawan* to portray the fate of Malay tradition.

The third point this study wishes to make is that although external social and political factors are important in shaping the fortunes and nature of *bangsawan*, they are not the total explanation. *Bangsawan* did not merely reflect or mirror cultural change. In fact, the performers themselves were actively creative and innovative and were able to intervene in the 'making' of *bangsawan*, though admittedly within certain socio-economic, political, structural, and historical constraints. In this regard, it must be stressed that *bangsawan* was one of the new forms of entertainment created by non-Europeans in Malaya as a response to the cultural activities of Europeans, activities which were regarded by the non-Europeans as attractive but from which they were excluded or which were beyond their reach. The new non-European theatre was open to people of all ethnic backgrounds, including the European. Free to innovate and adapt to audience preferences, *bangsawan* performers in the early twentieth century created an interesting and appealing heterogeneity—interesting and appealing to their heterogeneous audience.

The performers continued to innovate and adapt, even when *bangsawan* was declining in the 1940s and 1950s. Many troupes assumed

Japanese names and performed Japanese propaganda plays to earn food and obtain medicine during the Occupation; they included more realistic modern-style Malay plays and Malay historical plays in the 1950s; and they experimented with *bangsawan jenaka* in the 1960s.

In order to survive today, however, *bangsawan* performers who are employed by the government or the universities and/or are contracted to Radio and Television Malaysia have been inclined to follow the government's guidelines on national culture. The *bangsawan* performances which are shown on television or staged at State functions have become increasingly Malayized. The performers have once again reshaped *bangsawan* to suit the times, but this has resulted in the Malayization of the form, which the government has projected as traditional. Such dependence on State sponsorship compromises the independence of the performers and their ability to further reshape and innovate, and it curtails any efforts to make *bangsawan* popular again for all ethnic groups. *Bangsawan* has become a State-sponsored artefact.

Finally, this book asserts that musical and cultural syncretism in *bangsawan*'s development is the result of non-musical–cultural factors. As stressed in the Preface, interaction does not happen automatically or mechanically when two or more cultures come into contact. Nor is syncretism a result of 'compatibility' or 'similarity' of musical 'traits'.

Syncretism occurred in *bangsawan* in the early twentieth century as a result of the following factors. As commercial theatre, *bangsawan* had to adapt to the tastes of the urban population. In particular, Western elements were adopted as they were 'modern' and 'up-to-date' and it was 'prestigious' to perform and listen to the music of the British. Musical interaction also took place because of the close relations among *bangsawan* performers of different ethnic groups who lived and toured together, and learnt from and helped one another. Exposure through technological innovations and the mass media played an important role in promoting cultural interaction as well.

In addition to the above, there remained an overriding factor, namely the degree of control imposed by governments over the arts and artistic expression. In the early twentieth century, the British colonial authorities had little interest in imposing censorship or control over *bangsawan* because it did not threaten their prestige and status; thus, musical interaction could occur freely. However, since the 1970s, with the Malaysian government's attempts to intervene in the performing arts, a lesser degree of musical interaction has taken place. *Bangsawan* has become increasingly Malayized. Not only has *bangsawan* become less syncretic, it has also lost its creativity, flexibility, and adaptability as a consequence of government sponsorship. The present-day *bangsawan* is artificial. It lacks dialectical interplay between audience and players and critical thinking in the texts and music. It does not have popular commercial appeal. Government intervention has had a dampening effect on intercultural interaction and creativity in the case of *bangsawan*.

This is not to say that no musical syncretism or creativity is taking place in Malaysia today. Nor is it to suggest that the government has been able to exert its control over all the arts as it has over *bangsawan*. Some performing arts groups which are independent of the government and command popular support continue to exist. Indeed, some groups even challenge the government's attempts to achieve cultural hegemony over Malaysian society. In response to the national culture policy and the increasing ethnic polarization in the country, a recent revival of Malay, Chinese, and Indian arts and festivals has occurred. These arts and festivals have become emblems of ethnicity (Tan, 1988b and 1988c).

At the same time, new forms of popular music which evoke popular support and which promote syncretism have also emerged. Like *bangsawan* music of the 1920s and 1930s, these new musical forms have been inspired by internationally distributed popular music as well as local music of various ethnic origins. Popular music groups such as Asiabeat and singer-composers like Manan Ngah and Hang Mokhtar combine Western electronic and indigenous instruments and turn to Malay, Chinese, and Indian music for their rhythmic and melodic ideas (Tan, 1988b).

Chinese cultural groups have incorporated Malay music, dances, and dramatic themes into their performances as well; many such groups continually play Malay folk-songs like 'Tanah Air Ku', 'Air Didik', and 'Inang Cina' (arranged by Lee Soo Sheng), and new compositions incorporating local dance rhythms. One example of the latter is Saw Yeong Chin's 'Malay Dance' based on the *ronggeng* rhythm.

Contemporary dance choreographers such as Marion D'Cruz (Five Arts Centre) and Leong Wai Kein (Kwangsi Association) have also combined Chinese, Malay, and modern dance movements and music in their works. Ramli Ibrahim (Sutra Dance Co.) has mixed Indian, Malay, and modern dance movements in his choreography.

What this study wishes to stress is that the arena for creative musical and cultural interaction has shifted away from *bangsawan* to other forms of art. Such artistic shifts are processes which inevitably accompany change in 'structures of feeling', societies, and governments. The unfailing creativity of individual human beings will ensure that artistic forms which are syncretic or adaptive will always emerge. What is tragic, however, is that the artistic forms of many societies are disappearing before our eyes without documentation. This study is an attempt to document the social and stylistic history, as well as the fate, of one such form—*bangsawan*—in the twentieth century.

Appendices

Musical Transcriptions

Key to Transcriptions

WESTERN notes are used in the transcriptions but letters which stand for 'drum syllables', that is, standard Malay onomatopoeic representations of the drum strokes, are employed so that the timbre of the drum stroke can be better represented. I was taught to play the *rebana* using these drum strokes.

d	drum syllable 'dung' (used by *bangsawan* musicians), undamped stroke played by the right hand, striking drum towards the centre of drum head producing a deep, resonant sound
t	drum syllable 'tak', light, sharp stroke striking drum near the rim
g	gong syllable 'gung', undamped stroke on gong striking drum at the centre
〰〰〰	vocal vibrato

trill (if vocal vibrato is wide enough for two pitches)

turn

mordent

↑ pitch is slightly higher than indicated note

↓ pitch is lower than indicated note

two notes joined by a glide (glissando)

note is attacked by a glide from a lower pitch

single appoggiatura

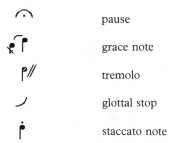

pause

grace note

tremolo

glottal stop

staccato note

TRANSCRIPTION 6.1
Lagu Melayu: 'Hiburan Raja Ahmad Beradu'

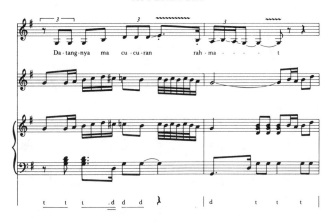

STANZA II · only voice part transcribed

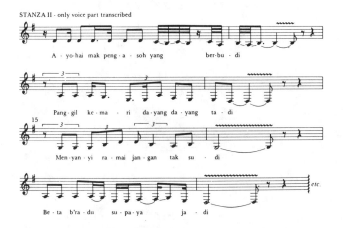

Source: 78 r.p.m. record (1930s), His Master's Voice (P 12761).

TRANSCRIPTION 6.2
Lagu Padang Pasir/Arab: 'Telek Ternang'

Source: 78 r.p.m. record (1930s), His Master's Voice (P 12763).

TRANSCRIPTION 6.3
Lagu Padang Pasir/Arab: 'Gambos Sri Makam'

Source: 78 r.p.m. record (1930s), His Master's Voice (P 12803).

TRANSCRIPTION 6.4
Lagu Jawa: 'Sinandung Jawa'

Source: 78 r.p.m. record (1930s), Chap Kuching (NG 73).

TRANSCRIPTION 6.5
Lagu Hindustan: 'Paraber'

Repeat of B and A [Text of B when repeated:
Wokarim bernepa, Dia boleh buat seberang apa].

Source: 78 r.p.m. record (1930s), Chap Singa (QF 35).

TRANSCRIPTION 6.6
Lagu Hindustan: 'Mostikowi'

Transcribed a tone lower

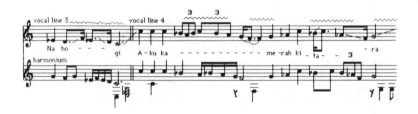

Source: 78 r.p.m. record (1930s), Chap Singa (QF 36).

TRANSCRIPTION 6.7
Lagu Klasik/Opera: 'Penceraian Jula Juli dengan Sultan'

Source: 78 r.p.m. record (1930s), Chap Kuching (NG 30).

TRANSCRIPTION 6.8
Lagu Cina: 'Shanghai Street'

Source: 78 r.p.m. record (1930s), His Master's Voice (P 15978).

APPENDIX 2
Synopses of Six *Bangsawan* Plays

THESE synopses provide the bases for the analysis and comparison of the scene types and stock characters in Chapter 6. Standard scene types and stock characters were used in the six plays which originated from different countries. The scene types were the reference points for performers who knew the conventions which corresponded with each of them. Four different summaries of the foreign play *Hamlet* are also presented to show how *bangsawan* scene types and stock characters were adapted.

I. *Jula Juli Bintang Tiga* (*cerita klasik/opera*)

This story is based on a 78 r.p.m. recording of the play by the Gramophone Co. Ltd., Dum Dum, India, under the label of Chap Kuching or Cat Label (NG 29–NG 32). Advertisements for performances of the play were made in newspapers from the turn of the century. Veteran performers say that this is one of the most popular *bangsawan* plays. As the category *cerita klasik* or *opera* implied, the characters wore Western costumes (their own version) and adapted songs from the West.

Scene i: Takhta Kerajaan di Negeri Zamin Tawaran
[Throne or Reception Hall at the Palace in Zamin Tawaran]

Sultan Darshah Alam of Zamin Tawaran Kingdom gives an audience to his court officials. He asks about his state and his people. His court officials answer that all is well. Since there are no problems that require his attention, the Sultan announces that he is going to play ball by the beach.

Scene ii: Taman di Tepi Laut [Garden by the Sea]

While playing ball the King loses his sacred ring which is called 'Mustika Bumi' (magic stone of the earth). The ring is also the symbol of the ruler. The Sultan promises to give anything to the person who can find the ring. He orders his clown servant Adam and his officials to look for the ring.

Meanwhile, Jula Juli Bintang Tiga, the third daughter of the King of the Heavens, has been ordered by her father to look for a husband on earth. She flies across the stage with the sacred ring in her hand. The Sultan asks for the ring. She says she will return the ring if the Sultan fulfils her three conditions: (a) the Sultan has to marry her; (b) the Sultan cannot ask for her real name: (c) the Sultan cannot inquire about her background (where she came from, her parents, etc.). The Sultan agrees to all these conditions, brings her back to his palace, and marries her.

Scene iii: Takhta Kerajaan Istana

The Sultan meets with his court officials. In the course of their discussion it is revealed that one year has passed. The Sultan and Jula Juli Bintang Tiga now have a child named Baharom Alam. The court officials say that some foreigners are visiting the kingdom and wish to see the queen. They cannot introduce the queen without knowing her name or anything about her.

The Sultan calls for his wife and demands to know her background. She replies that if the Sultan wishes to know her origins, then he must bring her to the place where he first found her.

Scene iv: Jalan [Road]

The Sultan brings Jula Juli Bintang Tiga to the place where they first met. He is angry with her.

Scene v: Taman di Tepi Laut

Jula Juli tells him her name and her background. A goose (angsa) descends from the heavens. Jula Juli sits on the goose and ascends into the clouds. The Sultan faints.

Scene vi: Kayangan [Heaven]

Jula Juli Bintang Tiga sits with her two sisters, Jula Juli Bintang Satu and Jula Juli Bintang Dua, on some paper or cardboard stars. Jula Juli Bintang Tiga asks her two sisters to go down to earth with the fairies (pari-pari). She wishes them to give her son a special bow and arrow called panah pancawarna (literally meaning multicoloured bow and arrow), which has supernatural powers.

The two sisters and their fairies carry the panah pancawarna to earth.

Scene vii: Istana Zamin Tawaran [Palace of Zamin Tawaran]

Baharom Alam, Jula Juli Bintang Tiga's son, fights with a raksasa (giant, demon) using an ordinary bow and arrow. He kills the giant. Suddenly the giant's face transforms into that of Baharom Alam's father. Baharom Alam realizes that his father had changed into a giant after he forced Jula Juli Bintang Tiga to reveal her identity. Baharom Alam has murdered his own father.

Baharom Alam is about to kill himself when his aunts Jula Juli Bintang Satu and Jula Juli Bintang Dua come down from kayangan with their fairies. They persuade him not to commit suicide and tell him that his father will live again one day. They give him the panah pancawarna and tell him that he can achieve anything he wishes with the assistance of the special bow and arrow.

Placing the bow and arrow over his father's dead body, Baharom Alam prays that his father will rise from the dead. The Sultan wakes up. Baharom Alam then asks for his mother and Jula Juli Bintang Tiga descends from the clouds.

Seeing the family reunited, Jula Juli Bintang Satu and Jula Juli Bintang Dua ascend with their fairies to kayangan.

II. *Puteri Bakawali* (*cerita Hindustan*)

This play was performed by the Bangsawan Sri USM troupe on 2 July 1986. The following synopsis is taken from the script written by Alias Manan, one of the teachers and directors of the troupe. Alias Manan based the script on bangsawan performances of the play in the 1930s. Performances of this play had been advertised in the newspapers since the turn of the century.

Scene i: Takhta Kerajaan Tajul Bahri di Singgah-sana Balai Penghadapan
[Palace Reception Hall of the Kingdom of Tajul Bahri]

Sultan Tajul Arif holds an audience with his viziers (*wazir*) and court officials. He inquires about the state of his kingdom and his people. They answer that all is well. In turn, the court officials ask the king about his health. The king is worried about his blindness and wants to know its cause. According to the state astrologer (*ahli nujum negara*), the king became blind because a golden barking deer (*kijang mas*) darted across his path while he was hunting. Only the flower Bunga Bakawali (Bakawali Flower), which may be found in Taman Bolkis (Garden of Bolkis), can cure the king. The astrologer says that the garden has never been entered by any human being, insect, or animal. It is guarded by a genie (*jin*), ghost or spirit (*mambang*), and fairies (*pari-pari*). No one can pluck this flower except the king's son Tajul Muluk.

Tajul Muluk agrees to try. The two sons of the premier vizier (*wazir perdana*), Ahmad and Muhamad, volunteer to go with him. As a prayer and offering for their safe journey, food and money are given to the poor and to the mosque.

Scene ii: Jalan [Road]

The three young men reach a three-road crossing and decide to split up. Ahmad and Muhamad agree to follow the roads which pass through seas of mud and ashes respectively while Tajul Muluk decides to take the road that passes a sea of fire. They agree to meet at a certain junction after a period of time.

As soon as Tajul Muluk leaves, both Ahmad and Muhamad go to the market instead to enjoy themselves. They plan to meet at the junction at the designated time.

Scene iii: Gua Batu [Stone Cave]

Tajul Muluk arrives at a cave after crossing the sea of fire. He falls asleep. A *garuda* (Vishnu's eagle) by the name of Gurda swoops down, catches Tajul Muluk, hurls him down, and threatens to eat him. Tajul Muluk begs for pity. Since Tajul Muluk is handsome, Gurda decides not to kill him but asks him to marry his daughter. Tajul Muluk says he does not want to marry a bird. In a good mood, Gurda does not force the marriage but asks Tajul Muluk to call him grandfather. Gurda leaves.

Princess Nurul Asyikin, the daughter of Gurda, appears. After threatening to kill Tajul Muluk for not wanting to speak to her, she falls in love with him. They flirt with each other.

Gurda returns. Both lovers run off. Gurda calls his daughter and tells her that he cannot find her a husband. Gurda declares that he should have squeezed Nurul Asyikin to death long ago. She screams for help and Tajul Muluk rushes to help her. Tajul Muluk brushes her cheek when she says that it hurts. Gurda slaps Tajul Muluk. This time, Nurul Asyikin pats his cheek. Gurda declares that since both of them have committed sins, they have to be punished. Their punishment is marriage! They happily agree and Gurda marries them.

When the two lovers are alone, Tajul Muluk tells Nurul Asyikin his reason for coming. She says that her father is the guard of Taman Bolkis. She has an idea. They pretend to fight to deflect Gurda's attention. Nurul Asyikin agrees to stop fighting. She will tell Gurda why they are quarrelling if Gurda swears upon the name of Nasar Sulaiman (the Vulture Sulaiman who is his superior) that he will not become angry. Gurda agrees. After much coaxing, Gurda decides to help

Tajul Muluk. He asks his friend, Maharaja Tikus (the King of the Mice), to dig a tunnel from his palace to Taman Bolkis. Tajul Muluk says goodbye to Nurul Asyikin and promises to come back for her. He sits on the Maharaja Tikus and they both leave.

Scene iv: Taman Bolkis

Princess Bakawali is sleeping in Taman Bolkis. She is guarded by the genie and fairies. Tajul Muluk enters. He climbs up the dais or sleeping platform (*geta-puterakna*), picks the Bakawali flower, and takes the ring from the princess' finger.

When her father, Maharaja Indar, finds out that she has lost her flower and her ring, he gets angry and sings that it is better for her to die. The ring is the symbol of the ruler. The fairies beg him not to kill her. She is ordered to go down to earth dressed as a man to look for the ring and flower. She is not allowed to return without them.

Scene v: Jalan

Ahmad and Muhamad meet Tajul Muluk at the three-way crossing. All three have a flower each. They tell each other how they obtained the flowers. They decide to test the powers of their flowers on a blind man who passes by. Ahmad and Muhamad's flowers cause pain while Tajul Muluk's flower makes the blind man's eyes feel cool. He is able to see.

Ahmad and Muhamad suggest that they travel a bit before going back. They want to see a beautiful fish in a lake near by. Tajul Muluk goes with them.

Scene vi: Pemandangan Tasik [View of the Lake]

While Muhamad pretends to show Tajul Muluk the golden fish in the lake, Ahmad pushes him. Before Tajul Muluk falls into the lake, Muhamad steals the flower from him. Both Ahmad and Muhamad leave.

Fatimah, a village woman who comes to fetch water from the lake, saves Tajul Muluk. Tajul Muluk pretends to be Abdul, a merchant who has been robbed and thrown into the lake. Fatimah takes him home.

Scene vii: Rumah Pondok [Hut]

After hearing Abdul's story, Fatimah's husband Ali says he is welcome to live with them. They tell him that they are farmers. They grow bananas, maize, and vegetables. Abdul asks Fatimah to make cakes for him to sell at the market.

Scene viii: Kerajaan Tajul Bahri [Government of Tajul Bahri]

The Sultan asks for news of his son and the vizier's two sons. Just as the vizier is about to say that he has not heard anything, Ahmad and Muhamad enter. They say that Tajul Muluk did not meet them at the designated time and place. They show the chief astrologer the flower. The chief astrologer declares it to be real. As soon as he puts the flower on the Sultan's eyes, the latter is able to see again. In return, the king grants the two brothers freedom to do anything they like for forty days and nights. The king promises to pay for their expenses.

Just as Ahmad and Muhamad leave, a young boy named Shahrat appears and wishes to see the king. He says that he has been travelling from kingdom to kingdom searching for knowledge. He had heard that the government of Tajul Bahri is prosperous and just. He has come to pay his respects. Pleased with Shahrat's praises, the Sultan asks his chief vizier to give the boy a job. He is made the keeper of the key to the treasures of the palace. The Sultan asks his vizier to give alms to the poor and the mosque to thank God for the return of his eyesight.

Scene ix: *Jalan*

Abdul sells cakes. Ahmad and Muhamad pass by and say they want to buy some cakes. After eating, they pretend to choke. While Abdul goes to get water for them, they run off without paying him. Ali and Fatimah insist on reporting this theft to the Sultan.

Scene x: *Balai Penghadapan [Audience Hall]*

The Sultan asks his officials whether they have heard from Tajul Muluk. The chief vizier says that he has sent out a search party. Ali, Fatimah, and Abdul enter. They complain about the theft to the Sultan. The Sultan declares that Abdul will be punished if he is lying and asks Abdul to identify Ahmad and Muhamad. He points to the two culprits. Ahmad and Muhamad deny that they stole the cakes. After all, the Sultan had given them so much money to spend.

Shahrat begs for forgiveness and reports that there is a thief in the audience hall. He asks the Sultan to order that all doors be closed. He then points at the ring that Abdul is wearing. He says that the ring belongs to his father. Shahrat reveals 'himself'. Actually, she is the Princess Bakawali dressed like a man. She says that Abdul was the one who stole the flower and ring from her and Ahmad and Muhamad had tricked Abdul.

Abdul takes off his poor man's clothes. After seeing him, the Sultan descends from his throne to hug his son. Ahmad and Muhamad are sentenced to life imprisonment. Tajul Muluk begs the Sultan to forgive Ahmad and Muhamad but to let this be a lesson to all humans on earth. They are forgiven.

Gurda arrives with Nurul Asyikin. Maharaja Indar also appears to take his daughter back. He asks the Sultan to plant the Bunga Bakawali so that it will survive for a long time on earth. Before she leaves, Princess Bakawali asks for her ring. Tajul Muluk replies that he cannot part with it. It would be like losing his life. Besides, he is sad that she is going back to *kayangan*. The ring would serve as a reminder of her. If she really wants the ring back, she has to cut it off his finger. The Princess lets him keep the ring. Father and daughter ascend to heaven.

Gurda tells the Sultan that Nurul Asyikin is actually the daughter of the king of a country called Tajul Naim. Gurda had taken her when she was playing in her father's garden. He leaves Nurul Asyikin and goes back.

Following the custom of Tajul Arif, the Sultan declares forty days and nights of festivities to celebrate the wedding of his son to Nurul Asyikin.

III. *Laksamana Bentan* (*cerita Melayu*)

This play was very popular in the 1920s and 1930s. Veteran *bangsawan* performers say that it is the first Malay play performed in the history of *bangsawan*. According to Suki, the Sultan of Bentan who was invited to see the premiere performance 'stood up' when the performer playing the Sultan came on stage. This synopsis is based on two separate performances: (a) by the Bangsawan Sri USM troupe which performed in Taiping (Perak) in conjunction with the coronation of the Sultan of Perak on 22 December 1985; and (b) by the Kuala Lumpur group for PATA in Kuala Lumpur on 11 April 1986. Scripts were written by Alias Manan and Rahman B. respectively for the performers of the two groups.

Scene i: Singgah-sana Kerajaan Bentan
[Court Audience at the Palace of Bentan]

The Sultan of Bentan sits on his throne surrounded by the prince (Raja Muda Bentan, heir to the throne of Bentan), two princesses (Tengku Wan Senari, eldest daughter of the Sultan and Tengku Wan Entah, second daughter of the Sultan), officials, servants, and maids. The Sultan asks his officials about the state of his country and his people. The officials answer that all is well. His son and two daughters are also well.

Suddenly, two merchants arrive wishing to see the Sultan. They complain that they have been robbed by a band of pirates headed by Megat Alang DiLaut in the Sea of Bentan. The Sultan asks his Temenggong (treasurer) to repay the merchants and orders the Admiral of his fleet, Raja Andak Raja Laksamana, to destroy the pirates.

Scene ii: Taman Banjaran Sari [Garden of Banjaran Sari]

Tengku Wan Entah and her maids are playing and singing. The Laksamana enters the garden to see her. He puts his small single-edged dagger (*tumbok lada*) on the table. They exchange greetings through song. Suddenly, Kembang Cina, the chief maid-in-waiting, hurries in and announces that Tengku Wan Entah's brother and sister are here. The Laksamana leaves in a hurry and forgets his dagger. Tengku Wan Senari sees the dagger and asks Wan Entah if anyone had entered the garden. Wan Entah refuses to answer. Wan Senari gets angry and accuses her of 'dishonouring the good name of the family of Bentan' (*mencemarkan nama baik keluarga Bentan*). She is about to stab her sister with the dagger when her brother stops her. Wan Senari gives him the dagger and leaves. Raja Muda threatens Kembang Cina and forces her to tell him who entered the garden. She breaks into hysteria (*latah*) before saying that it was the Laksamana.

Scene iii: Sebuah Pulau [An Island]

Pirates are gambling, cheating, and quarrelling with each other. They make a lot of noise. Megat, their chief, reprimands them. Megat describes his background to the audience (in verse). His mother is of royal blood but she had to leave the court when she married an ordinary man. Suddenly, one of his pirates announces that the enemy is seen. Megat orders his pirates to get their boats and weapons ready.

Scene iv: Di dalam Bahtera Laksamana [In the Vessel of Laksamana]

While Raja Laksamana orders his warriors to get ready for the attack, he is surprised to find the Raja Muda in the vessel. He had come to fight Megat as well as to confront the Laksamana about his sister. The Raja Muda asks the Laksamana how he is going to fight without a weapon. He takes out the dagger found in Wan Entah's garden. Just then, they hear shouts. The pirates and the Laksamana's warriors fight. The Raja Muda is stabbed by a pirate. The

Laksamana asks Megat to kill him because the heir to the throne of Bentan is dead.

Overcome with sadness, Megat repents, asks the Laksamana to stand up, gives his *keris* (dagger) to the Laksamana, kneels, tears his clothes, and beats his chest. Megat begs the Laksamana to make him his slave (*hamba orang tawanan*). The Laksamana ties his hands with a black cloth (a sign of captivity), lowers the flag of the ship to mourn the death of the Raja Muda, and sails home.

Scene v: Kerajaan Bentan [Palace of Bentan]

The Sultan asks for news of Laksamana Bentan. Just as the Raja Temenggung says he has not heard anything, the Laksamana enters and pays his respects. Megat is ordered in. He swears he will not be a pirate any more and asks for forgiveness. The Sultan forgives and frees him. He asks the Temenggung to give him and the other pirates a plot of land each so that a village could be set up with Megat as the headman.

The Sultan then looks around for his son. When he hears that the Raja Muda has been killed by pirates, he feels ill, pauses a while and then asks the Temenggung to inaugurate his daughter Tengku Wan Senari as the heir to the throne after 44 days of mourning. All flags are to be lowered for these forty-four days.

Scene vi: Pemandangan Jalan dalam Kampung [A Road in the Kampong]

Megat hides and waits for Wan Entah. When he sees the princess walking pass on her way to the garden, he praises and teases her. The Laksamana comes along and scolds Megat, saying that he loves her. Megat laughs. The two men compete with each other (through verse) and later start fighting. Megat loses, of course. The Laksamana leaves.

While he is recovering from the duel, Wan Senari passes by. After hearing what has happened, she asks him if he still keeps 'venomous poison' (*racun berbisa*). She wants to test the Laksamana's love for her sister and asks if he has an 'antidote for the poison' (*penawar*) as well. Megat replies that he has. Megat gives her the poison and leaves.

Scene vii: Pemandangan Sebuah Taman Lengkap dengan Tempat Tidur
[Private Garden with a Platform for Sleeping]

While Wan Entah plays with her maids, Wan Senari puts some of the poison in the drink of Wan Entah and goes for a walk. Wan Entah drinks, gets sick, coughs, and faints.

The Laksamana is called. Struck with grief, he sings and draws his *keris* to kill himself declaring there is no point in living any more. Wan Senari asks him to find someone else. The Laksamana replies that even angels from the sky cannot replace Wan Entah. Ashamed of herself, Wan Senari calls for Megat.

Megat walks in gloating and teases the Laksamana. He says that the Laksamana is crying like a child thirsting for milk and that it is shameful to cry in front of so many people. Megat goes near Wan Entah and annoys the Laksamana further by touching Wan Entah's hand and forehead. The Laksamana controls his jealousy as Megat promises a cure. Megat asks for a glass of water, mumbles some prayers, puts a piece of elephant tusk in the glass, and sprinkles some of the water on Wan Entah's forehead and body. He then drinks some of the water and spits the water all around, making sure that it hits the Laksamana.

Wan Entah wakes up. Wan Senari asks the Temenggung to marry the couple and to install them as King and Queen of Bentan. Wan Senari will go to Bangka because Bangka is part of Bentan and has no ruler. The Laksamana orders some of the people to go with her and build her a palace. Megat is asked to take care of Wan Senari. Wan Entah asks for forgiveness. Wan Senari hugs her and forgives everyone. As she leaves, all wish her a safe journey.

IV. *Laila Majnun* (*cerita Arab*)

This synopsis is based on interviews with Minah Alias and Mat Hashim and 78 r.p.m. recordings of the play in the 1930s. The records were produced by the Gramophone Co. Ltd., Dum Dum, India, under the label of His Master's Voice [P 12800–P 12805]. The play has been performed since the early twentieth century. It has been described by veteran performers as 'the Arab version of *Romeo and Juliet*'.

Scene i: Rumah Saudagar Abdullah [House of the Merchant Abdullah]

Majnun's father, a rich businessman, and his mother discuss sending their son to school. They agree that he needs education. Majnun and his servant, Selamat, leave for school.

Scene ii: Sekolah [School]

Majnun meets Laila, the daughter of the teacher. They study together and fall in love.

Scene iii: Rumah Saudagar Abdullah

Majnun's parents are very sad because their son does not seem to want to eat or sleep. When they pressure him to tell them why he is not himself, Majnun reveals to them his love for Laila. Majnun's father decides to see Laila's parents about arranging marriage for the two lovers.

Scene iv: Sekolah

The businessman meets with the teacher. The father of Laila does not approve of Majnun. Laila's mother wants her daughter to marry someone else. She asks Majnun's father to take him away from the school.

Majnun's father goes home and tells his son to look for someone else to marry.

Scene v: Rumah Saudagar Abdullah

Selamat, the clown servant, helps Majnun to meet secretly with Laila. Majnun disguises himself as a blind beggar, wears beggar's clothes, and carries a stick. Selamat guides him.

Scene vi: Sekolah

Majnun and Selamat meet with Laila but they are caught by the teacher. He beats Laila and Majnun.

Scene vii: Rumah Saudagar Abdullah

Majnun is so lovesick that he turns mad. He runs out of the house. His father, his mother, and Selamat look for him.

Scene viii: Sekolah

Laila also becomes mad. She sees Majnun's face. She remembers the times with Majnun and imagines Majnun singing to her. Selamat comes to tell her that Majnun has disappeared. Laila runs away.

Scene ix: Padang Pasir [Desert]

Majnun and Laila sing of their fate as they run in different directions. Finally they meet. A strong wind blows, uprooting trees. They both die, one on top of the other. The parents of both Majnun and Laila arrive but it is too late. The parents sing of their fate.

V. *Sam Pek Eng Tai* (*cerita Cina*)

This synopsis is based on interviews with Minah Alias who used to play the role of Eng Tai in the 1930s and 1940s. *Sam Pek Eng Tai* was one of the popular Chinese plays performed by *bangsawan* troupes from the turn of the century. According to *bangsawan* performers, it is the Chinese version of *Romeo and Juliet* and *Laila Majnun*. A Chinese director is usually borrowed from the Chinese Opera troupe to help direct the play and the music when *Sam Pek Eng Tai* was performed in the 1930s.

Scene i: Rumah Tionghua Kaya [Rich Chineseman's House]

Eng Tai tells her rich merchant parents that she wishes to study in Hang Chiu. Her parents try to persuade her to study in her own hometown. All the students at Hang Chiu are males. As a woman, she cannot go there.

Scene ii: Rumah Tionghua

One afternoon, Eng Tai dresses herself up as a man. While her parents are having tea, she slips in and sits next to her mother. Her father becomes angry when Eng Tai (dressed as a man) says that she loves her mother. He beats her for flirting with his wife. Her hat falls off and her long plaited hair drops down.

Scene iii: Rumah Tionghua Miskin [Poor Chineseman's House]

Sam Pek tells his mother (a cake-seller) who is sick that he wishes to study in Hang Chiu. His mother says that she has no money to send him. Nevertheless, he leaves with his brush and paper, wearing torn dirty clothes.

Scene iv: Jalan [Road]

While Sam Pek is walking to Hang Chiu, he meets Eng Tai (disguised as a man) riding on a horse. Eng Tai befriends Sam Pek and offers him a ride on her horse. Not knowing that she is female, he accepts her offer.

Scene v: Sekolah [School]

During registration, all the students pay their fees. Sam Pek has no money. Eng Tai pays for him. The teacher assigns the students their rooms. Eng Tai is shocked when Sam Pek volunteers to share a room with her.

Scene vi: Kebun Bunga [Flower Garden]

Eng Tai tries to suggest to Sam Pek that she is a woman. First, she admires the flowers in the garden and says that she loves flowers. Sam Pek thinks she is crazy because to him, only women love flowers. Secondly, Eng Tai likens Sam Pek to a bee and she a flower. Again, Sam Pek thinks she is out of her mind to suggest that analogy of the male and female. Thirdly, Eng Tai pats Sam Pek's lap. He tells her not to do it because they are both men. Fourthly, Eng Tai sees the statues of a god and a goddess on an altar near by and says that they are like the pair of statues. Lastly, she asks him to look at the fish in the pond. Like Sam Pek who always follows Eng Tai, the male fish always follows the female fish. Bewildered and frustrated, Sam Pek says that Eng Tai is crazy and walks away.

Scene vii: Sekolah

Sam Pek and Eng Tai return late. Both of them are caned and fined. They have to give twelve pencils to the teacher. Sam Pek cannot afford the fine and Eng Tai helps him.

Scene viii: Taman Dekat Sungai [Garden near the River]

Eng Tai wishes to bathe in the river. She tells Sam Pek not to follow her. He goes anyway since he thinks they are both men. She insists that he bathe first and then wait for her far away. While she is bathing, he peeps. Shocked that Eng Tai is a woman, he collapses. Eng Tai comes over and tells him that she had given him so many clues before. Both declare their love for one another. Sam Pek says that he is poor. He cannot possibly marry Eng Tai.

Scene ix: Rumah Tionghua Kaya

A rich businessman from Shanghai comes to see Eng Tai's father to ask for his daughter's hand in marriage. Eng Tai's father sends a servant to bring her home.

Scene x: Sekolah

Both Sam Pek and Eng Tai are studying. The teacher gives Eng Tai a letter from her mother. She reads it and says that she has to go home. Both lovers cry and sing of their fate.

Scene xi: Rumah Tionghua Kaya

Eng Tai does not want to marry the rich businessman. She sends a bird with a letter for Sam Pek to tell him the news. Sam Pek falls ill after reading the letter and sends her another letter (also by means of a bird). He tells her he is going to die. He asks her to go to his grave and poke the hole for the joss-stick with her hairpin.

Scene xii: Rumah Tionghua Kaya

After the official ceremony, on the day of her marriage, Eng Tai asks her new husband for permission to visit her friend's grave. He agrees.

Scene xiii: Kubur [Grave]

Everyone at the wedding accompanies her. At the grave, Eng Tai prays and pokes the hole for the joss-stick with her hairpin. The grave breaks into two. Eng Tai disappears into the grave. Two butterflies appear. Angry, Eng Tai's father digs the grave up and finds a pair of stones. He separates the two stones so that the lovers cannot be together. But their spirits had already joined. From the stones grow two bamboo trees. Eng Tai's new husband becomes crazy. He leaves. Fairies descend from the heavens to rejoice the joining of the two spirits of Eng Tai and Sam Pek.

VI. Comparison of Four Versions of *Hamlet*

The four versions are summaries of (a) *Hamlet, Prince of Denmark* by Kean (1859), reproduced in 1971; (b) a story told to me by veteran actress Minah Alias; (c) a description of *Hamlet* by R. O. Windstedt (Federated Malay States Civil Service) for the *Malay Mail* and reprinted by the *Straits Echo* (14 November 1908); and (d) a review of *Hamlet* printed in the *Times of Malaya* (11 January 1912).

The characters from the four versions include

Hamlet—Prince of Denmark

Queen Gertrude—mother of Hamlet and wife of King Claudius

King Claudius—brother of Hamlet's father and Hamlet's uncle who married Gertrude after the death of her husband

Polonius—Prime Minister

Ophelia—daughter of Polonius

Laertes—son of Polonius

Marcellus—guard

Bernado—guard

Rosencrantz—courtier

Guildenstern—courtier

Osric—courtier

PC 22—police guard

Published Script by Charles Kean (1895)	*Minah Alias's Version*	*Winstedt's Review (1908)*	*Times of Malaya Review (1912)*
	Scene i: Garden	*Scene i: Palace room*	*Scene i: Garden*
	Claudius asks Queen Gertrude to put a poisonous leaf in the King's ear while he is sleeping. Gertrude follows his instructions. The King dies. The Queen shouts for help. People come, and they say it must be a snake which has bitten the King. Hamlet comes out and sees his father dead. He swears that he will not take off his black clothes till he finds out why his father died.	King Claudius addresses Queen Gertrude about Hamlet's sanity. Polonius hurries off to find out about Hamlet's sanity. A clown sings to introduce himself.	Sultana Gertrude sings of her love for Claudius while her husband sleeps. Claudius brings poison and asks her to put it in the King's ear. Gertrude does so. The King scratches his ear and dies. Hamlet sings '*Idop-kah mati-kah.*' (Is he alive or dead?)

Act I

Scene i: A platform before the castle

The ghost appears before Horatio and the two guards (Marcellus and Bernado) who are taking care of the coffin of the King.

Scene ii: A room of state in the palace

Laertes asks for permission to leave for France. Hamlet laments the death of his father. Horatio, Bernado, and Marcellus report that they saw the ghost of the king. Hamlet says he will visit the grave.

Scene iii: A room in Polonius' house

Ophelia and Polonius bid Laertes farewell. Ophelia declares her love for Hamlet. Polonius asks her to marry Hamlet.

Scene ii: Graveyard

Two clowns (Sunday and Monday) go back and forth, scared. The ghost appears. The two clowns run off to call Hamlet. Hamlet visits the grave. His father's spirit appears and tells Hamlet that he had been poisoned by his mother and that his mother and uncle are lovers. Hamlet is angry and declares that he will find out the truth.

Scene ii: Graveyard

The clowns sleep at the foot of the coffin. The ghost appears. Scared, the clowns look into the coffin. One moment the corpse is there, the next it is gone. Terrified, the clowns exit to fetch Hamlet.

The curtain re-opens. The clowns, Polonius, Horatio, and Hamlet are at the grave. The ghost appears. Horatio and the clowns are scared. The ghost reveals the story and vanishes.

Scene ii: Graveyard

The Constables Marcellus and Bernado ask PC 22 to take care of the grave. The ghost appears. PC 22 is scared. He telephones the officer who reports to Hamlet.

At the stroke of twelve, the ghost appears. Hamlet recognizes the ghost as his father. The ghost tells Hamlet how he was murdered.

Published Script by Charles Kean (1895)	Minah Alias's Version	Winstedt's Review (1908)	Times of Malaya Review (1912)
Scene iv: The platform at night			
Hamlet, Horatio, and Marcellus enter. The ghost appears.			
Scene v: More remote part of platform			
The ghost and Hamlet re-enter. The ghost tells Hamlet the whole story. All three are made to swear that they will not speak of this to anyone.			
Act II			
Scene i: A room in Polonius' house	*Scene iii: House of Ophelia*	*Scene iii*	
Ophelia tells her father that Hamlet came to see her, held her, and left.	Hamlet asks everyone to go to the house of Ophelia.	Hamlet sings how a play shall be devised to prick the King's conscience.	

Scene ii: A room in the castle

The King discusses Hamlet's transformation with the Queen. He asks his courtiers (Rosencrantz and Guildenstern) to visit Hamlet. Polonius enters and says that Hamlet has gone mad. He reads Hamlet's love letter to Ophelia. Polonius wishes to confront Hamlet about the matter. Hamlet comes in reading. Polonius asks him questions. His answers make sense. Polonius decides to leave and plan a meeting between Ophelia and Hamlet. Hamlet plans to have a play staged, and he gets the actors together.

Act III

Scene i: A room in the castle

The two courtiers return to invite the King and Queen to the play. The King and Queen hope that the cause of Hamlet's wildness is his love for Ophelia. They send for Hamlet so that he can meet Ophelia.

Scene ii: Opera

Hamlet invites everyone including Claudius, Gertrude, Ophelia, and Laertes to the performance.

The dumb show (as in Scene 1) is performed. Hamlet sits with the audience and

Scene iv: Dumb-show

Hamlet puts on a show where a sleeping person is poisoned. Hamlet roams about saying 'I'm . . . clever . . .' A clown watches the face of the King and Queen and detects agitation.

Scene iii: Outside the theatre

Hamlet arranges with the players of a neighbouring theatre to stage a representation of the murder. He invites Claudius and Gertrude who get free admission. People of many ethnic origins come to the performance.

Published Script by Charles Kean (1895)	Minah Alias's Version	Winstedt's Review (1908)	Times of Malaya Review (1912)
Hamlet and Ophelia enter. Ophelia remembers Hamlet's sweet words to her. Hamlet accuses her of being dishonest. Hamlet says that he does not love her anymore and asks her to join a convent. Feeling dejected, Ophelia leaves.	narrates the story. The Queen stops the performance just as the actress puts poison into the ear of the King. She leaves. Hamlet shouts that she has killed her husband and that he will find out the truth soon.		*Scene iv: Theatre* The Queen and her lover are affected by the performance.
The play *Mouse Trap* is performed. It is about a murder in Vienna. In the play, the King's nephew puts poison into the King's ears when he is sleeping. Claudius stops the play. Rosencrantz, Guildenstern, and Polonius tell Hamlet that his mother wishes to see him.			

Scene v: Palace

The King, Queen, and Polonius are in consultation. The King says that Hamlet is moody and should get married soon. Polonius brings Ophelia. Hamlet strolls in.

Hamlet refuses to marry Ophelia. He spits and spurns her. She leaves the stage and falls into a pond. The King enters and repents.

Scene v: Palace

Laertes asks for permission to leave for France.

Scene vi: Palace

Ophelia and Hamlet meet. Hamlet had killed her father by mistake. Now he refuses to marry her. He takes back her engagement ring and knocks her down eight times.

Scene vii

After nineteen verses to the air of 'Ah Che La Morte', Ophelia plunges into the sea.

Scene ii: A room in the palace

The King wants to send Hamlet away to England.

Scene iii: The Queen's chamber

The Queen and Polonius are discussing Hamlet when the latter comes in. Polonius hides. Hamlet says that the Queen has offended his father by marrying Claudius. She wants to call someone but he makes her sit still. She asks him if he is going to kill her. Polonius shouts 'help'. Thinking that it is a rat, Hamlet stabs Polonius. Hamlet shows his mother the picture of his father and accuses her of being a murderer. The ghost appears and prods Hamlet on. The Queen cannot see the ghost and thinks Hamlet has gone mad. She says that he is creating everything in his head. She says she repents and leaves.

Scene v: Palace

Laertes leaves for overseas.

Scene vi: Palace

Hamlet meets with Ophelia. He says that he does not want a wife that lies. He knows that there is someone else in the palace besides her. Ophelia insists that there is no one else. Hamlet stabs at the curtains. Ophelia cries and Polonius drops dead. Ophelia goes mad.

Scene vii

Ophelia is so depressed that she commits suicide. She walks into the river carrying a flower, singing and asking why Hamlet left her.

Published Script by Charles Kean (1895)	Minah Alias's Version	Winstedt's Review (1908)	Times of Malaya Review (1912)
Act IV			
Scene i: A room in the castle			*Scene viii: Palace*
The King sends Hamlet away to England for his own safety since he has killed someone. Ophelia weeps for the death of her father. Laertes returns from France. When he finds out that his father had died, he calls for revenge.			The Queen and King decide that Hamlet must not be suspicious. Claudius sends Hamlet after Laertes with a letter.
Bernado brings a letter from Hamlet saying he has returned and that he wishes to see the King. The King plots with Laertes to kill Hamlet. They will dip the tip of the sword in poison and prepare a poisonous drink. The Queen enters and says that Ophelia fell into a brook while weeping and died.			*Scene ix: Mid-ocean* Hamlet jumps from his ship on to a cruiser going back to Denmark. *Scene x* Hamlet turns up at the court and tells his mother about England. The King arranges for Laertes to kill Hamlet. He prepares two glasses (one with poison and the other without).

Act V

Scene i: Churchyard

The two clowns dig the grave of Ophelia. They discuss whether she should be given a Christian burial. Hamlet enters and is told that the grave is for a woman who has committed suicide. Priests enter, followed by Ophelia's coffin, Laertes, the King, and the Queen. Each one says a prayer for Ophelia. Laertes grapples with Hamlet and is stopped by the King and the Queen.

Scene ii: Hall in the castle

Osric (courtier) comes and tells Hamlet that the King has laid a wager on his head. Hamlet agrees to fight.

Scene viii: Grave

Hamlet wears black and covers his face with a black mask so that he will not be recognized. People say kind words and throw flowers over the coffin. Laertes declares his love for Ophelia and says he will take revenge for her death. Hamlet takes his mask off and says it is he who has killed her. Hamlet is prepared to fight. They are stopped by the Queen.

Scene ix: Palace

Hamlet shows his father's photograph to his mother and says that the man was good. He shows her Claudius' photo and says the man is evil. Hamlet's mother says Hamlet is mad and must die.

Published Script by Charles Kean (1895)	Minah Alias's Version	Winstedt's Review (1908)	Times of Malaya Review (1912)
Scene iii	*Scene x: Palace*	*Scene vi: Palace*	*Scene xi: Palace*
Hamlet and Laertes play sword. The King asks Hamlet to drink first. Hamlet wishes to fight instead. The Queen drinks from the cup and falls. Laertes wounds Hamlet. They exchange rapiers and Hamlet wounds Laertes. Laertes says the King is to be blamed: his mother had been poisoned. Hamlet stabs the King. Laertes asks to exchange forgiveness since his father was killed by Hamlet. Hamlet takes the cup, drinks, and dies.	The King asks Laertes to kill Hamlet so that he can become the next king. They put poison at the tip of the sword and in a glass of drink. Hamlet and Laertes fight with the sword. Gertrude drinks from the poisoned cup and dies. Hamlet is hurt. Hamlet stabs Laertes. Hamlet is carried by four friends to the top of the hill. Everyone says 'The Last King of Denmark'.	Hamlet and Laertes fight. Laertes falls. The Queen drinks poison. The King is stabbed by Hamlet. Hamlet draws the scimitar across his throat and dies. Polonius is spared and looks at the dead bodies.	Hamlet and Laertes fight. Hamlet is cut at the wrist. Laertes is stabbed. Gertrude grabs the poison, drinks it, and dies. Hamlet gives Claudius a choice of the cutlass or poison. Claudius declines but when he sees that the audience wants him to die, he chooses the poison. Hamlet raises the cutlass and cuts his own throat.

APPENDIX 3
Categories of *Lagu* and Their Dramatic Uses
in *Puteri Gunong Ledang*

THIS table is based on an analysis of seven 78 r.p.m. records of the 1930s (His Master's Voice, P 12760–P 12766). It shows the relationship between *lagu* and dramatic situation in *Puteri Gunong Ledang* (analysed in Chapter 8).

Babak (Scene)	Synopsis of Events	Lagu (Musical Piece)
1. *Taman* (Garden)	The cock crows. The clock strikes five times. It is five o'clock in the morning. The maids and servants of the palace of Sultan Mansur Shah of Malacca are up. Che Wan Gayah, nursemaid (*inang*) to the heir to the throne (Raja Ahmad), asks the maids and servants to get ready quickly. She then describes Raja Ahmad and gives him advice.	'Che Wan Gayah' [Song of Che Wan Gayah], *lagu asli*, sung by Che Wan Gayah, male servant, and chorus
	Raja Ahmad accepts the advice. He will study the Koran and learn about the world. He is going to see his father, the Sultan.	'Guridam Raja Ahmad' [Couplet of Raja Ahmad], *lagu asli*, sung by Raja Ahmad
	Bujang Kelana, one of the ministers, comes to tell the nursemaid that the Sultan wants to see his son. She replies, 'Yes'.	'Penchak Silat' [Malay Art of Self-defence], *lagu inang*, sung by the minister, nursemaid, and chorus
	Nursemaid tells Raja Ahmad that he has been summoned to see the Sultan. Before he prepares himself to see his father, he calls the maids-in-waiting to sing for him.	'Hiburan Raja Ahmad Beradu' [Song of Entertainment for Raja Ahmad While He Rests], *lagu asli*, sung by Raja Ahmad, nursemaid, and chorus
2. *Istana Kerajaan Melaka* (Palace of Government of	The Sultan of Malacca meets his chiefs and ministers. The ministers and the people are sad that the Queen has passed away. They sing that the palace is so quiet. The people want a queen.	'Percintaan Baginda Yam Tuan' [The Love of His Highness], *lagu asli*, sung by the Sultan, Sang Stia,

Babak (Scene)	Synopsis of Events	Lagu (Musical Piece)
Malacca)	The Sultan says that he will only marry an extraordinary princess. The warrior, Sang Stia, suggests that they call the shaman.	and ministers
3. *Kampung* (Village)	Sang Stia is sent to fetch the *pawang* (shaman) Tok Ngah and his wife.	'Tok Ngah Pawang' [Shaman Tok Ngah], *lagu masri*
4. *Istana* (Palace)	Tok Ngah and Mek Ngah go into trance. They say that the Princess who lives on Gunong Ledang is a good match. The Laksamana and Sang Stia are sent to ask for her hand. They take Tun Mamad, the headman of Indragiri, with them. Tun Mamad brings some men to help clear the path.	'Telek Ternang' [Going into Trance Using a Water Jar], *lagu inang*
5. *Hutan* (Forest)	The Laksamana, Sang Stia, and Tun Mamad climb the mountain. Halfway up, they find they cannot climb any further as the wind is too strong and the path too difficult. Tun Mamad continues to climb with a few of his men while the Laksamana and Sang Stia wait. Tun Mamad asks a sage about the fruits there.	'Seloka Buah Mempelam' [Stanza of the Mango Fruit], *lagu asli*, sung by Tun Mamad and sage 'Seloka Buah Rambutan' [Stanza of the Rambutan Fruit], *lagu asli*, sung by Tun Mamad and sage
	As Tun Mamad and his men approach the 'singing bamboos', the wind becomes so strong, that the climbers feel they may be blown away. There is thunder and lightning.	'Tangisan Buluh Perindu' [Cry of the Singing Bamboos], *lagu asli/lagu nasib*
6. *Taman*	They come upon a garden. They meet an old woman called Dang Raya Rani, the Guardian of the Princess of Gunong Ledang. She asks Tun Mamad who he is and why he is there. He gives his name and states his reasons. She goes in to consult the Princess.	'Dang Raya Rani', *lagu inang*, sung by Dang Raya Rani and Tun Mamad

Babak (Scene)	Synopsis of Events	Lagu (Musical Piece)
	Another older woman, Nenek Kebayan, appears. She says that the Princess will accept the Sultan's offer of marriage if she is given the following: (a) a bridge of gold and a bridge of silver from the foot of the mountain to the palace; (b) seven trays of sandflies' hearts (c) seven trays of mosquitoes' hearts; (d) seven barrels of young areca-nut water; (e) seven barrels of tears; (f) a bowl of Sultan Mahmud's blood; and (g) a bowl of Raja Ahmad's blood. (The old woman is actually the Princess herself in disguise.)	'Nenek Kebayan dan Tun Mamad' [Fairy Godmother and Tun Mamad], *lagu masri*, sung by Nenek and Tun Mamad

'Pinang Mas Kahwin' [Song of Dowry for Marriage], *lagu asli*, sung by Nenek |
| 7. *Istana* | Tun Mamad, Laksamana, and Sang Stia return to the palace. The Sultan says that he can provide all that the Princess requested except the blood of his son. Tok Ngah and Mek Ngah sing that the Princess does not intend to marry the Sultan. The Sultan declares that God knows the truth and to Him he will return. The people ask God to bless and keep their Sultan. | 'Baginda Yamtuan Melaka' [His Highness the Sultan of Malacca], *lagu inang*, sung by Tok Ngah, Mek Ngah, Tun Mamad, Sang Stia, and the Sultan. |

Glossary

abang	brother
adinda	sister
aguk kebesaran	ornamental medallion for royalty
ahli nujum negara	state astrologer
alat à la Hindustan	Hindustani instrument
alat melodi	melodic instrument
alat rentak	rhythmic instrument
alat tali	stringed instrument
alat tiupan	wind instrument
anak	child
angsa	goose
Apa khabar?	How are you?
Arab	Arabic
asli	traditional; original; name of slow sad song of Malay origin; rhythmic pattern
atap genting	tiled roof
awan	clouds
babak	scene; scene type
bahasa pasar	colloquial language
baju dalam	inner shirt
baju kurung	Malay traditional dress for women
baju luar	outer coat
bangsawan	nobility; of good birth; Malay opera
bangsawan jenaka	comic *bangsawan*
barshat	rhythmic pattern of Indian origin
beras	rice
berbakti	serve
beta	I, me (term used by royalty)
betul	correct (term used by *bangsawan* performers to mean 'realistic')
bintang	star
biola	violin
boria	popular theatre (comprising dance, song, and sketch) originating from Penang
buka panggung	opening ritual in traditional theatre for propitiating spirits
bunga	flower; ornament
bunga telur	eggs given out during weddings
cai luong	popular theatre of Vietnam

cari makan	make a living
cerita	story or tale
cerita sejarah Melayu	Malay historical tales
Cina	Chinese
cinta	love
dalang	puppeteer
dendang	musical piece
dinding papan	wooden walls
dok	cylindrical drum with one head struck by the fingers of one hand
dondang sayang	love-song; type of slow sad dance-song
drama moden	modern drama
'drop sin'	curtains (drop scene)
extra turn	extra turn (entertainment between scenes)
fesyen	fashion
gambos [*gambus*]	rhythmic pattern; instrument; dance-song of Middle Eastern origin
gamelan	Javanese or Malay instrumental ensemble
garuda	Vishnu's eagle
gaya pertuturan	manner of speech
gedombak	one-sided goblet drum
gendang	barrel-shaped drum
getaputerakna	sleeping platform; dais
gong	flat or bossed gong
gongan	gong cycle, period of time between two strokes on a big gong
gua batu	stone cave
gunung	mountain
halus	fine, refined, elegant
Hari Raya	feast day marking the end of the fasting month in the Muslim calendar
hikayat	tale, story, romance
hilang royat	formula for closing scene in *wayang Siam*
Hindustan	Hindustani
hutan	forest, jungle
inang	nursemaid; lively dance-song of Malay origin; rhythmic pattern
irama	tempo (concept includes metre and rhythm)
irama dua	double density; twice the number of notes per unit of time
istana	palace
jalan	road
jalar	curtain
Jawa	Javanese
jin afrit	an evil spirit, often featured in *bangsawan*
joget	popular Malay dance; happy dance song of Portuguese origin; rhythmic pattern
joget gamelan	gamelan ensemble or dance originating from the Pahang/Trengganu courts
kain hitam	black cloth
kain samping	sarong
kampung	village

kasar	coarse
kasih sayang	love
kaya	rich
kayangan	heaven; cloud
kebaya labuh	knee-length blouse
kebun bunga	flower garden
kecapi	stringed instrument
kerah	labour
keramaian	celebration; gathering
keris kerajaan	state kris
ketoprak	popular theatre originating from Java in the nineteenth century
khemah gedung besar	big godown-like tent
kijang emas	golden barking deer
klasik	classical
komedi Melayu	Malay comedy
komedi stambul	popular theatre originating from Java in the late nineteenth century; *stambul* means Istanbul
kompang	frame drum with goat skin tacked to the frame
kota bam	painted flats at side of *bangsawan* stage
kroncong	popular music with Portuguese characteristics originating from Java
kubur	grave
kuda kepang	type of horse-dance originating from Java
kugiran	band
kuntau	Chinese art of self-defence
lagu	song; musical piece
lagu buka tirai	curtain-opening song
lagu cakap	song for speaking
lagu dagang	foreign song
lagu gad	instrumental background music played during *bangsawan* scenes
lagu garang	fierce song
lagu hiburan	song for entertainment
lagu kahwin	marriage song
lagu kayangan	song for heaven scene
lagu nasib	song of fate
lagu pelawak	song for the clown or comedian
lagu pembuka	opening song
lagu pengasoh/inang	song for the nursemaid
lagu penutup	closing song
lagu riang	happy song
lagu sedih	sad song
lagu silat	*silat* song
lagu strit	song for street scene
lagu taman	garden song
lakon bassac	popular theatre of Kampuchea
lalang yang ditiup angin	long grass blown by the wind
langgam jawa	literally Javanese song, a type of *kroncong*
latah	hysteria
laut	sea
lawak	comedy

leher tutup	closed neck; collar, when used in relation to *baju dalam*
likay	a form of Thai opera
luas betul	very wide
ludruk	popular theatre of East Java
mahkota	crown
maju	progress
makyong	traditional theatre originating from Patani
mambang	a kind of spirit
manusia	people
marwas	double-headed cylindrical hand drum
masri	dance-song of Middle Eastern origin; specific rhythmic pattern
mek mulung	type of traditional theatre from Kedah
menadah tangan berdoa	hands lifted in Muslim prayer
menora	type of traditional theatre of Southern Thai origin
merantau tempat	see the world
merayu	appeal
merdeka	independence
Mesir	Egypt
miskin	poor
mistri	set designer in *bangsawan*
mitos	myth
moden	modern
nasi kunyit	yellow rice (cooked)
nasib	fate; destiny; luck
nasyid	type of Arabic cantillation of poetry with noble and Islamic themes
nenek	grandmother; grandparent
nobat	ensemble played in Malay courts for special ceremonies, e.g. installations of Sultans
orang muda	(literally 'young person') hero
orkestra Melayu	Malay orchestra
Padang Pasir	(literally 'field of sand', 'desert') Middle East
panah pancawarna	multicoloured bow and arrow
pantun	type of poetry with *a b a b* rhyme scheme, first couplet = allusion, second couplet = meaning
pari-pari	fairies
pasar malam	night market
patahan lagu	melodic interludes or cadential phrases
patik	I, me (way of referring to oneself when addressing royalty)
pelajaran	education
pelawak	comedian, clown
pélog pathet nem	Javanese mode
pembangunan	development
pendek-panjang	short-tall
perang	war
pergerakan	movements
pohon beringin	banyan tree
raja	king
raksaksa	giant

rakyat	the people, the masses
ramvong	social dancing; dance of Thailand
rebab	three-stringed bowed instrument
rebana	Malay frame drum
rentak	rhythmic pattern
ronggeng (asli)	ensemble accompanying social dancing in which couples dance and exchange verses; Malay social dance
rumah	house
'said wing'	side-wing
sandiwara	theatrical production which is scripted, directed by a director, and dwelling on nationalistic or philosophical themes
sejarah	history
sekolah	school
selampit	sash
seluar	pants
sembah	(literally 'greetings') in relation to *bangsawan*, greetings to the Sultan requiring the pressing of ten fingers to the head
seronok	happy
serunai	quadruple-reed wind instrument
siku di lutut	sit with knees bending at an angle
silat	Malay art of self-defence
sri panggung	heroine
stamboul	a type of Javanese popular theatre (see *komedi stambul*)
strit	street
surat kepujian	letter of praise
syair	Malay verse form with *a a a a* rhyme
takhta kerajaan istana	throne or reception hall of palace
taman	garden
tanjak	head-dress
tauke	businessman; proprietor
tauladan	example, model
teater tradisional	traditional theatre
tebuk	cut out
timbul royat	formula for opening scene in *wayang Siam*
tirai	backdrop; curtain
tiruan wayang Parsi	imitation Parsi theatre
tonil	Dutch term for play; theatrical production of contemporary plays which are scripted and directed
watak	character
wayang	theatre
wayang kulit	shadow theatre
wayang mati	dead theatre
wayang Parsi	Parsi theatre
wayang peranakan	*peranakan* (locally born Chinese) theatre
wayang stambul	*stambul* theatre (see *komedi stambul*)
zapin	dance-song of Middle Eastern origin; specific rhythmic pattern
zarzuela	opera originating from the Philippines in the late nineteenth century

Bibliography

Books, Articles, and Theses

A. Samad Hassan (1977), 'Senarai Koleksi Piring Hitam di Jabatan Pengajian Melayu' [List of the Collection of Records at the Department of Malay Studies], BA dissertation, Universiti Malaya.

Abdul Fatah Karim (1980), 'Lagu Melayu Asli' [Malay Asli Songs], in *Gendang Gendut: Pameran Alat-alat Muzik Tradisional Malaysia* [Gendang Gendut: Exhibition of Traditional Musical Instruments of Malaysia], Kuala Lumpur: Kementerian Kebudayaan, Belia dan Sukan.

Al-Faruqi, Lois Ibsen (1985), 'Music, Musicians and Muslim Law', *Asian Music*, XVII(1): 3–36.

_____ (1987), 'The Cantillation of the Qu'ran', *Asian Music*, XIX(1): 2–25.

Arena Wati (1973), *Silsilah Melayu dan Bugis* [by Raja Ali-al Haji], Kuala Lumpur: Pustaka Antara.

Arnold, Alison (1988), 'Popular Film Song in India: A Case of Mass-market Musical Eclecticism', *Popular Music*, 7(2): 178–88.

Austin-Broos, Diane J. (1987), *Creating Culture*, Sydney: Allen & Unwin.

Baharudin Latif (1989), 'Kemunculannya' [Its Emergence], in Perbadanan Kemajuan Filem Nasional Malaysia, *Cintai Filem Malaysia* [Love Malaysian Films], Kuala Lumpur.

Bailey, Peter (1978), *Leisure and Class in Victorian England: Rational Recreation and the Contest for Control, 1830–1885*, London: Routledge & Kegan Paul.

Balwant Gargi (1962), *Theatre in India*, New York: Theatre Art Books.

Barnes, C. (1980), 'Vaudeville', in S. Sadie (ed.), *The New Grove Dictionary of Music and Musicians*, London: Macmillan Publishers Ltd., Vol. 19.

Barthes, Roland (1972), *Mythologies*, London: Paladin Grafton Books.

_____ (1977), *Image, Music, Text*, Oxford: Oxford University Press.

Becker, Alton (1979), 'Text-building, Epistemology, and Aesthetics in Javanese Shadow Theater', in Alton Becker and A. Yengoyan (eds.), *The Imagination of Reality*, Norwood, NJ: Ablex.

Becker, Alton and Yengoyan, A. (eds.) (1979), *The Imagination of Reality*, Norwood, NJ: Ablex.

Becker, Judith (1976), 'Kroncong, Indonesian Popular Music', *Asian Music*, VII(1): 14–19.

Becker, Judith and Becker, Alton (1981), 'A Musical Icon: Power and Meaning in Javanese Gamelan Music', in Wendy Steiner (ed.), *The Sign in Music and Literature*, Austin: University of Texas, pp. 203–15.

Bedlington, Stanley S. (1978), *Malaysia and Singapore: The Building of New States*, Ithaca: Cornell University Press.

Behague, Gerard (1973), 'Bossa and Bossas: Recent Changes in Brazilian Urban Popular Music', *Ethnomusicology*, 17(2): 209–33.

_____ (1980a), 'Latin America [Sub-section on Popular Music]', in S. Sadie (ed.), *The New Grove Dictionary of Music and Musicians*, London: Macmillan Publishers Ltd., Vol. 10.

_____ (1980b), 'Tango', in S. Sadie (ed.), *The New Grove Dictionary of Music and Musicians*, London: Macmillan Publishers Ltd., Vol. 18.

_____ (1986), 'Musical Change: A Case Study from South America', *The World of Music*, XXVIII(1): 16–25.

Bendix, Reinhard (1968), *State and Society*, Berkeley: University of California Press.

Blacking, John (1973), *How Musical Is Man?* Seattle: University of Washington Press.

_____ (1977), 'Some Problems of Theory and Method in the Study of Musical Change', *Yearbook of the International Folk Music Council*, 9: 1–26.

_____ (1981), 'The Problem of "Ethnic" Perceptions in the Semiotics of Music', in Wendy Steiner (ed.), *The Sign in Music and Literature*, Austin: University of Texas, pp. 184–94.

_____ (1986), 'Identifying Processes of Musical Change', *The World of Music*, XXVIII(1): 3–12.

Blades, James (1984a), 'Woodblock', in S. Sadie (ed.), *The New Grove Dictionary of Musical Instruments*, London: Macmillan Publishers Ltd., Vol. 3.

_____ (1984b), *Percussion Instruments and Their History*, London: Faber & Faber Ltd.

Blum, Stephen (1975), 'Towards a Social History of Musicological Technique', *Ethnomusicology* , 19(2): 207–31.

Boen S. Oemarjati (1971), *Bentuk Lakon dalam Sastra Indonesia* [Drama Form in Indonesian Literature], Jakarta: Gunung Agung.

Bourdieu, Pierre (1978), *Outline of a Theory of Practice*, trans. Richard Nice, Cambridge: Cambridge University Press.

Brandon, James (1967), *Theatre in Southeast Asia*, Cambridge: Harvard University Press.

Brockett, Oscar G. (1980), *The Essential Theatre*, 2nd edn., New York: Holt, Rinehart & Winston.

Brown, C. C. (trans.) (1970), *Sejarah Melayu (Malay Annals)*, Kuala Lumpur: Oxford University Press.

Brown, H. M. (1980), 'Band', in S. Sadie (ed.), *The New Grove Dictionary of Music and Musicians*, London: Macmillan Publishers Ltd., Vol. 2.

Burke, Peter (1981a), 'People's History or Total History', in Raphael Samuel (ed.), *People's History and Socialist Theory*, History Workshop Series, London: Routledge & Kegan Paul.

_____ (1981b), 'The "Discovery" of Popular Culture', in Raphael Samuel (ed.), *People's History and Socialist Theory*, History Workshop Series, London: Routledge & Kegan Paul.

Butcher, J. D. (1979), *The British in Malaya 1880–1941: The Social History of a European Community in Colonial Southeast Asia*, Kuala Lumpur: Oxford University Press.

Camoens, Cantius Leo (1981), 'History and Development of Malay Theatre', MA dissertation, University of Malaya.

_____ (1982), 'The Wayang Parsi, Tiruan Wayang Parsi, Komidi Melayu and the Bangsawan, 1887–1895', *Malaysia in History*, 25: 1–20.

Chase, Gilbert (1976), 'Musicology, History, and Anthropology', in J. W. Grubbs (ed.), *Current Thought in Musicology*, Austin: University of Texas.

Chopyak, James (1986), 'Music in Modern Malaysia: A Survey of the Musics Affecting the Development of Malaysian Popular Music', *Asian Music*, XVIII(1): 111–38.

_____ (1987), 'The Role of Music in Mass Media, Public Education and the Formation of a Malaysian National Culture', *Ethnomusicology*, 31(3): 431–54.

Cohn, Bernard (1980), 'History and Anthropology: The State of Play', *Contemporary Studies in Society and History*, 22(2): 198–221.

Coplan, David (1982), 'The Urbanisation of African Music: Some Theoretical Observations', in Richard Middleton and David Horn (eds.), *Popular Music 2: Theory and Method*, Cambridge: Cambridge University Press.

_____ (1988), 'Musical Understanding: The Ethnoaesthetics of Migrant Workers' Poetic Song in Lesotho', *Ethnomusicology*, 32(3): 337–68.

D'Cruz, Marion (1979), 'Joget Gamelan', MA dissertation, Universiti Sains Malaysia.

Danielson, Virginia (1987), 'The Qu'ran and the Qasidah: Aspects of the Popularity of the Repertory Sung by Umm Kulthum', *Asian Music*, XIX(1): 26–45.

Daud Hamzah (1973), 'Aliran Muzik Malaysia, Khasnya Jenis Suka Ramai dan Cara-cara ke Arah Yang Lebih Sihat dalam Konteks Keperibadian Malaysia' [Trends in the Music of Malaysia, Focusing on Popular Music and the Ways towards Making It More Healthy in the Context of Malaysian Identity], in KKBS, *Asas Kebudayaan Kebangsaan* [Basis of National Culture], Kuala Lumpur, pp. 234–42.

Dick, Alastair and Sen, Devdan (1984), 'Tabla', in S. Sadie (ed.), *The New Grove Dictionary of Musical Instruments*, London: Macmillan Publishers Ltd., Vol. 3.

Dobbs, Jack Percival Baker (1972), 'Music and Dance in the Multi-Racial Society of West Malaysia', M.Phil. dissertation, University of London.

_____ (1984), 'Rebana', in S. Sadie (ed.), *The New Grove Dictionary of Musical Instruments*, London: Macmillan Publishers Ltd., Vol. 3.

Edrus, A. H. (1960), *Persuratan Melayu: Drama dan Perkembangan Bahasa Melayu* [Malay Literature: Drama and the Development of the Malay Language], Singapore: Qalam Printers.

Emerson, Rupert (1964), *Malaysia: A Study in Direct and Indirect Rule*, Kuala Lumpur: University of Malaya Press.

Erlmann, Veit (1983), 'Marginal Men, Strangers and Wayfarers: Professional Musicians and Change among the Fulani of Diamare (North Cameroon)', *Ethnomusicology*, 27(2): 187–226.

Fabbri, Franco (1982), 'What Kind of Music?', in Richard Middleton and David Horn (eds.), *Popular Music 2: Theory and Method*, Cambridge: Cambridge University Press.

Firdaus Haji Abdullah (1985), *Radical Malay Politics: Its Origins and Early Development*, Kuala Lumpur: Pelanduk Publications.

Fiske, John (1982), *Introduction to Communication Studies*, London: Methuen.

Foulcher, Keith (1977), 'Perceptions of Modernity and the Sense of the Past: Indonesian Poetry in the 1920s', *Indonesia*, 23: 39–58.

Furnivall, J. S. (1968), 'The Political Economy of the Tropical Far East', in Reinhard Bendix (ed.), *State and Society*, Berkeley: University of California Press.

Gallop, Rodney (1934), 'The Folk Music of Eastern Portugal', *Musical Quarterly*, 20.

Geertz, Clifford (1973a), *The Interpretation of Cultures*, New York: Basic Books Inc.

_____ (1973b), 'Ideology as a Cultural System', in Clifford Geertz, *The Interpretation of Cultures*, New York: Basic Books Inc.

_____ (1973c), 'Deep Play: Notes on the Balinese Cockfight,' in Clifford Geertz, *The Interpretation of Cultures*, New York: Basic Books Inc.

Ghazalie Shafie (1979), 'Keperibadian Nasional Belum Lahir' [National Identity Has Not Emerged], in *Dewan Masyarakat*, 17(8), 15 August.

Ghulam Sarwar (1976), 'The Kelantan *Mak Yong* Dance Theatre: A Study of Performance Structure', Ph.D. dissertation, University of Hawaii.

_____ (n.d.), 'Bangsawan: The Malay Opera', Mimeo.

Giddens, Anthony (1979), *Central Problems in Social Theory: Action, Structure and Contradiction in Social Analysis*, Cambridge: Cambridge University Press.

Goldsworthy, David (1979), 'Melayu Music of North Sumatra,' Ph.D. dissertation, Monash University.

Gramophone and Typewriter Ltd., The (1903), 'Volkdige Catalogus der Maleische Gramophone Records', Amsterdam.

Grenfell, Newell (1979), *Switch On Switch Off*, Kuala Lumpur: Oxford University Press.

Gronow, Pekka (1963), 'Phonograph Records as a Source for Musicological Research', *Ethnomusicology*, 8(3): 225–8.

_____ (1975), 'Ethnic Music and Soviet Record Industry', *Ethnomusicology*, 19(1): 91–9.

_____ (1981), 'The Record Industry Comes to the Orient', *Ethnomusicology*, 25(2): 251–82.

Grubbs, J. W. (with the assistance of Baltzer, R. A., Blount, G. L., and Perkins, L.) (1976), *Current Thought in Musicology*, Austin: University of Texas.

Gullick, J. M. (1958), *Indigenous Political Systems of Western Malaya*, London: University of London.

_____ (1963), *Malaya*, London: Ernest Benn Ltd.

_____ (1978), *Syers and the Selangor Police 1857–1897*, Kuala Lumpur: Malaysian Branch of the Royal Asiatic Society.

_____ (1981), *Malaysia: Economic Expansion and National Unity*, London: Westview Press.

_____ (1988), *Kuala Lumpur 1880–1895: A City in the Making*, Kuala Lumpur: Pelanduk Publications.

H. S. L. (1924), *Penghiboran Hati*, Penang: Criterion Press Ltd.

Hamm, Charles (1980), 'Popular Music [Sub-sections on North America to 1940 and since 1940]', in S. Sadie (ed.), *The New Grove Dictionary of Music and Musicians*, London: Macmillan Publishers Ltd., Vol. 15.

Hatley, Barbara (1979), 'Ketoprak Theatre and the Wayang Tradition', Centre of Southeast Asian Studies Working Paper No. 19, Melbourne: Monash University.

_____ (1983), 'Theatrical Imagery and Gender Ideology in Java', Paper presented at the Conference on Cultural Construction of Gender in Insular Southeast Asia, Princeton, 8–11 December.

_____ (1985), 'Ketoprak: Performance and Social Meaning in a Javanese

Popular Theatre Form', Ph.D. dissertation, University of Sydney.

Herskovits, Melville J. (1958), *Acculturation: The Study of Culture Contact*, 2nd edn., Gloucester, Mass.: Peter Smith.

Hind, H. and Baines, A. (1980), 'Military Band', in S. Sadie (ed.), *The New Grove Dictionary of Music and Musicians*, London: Macmillan Publishers Ltd., Vol. 12.

Hobsbawm, Eric and Ranger, Terence (1983), *The Invention of Tradition*, Cambridge: Cambridge University Press.

Honjo, M. (ed.) (1984), *Urbanization and Regional Development*, Singapore: Maruzen Asia.

Hood, Mantle (1971), *The Ethnomusicologist*, New York: McGraw-Hill.

Ismail Samaat (1984), 'Penghibur Melayu Masakini', BA dissertation, Universiti Malaya.

Ismail Zain (1977), 'Cultural Planning and General Development in Malaysia', Kuala Lumpur: Kementerian Kebudayaan, Belia dan Sukan Malaysia.

Jacobs, Arthur (1977), *New Penguin Dictionary of Music*, Harmondsworth: Penguin.

Jomo Kwame Sundaram (1984), 'Malaysia's New Economic Policy: A Class Perspective', *Pacific Viewpoint*, 25(2): 153–72.

Kahn, Joel (1992), 'Class, Ethnicity and Diversity: Some Remarks on Malay Culture in Malaysia', in Joel Kahn and Francis Loh (eds.), *Fragmented Vision: Culture and Politics in Contemporary Malaysia*, Sydney: Asian Studies Association of Australia/Allen & Unwin, pp. 158–78.

Kahn, Joel and Loh, Francis (eds.) (1992), *Fragmented Visions: Culture and Politics in Contemporary Malaysia*, Sydney: Asian Studies Association of Australia/Allen & Unwin.

Kamal Salih and Mei Ling Young (1984), 'Malaysia: Urbanization in a Multi-ethnic Society—Case of Peninsular Malaysia', in M. Honjo (ed.), *Urbanization and Regional Development*, Singapore: Maruzen Asia.

Kartomi, Margaret (1981), 'The Processes and Results of Musical Culture Contact: A Discussion of Terminology and Concepts', *Ethnomusicology*, 25(2): 227–49.

_____ (1984a), 'Gambus', in S. Sadie (ed.), *The New Grove Dictionary of Musical Instruments*, London: Macmillan Publishers Ltd., Vol. 2.

_____ (1984b), 'Gambusan', in S. Sadie (ed.), *The New Grove Dictionary of Musical Instruments*, Vol. 2.

_____ (1987), Review of Bruno Nettl's *The Western Impact on World Music: Change, Adaptation and Survival*, in *Yearbook for Traditional Music*, 19.

_____ (1988), 'Kapri: A Synthesis of Malay and Portuguese Music on the West Coast of North Sumatra', in R. Carle (ed.), *Cultures and Societies of North Sumatra*, Hamburg: University of Hamburg.

_____ (ed.) (1978), *Studies in Indonesian Music*, Centre of Southeast Asian Studies, Monash Papers on Southeast Asia, No. 7, Melbourne.

Kassim Ahmad (ed.) (1973), *Hikayat Hang Tuah*, Kuala Lumpur: Dewan Bahasa dan Pustaka.

Kaufmann, Walter (1968), *The Ragas of North India*, Bloomington: Indiana University Press.

Kean, Charles (1971), *Hamlet Prince of Denmark*, reprint of 1859 version, London: Cornmarket Press.

Kimberlin, Cynthia Tse (1988), 'Cultural Policy and Contemporary Music

Change in Ethiopia', Paper presented at the Symposium of the International Musicological Society and Festival of Music, Melbourne, 28 August– 2 September.

KKBS (Kementerian Kebudayaan, Belia dan Sukan Malaysia or Ministry of Culture, Youth and Sports Malaysia) (1973), *Asas Kebudayaan Kebangsaan* [Basis of National Culture], Kuala Lumpur.

_____ (1977), 'Rumusan Bengkel Bangsawan 1977' [Summary of the Bangsa- wan Workshop 1977], Kuala Lumpur.

_____ (1980), 'Kompang', Kuala Lumpur.

Knaap, Otto (1903), 'A. Mahieu', *De Indische Bond*, 18 and 25 July, translated in *Tong Tong*, 16(1 March 1971) and 21(15 May 1971).

Kornhauser, Bronia (1978), 'In Defence of Kroncong', in Margaret Kartomi (ed.), *Studies in Indonesian Music*, Centre of Southeast Asian Studies, Monash Papers on Southeast Asia, No. 7, Melbourne, pp. 104–83.

Krishen Jit (1979), 'Teater Moden Malaysia—Satu Essei Retrospektif', *Dewan Sastra* (March).

Kua Kia Soong (ed.) (1985), *National Culture and Democracy*, Petaling Jaya: Kersani Penerbit-Penerbit Sdn. Bhd.

Kumpulan Noor El-Kawakib Papar, Sabah (n.d.), 'Lagu-lagu Nasyid'.

Lamb, Andrew (1980a), 'March [Sub-section on 19th- and 20th-Century Military and Popular Marches]', in S. Sadie (ed.), *The New Grove Dictionary of Music and Musicians*, London: Macmillan Publishers Ltd., Vol. 11.

_____ (1980b), 'Popular Music [Sub-section on Europe to World War II]', in S. Sadie (ed.), *The New Grove Dictionary of Music and Musicians*, London: Macmillan Publishers Ltd., Vol. 15.

_____ (1980c), 'Waltz', in S. Sadie (ed.), *The New Grove Dictionary of Music and Musicians*, London: Macmillan Publishers Ltd., Vol. 20.

Lapena-Bonifacio, Amelia (1972), *The 'Seditious' Tagalog Playwrights: Early American Occupation*, Manila: Zarzuela Foundation of the Philippines, Inc.

Larkin, John A. (1978), 'The Capampangan Zarzuela: Theater for a Provincial Elite', in Ruth McVey (ed.), *Southeast Asian Transitions Approaches through Social History*, New Haven and London: Yale University Press, pp. 158–90.

Loh Fook Seng (1975), *Seeds of Separatism*, Kuala Lumpur: Oxford University Press.

Lomax, Alan (1968), *Folk Song Style and Culture*, Washington, DC: American Association for the Advancement of Science.

Lord, A. B. (1976), *The Singer of Tales*, New York: Atheneum.

Makepeace, Walter; Brooke, Gibert E.; and Braddell, Roland St. J. (1921), *One Hundred Years of Singapore*, London: John Murray.

Malaysia (1977), *Laws of Malaysia, Act 182, Theatres and Places of Public Amusement (Federal Territory) Act 1977*, Kuala Lumpur: Government Printers.

_____ (1986), *Fifth Malaysia Plan, 1986–1990*, Kuala Lumpur: National Printing Department.

Manderson, Lenore (1980), *Women, Politics and Change: The Kaum Ibu UMNO Malaysia, 1945–1972*, Kuala Lumpur: Oxford University Press.

Manuel, Peter (1988), 'Popular Music in India: 1901–86', *Popular Music*, 7(2): 157–76.

Manusama, A. Th. (1922), *Komedie Stamboel of De Oost-Indische Opera*, Batavia.

Matheson, Virginia and Andaya, Barbara Watson (ed.) (1982), *Tuhfat al-Nafis* by Raja Haji Ahmad and Raja Ali Haji, Kuala Lumpur: Oxford University Press.

Matusky, Patricia (1980), 'Music in the Malay Shadow Puppet Theatre (Vols. I and II)', Ph.D. dissertation, University of Michigan.

_____ (1985), 'An Introduction to the Major Instruments and Forms of Traditional Malay Music', *Asian Music*, XVI(2): 121–82.

May, E. (ed.) (1980), *Musics of Many Cultures: An Introduction*, Berkeley: University of California Press.

McVey, Ruth (ed.) (1978), *Southeast Asian Transitions Approaches through Social History*, New Haven and London: Yale University Press.

Merriam, Alan (1955), 'The Use of Music in the Study of a Problem of Acculturation', *American Anthropologist*, 57: 28–34.

_____ (1964), *The Anthropology of Music*, Evanston: Northwestern University Press.

Middleton, Richard and Horn, David (eds.) (1981), *Popular Music 1: Folk or Popular? Distinctions, Influences, Continuities*, Cambridge: Cambridge University Press.

_____ (1982), *Popular Music 2: Theory and Method*, Cambridge: Cambridge University Press.

Ministry of Information (1975), *Inilah Radio/TV Malaysia* [This is Radio/TV Malaysia], Kuala Lumpur: Government Printer.

Mohd. Anis Md. Nor (1990), 'The Zapin Melayu Dance of Johore: From Village to a National Performance Tradition,' Ph.D. dissertation, University of Michigan.

Mohd. Taib Osman (1974), *Traditional Drama and Music of Southeast Asia*, Kuala Lumpur: Dewan Bahasa dan Pustaka.

_____ (1975), *Warisan Puisi Melayu* [Heritage of Malay Poetry], Kuala Lumpur: Dewan Bahasa dan Pustaka.

_____(1984), *Bunga Rampai: Aspects of Malay Culture*, Kuala Lumpur: Dewan Bahasa dan Pustaka.

Mulk Raj Anand (1951), *The Indian Theatre*, New York: Roy Publishers.

Mustapha Kamil Yassin (1974), 'The Malay Bangsawan', in Mohd. Taib Osman (ed.), *Traditional Drama and Music of Southeast Asia*, Kuala Lumpur: Dewan Bahasa dan Pustaka.

Nanney, Nancy (1983), 'An Analysis of Modern Malaysian Drama', Ph.D. dissertation, University of Hawaii.

Nettl, Bruno (1965), *Folk and Traditional Music of the Western Continents*, Englewood Cliffs, NJ: Prentice-Hall.

_____ (1972), 'Persian Popular Music in 1969', *Ethnomusicology*, 16: 218–39.

_____ (1980), 'Ethnomusicology: Definitions, Directions, and Problems', in E. May (ed.), *Musics of Many Cultures, An Introduction*, Berkeley: University of California Press.

_____ (1983), *The Study of Ethnomusicology, Twenty-nine Issues and Concepts*, Urbana: University of Illinois Press.

_____ (1985), *The Western Impact on World Music, Change, Adaptation and Survival*, New York: Schirmer Books.

_____ (1986), 'World Music in the Twentieth Century: A Survey of Research on Western Influence', *Acta Musicologica*, 53: 360–73.

_____ (ed.) (1978), *Eight Urban Musical Cultures: Tradition and Change*, Urbana: University of Illinois Press.

Ong, Walter J. (1982), *Orality and Literacy, The Technologizing of the Word*, London: Methuen.

Ortner, Sherry B. (1984), 'Theory in Anthropology Since the Sixties',

Comparative Studies in Society and History, 26(1): 126–66.

Owen, Barbara and Dick, Alastair (1984), 'Harmonium', In S. Sadie (ed.), *The New Grove Dictionary of Musical Instruments*, London: Macmillan Publishers Ltd., Vol. 2.

Pacholczyk, Jozef (1980), 'Secular Classical Music in the Arabic Near East', in E. May (ed.), *Musics of Many Cultures, An Introduction*, Berkeley: University of California Press.

Peacock, James (1968), *The Rites of Modernization: Symbols and Social Aspects of Indonesian Proletarian Drama*, Chicago: University of Chicago Press.

Perbadanan Kemajuan Filem Nasional Malaysia (Association for the Development of Malaysian National Films) (1989), *Cintai Filem Malaysia* [Love Malaysian Films], Kuala Lumpur: Perbadanan Kemajuan Filem Nasional Malaysia.

Perkins, J. F.; Kelly, A.; and Ward, J. (1976), 'On Gramophone Company Matrix Numbers 1898 to 1921', *The Record Collector*, 23(3 and 4), May.

Powers, Harold S. (1980), 'India [Sub-section on Tala]', in S. Sadie (ed.), *The New Grove Dictionary of Music and Musicians*, London: Macmillan Publishers Ltd., Vol. 9.

Racy, Ali Jihad (1976), 'Record Industry and Egyptian Traditional Music: 1904–1932', *Ethnomusicology*, 20(1): 23–48.

Rahmah Bujang (1975), *Sejarah Perkembangan Drama Bangsawan di Tanah Melayu dan Singapura* [The History of the Development of Bangsawan Drama in Malaya and Singapore], Kuala Lumpur: Dewan Bahasa dan Pustaka.

_____ (1987), *Boria: A Form of Malay Theatre*, Local History and Memoirs, Singapore: Institute of Southeast Asian Studies.

Ramesh Bhatt (1956), *Souvenir, 70th Anniversary of the College of Indian Music, Dance and Dramatics*, Baroda: College of Indian Music, Dance and Dramatics.

Randel, Don Michael (1978), *Harvard Concise Dictionary of Music*, Cambridge: Harvard University Press, Belknap Press.

Robinson, J. B. (1984), 'Band', in S. Sadie (ed.), *The New Grove Dictionary of Musical Instruments*, London: Macmillan Publishers Ltd., Vol. 2.

Roff, W. R. (1967), *The Origins of Malay Nationalism*, Kuala Lumpur: University of Malaya Press.

_____ (1972), *Bibliography of Malay and Arabic Periodicals, 1876–1941*, London: Oxford University Press.

Root, Deane (1977), *American Popular Stage Music, 1860–1880*, Michigan: UMI Research Press.

Sadie, S. (ed.) (1980), *The New Grove Dictionary of Music and Musicians*, London: Macmillan Publishers Ltd.

_____ (ed.) (1984), *The New Grove Dictionary of Musical Instruments*, London: Macmillan Publishers Ltd.

Samuel, Raphael (ed.) (1981), *People's History and Socialist Theory*, History Workshop Series, London: Routledge & Kegan Paul.

Schwandt, Erich (1980), 'March [Sub-section on the Military March to the 1820s]', in S. Sadie (ed.), *The New Grove Dictionary of Music and Musicians*, London: Macmillan Publishers Ltd., Vol. 11.

Scott, James C. (1985), *Weapons of the Weak: Everyday Forms of Peasant Resistance*, New Haven: Yale University Press.

Sheppard, Mubin (1972), *Taman Indera: A Royal Pleasure Ground*, Kuala Lumpur: Oxford University Press.

Shiloah, Amnon (1986), 'The Traditional Artist in the Limelight of the Modern City', *The World of Music*, XXVIII(1): 87–98.

Shiloah, Amnon and Cohen, Erik (1983), 'The Dynamics of Change in Jewish Oriental Ethnic Music in Israel', *Ethnomusicology*, 27(2): 227–52.

Short, Anthony (1975), *The Communist Insurrection in Malaya, 1948–1960*, New York: Crane, Russak & Co.

Shri Chandravadan C. Mehta (1956), 'A Hundred Years of Gujerati Stage', in Ramesh Bhatt (ed.), *Souvenir, 70th Anniversary of the College of Indian Music, Dance and Dramatics*, Baroda: College of Indian Music, Dance and Dramatics.

Sidney, R. J. H. (1926), *Malay Land, 'Tanah Melayu': Some Phases of Life in Modern British Malaya*, London: C. Palmer.

Signell, Karl (1977), *Makam: Modal Practice in Turkish Art Music*, Series D(4), Washington, Seattle: Asian Music Publications.

Skeat, Walter William (1967), *Malay Magic*, New York: Dover Publication Inc.

Skillman, Teri (1986), The Bombay Hindi Film Song Genre: A Historical Survey', *Yearbook for Traditional Music*, 18.

Smithies, Michael (1971), 'Likay: A Note on the Origin, Form and Future of Siamese Folk Opera', *Journal of the Siam Society*, 59(1): 33–63.

Solehah Ishak (1987), *Histrionics of Development: A Study of Three Contemporary Malay Playwrights*, Kuala Lumpur: Dewan Bahasa dan Pustaka and Kementerian Pendidikan Malaysia.

Steiner, Wendy (ed.) (1981), *The Sign in Music and Literature*, Austin: University of Texas.

Stevenson, Rex (1974), 'Cinemas and Censorship in Colonial Malaya', *Journal of Southeast Asian Studies*, 5(2).

S. Sumantri (n.d.), 'Komedi Stambul 1900–1925', Mimeo.

Sweeney, Amin (1972), *The Ramayana and the Malay Shadow-play*, Kuala Lumpur: Penerbit Universiti Kebangsaan Malaysia.

_____ (1980), *Authors and Audiences in Traditional Malay Literature*, Berkeley: Centre for Southeast Asian Studies, University of California.

Swettenham, F. A. (1895), *Malay Sketches*, London: Graham Brash.

Talbot, Michael (1980), 'Ragtime', in S. Sadie (ed.), *The New Grove Dictionary of Music and Musicians*, London: Macmillan Publishers Ltd., Vol. 15.

Tan Sooi Beng (1980), 'Chinese Opera in Malaysia: Changes and Survival', *Review of Southeast Asian Studies*, 10: 29–45.

_____ (1984a), *Ko-tai: Chinese Street Theatre in Malaysia*, Singapore: Institute of Southeast Asian Studies.

_____ (1984b), 'An Introduction to the Chinese Glove Puppet Theatre', *Journal of the Malaysian Branch of the Royal Asiatic Society*, LVII(1): 40–55.

_____ (1988a), 'The Thai *Menora* in Malaysia; Adapting to the Penang Chinese Community', *Asian Folklore Studies*, XLVII(1): 19–34.

_____ (1988b), 'The Performing Arts in Malaysia: State, Society and the Entertainment Industry', Paper presented at the Symposium on 'Culture and Politics in Contemporary Malaysia', Monash University, Melbourne, 18–19 November.

_____ (1988c), 'The *Phor Tor* Festival in Penang: Deities, Ghosts and Chinese Ethnicity', Centre of Southeast Asian Studies Working Paper No. 51, Melbourne.

Tax, Sol (ed.) (1952), *Acculturation in the Americas*, Proceedings of the 29th International Congress of Americanists, Chicago, Vol. 2.

Tewari, Laxmi Ganesh (1974), 'Folk Music in India: Uttar Pradesh', Ph.D. dissertation, Wesleyan University.

Thomas, Phillip (1986), *Like Tigers around a Piece of Meat*, Singapore: Institute of Southeast Asian Studies.

Thompson, E. P. (1978), *The Poverty of Theory and Other Essays*, New York: Monthly Review Press.

Treitler, Leo (1984), 'What Kind of Story Is History?', *Nineteenth Century Journal*, VII(3): 363–73.

Turner, Victor (1986a), *The Anthropology of Performance*, New York: PAJ Publications.

_____ (1986b), 'Images and Reflections: Ritual, Drama, Carnival, Film and Spectacle in Cultural Performance', in Victor Turner, *The Anthropology of Performance*, New York: PAJ Publications.

Van Aalst, J. A. (1966), *Chinese Music*, New York: Paragon Book Reprint Corp.

Vaughan, V. D. (1975), *Manners and Customs of the Chinese of the Straits Settlements*, reprint, Singapore: Oxford University Press.

Wachsmann, Klaus P. (1961), 'Criteria for Acculturation', *Report of the Eighth Congress of the International Musicological Society*, pp. 139–49.

Wade, Bonnie (1980), 'India [Sub-section on Folk Music]', in S. Sadie (ed.), *The New Grove Dictionary of Music and Musicians*, London: Macmillan Publishers Ltd., Vol. 9.

Wallis, Roger and Malm, Krister (1984), *Big Sounds from Small Peoples: The Music Industry in Small Countries*, London: Constable & Co. Ltd.

Wan Abdul Kadir (1983), 'Taman Hiburan: Satu Penilaian Sosial' [Entertainment Parks: A Social Study], *Purba*, 2: 96–102.

_____ (1988), *Budaya Popular Dalam Masyarakat Melayu Bandaran* [Popular Culture in Urban Malay Society], Kuala Lumpur: Dewan Bahasa dan Pustaka.

Want, John (1976), 'The Great Beka Expedition 1905–6', *The Talking Machine Review—International*, 41 (August).

Waterman, Richard (1952), 'African Influence on the Music of the Americas', in Sol Tax (ed.), *Acculturation in the Americas*, Proceedings of the 29th International Congress of Americanists, Chicago, Vol. 2.

Wiant, Bliss (1965), *The Music of China*, Hong Kong: Chung Chi Publications.

Williams, Raymond (1977), *Marxism and Literature*, London: Oxford University Press.

_____ (1981), *Culture*, London: Fontana Paperbacks.

_____ (1983), *Towards 2000*, London: Hogarth Press.

Wise, Michael (comp.) (1985), *Travellers' Tales of Old Singapore*, Singapore: Times Books International.

Wolf, Eric (1982), *Europe and the People Without History*, Berkeley: University of California Press.

Yengoyan, A. (1979) 'Cultural Forms and a Theory of Constraints' in Alton Becker and A. Yengoyan (eds.), *The Imagination of Reality*, Norwood, NJ: Ablex.

Yeo, Stephen and Yeo, Eileen (eds.) (1981), *Popular Culture and Class Conflict 1590–1914: Exploration in the History of Labour and Leisure*, Sussex: Harvester Press.

Yung, Bell (1983a), 'Creative Process in Cantonese Opera I: The Role of Linguistic Tones', *Ethnomusicology*, 27(1): 9–47.

_____ (1983), 'Creative Process in Cantonese Opera II: The Process of *T'ien Tz'u* [Text Setting]', *Ethnomusicology*, 27(2): 297–318.

_____ (1989), *Cantonese Opera: Performance as Creative Process*, Cambridge: Cambridge University Press.

Za'aba (Zain al-Abidin bin Ahmed) (1939), 'Modern Developments', *Journal of the Malayan Branch of the Royal Asiatic Society*, 17(3): 142–62.

_____ (1941a), 'Recent Malay Literature', *Journal of the Malayan Branch of the Royal Asiatic Society*, 19(1): 1–20.

_____ (1941b), 'Malay Journalism in Malaya', *Journal of the Malayan Branch of the Royal Asiatic Society*, 19(2): 244–50.

Zonis, Ella (1973), *Classical Persian Music: An Introduction*, Cambridge: Harvard University Press.

Newspapers

Berita Harian, 1966, 1977–88.
Berita Minggu, 1966, 1982–5.
Bintang Timor (Penang), 1900.
Bintang Timor (Singapore), 1894–5.
Bintang Timur, 1980.
Bumiputra, 1933–4.
Chahaya Pulau Pinang, 1904–6.
Idaran Zaman, 1925, 1929.
Majlis, 1932–40, 1946, 1947.
Malacca Guardian, 1928–40.
Mingguan Malaysia, 1978–83.
Mingguan Timor, 1980.
National Echo, 1970–88.
New Straits Times, 1970–90.
New Sunday Times, 1970–90.
Penang Shimbun, 1942–4.
Pinang Gazette and Straits Chronicle, 1892–6.
Sahabat, 1939–40.
Saudara, 1928–36.
Star, 1984–90.
Straits Echo, 1903–40.
Straits Times, 1930–5.
Sunday Gazette, 1932–8.
Tantuan Muda, 1926.
Times of Malaya, 1904–49.
Utusan Melayu, 1945–8.
Utusan Malaysia, 1978–88.
Utusan Zaman, 1963.
Warta Jenaka, 1936–41.
Warta Malaya, 1933, 1936, 1941.

78 r.p.m. Records (1930s)

Bangsawan Stories (taped from the 78 r.p.m. record collection donated by Naina Merican to Universiti Malaya).

Cerita Jula Juli Bintang Tiga (Malay Drama), Sung by Dean's Grand Opera, S. Moutrie and Co., Dum Dum, India: Chap Kuching, NG 29–NG 32.

Songs:
'Kehilangan Cincin', NG 29.

'Teribet Jula Juli', NG 29.
'Pertanyaan Nama', NG 30.
'Penceraian Jula Juli', NG 30.
'Telesmat Bintang Satu dan Dua', NG 31.
'Pari-pari Biangkot', NG 32.
'Puja Kamati Dasa Alam', NG 32.

Cerita Laila Majnun, Sung by Che Norlia, Salleh Aspoo, and Che Jot Gramophone Co. Ltd., Dum Dum, India: His Master's Voice, P 12800—P 12805. Song categories (in brackets) appear on the record labels.

Songs:
'Laili Majnun Ka 1' (Lagu Melayu), P 12800.
'Ya Aini' (Lagu Melayu), P. 12800.
'Sambot Kekasih' (Lagu Melayu), P 12801.
'Marah Hati' (Lagu Melayu), P 12801.
'Nasib Mengenang Diri' (Nasib Malay), P 12802.
'Karangan Hati' (Lagu Melayu), P 12802.
'Masri Kelantan' (Lagu Melayu), P 12803.
'Gambos Sri Makam' (Gambos), P 12803.
'Gambos Berahi' (Gambos), P 12804.
'Nasib Pandan' (Nasib), P 12804.
'Nasib Ketinggalan Ka 1/2' (Nasib), P 12805.

Cerita Noor-E-Islam (Hindustani Drama) [8 songs—names of songs not listed], Sung by Miss Tijah and Dean Opera Co., India: Chap Singa [Lion Label], QF 34–QF 37 (distributed by M. E. and T. Hemsley, Singapore).

Cerita Puteri Gunong Ledang, Music by M. A. Pochik and Ahmad, Gramophone Co. Ltd., Dum Dum, India: His Master's Voice, P 12760–P 12766.

Songs:
'Che Wan Gayah' (Lagu Melayu), Sung by Che Asmah and Shariff, P 12760.
'Gurindam Raja Ahmad' (Lagu Melayu), Sung by Shariff, Asmah, and Derma, P 12760.
'Penchak Silat' (Lagu Melayu), Sung by A. Shariff, K. Ahmad, and Che Asmah, P 12761.
'Hiboran Raja Ahmad Beradu' (Lagu Melayu), Sung by Che Asmah, Shariff, and Rahmah, P 12761.
'Perchinta'an Baginda Yamtuan' (Lagu Melayu), Sung by Syed Ali Al Attass and Shariff, P 12762.
'Tok Ngah Pawang Bomor' (Lagu Melayu), Sung by Shariff and Chorus, P 12762.
'Telek Ternang' (Lagu Melayu), Sung by Syed Ali Al'Attass, Che Asmah, and Shariff, P 12763.
'S'loka Buah Mempelam' (Lagu Melayu), Sung by Che Derma and K. Ahmad, P 12763.
'S'loka Buah Rambutan' (Lagu Melayu), Sung by Che Derma and K. Ahmad, P 12764.
'Tangisan Buluh Perindu' (Lagu Melayu), Sung by Che Asma, and K. Ahmad, P 12764.
'Dang Raya Rani' (Lagu Melayu), Sung by Derma and K. Ahmad, P 12765.
'Nenek Kebayan dan Tun Mamat' (Lagu Melayu), Sung by Che Asmah and K. Ahmad, P 12765.

'Pinang Mas Kahwin' (Lagu Melayu), Sung by Che Asmah and K. Ahmad, P 12766.

'Baginda Yamtuan Melaka' (Lagu Melayu), Sung by Syed Ali Al'Attass, Shariff, Che Asmah, and Chorus, P 12766.

Bangsawan Songs (taped from the 78 r.p.m. record collection donated by Naina Merican and Y. M. Ibrahim to Universiti Malaya). Song categories (in brackets) appear on the record labels.

'Alang Asyik' (Malay), Merry Opera Co., Gramophone Co. Ltd., Dum Dum, India: His Master's Voice, P 7613.

'Alrat' (Malay) Merry Opera Co., Gramophone Co. Ltd., Dum Dum, India: His Master's Voice, P 7611.

'Amal Berhaman' (Malay), Merry Opera Co., Gramophone Co. Ltd., Dum Dum, India: His Master's Voice, P 7608.

'Anak Koe' (Stamboel), Ahmad C. B., India: Chap Singa, QF 89 (distributed by M. E. and T. Hemsley, Singapore).

'Antah Hairani' (Malay), Merry Opera Co., Gramophone Co. Ltd., Dum Dum, India: His Master's Voice, P 7269.

'Azim Zaliha' (Malay), Merry Opera Co., Gramophone Co. Ltd., Dum Dum, India: His Master's Voice, P 7201.

'Baba Mustafa' (Malay), Merry Opera Co., Gramophone Co. Ltd., Dum Dum, India: His Master's Voice, P 7424.

'Banjaran Sari' (Malay), Merry Opera Co., Gramophone Co. Ltd., Dum Dum, India: His Master's Voice, P 7197.

'Boenga Tandjoeng' (Stamboel, 1927), Miss Riboet v/h Maleisch Operette Gezelschap Orion, Carl Lindstrom A. G., Germany: Beka, 27801.

'Bunga Shiher' (Malay), Merry Opera Co., Gramophone Co. Ltd., Dum Dum, India: His Master's Voice, P 7751.

'Burong Puteh' (Malay), Merry Opera. Co., Gramophone Co. Ltd., Dum Dum, India: His Master's Voice, P 7268.

'Chahaya Alam' (Malay), Merry Opera Co., Gramophone Co. Ltd., Dum Dum, India: His Master's Voice, P 7065.

'Cahaya Udara' (Malay), Merry Opera Co., Gramophone Co. Ltd., Dum Dum, India: His Master's Voice, P 7269.

'Chinta Brahi' (Malay), Merry Opera Co., Gramophone Co. Ltd., Dum Dum, India: His Master's Voice, P 7615.

'Djoela Djoeli Bintang III' (Stamboel), Miss Riboet, Maleisch Operette Gezelschap Orion, Carl Lindstrom A. G., Germany: Beka, 27817.

'Dondang Sayang' (Malay), Miss Tijah and K. Dean, Gramophone Co. Ltd., Dum Dum, India: Chap Kuching, NG 1.

'Dul I Bahar' (Malay), Merry Opera Co., Gramophone Co. Ltd., Dum Dum, India: His Master's Voice, P 7424.

'Gambos Kayangan' (Malay), Merry Opera Co., Gramophone Co. Ltd., Dum Dum, India: His Master's Voice, P 7751.

'Gurindam Jawa' (Pelahan), Julia with Osman-Ahmad Orchestra, Columbia Graphophone Co.: GEM 166.

'Haris Padilah' (Malay), Merry Opera Co., Gramophone Co. Ltd., Dum Dum, India: His Master's Voice, P 7203.

'Heyrdonia' (Malay), Merry Opera Co., Gramophone Co. Ltd., Dum Dum, India: His Master's Voice, P 7205.

'Inang Sarget' (Stamboel), Miss Riboet, Maleisch Operette Gezelschap Orion

Carl Lindstrom A. G., Germany: Beka, 27767.

'Indera Sabah' (Malay), Merry Opera Co., Gramophone Co. Ltd., Dum Dum, India: His Master's Voice, P 7615.

'Jin Pujok', City Opera, Carl Lindstrom A. G., Germany: Beka, 26530.

'Johan Maligar' (Malay), Merry Opera Co., Gramophone Co. Ltd., Dum Dum, India: His Master's Voice, P 7201.

'Kembang Delima', S. Mohamad Harmonium Orchestra, Columbia: CEL 8118.

'Kontang Konteng' (Malay comic song), Sooin with City Opera Orchestra, Columbia Graphophone Co.: 15684.

'Laila Majnun Part I and II', Che Saimah and Party, Gramophone Co. Ltd., Dum Dum, India: His Master' Voice, P 16494.

'Lal Pari' (Malay), Merry Opera Co., Gramophone Co. Ltd., Dum Dum, India: His Master's Voice, P 7198.

'Mahbob' (Malay), Merry Opera Co., Gramophone Co. Ltd., Dum Dum, India: His Master's Voice, P 7611.

'Mary Tukang Kebon' (Malay), Merry Opera Co., Gramophone Co. Ltd., Dum Dum, India: His Master's Voice, P 7205.

'Merak Mas' (Malay), Merry Opera Co., Gramophone Co. Ltd., Dum Dum, India: His Master's Voice, P 7748.

'Muri Alam' (Malay), Merry Opera Co., Gramophone Co. Ltd., Dum Dum, India: His Master's Voice, P 7748.

'Nasib Ali Baba' (Malay), Merry Opera Co., Gramophone Co. Ltd., Dum Dum, India: His Master's Voice, P 7197.

'Nasib Kamrulzaman' (Malay), Merry Opera Co., Gramophone Co. Ltd., Dum Dum, India: His Master's Voice, P 7608.

'Noor Ashik' (Malay), Merry Opera Co., Gramophone Co. Ltd., Dum Dum, India: His Master's Voice, P 7067.

'Noor Bakar' (Malay), Merry Opera Co., Gramophone Co. Ltd., Dum Dum, India: His Master's Voice, P 7268.

'Pemuda Semarang', S. Mohamad Harmonium Orchestra, Columbia: CEL 8119.

'Perak Sabah' (Malay), Merry Opera Co., Gramophone Co. Ltd., Dum Dum, India: His Master's Voice, P 7198.

'Raja Strit' (Malay), Merry Opera Co., Gramophone Co. Ltd., Dum Dum, India: His Master's Voice, P 7613.

'Salam Taksim', Miss Tuti, Dramatic Arbab Rumba Arts Bangsawan, Odeon: Str. 2394.

'Sambot Kekaseh' (Malay), Che Norlia and Salleh Aspoo, Gramophone Co. Ltd., Dum Dum, India: His Master's Voice, P 12801.

'Saridam' (Malay), Merry Opera Co., Gramophone Co. Ltd., Dum Dum, India: His Master's Voice, P 7203.

'Selamat Tinggal' (Malay), Merry Opera Co., Gramophone Co. Ltd., Dum Dum, India: His Master's Voice, P 7263.

'Senaran Bintang' (Malay), Merry Opera Co., Gramophone Co. Ltd., Dum Dum, India: His Master's Voice, P 7619.

'Seri Serdang' (Malay), Merry Opera Co., Gramophone Co. Ltd., Dum Dum, India: His Master's Voice, P 7433.

'Shah Kobat' (Malay), Merry Opera Co., Gramophone Co. Ltd., Dum Dum, India: His Master's Voice, P 7433.

'Shanghai Street' (Malay), Che Norlia, Gramophone Co. Ltd., Dum Dum, India: His Master's Voice, P 15978.

'Simpolan Massri', City Opera, Carl Lindstrom A. G., Germany: Beka, 26419.

'Sinandung Jawa' (Lagu), Miss Tijah, Gramophone Co. Ltd., Dum Dum, India: Chap Kuching [Cat Label], NG 73.

'Sinaran Ajaib' (Malay), Merry Opera Co., Gramophone Co. Ltd., Dum Dum, India: His Master's Voice, P 7620.

'Siti Rukiah' (Malay), Merry Opera Co., Gramophone Co. Ltd., Dum Dum, India: His Master's Voice, P 7065.

'Slendang Mayang' (Stamboel), Miss Riboet, Maleisch Operette Gezelschap Orion, Carl Lindstrom A. G., Germany: Beka, 27751.

'Tilana' (Malay), Merry Opera Co., Gramophone Co. Ltd., Dum Dum, India: His Master's Voice, P 7263.

'Tozin Kiss' (Malay), Merry Opera Co., Gramophone Co. Ltd., Dum Dum, India: His Master's Voice, P 7619.

'Yatim Piatu' (Malay), Merry Opera Co., Gramophone Co. Ltd., Dum Dum, India: His Master's Voice, P 7620.

Interviews (Taped and Transcribed)

Bangsawan Proprietors, Performers, and Musicians

Pak Abdullah Abdul Rahman (born in 1927, *bangsawan* villain), Kuala Lumpur, 13 April 1986.

Pak Ahmad B. (born in 1931, *bangsawan* hero), Kuala Lumpur, 20 April 1986.

Pak Ahmad C. B. (born in 1915, *bangsawan* hero, song composer, proprietor of Rayuan Asmara), Kuala Lumpur, 17 April 1986.

Mak Ainon Chik (born *c.*1918, *bangsawan* heroine, also known as 'Grete Garbo of Malaya'), Kuala Lumpur, 15 April 1986; 26 June 1986.

Pak Alias Abdul Manan (born *c.*1920, *bangsawan* hero, proprietor of Sri Timur Bangsawan), Penang, 25 December 1985.

Pak Aziz (born in 1914, *bangsawan* and *ronggeng asli rebana* player and violinist), Penang, 13 January 1986.

Tok Bakar M. (born in 1906, proprietor of Rahman Star Opera and Bintang Timor Opera), Kuala Lumpur, 13 March 1986.

Mak Kamariah Noor (born in 1930, *bangsawan* singer), Kuala Lumpur, 20 April 1986.

Pak Mahmud Jun (born in 1921, *bangsawan* hero), Kuala Lumpur, 26 June 1986.

Mak Marshita (born in 1923, *bangsawan* heroine), Singapore, 7 January 1987.

Pak Mat Arab (born in 1920, *bangsawan* comedian/clown), Kuala Lumpur, 18 April 1986.

Pak Mat Hashim (born in 1930, *bangsawan* and *ronggeng asli* accordion and *rebana* player), Penang, 16 December 1985; 5 January 1986.

Mak Menah Yem (born *c.*1915, *bangsawan* heroine, also known as 'Queen of Dance', wife of the deceased proprietor of the Grand Nooran Opera, Pak Yem), Kuala Lumpur, 16 April 1986.

Mak Minah Alias (born *c.*1921, *bangsawan* heroine, wife of Pak Alias), Penang, 27 July 1986.

Pak Rahim B. (born in 1935, *bangsawan* hero), Kuala Lumpur, 16 February 1986.

Pak Rahman B. (born in 1933, proprietor of Rahman Star Opera, *bangsawan* hero), Kuala Lumpur, 27 February 1986; 23 January 1987.

Mak Saniah or Sri Kandi (born in 1938, *bangsawan* heroine), Kuala Lumpur, 21 February 1986.

Soliano, Alfonso (born in 1925, *bangsawan* musical director, composer, pianist) Kuala Lumpur, 17 April 1986.

Tok Shariff Medan (born *c.*1901, *bangsawan* hero), Singapore, 8 January 1987.

Pak Suki or Marzuki Nordin (born in 1902, *bangsawan* hero, proprietor of Dian Sandiwara, also known as 'The King of Bangsawan'), Kuala Lumpur, 29 April 1986; 22 January 1987.

Pak Wan Pekak (born in 1914, *bangsawan* and *ronggeng asli* violinist), Penang, 5 February 1986.

Tok Wan Said Tahir (born in 1902 or 1903, *bangsawan* hero, proprietor of Wan Man Sri Bangsawan), Alor Star, 21 December 1985.

Pak Yahya Sulong (born *c.*1925, *bangsawan* comedian/clown, drummer), Kuala Lumpur, 15 April 1986.

Others

Ashok Roy (Indian musician teaching at Monash University), Melbourne, 13 July 1988.

Gwee Thian Hock (producer of *wayang peranakan* [*peranakan* theatre] in Singapore and *bangsawan* fan), Singapore, 13 January 1986.

William Tan (*dondang sayang* singer, performer in *wayang peranakan* in Singapore), Singapore, 17 January 1986.

Index

Numbers in italics refer to plates.

A. SAMAD HASSAN, 29
Abdul Azziz, 110
Abdul Fatah Karim, 85, 87
Abdul Rahman, Tunku, 170
Abdul Wahab, 72
Abdullah, S., 29
Abdullah, Sheik, 81
Abdullah Abdul Rahman, 63–6, 68, 167
Abu Bakar, 28
Advertisements, 11–13, 15, 17, 20, 27, 30,
    36, 41–2, 46–50, 54–7, 171–3, 180
Ahmad, 3, *10*
Ahmad, Sultan, 101
Ahmad B., 168, 187
Ahmad C. B., 169, 174
Ahmad Jaafar, 29
Ahmad Kassim, 72
Ahmad Shariff, 133
Ahmat Pochu, 33
Ainon Chik, 62, 64–5, 70–2, 166, 169,
    187, *31*
Albar, S., 29
Al-Faruqi, Lois Ibsen, 91–2
Alford, K. J., 137
'Alhamdulilah', 5
Ali Abdul Rahman, 5
Alias Manan, 1–3, 5, 7, 31, 64–5, 70–1,
    79, 104, 175, 178, 187–8, *7*
Aman Belon, 65, 165
Amateur: theatre groups, 82; wireless
    associations, 12
Amazah Damnah, 51
American Ragtime Octette, 139
Amusement parks, 13–14, 30–1, 169
'Anak Koe', 159
Anarkali, Miss, 41
Andaya, Barbara Watson, 144
Andjar Asmara, 52
Antido Vod-a-Vil Coy, 76
Arah Bangsawan, 68, 165
Arnold, Alison, 102
Ashok Roy, 94

Asiabeat, 194
Asli, 143–6
Asmara Dana, 169
Atap Genting Atap Rembia, 175
Atimah, Miss, 38
Audience, 26–9, 103
Austin-Broos, Diane J., x
Awang Had Salleh, 175
Aziz Deraman, 178

BABA BANGSAWAN, 76, 82
Baba Melaka, 170
Babak, see Scene types
Babjan, 61
Babjee, A., 18
Backdrops, 104–7, 19
'Baginda Yam Tuan Melaka', 147–8
Baharudin Latif, 167
Bahroodin Ahmad, 179
Bai Kassim, 138
Bailey, Peter, viii
Bakar M., 62, 170, 174
Bakhtiar Effendi, 52
Balwant Gargi, 16
Bangsawan: adaptability, 44–57; decline,
    165–75, 191; development, 16–18,
    190–1; as new theatre form, vii, 7,
    18–25, 189–91; popularity, 25–32;
    revival, 1–7, 175–8, 191–2; as urban
    commercial theatre, 18–24, 32, 58, 189,
    193; variety in, 35–40, 190, *19–27*
Bangsawan associations, 1, 175, 178
'Bangsawan di Utara', 174
Bangsawan jenaka, 174, 193
Bangsawan Seri Dagang Suria Jaya, 179
Bangsawan Sri USM, 6, 83, 104, 150,
    178–9, 187
Bangsawan troupes, 16–18, 26, 29–31,
    68–9, 165, 175, 179
Bangsawan Workshop: (1977), 178;
    (1985), 1–7, *1–12*
'Bangun Anakku', 174

Banjo, 156
Barshat, 160
Barthes, Roland, ix
Bartholemeuz, Mr, 43
Bawang Merah Bawang Puteh, 123, 169
Beach Combers, 13
Becker, Alton, 6, 109
Becker, Judith, 6, 155
Bedlington, Stanley S., 166–7
Behague, Gerard, 132, 137–8, 163
Beka Records, 10, 29, 158, 164, 183
'Bercerai Kasih', 153–5
Berita Harian, 174–5, 178–9, 188
Berita Minggu, 52, 174
Besan Bioscope Co., 9
Bintang Emas Malay Opera, 170
Bintang Timor, 17–18, 21, 25–6, 33
Bintang Timur, 33, 178–9
Bintang Timur Opera, 170, 174
Blacking, John, ix–x
Blades, James, 77, 82
Blum, Stephen, viii
Boen S. Oemarjati, 53, 59
'Boenga Mawar', 144
'Boenga Tandjung', *see* 'Bunga Tanjung'
Bolero Opera, 52
Boria, 9, 179, 192
Bourdieu, Pierre, x
Boxing matches, 41
Braddell, Roland St. J., 82
Brandon, James, vii, 6, 18, 130
Brish, Catharine de, 63
Britania Opera Co., 18
British Cinematograph, 9
British in Malaya, 8, 26–7, 31, 33–4, 75, 82, 99–100
Brockett, Oscar G., 130
Brooke, Gilbert E., 82
Brown, H. M., 81
Buat Menyapu Si Air Mata, 175
Buka panggung ceremony, 20, 190
Bukan Lalang Ditiup Angin, 176
Bumiputra, 44
'Bunga Tanjung', 144, 158, 162, 164, 183–6
Burke, Peter, viii
Burong Pipit Makan Jagong, 168
Butcher, J. D., 31, 100

CABARETS, 14, 30, 33
Cai luong, 18
Camoens, Cantius Leo, vii, 16, 33, 52, 59, 166–70, 174
Cantarfischer, Miss Van, 60
Carl Lindstrom Records, 10, 99
Cathay-Keris Productions, 167–8
Cathay Productions, 167

'Cempaka Sari', 5
Censorship, 99–100, 167, 177
Chahaya Pulau Pinang, 23, 26, 32–3, 43, 73
Chap Kuching records, 29–30, 77, 79–80, 92, 96, 104
Chap Singa records, 29, 80, 93
Charity performances, 26, 32, 37, 49–50, 170
Chase, Gilbert, ix
'Che Wan Gayah', 146
Cheah Chin Keong, 69
Chempaka, 32
Child performers, 61, 66
Chinese: *bangsawan* groups, 26, 29, 76; cultural groups, 194; influence on *bangsawan*, 97–8, 190; opera, 14, 29, 188; plays in *bangsawan*, 35
Choong Wah Cinema, 10
Chopyak, James, 151, 153, 164
Chorus dancing, 44
Chow Chow Maraba, 58
City Opera, 59, 62, 68–9, 76
Clarino, Purita, 65
Clowns, 39–40, 110, 112, 124
Cohen, Erik, x
Cohn, Bernard, ix
'Colonel Bogey', 137
Columbia, 10, 29, 99
Comedy-dramas, 47
Comedy Pusi Indra Bangsawan, 18, 21, 25–6
Comic sketches, 39
Conventions in *bangsawan*, 103–30
Coplan, David, ix–x
Cordelier Hicks Co.'s Theatre Parisien, 14, 75
Costumes, 1–2, 110–11, 115–24, 181, *3–34, 24, 27, 33–34, 45–48*
Criterion Press Ltd., 157
Crystal Follies, 44
'Cumparsita', 138

DADRA TALA, 94, 101, 160
Dance: bands, 76–7, 79, 82; halls, 14, 44
Dandan Setia, 179
Danielson, Virginia, 101
Damisa Company, 179, 187
Dara dan Stia, 21
Daud Hamzah, 149, 163–4
D'Cruz, Marion, 101, 164, 194
D'Cruz, Santiago, 81–2
Dean, K., 29, 33, 39, 51, 68
Dean Tijah Opera, 68
Dean's Opera, 18, 21, 25–6, 30, 36–7, 39, 41, 44
Dean's Union Opera, 47–9

Dendang, 77
Department of Information, 177
Desert Thief of Baghdad, 41
DHR Company, 187
Dian Sandiwara, 62, 170
Dick, Alastair, 73
Dikir barat, 192
Dja's Dardanella troupe, 52–6, 60
Djoela Djoeli Bintang Tiga, 133, 137, 155, 164
Dobbs, Jack Percival Baker, 77
Dok, 153
Dondang sayang, 5
'Donou Walen', 133
Drama moden, 175

EASTERN AND ORIENTAL HOTEL DANCE HALL, 44
Echon, Miss, 61
Eddie's High Steppers, 44
Edrus, A. H., 16, 33, 73
Elite Anglo-American Troubadours, 14, 75
Elysee Cabaret, 44
Emergency and *bangsawan*, 166–74
Emerson, Rupert, 8
Empire Theatrical Co., 16
Empress Victoria Jawi Peranakkan Theatrical Company, 17–18
Ethnic riots, 166, 176
Ethnomusicology, viii–ix
Evans, W., 26
Evergreen Kronchong Party, 12
Experimental theatre, 176
Extra turns, 35, 37–8, 58, 110, 140, 144, 147, 149, 156, 163–4, 176, 181, *28–29, 32*

FAIRYLAND, 13
Faridah Hanim, 49, 51
Faundi, Leo, 37
Federal Land Development Authority (FELDA), 175
'Femme Qui Tue', 138
Festivals and *bangsawan*, 32
Filipino musicians, 63, 81, 99
Football teams, 64, 70
Forum on Bangsawan Music, 137
Foxtrot, 141–3
Frank J. Sidney Co., 39, 41–2
Frank Oriental Melodians, 12
French Cinematograph, 9
Fun and Frolic Park, 14

GAIETY STARS POLITE VAUDEVILLE AND SPECIALTY CO., 75
Gaiety Theatre, 138
Gambos, 153

'Gambos Sri Makam', 90–2, 98, 153, 198–200
Gamelan, 6, 101, 177
Gaylads Musical Party, 12, 39
Genani Star Opera, 5, 32, 61–2, 64, 69
Gendang, 153
Ghazalie Shafie, 176
Ghulam Sarwar, 1, 71, 130, 178, 181
Giddens, Anthony, x
Gima, 144
Ginufifah, 26
Goldsworthy, David, 80, 86, 101, 144, 149, 163–4
Gongan, 6
Government: and *bangsawan*, vii–viii, 1, 7, 175–9, 186–7, 191–3; control of cultural activities, 177, 188, 191–4; and syncretism, x
Gramophone and Typewriter Ltd., 10, 144, 147, 149, 156
Gramophone Co. Ltd., 33, 77, 79–80, 84, 90, 92, 97, 99, 102, 104, 132–3, 183
Grand Bangsawan, 76
Grand Jubilee Opera, 61, 66
Grand Nooran Opera, 26, 68, 166, 170
Grand Opera Co., 16, 26, 35
Grand Records, 29
Great Eastern Park, 13
Greek tragedies, 52
Grenfell, Newell, 176
Gronow, Pekka, 10, 99, 102
Gul Bakawali, 118, 179
Gullick, J. M., 8, 33, 74, 81

HAMBA ALLAH, 192
Hamlet, 96, 104, 117, 124–9, 134, 179, 219–31, *23*
Hang Mokhtar, 194
Hang Tuah, 169–70
Happy Go-Lucky Party, 28
Harmonium, 73, 80, 150, 153, 159
Hasan Kechi, 69
Hatley, Barbara, 18, 130
Hatta Azad Khan, 188
Henry Dallas Musical Comedy Co., 75
Herskovits, Melville J., ix
Herto Brabant, 26
'Het Lied Van Tandjoeng Katoeng', 149
'Hiburan Raja Ahamd Beradu', 84–8, 98, 196–7
Hikayat Hang Tuah, 144
Hindu Sabah Tamil School, 13
His Master's Voice, 29, 77, 80, 84, 90, 97, 104, 174, 183
History Workshop, viii
Ho Ah Loke, 167
Hobsbawm, Eric, x

Hollywood Park, 13
Hood, Mantle, viii
Housen, H., 16
H. S. L., 157, 158
Hu Yew Seah Orchestra, 12
Hurley, Mr., 74

IDARAN ZAMAN, 18, 38, 58, 76
Illusionists, 40–1
Immigration, 8
Inang, 146–8, 151, 162, 164
'Inang-Sarget', 164
Indera Saba, 16
Indian: influence, 78, 95–7, 131, 159, 163, 190, *43*; theatrical troupes, 14
Indonesian *sandiwara* troupes, 52–3, 56, 169
Indra Bangsawan, 69
Institut Teknologi Mara, 177
Internal Security Act (1960), 188
International Dramatic Co., 39, 41–2, 69
International Opera of Java, 77
Irama, 132; *Cina*, 161; *Hindustan*, 159–61; *Jawa*, 155–9; *Melayu*, 143–50; *Orang Putih*, 132–43; *Padang Pasir*, 150–5
Ismail Zain, 177

JAAFAR TURKI, 33
Jaar, Mr, 29
Jacoba, Miss, 28, 44
Jacobs, Arthur, 76
Jahara, Miss, 69
Jalil Shah, 26
Japanese Occupation, 165–6, 193
Javanese influence, 72–3, 131, 156, 190, *21–22*
Jawi Peranakan, 33
Jawi Peranakan Party, 13
Jazz, 76–8
Joget, 14, 148–50, 162; *gamelan*, 101, 164; *moden*, 169
'Joget Hitam Manis', 5, 181
Jomo Kwame Sundaram, 176
'Jong Kina', 38
Joplin, Scott, 139
Jula Juli Bintang Tiga, 26, 29, 77, 79, 95, 103–4, 108–9, 134–5, 141, 144, 150, 209–10, *25–26*

KAAI'S ROYAL HAWAIIAN TROUBADOURS, 76
Kaharvā tāla, 95, 102, 161
Kahn, Joel, x, 186, 192
Kartomi, Margaret, ix–x, 82, 86
Kassim Ahmad, 144
Kaufmann, Walter, 94–5
Kean, Charles, 125–6

Kecapi, 144
Kelly, A., 33
Keris Film Productions, 167
Ketoprak, 18, 109
Kiah, Miss, 44
Kiah Opera, 21, 56
Kimberlin, Cynthia Tse, x
King of Siam, 28
King Street Parsee Theatre, 14
Kinta Opera Co., 61
Klimanoff, Adolf, 40
Knaap, Otto, 59, 74, 155–6
Komedi stambul, 18, 33, 59, 74, 77, 133, 137–8, 155–6
Komet Opera, 68–9
Kornhauser, Bronia, 86, 92, 101, 155
Krishen Jit, 53
Kroncong, 9, 92–3, 101, 155–9, 164, *39*
'Kroncong Pulau Jawa', 164
Kugiran, 175
Kumpulan Dagang Bangsawan, 170

LAGU, 131–63, 191, 229–31; *asli*, 144, 161–2, 164; *cakap*, 133, 145, 147; *Cina*, 83, 97–8; *dagang*, 137; *gad*, 131, 137; *gambos*, 153; *garang-garang*, 137; *hiburan*, 145; *Hindustan*, 83, 93–5, 98; *Jawa*, 83, 92–3, 98; *kayangan*, 141; *klasik*, 83, 95–8; *masri*, 161–2; *Melayu*, 83–8, 98; *nasib*, 4, 94–5, 144, 151, 153; *Padang Pasir/Arab*, 83, 88–92, 98; *pelawak*, 147; *pengasoh/inang*, 145, 147; *riang*, 144, 146; *sedih*, 144; *strit*, 140, 145; *taman*, 135, 141, 145
'Lagu Sambut Kekasih', 80, 181–3
'Lagu Silat', 149
Laila Majnun, 10, 29, 77, 80, 90, 103–4, 109, 124, 150, 161, 216–17
Lake Band, 63
Lakon bassac, 18
Laksamana Bentan, 6, 47, 56, 69, 103–4, 108–9, 111, 115, 121–3, 150, 170, 179, 213–16, *45–47*
Laksamana Mati Dibunuh, 6, 59, 169–70, 179, 181, 186, 188, *48*
Lakuan Inder Sabah, 41
Lamb, Andrew, 82, 132, 134, 136–9, 163
Langgam jawa, 92, 101
Lanner, Joseph, 132
Lapena-Bonifacio, Amelia, 18
Larkin, John A., 18
Latin American influence, 77, 131, 163, 190
Leavitt, M. B., 14
Lee Soo Sheng, 194
Leo, A., 37
Leong Wai Kein, 194

Licences for performances, 100
Likay, 18
Lim Choon Sim, 28
Lithograph presses, 47, 59
Loh Fook Seng, 58
Loh, Francis, 188
Loke Wan Tho, 167–8
Lolita, 38
Lomax, Alan, 101
Lord, A. B., 6
Ludruk, 18

'MA INANG', 147
Madame HMV Troupe, 47, 51, 56
Mahieu, August, 18, 74, 133, 155
Mahmud Jun, 61–2, 66, 79, 156, 166–8, 170
Mahsuri, 6, 179
Maimoon, Miss, 29, 33
Maimoon Opera, 47, 49
Makepeace, Walter, 82
Makyong, 6, 71
Malacca Guardian, 26, 28, 31–2, 37, 41, 43, 53, 60, 109–10
'Malay Dance', 194
Malay Film Productions, 167
Malay historical plays, 47, 52, 168, 170, 179, 189, 193
Malay intelligentsia: and *bangsawan*, 51–2; and *sandiwara*, 52
Malay Translation Bureau, 47
Malaya Opera, 18
Malaya Tribune, 9, 12–13, 29–30, 37, 47, 49, 51, 56
Malayan Communist Party, 167
Malayan Opera, 39, 58
Malayan People's Anti-Japanese Army, 166
Malayization of *bangsawan*, 178–87, 193
Malm, Krister, x
Mamat Mashor, 16
Mamat Pushi, 16
Manan, A., 51
Manan Ngah, 194
Manderson, Lenore, 71
Manohar Company, 188
Manuel, Peter, 95, 102, 164
Manusama, A. Th., 18, 74, 77, 133, 137–8, 155
'Maple Leaf Rag', 139
Maracas, 153
Marathi theatre, 164
March, 136–7
Mariam, Tengku, 101
Martinez, C., 29, 33, 81–2
Marwas, 153
'Mas Merah', 162

Mash company, 187
Masri, 150–2, 162, 164
Mat Arab, 62, 65, 68, 166, 187, *31*
Mat Hashim, 2–3, 7, 63–4, 81, 83, 100, 164, 187, *10*
Matheson, Virginia, 144
Matsuo's Japanese Cinematograph, 9
Matusky, Patricia, 6, 161, 163–4
Menah Yem, 26, 31, 62, 65, 67, 70–1, 77–8, 163, 166, 187, *32*
Mendietta, Eddie, 45
Merchant of Bagdad, 26
Merriam, Alan, viii–x
Messrs. S. Moutrie and Co., 30
Michelle, W. C., 110
Middle Eastern influence, 88–92, 131, 150–3, 163, 190, *24, 27*
Mignon, Miss, 39
Minah Alias, 1–2, 5, 7, 61, 63–4, 66–7, 71, 80–1, 94, 99, 101, 125, 134, 166, 175, 178, 181, 183, 187–8, *9, 12, 35*
Mingguan Malaysia, 179
Ministry of Culture, Youth and Sports, 1, 3, 137, 176–81, 186
Ministry of Information, 177
Miss Riboet Orient Opera, 66, 158
Mobile theatres, 170
Mohamad Hasan, 144
Mohd. Anis, 147, 153, 192
Mohd. Bahroodin Ahmad, 5
Mohd. Nor Ismail, 179
Mohd. Taib Osman, 59, 100
Moonlight Opera Co., 20, 28, 46–7, 61
'Mostikowi', 94, 98, 161, 204–5
Motilal Chemical Company, 10
Movies and movie industry, 9–10, 28–9, 32–3, 167, 191–2
Mulk Raj Anand, 16
Multi-ethnic character of *bangsawan*, vii–viii, 7, 16–18, 26–9, 35–7, 60–4, 99, 190, 193, *20, 24*
Music in *bangsawan*, 83–100, 131–64, 181–6
Musical instruments, 73–81
Mustapha Kamil Yassin, vii, 5, 175, 189
Mutiara, 10

NACTER, ANN, 38
Naina Merican, xi
Najib Nor, 192
Nani, Miss, see Minah Alias
Nani bin Al. Hj. Osman, 51
Nani bin Haji Omar, 5, 63–4, 69
Nanney, Nancy, 52, 124, 175–6
'Nasib Pandan', 77, 150–1
Nasyid, 177
National culture policy, 176–9, 192

Nationalism and *bangsawan*, 51–2, 168, 170, 189, 191
Nettl, Bruno, ix, 89, 91, 100, 149
New Economic Policy (NEP), 176
New Elphinstone Theatrical Co., 14
New Straits Times, 176–7, 179, 186, 192
New Sunday Times, 179, 188
Noonmim Ainmim, 51
Noor-E-Islam, 29, 80, 93–4, 160–1
Noor K. K., 174–6
Nooran Opera, 18, 25–7, 31–2, 37, 39, 41–3, 77
Noordin Hassan, 176
Norlia, Miss, 29, 97
Normah Amateur Dramatic Party, 25
Nostalgia Laguku, 192
Novel, 52
Novelty and spectacle, 40–3
Nut, Inche, 81
Nyai Dasima, 26, 45, 53, 59

ODEON, 29
Oemar, Prof., 76
Ohaiyo Gozaimas Opera, 165
Omar, Sheik, 61
Omar bin Osman, 18
Ong Peng Hock, 62, 68
Ong, Walter J., 6
Opera Indra Permata, 38, 58, 60
Opera of Singapore, 51
Opera Stamboul, 16
Oriental Malay Opera Company, 20, 39
Oriental Opera, 63
Orion troupe, 52–3, 60
Orkes Radio Malaysia, 63
Orkes RTM, 73
Orkestra Dungun, *41*
Orkestra Melayu, 73–81, 175, *36*
Ortner, Sherry B., viii–xi
Osman, O. B., 37
Owen, Barbara, 73

PACHOLCZYK, JOZEF, 89
Pak Hitam Dagang, 176
Panji Semerang, 119
Pantomime, 39–40
Pantun, 3, 6, 102, 144
'Paraber', 93–4, 98, 160, 203–4
Parlophone, 29
Parsi theatre, 14, 16, 29, 159, 164
Past and Present, viii
'Patah Hati', 164
Pathe, 10, 29, 99
Paul Whiteman's Band, 141
Peacock, James, 18
Penang Amateur Dramatic Society, 74
Penang Baba Bangsawan, 38

Penang Band, 74–5, 132, 137–8
Penang Concert Orchestra, 12
Penang Festival, 6, 175
Penang Lichi Seah Orchestra, 12
Penang Nyo Nya Bangsawan, 26–7
'Penceraian Jula Juli dengan Sultan', 95–8, 134, 205–7
Penghiboran Hati, 157
Peninsula Opera, 18, 76
Pentas Opera, 192
Perawan Kampung, 179
Percussion instruments, 77
Performers: and film industry, 167–8; and musical change, x; promotion of, 60–82
Perkins, J. F., 33
Pertubuhan Seni Bangsawan Negara (PESBANA), 175
Philips sisters, 42
Piedro, A., 52
Pinang Gazette and Straits Chronicle, 14, 16, 75, 81
Pitroff, Alexis, 39
Plays, 35–7, 45–51, 56; synopses, 209–31
Pokar, Haji (Ging), 62
Police Act (1967), 177
Political events and *bangsawan*, xi, 59, 170, 174
Pop yeh yeh bands, 175
Popular music, 176, 194
Population, 8–9
Portuguese influence, 149, 155, 164
Powers, Harold S., 102, 160
Princess Nilam Chahaya, 26
Printing Presses and Publications Act (1988), 188
'Puja Kamati Darsha Alam', 144–5, 150, 161
Punjab Mail, 49
Pushi Indera Bangsawan, 16, 33
Puteri Bakawali, 103–4, 109, 112, 210–13
Puteri Gunong Ledang, 29, 77, 80, 84, 88, 144, 146–7, 151, 170, 174, 229–31
Putri Sa'Dong, 192

RADEN MAS, 2–6, 178–9, 181, *11*
Radio, 12, 30
Radio and Television Malaysia, 177, 193
Radio Malaysia, 174
Ragtime, 76, 139–41
Rahim B., 63, 174–5, 179, 187, *34*
Rahmah Bujang, vii, 5, 33, 179, 189
Rahman B., 62, 65–6, 70, 99, 165, 170, 175, 179, 181, 187, *33*
Rahman Star Opera, 62, 165, 170
Raja Bersiong, 120
Rajan, B. S., 10, 32
Ramlee, P., 192

Ramli Ibrahim, 194
Rampai Rampaian, 58
Rancangan Lima Tahun untuk
  Pembangunan Teater Bangsawan, 178
Randel, Don Michael, 82
Ranger, Terence, x
Rayuan Asmara, 169
Rebana, 77, 80, 82, 84, 100, 143–4, 150,
  153, 155, 162, *37, 38*
Recordings, xi, 10–13, 29–30, 104, 131,
  13–18
Rentak, 132, 164
Reward of Virtue, 51
Rezels Troupe, 12
Rhynal, Camille de, 138
Riboet, Miss, 29, 33, 52–3, 56, 66, 158,
  164
Robinson, J. B., 75, 78
Rodriguez, Gerardo Matos, 138
Roff, W. R., 9, 30–1, 51, 59
Rohani B., 63
Ronggeng asli, 3, 5, 14, 86, 100–1, 147,
  164, 181, *40*; ensemble, 3, 6, 80, 143–4,
  147, 159, 163, 169, 181, *10*
Root, Deane, 75
Rosas, Juventino, 132
Rose Opera, 28, 44, 51, 60
Royal Opera, 62, 68
Royal Ruby Opera, 12, 30, 57
Royal Star Opera, 170
Royal Zainab Opera, 32
Ruby's Grand Opera, 64
Ruby's Rhythmic Orchestra, 82

SAADIAH, 68–9
Sabrul Jamil Football Club, 28
Sadie, S., 141
Said Haji Hussein, 59
St George's Secondary School, 179
Salim, H. M., 174
Salmah, Miss, 29, 33
Saloma, 192
Salomme Revue, 44
Sam Pek Eng Tai, 35, 104, 109, 115–16,
  124, 217–19
Samuel, Raphael, viii
Sandiwara, 18, 52, 58–9, 115, 168–70,
  175, 191, *42–44*
Sandiwara Cahaya Timor, 168
Sandiwara Senang Hati, 168
Saudara, vii, 28, 32, 45, 49, 51, 100, 186
Saw Yeong Chin, 194
Scene types, 103–10, 130
Sedition Act, 188
Sejarah Melayu, 84
Sekolah Melayu, 33
Selangor State Band, 63, 74, 81

'Selendang Majang', 164
Semangat Pemuda, 168
Sen, Devdan, 73
Seri Kembangan Opera, 170
'Seri Mersing', 162, 164
Seri Rani Opera, 170
'Seri Serdang', 80
Shahrom Hussain, 59
Shakespeare plays, 52
'Shanghai Street', 80, 97–8, 102, 140, 208
Shariff Medan, 168
Sharom Ahmat, 178
Shaw Brothers, 10, 31, 61, 167
Shiloah, Amnon, x
Short, Anthony, 167
Short story, 52
Shri Chandravadan Mehta, 16
Signell, Karl, 89–91, 101
Siku di lutut, 1, *1*
Silat, 2, *7*
Sinandung, 163
'Sinandung Jawa', 80, 92–3, 200–3
Singapura di Waktu Malam, 32
Siti Aishah bt. Yahya, 1
'Siti Payung', 5, 92, 181
Smith, Miss Dora van, 60
Smithies, Michael, 18
Social change: and literature, 59; and
  theatre, 51–2, 58, 191
Social clubs, 9, 31
Soliano, Alfonso, 29, 63, 66, 70, 78, 81,
  99, 169–70
Soliano, Jerry, 63
Soliano, Pacita, 63
Soliano, Rupino, 37, 63
Songs, 10, 37–9
Sousa, John Philip, 137
Sree Penang Theatrical Co., 25
Sri Majlis Kronchong Party, 12
'Sri Siantar', 4, 181
Sri Temiang, 176
Sri Timur Bangsawan, 175
Stage sets, 21–3, 104–7
'Stambol Satoe' 155, 157–8
Stambul, 155–9, 164
Star, 64, 178–9
Star Opera Co., 18, 20, 28, 38, 58, 110
Starlight Opera Co., 60–1, 68, 71
Stars in *bangsawan*, 60–72
Stevenson, Rex, 100
Stock characters, 103, 110–30
Straits Cinematography Co., 76
Straits Echo, vii, 9–11, 13–16, 18, 20–1,
  23, 25–30, 32–51, 53– 61, 69, 74–7,
  79, 82, 100, 104, 110–12, 124, 126–9,
  132, 137–8, 140–1, 157, 162, 186
Straits Opera, 16, 26

Straits Times, 9–10, 14, 25, 28–9, 44, 56
Strauss, Johann, 132
Suasana Dance Co., 192
Suki, Pak, 28, 62, 65, 67–9, 170, 187
Sultan Idris Training College, 47–9, 52, 59
Sultan of Deli, 16, 26
Sultan of Kedah, 26
Sultan of Kelantan, 26
Sultan of Langkat, 26
Sultan of Perak, 26
Sunday Gazette, 28, 44, 53
Sunshine Girl, 138
Sweeney, Amin, 6, 103, 108, 130
Syair, 4, 6, 47, 86, 96, 98, 101
Syed Alwi, 69, 176, 192
Syncretism, ix–x, 193–4

TABLA, 73, 80, 159
Tai Sun Cantonese Musical Party, 13
Talbot, Michael, 139
Tambi Ketjik, 147, 149
Tambourine, 153
Tan, K. C., 51
Tan Kam Choon, 64, 60
Tan Sooi Beng, 33, 163, 176, 186, 194
Tan Tjeng Bok, 60–1
Tan, Y. L., 18
Tango, 137–9
Tantuan Muda, 51–2
Tari inang, 147
Tari lilin, 147
Tari payung, 147
Tari piring, 147
Tay Boon Teck, 16
Tchaya Timoer troupe, 52
'Telek Ternang', 88–90, 98, 151–2, 198
'Telesmat Bintang Satu dan Dua', 77, 135–6, 141–3
Television and *bangsawan*, 176, 179, 187
Tengku Sulung Mati Digantung, 6, 179
'Teribet Jula Juli', 135–6
Terpaksa Menikah, 10, 29, 49
Tewari, Laxmi Ganesh, 94
Theatrical troupes, 14, 75
Thomas, E., 28
Thompson, E. P., x
Ticket prices, 23–5, 30, 34
Tiga Kekasih, 10
Tijah, Miss, 29, 33, 92
Times of Malaya, 9–10, 20, 28, 32–4, 37–40, 44–5, 52–3, 60, 64, 75–7, 81, 104, 124–9, 138, 140, 163
Tio, T. D., 33
Tonil, 18, 52–3, 58
Torio, J., 37
Town Band, 39, 138

'Track-tack-tack', 58
Traditional Malay theatre: and *bangsawan*, vii, 1, 5–7, 18–25, 115, 124, 131, 189–91; definition, vii
Treitler, Leo, x
Trengganu royal family, 26
'Tudung Periok', 164
Tuhfat al-Nafis, 144
Turner, Victor, ix–x

Ud, 153
Ukelele, 156
Umm Khulthum, 101
Union City Opera, 81
United Malays National Organization (UMNO), 170, 174
Universiti Kebangsaan Malaysia, 177
Universiti Malaya, xi, 177
Universiti Sains Malaysia, 1, 177–8
Universities and University Colleges Act, 188
Urban entertainment, 9–16
Utih, 186
Utusan Malaysia, 179
Utusan Melayu, 170
Utusan Zaman, 174

VAN AALST, J. A., 102
Variety performances, 58
Vaudeville turns, 20, 44–5, 59
Vaughan, V. D., 14
Victor Talking Machine Co., 10, 99

WADE, BONNIE, 94–5
Wages, 65–6, 167–8
Wales Minstrel Party of Singapore, 9
Wallis, Roger, x
Waltz, 132–6
Wan, Tok, 58, 68, 70–2, 164–5, 187, *30*
Wan Abdul Kadir, vii, 12–13, 100, 167
Wan Man Sri Bangsawan, 61, 71
Wan Pekak, 3, 169, 187, 10
Want, John, 10
Ward, J., 33
Watak, see Stock characters
Waterman, Richard, ix
Wayang Aishah Indra Mahkota Theatrical Co., 18, 25, 38, 41, 58
Wayang Inche Baba Orchestra, 37
Wayang Inche Puteh Theatrical Co., 18, 41, 58
Wayang Jupiter, 69
Wayang Kassim, 18, 23, 28, 32, 35, 37–41, 44, 58, 61, 69, 74, 110
Wayang Komedi India Ratoe, 38–9, 69, 74, 140
Wayang kulit, 6, 177

Wayang Parsi, 58, 73, 76
Wayang Siam, 108–9, 115, 124, 130
Wayang stambul, 33
Wayang Yap Chow Thong, 16, 18, 23, 25–6, 28, 32, 38, 44, 73–4
Wembley Amusement Park, 14, 28
Wembley Cabaret, 44
Western: influence, 35, 44–5, 47–9, 74–9, 95–7, 131–43, 161–3, 175, 189–90, 193; touring theatre groups, 14, 29, 39, 75
White, Maytum, 141
Wiant, Bliss, 101
Willard Opera Company, 14, 75
Williams, Mr, 39
Williams, Raymond, ix–x
Williamson and Maher's Chicago Tourist Minstrel and Variety Co., 14, 75
Winstedt, R. O., 74, 104, 126
Wise, Michael, 127
Women in *bangsawan*, 71–2
Wonders of the Deep, 41

YAHAYA AHMAD, 3
Yahya Sulong, 63, 70
Yap Chow Thong, 16
Yem, Pak, 31, 65, 71, 166
Yeo, Eileen, viii
Yeo, Stephen, viii
Yung, Bell, 102, 161

ZA'ABA, 30, 51–2, 59
Zakaria Ariffin, 192
Zanibar Royal Theatrical Co., 18
Zapin, 152–5, 192; *Arab*, 153; *Melayu*, 153
Zarzuela, 18
Zonis, Ella, 91–2, 101
Zubedah, Che, 101
Zubir Said, 29
Zuraidah Ahmad, 5